Development-Induced Displacement and Resettlement in Vietnam

This book explores the complex legal, cultural, economic and human rights issues associated with development-induced displacement and resettlement (DIDR) in Vietnam.

As in many parts of the world, urban expansion and large-scale infrastructure projects in Vietnam often rely on forced land acquisition, which can result in the involuntary resettlement of households and entire communities. This book examines the adequacy of monetary and in-kind compensation and the support that resettlees need for successful integration into host communities and for sustainable livelihoods and improved well-being. It presents new paradigms and practices that place affected households at the centre of project planning and implementation to fully address the needs of the most vulnerable. This includes women, the elderly, and ethnic minority groups. Bringing together research evidence, practical experience, and insights of distinguished researchers, this book is the first to systematically examine DIDR in Vietnam, a single-party state seeking to balance state interests with the demands of investors and civil society for human rights and participation by affected people.

Combining the latest evidence and research findings on development-induced displacement and resettlement in Vietnam with practical experiences in project implementation, this book will be a useful guide for researchers across development, migration, and Southeast Asian Studies, as well as practitioners and policy makers. Its lessons will also be relevant to other countries facing rapid development.

Nguyen Quy Nghi is Senior Social Development Specialist for The World Bank in Washington DC.

Jane Singer is Professor in the Department of Global Studies at Kyoto University of Foreign Studies.

Routledge Studies in Development, Displacement and Resettlement

This series is concerned with the complex global issue of forced migration, from its causes and resulting implications to potential responses and solutions. With the numbers of forcibly displaced people around the world hitting record levels in recent years, including refugees, internally displaced persons, and asylum seekers, this is an issue that affects not only those communities and countries that people are fleeing from but also those they are fleeing to.

The series will explore the various mechanisms by which people undergo forced movement, such as war, conflict, environmental disaster, development projects, persecution, ecological degradation, famine, human trafficking, and ethnic cleansing. It also seeks to promote a fuller understanding of the implications of forced displacement and how scholars, policy-makers, NGO advocates, and those working in the field can collectively develop adequate responses.

Climate Change, Disasters, and Internal Displacement in Asia and the Pacific
A Human Rights-Based Approach
Edited by Matthew Scott and Albert Salamanca

Resettlement in Asian Countries
Legislation, Administration and Struggles for Rights
Edited by Mohammad Zaman, Reshmy Nair and Shi Guoqing

Child Rights and Displacement in East Africa
Agency and Spatial Justice in Planning Policy
Cherie C. Enns and Willibard J. Kombe

Development-Induced Displacement and Resettlement in Vietnam
Exploring the State – People Nexus
Edited by Nguyen Quy Nghi and Jane Singer

For more information about this series, please visit: www.routledge.com/Routledge-Studies-in-Development-Displacement-and-Resettlement/book-series/RSDR

Development-Induced Displacement and Resettlement in Vietnam

Exploring the State – People Nexus

Edited by
Nguyen Quy Nghi and Jane Singer

Routledge
Taylor & Francis Group
LONDON AND NEW YORK

First published 2023
by Routledge
4 Park Square, Milton Park, Abingdon, Oxon OX14 4RN

and by Routledge
605 Third Avenue, New York, NY 10158

Routledge is an imprint of the Taylor & Francis Group, an informa business

British Library Cataloguing-in-Publication Data
A catalogue record for this book is available from the British Library

Library of Congress Cataloging-in-Publication Data
Names: Nguyen, Quy Nghi, editor. | Singer, Jane (Professor of environmental education), editor.
Title: Development-induced displacement and resettlement in Vietnam : exploring the state – people nexus / edited by Nguyen Quy Nghi and Jane Singer.
Description: Abingdon, Oxon ; New York, NY : Routledge, 2023. | Series: Routledge studies in development, displacement and resettlement | Includes bibliographical references and index.
Identifiers: LCCN 2022015723 (print) | LCCN 2022015724 (ebook) | ISBN 9780367761639 (hardback) | ISBN 9780367761660 (paperback) | ISBN 9781003165774 (ebook)
Subjects: LCSH: Forced migration—Vietnam. | Internally displaced persons—Government policy—Vietnam. | Internally displaced persons—Legal status, laws, etc.—Vietnam. | Economic development projects—Social aspects—Vietnam. | Rural development—Social aspects—Vietnam.
Classification: LCC HB2104.5.A3 D435 2023 (print) | LCC HB2104.5.A3 (ebook) | DDC 304.8/109597—dc23/eng/20220706
LC record available at https://lccn.loc.gov/2022015723
LC ebook record available at https://lccn.loc.gov/2022015724

ISBN: 978-0-367-76163-9 (hbk)
ISBN: 978-0-367-76166-0 (pbk)
ISBN: 978-1-003-16577-4 (ebk)

DOI: 10.4324/9781003165774

Typeset in Times New Roman
by Apex CoVantage, LLC

Contents

List of figures viii
List of tables ix
List of boxes xi
List of contributors xii
Foreword by Frank Vanclay xv
Acknowledgments xviii
List of acronyms and abbreviations xix

Introduction 1
NGUYEN QUY NGHI AND JANE SINGER

PART 1
Legal framework on land acquisition and resettlement in Vietnam 9

1 **Land acquisition legal framework in Vietnam: balancing public and private interests** 11
PHAN TRUNG HIEN

2 **Local governments as catalysts for enhancing resettlement outcomes in infrastructure development** 28
LE ANH TUAN

3 **Noncompliance with land acquisition and resettlement in Vietnam: a policy tools approach** 42
NGUYEN VAN DANG

PART 2
Agricultural land conversion, urbanization, and farmers' responses 63

4 Urbanization and land acquisition in Hue's peri-urban areas: challenges and the way forward 65
NGUYEN QUANG PHUC

5 Agricultural land appropriation for urban development: villagers learn to cope with the state and adapt to the market 82
NGUYEN VAN SUU

6 "Good" versus "bad" urbanization: land appropriation impacts in two peri-urban villages in Hanoi 100
NGUYEN THI THANH BINH

PART 3
Navigating resettlement practices in large infrastructure projects 119

7 Development-induced peri-urban resettlement: livelihood opportunities, but at what cost? 121
JANE SINGER, PHAM HUU TY AND THI KINH KIEU

8 How to deal with hunger? Household strategies and rural livelihood diversification at a dam-induced resettlement site 137
NGA DAO

9 Dam-induced resettlement in Vietnam: proposing a socially sustainable model 160
NGUYEN QUY NGHI AND PHAN HUYEN DAN

10 Post-resettlement integration into host communities: evidence from a cross-sectional survey of large infrastructure projects in Vietnam 185
NGUYEN QUY NGHI, NGUYEN THI MINH PHUONG AND DO THI LE HANG

PART 4
Addressing emerging and dormant issues in resettlement programs 213

11 Breaking the vicious cycle: how the private sector can contribute to solving resettlement dilemmas 215
DINH THI NGOC BICH

12 Excitement or anxiety: psychological aspects of development-induced resettlement 242
DO THI LE HANG, NGUYEN QUY NGHI AND NGUYEN THI MINH PHUONG

13 Gender-impact assessment: toward a universal application in large development projects in Vietnam 255
PHAM THI DIEU MY

Index 275

Figures

2.1	Provincial prices versus market prices (36 samples)	35
2.2	Satisfaction of PMUs with LFDC services	38
4.1	The dual-price system of land	74
4.2	Use of compensation money	75
9.1	Changes in regulations on compensation in the *Land Laws* during the period 1987–2013	167
9.2	Percentage of satisfaction with project implementation (NIAPP & ASEC 2018)	173
10.1	Percentages of households reporting no support/relationship in specific events/organization: before and after relocation (%)	202
10.2	The structure of a three-tiered resettlement program	204
11.1	Analytical framework to assess PPP in NP project developed by Dinh (2015)	220
11.2	The landscape at the NP project site before land acquisition	223
11.3	Summary of grievance letters, by year, in the NP project	224
11.4	The Cao Lan ethnic minority display	236
12.1	Respondents' mood when learning of a project's impact on their land (with or without physical relocation)	244
13.1	The corporate social responsibility (CSR) pyramid	269

Tables

3.1	Facts about the three land-taking events	48
4.1	Compulsory land acquisition in Hue's peri-urban zones (2000–18)	69
4.2	Increase in land prices following the completion of projects	74
5.1	Compensation rate for agricultural land-use rights in Phú Điền in 2007	88
6.1	Types of houses in the two village communities in 2014 (%)	107
6.2	Village residents' opinions on overall advantages/ disadvantages of urbanization	112
6.3	Opinions of local people on recent urban expansion and development in their communities	113
7.1	Selected household survey results: Human and social capital	130
7.2	Selected household survey results: Cultural capital	133
8.1	Land use and agricultural structure in Tân Lập commune	140
9.1	Distribution of energy sources and projections (%)	162
9.2	Number of affected and relocated households due to the construction of some hydropower projects in Vietnam	163
9.3	Regulations on compensation when the state acquires residential land	164
9.4	Consultation activities during project preparation	170
10.1	Distance and travel time between the new and old places of residence	188
10.2	Distance to parents' houses after relocation in Son La province (km)	188
10.3	Frequency of visiting parents before and after relocation (%)	189
10.4	Description of livelihood activities in old and new places of residence among displaced Thai communities in Son La	195
10.5	Self-assessment of community engagement in the new residence	196
10.6	Concern about other people's opinions	197
10.7	Average scores on community engagement	197
10.8	Means of scores for mutual support in pre- and post-relocation periods	199
10.9	Level of mutual community support in pre- and post-relocation periods	200

10.10 Current participation rates in social organizations and activities (%) 200
10.11 Average number of activities or organizations joined by relocated households 203
12.1 Respondents' feelings upon the announcement of land acquisition 244
12.2 Comparison of moods among groups during resettlement process 246
12.3 Concerns of affected households upon land acquisition/ resettlement (by household types) 248
12.4 Concerns of the affected households upon land acquisition/ resettlement (by research location and relocation status) 249
12.5 Comparison of satisfaction with new living places among various population groups 251

Boxes

8.1	The story of Doi Village	146
8.2	The story of Long Coc Village	147
8.3	Lang's story	152
10.1	From Nga Tu So to Dong Tau: The occupational shift of resettled people	195
11.1	The development of compensation, support, and resettlement policies in Vietnam	216
11.2	International policies applied in the NP project	222
11.3	Resources of NPM for land conversion activities	229
11.4	Resettlement in Nam Song Cong relocation site	233
11.5	Vocational training and recruitment in the NP project	234
11.6	The establishment of the Cao Lan ethnic minority display corner	236
12.1	Psychological portraits of resettlement groups	247

Contributors

Dinh Thi Ngoc Bich, senior research fellow of the Center for Global Cooperation Research, University of Duisburg- Essen, holds a PhD from the Catholic University of Leuven in Belgium. Her research deals with public-private partnerships (PPPs); stakeholder engagement; and corporate social responsibility (CSR) compliance – mainly related to the role of the private sector in resettlement and compensation, climate change, and Sustainable Development Goals (SDGs).

Do Thi Le Hang is a senior researcher at the Institute of Psychology, Vietnam Academy of Social Sciences. She holds a PhD in psychology. Her research focuses on applied psychology; mental health; education; and ethnic and gender issues in resettlement.

Le Anh Tuan is an independent researcher with 20 years' experience in rural development. He has been a consultant in social development; resettlement; gender; agricultural extension; and diffusion of innovation for the World Bank, the Food and Agriculture Organization of the United Nations (FAO), and the International Rice Research Institute (IRRI). He also is interested in behavior change; in social capital and common-pool resources; and in exploring how to apply these interdisciplinary knowledges in development projects. He holds an MSc from James Cook University.

Nga Dao is a faculty member in the Department of Social Science at York University in Toronto. She is a human-environment geographer; an international development practitioner; and an environmental activist researching at the intersection of resource governance, political ecology, political economy, and livelihood change in Vietnam and Southeast Asia.

Nguyen Quang Phuc has been a lecturer in the University of Economics, Hue University, Vietnam since 2002. He is an expert in development studies, including rural development, land governance, urbanization, and livelihoods. He has been involved in a variety of development projects funded by the World Bank, the FAO, the government of Finland, and the government of Vietnam.

Nguyen Quy Nghi is Senior Development Specialist with the World Bank in Washington DC. He has 22 years' experience working on social development issues in government, non-governmental, and international organizations. His expertise spans community development; craft village development; migration; gender; reproductive health; family planning; HIV/AIDS prevention; involuntary resettlement; and ethnic minorities. In his current capacity, he is deeply involved in the implementation of the World Bank's Environmental and Social Framework (ESF); in social-impact assessment; and in mitigation measures for development-induced resettlement.

Nguyen Thi Minh Phuong is a senior researcher at the Institute of Sociology, Vietnam Academy of Social Sciences. She has 22 years' experience in rural sociology, specializing in social security; agricultural labor transformation; cooperatives; lands; villages; communities; education orientation for teenagers in rural families; and digital transformation in agriculture. She also provides advice to governmental agencies, international organizations, and NGOs.

Nguyen Thi Thanh Binh is a researcher at the Institute of Anthropology, Vietnam Academy of Social Sciences. She holds an MA in Anthropology from the University of Amsterdam and a PhD from the Australian National University. Her research interests are local political dynamics, social change, and culture in rural Vietnam.

Nguyen Van Dang is a researcher and lecturer at the Institute of Sociology and Development, Ho Chi Minh National Academy of Politics. His research focuses on theories of public governance and policy; institutional design of governing systems; land policy; and social policy. He holds a PhD in public governance and policy from Portland State University.

Nguyen Van Suu is Head of the Department of Anthropology at the University of Social Sciences and Humanities, Vietnam National University (VNU-USSH) in Hanoi. His research interests include the intersection of land, livelihoods, and development; urbanization; and state-society interactions. He coordinated the development of curricula in anthropology at the Department of Anthropology at VNU-USSH.

Pham Huu Ty is a researcher at the University of Agriculture and Forestry, Hue University. He holds an MSc in applied science from the University of Dalhousie in Canada and a PhD from the Faculty of Geosciences, Utrecht University. His research interests are land and water governance; resettlement; food security; livelihood; geographic information systems; and remote sensing.

Pham Thi Dieu My is Technical and Fundraising Adviser at the Centre for Social Research and Development (CSRD). She holds a master's degree in natural hazards and disasters from the Australian National University, and she is currently undertaking doctoral studies at the University of Potsdam. She has over

18 years' experience undertaking research and development projects in natural disasters, climate change response, and impact assessment.

Phan Huyen Dan is a researcher at the Institute for Family and Gender Studies, Vietnam Academy of Social Sciences. She holds an MA degree in international development and management from Lund University. She has been providing consultancies to governmental agencies, NGOs, and international organizations (including the Asian Development Bank and the World Bank). Her current research includes aging, family, gender studies, and involuntary resettlement.

Phan Trung Hien is an associate professor and Vice Dean of the Faculty of Law at Can Tho University, Vietnam and a Fulbright visiting scholar at the University of Washington School of Law. Since 1998, he has been a lecturer and an active researcher in law. His areas of expertise include the theory of state and law; administrative law; and Legal Methods, especially the law of compulsory land acquisition.

Jane Singer is a professor in the Department of Global Studies at Kyoto University of Foreign Studies. She holds a PhD in global environmental studies from Kyoto University. Her principal research focus is migration and displacement, with recent research investigating dam-displaced ethnic minority communities in Vietnam; disaster communication in Japan and Vietnam; and community resilience for transmigrants in Indonesia. She has previously coedited three books on community resettlement and resilience.

Thi Kinh Kieu is a lecturer at the University of Danang – University of Science and Education (UD-DUT). She holds a PhD from Kyoto University, focusing on the training of teachers in education for sustainable development (ESD). Her research focuses on two separate areas of interest: promoting the culture of sustainability in higher education institutions; and community-based development.

Frank Vanclay is Professor of Cultural Geography in the Faculty of Spatial Sciences at the University of Groningen in the Netherlands. He writes in the areas of social-impact assessment; the management of social issues associated with large projects; the social license to operate; business and human rights; social aspects of resource extraction; project-induced displacement and resettlement; and avoiding the "resource curse." He also facilitates training on land acquisition, resettlement, and social sustainability, as part of the University of Groningen summer school program.

Foreword

Being dispossessed of one's home or land – in other words, having it taken away and thus becoming displaced – has severe social, economic, and psychological impacts in many ways. Land is fundamental to the identity, lives, and livelihoods of rural people. And everyone needs a safe place in which to live, a home. Therefore, expropriation or forced eviction should never occur. Even when adequate compensation is provided (which has rarely been the case), considerable uncertainty, anxiety, and fear, as well as disruption, disturbance, and inconvenience, are created during the implementation of development projects of any kind: whether airports, bridges, business parks, dams, highways, industrial zones, railway lines, solar farms, urban development projects, wind farms, or whatever.

All too often, when projects need to acquire land, the compensation provided is not adequate, and the people who are displaced are made worse off. The negative social impacts and stresses associated with displacement affect every aspect of people's lives. In the "development-induced displacement and resettlement" (DIDR) discourse, the concept of "multi-dimensional stress" is typically used to describe this phenomenon. It is no wonder, therefore, that the first principle or objective of the resettlement standards of the World Bank and the International Finance Corporation is to avoid resettlement if at all possible.

But it should not have to be like that. New development projects will always need land, and inevitably people will have to make way for projects, which potentially may improve their lives. Thus, instead of making people worse off, resettlement associated with a development project should be seen as being an opportunity to improve the wellbeing of people in or near the project site.

We need to change the prevailing paradigm that currently allows states to expropriate land, pay minimal compensation, and conduct resettlement in appallingly bad and drawn-out processes. Instead, we must insist on a new regime of never resorting to expropriation, and always negotiating mutual agreements that make affected peoples better off, so that affected people willingly choose to participate in relocation in the full knowledge that they will be properly looked after. We need to think of the people who are to be resettled as key stakeholders and ensure that they also become beneficiaries. Thus, there needs to be effective benefit-sharing arrangements (or community development agreements) that are agreed on by projects and host communities. A critical issue for resettled people relates to what livelihood activities will be appropriate and sustainable in the new context. In all resettlement actions, attention needs to be given to providing support to ensure that all resettled people will continue to have ongoing viable livelihoods. This is likely to require the identification of possible alternative livelihood activities, appropriate training, and transition support. There is also a need to ensure that resettlement procedures (and projects that require the resettlement of people) are properly and professionally planned and executed in a timely fashion and in a manner consistent with respect for human rights.

Building collective capacity to improve resettlement practice is a personal goal of mine and one of the reasons why I facilitate training courses in better resettlement practice. I encourage all key players in development projects (especially project owners, decision-makers, planners, implementers) to imagine it was happening to them. What would they expect if they were in the way of a project and were being resettled? In my research and in the training courses I facilitate, I use the concept of "empathy" as an analytical tool and as a mechanism to enhance understanding of the social issues that arise in DIDR. I encourage all readers of this book to do the same. What would you expect if you were going to be resettled? How would you feel about the way you would be treated?

There is an increasing amount of scholarship and writing on DIDR, including the valuable contribution this book is making. It is good to see that more attention is now being paid to the many issues that need consideration in DIDR, for example: human rights; the gendered nature of impacts; vulnerability; the restoration (or preferably enhancement) of livelihoods; and improved participatory processes – all topics that are considered in this book. New models and methodologies have been developed to supplement (or perhaps replace) traditional approaches. One example of a new approach is Eddie Smyth's Social Framework for Projects, an excellent tool for analyzing, conceptualizing, and communicating about the social issues in projects, especially those that involve resettlement. An increasing number of works (including this book about Vietnam) are being written about specific locations, assisting in increasing the local relevance and practical applicability of the global learning on the topic of development-induced displacement and resettlement.

Despite this growing scholarship, some issues have remained under-considered, and it is good to see them being addressed in this book. Most importantly, an often-forgotten dimension in the resettlement process is host communities. Host communities usually experience many negative social impacts from resettlement processes, including increased demand on services; shortages; nuisance and annoyance; tension between newcomers and existing residents; and sometimes cultural differences. Sometimes, farmland is expropriated in order to make land available for housing people who were displaced elsewhere. If there is inequality between the host or receiving community and the resettlees, tensions can arise. If there was not fair compensation for the host community, there will be residual concerns that will make it very difficult for community cohesion to be re-established. As this book argues, much more attention needs to be given to the communities that will host resettled communities.

This book makes an excellent contribution to DIDR scholarship. Focusing on Vietnam, it brings together a distinguished and eminent group of researchers, mostly Vietnamese, who have contributed to a carefully designed book that addresses the key issues of importance in DIDR practice. Although specifically about Vietnam, many lessons will be relevant to other countries facing rapid growth. I am very pleased to be associated with this book.

Professor Frank Vanclay
Faculty of Spatial Sciences, University of Groningen, the Netherlands
Writer and instructor about land acquisition, resettlement, and social sustainability.

Acknowledgments

The editors would like to acknowledge the generosity of Kyoto University of Foreign Studies for providing financial assistance for the publication of this book. We would like to commend the expert editorial assistance provided by Carolyn Page of the Clear English Company. We would also like to warmly thank our families for their enduring support and understanding during the publication process.

Disclaimer

Acronyms and abbreviations

ADB	Asian Development Bank
AfDB	African Development Bank
BCSR	Board for Compensation, Support and Resettlement
BCGC	Board for Compensation and Ground Clearance
BDPA	Beijing Declaration and Platform for Action
BOT	build operate transfer
BT	build transfer
CDP	Community Development Plan
CPCs	Communal People's Committees
CPV	Communist Party of Vietnam
CSR	corporate social responsibility
CSRD	Centre for Social Research and Development
DARD	Department of Agricultural Rural Development
DCSR	Decision of Compensation, Assistance and Resettlement
DIDR	development-induced displacement and resettlement
DMS	detailed measurement survey
DoLISA	Department of Labour, Invalids and Social Affairs
DoNRE	Department of Natural Resources and Environment
DoF	Department of Finance
DoC	Department of Construction
DPs	displaced persons
DPC	District People's Committee
EMMA	International Conference on Economic Management in Minerals Activities
ERDB	European Bank for Reconstruction and Development
ERPs	economic restoration programs
ESD	education for sustainable development
ESS	Environmental and Social Standard
ESF	World Bank's Environmental and Social Framework
EVN	Electricity of Vietnam
FAO	Food and Agriculture Organization of the United Nations
FDI	foreign direct investment
FPIC	free, prior, and informed consent

GDP	gross domestic product
GIA	gender impact assessments
GIS	geographic information system
GRM	grievance redress mechanism
HCMC	Ho Chi Minh City
ha	hectares
HSD	honestly significant difference
IADB	Inter-American Development Bank
ICMM	International Council on Mining & Metals
IDIs	in-depth interviews
IEA	International Energy Agency
IFC	International Finance Corporation
IOL	inventory of losses
IRRI	International Rice Research Institute
IR	involuntary resettlement
LFDCs	Land Fund Development Centers
LUC	Land Use Certificate
LUR	Land Use Right
LURC	Land Use Right Certificate
MDGs	Millennium Development Goals
MIGA	Multilateral Investment Guarantee Agency
MOIT	Ministry of Industry and Trade, Vietnam
NGO	non-governmental organization
NP project	Nui Phao resettlement project
NPM	Nui Phao Mining
ODs	operational directives
ODA	official development assistance
OPs	operational policies
PAC	project-affected community
PAH	project-affected household
PAP	project-affected person
PCDP	Public Consultation and Disclosure Plan
PMU	Project Management Unit
PPC	Provincial People's Committee
PPP	public-private partnerships
RAP	Resettlement Action Plan
RPF	Resettlement Policy Framework
SD	standard deviation
SDGs	Sustainable Development Goals
SIAs	social-impact assessments
SN 1, SN 2	Sub-Network 1, Sub-Network 2
SPSS	Statistical Package for the Social Sciences
UN	United Nations
UNDP	United Nations Development Program
WB	World Bank

WHO	World Health Organization
VND	Vietnamese Đồng
WSSD	World Summit on Sustainable Development
WVS	World Values Survey

Introduction

Nguyen Quy Nghi and Jane Singer

It has been estimated that more than 15 million people are displaced each year due to infrastructure and other large-scale development projects (Cernea 2006). This number is increasing annually, particularly due to surging construction and urban expansion in developing countries like Vietnam, and much of this displacement is linked to involuntary land acquisition – carried out, at least putatively, in the public interest. Since the launch of the *Doi Moi* [economic reforms] in 1986, Vietnam has recorded impressive economic growth and social development, to which infrastructure investments have contributed a large share. However, large-scale infrastructure projects may not only confer the promise of enhanced livelihoods and living conditions for the greater public; they may also cause significant land acquisition impacts and forced resettlement. Many people in Vietnam have compulsorily ceded their land (residential, agricultural, garden, forest) and associated assets to infrastructure projects. Others have experienced economic displacement, retaining their homes but suffering financial and intangible impacts from loss of the productive basis for their livelihoods (MONRE 2015).[1]

The large body of academic literature on development–forced displacement and resettlement published over the last four decades clearly indicates that, although many infrastructure projects are now conceptualized (by investors and government alike) as socioeconomic development initiatives aimed at improving the lives of affected people, the result too often has been increased impoverishment – because those affected are unable to secure either land-based or diversified livelihoods post-resettlement. This has been true in Vietnam as well. As this book will illustrate, land acquisition, compensation, and resettlement are among the most significant challenges in implementing and completing investment projects in Vietnam. The Ministry of Planning and Investment estimates that, out of nearly 2,000 public investment projects in 2020, about 60 percent encountered problems due to site clearance and compensation.[2]

These obstacles have consequences not only for the project itself (including delayed progress, increased capital, failure to achieve goals, and contractors claiming compensation), but they also hinder the affected community from achieving project development objectives and developing the local economy (Fish 2011; Ha-Duong et al. 2015; Phuc et al. 2015). Although the causes of these delays are

DOI: 10.4324/9781003165774-1

varied, they partly reflect the dysfunction in the relationship between the government and the people. The World Bank (2011) estimated that about 70 percent of people's formal complaints in Vietnam are related to land acquisition and the resettlement process. Recent data suggest that this situation remains unchanged. From 2014 to 2018, MONRE received about 67,383 complaints[3] related to environmental affairs, most of which were land related.

Land acquisition, compensation, and resettlement are complicated matters that could seriously affect households if not appropriately managed. The first principle of large infrastructure construction is to avoid displacement whenever possible (see the World Bank's Environmental and Social Framework, among others). This is important because the great majority of resettlements studied over the past four decades have been found to have resulted in increased poverty and abject living conditions. When displacement is found to be unavoidable, investors should adopt a program to mitigate the risks of impoverishment as first outlined by Cernea (1997). Such a program could constitute a real opportunity to transform the lives of affected households, or it could prove a development failure.

In many policy statements of international financial institutions or governments, a resettlement plan must be conceptualized as a development program – one that allows affected resettlees to maximize their access to project benefits and to improve their living standards. How far has this principle been achieved in the context of Vietnam's rapidly evolving socialist-oriented market economy? Has it made affected people better off? We try to answer these questions in this book, and we outline directions for future research and intervention. We contend that development-induced resettlement requires multiple processes to be implemented effectively. In carrying out these processes, it is imperative that the views and concerns of all actors involved be expressed, considered, and discussed.

This also raises the important question of whether a single-party state like Vietnam can institutionally mediate the often-conflicting demands of project stakeholders, governments, local residents, and resettlees in an inclusive, transparent, and equitable fashion. At the household level, the process of resettlement proceeds from the notice of land acquisition (including resettlement impacts) to relocation and local integration. It entails several stages (including notification, inventory of loss, pricing, approval, publication, payment, handover, grievances, and enforcement), with many decisions being made at various levels. The basic resettlement mechanism in Vietnam emphasizes the crucial role of local authorities, who are responsible for contacting and negotiating with affected households on the compensation rate, relocation plan, and implementation schedule. This book, organized into 13 chapters in four parts, reflects differing perspectives on the issues that this policy raises in resettlement implementation on the ground.

Part 1 consists of three chapters focusing on legal aspects and policy instruments related to land acquisition and the resettlement process. In the first chapter, Phan Trung Hien discusses resolving conflicts and balancing public and private interests in land taking for development projects. This chapter also proposes effective approaches for resolving conflict between authorities and concerned individuals. The legal provisions on compensation have also been evolving (Dang 2017), from no mention in the 1987 *Land Law* to a government-determined compensation rate (*Land Law 1993*), market-level compensation (*Land Law 2003*) and market-level rates determined at the time of compensation (*Land Law 2013*). In Chapter 2, Le Anh Tuan covers the key issues that usually arise with development projects requiring major resettlement and how these issues could be addressed by enhancing the capability of Land Fund Development Centers (LFDCs) as the key actors in resettlement implementation. He discusses how to support LFDCs to improve resettlement outcomes in infrastructure development projects and to promote policy change as a long-term objective. In Chapter 3, Nguyen Van Dang introduces the "policy tool" approach that the government uses to implement land acquisition and resettlement. This chapter analyzes the characteristics of policy tools; their influence on the behavior of government officials as well as the public; and the oft-contested relationship between the government and the people. It explains why people often react adversely to – and even actively oppose – land acquisition and resettlement projects.

Part 2 is a collection of analytical chapters on the conversion of agricultural land to make way for urban development projects in the north (Red River Delta) and central regions of Vietnam. In Chapter 4, Nguyen Quang Phuc uses a case study in Hue city to demonstrate that compulsory land acquisition driven by rapid urbanization is an unbalanced and unfair process in terms of the costs and benefits distribution, equal participation and just compensation. These issues, along with the shirking of responsibility by decision-makers in policy implementation, create challenges that impede equitable and sustainable development. The chapter concludes with policy recommendations for institutional improvement in Vietnam's land governance. In Chapters 5 and 6, Nguyen Van Suu and Nguyen Thi Thanh Binh analyze how farmers in suburban Hanoi react and adapt to urban development projects. In Chapter 5, Nguyen Van Suu argues that, while farmers have been dissatisfied with the compensation packages offered by state authorities, many villagers have successfully adapted to new market opportunities by offering rental accommodations to tenants who come to study and work in the city. This involvement in rental housing and in non-agricultural work was not foreseen by state authorities, but it stems from the state's urban development of their home village and enables these former farmers to formulate new market-based livelihood strategies. In Chapter 6, Nguyen Thi Thanh Binh highlights positive aspects of agricultural land conversion for two communities affected by urban development projects. Despite receiving unfair compensation packages, many local residents have turned urbanization advantages (for example, the increased value of residential land) into development opportunities. After years of anxiety and turbulence, the lives of most households in the two communities have gradually stabilized as many have transitioned from farming to join the urban working class.

The chapters in Part 3 introduce resettlement programs related to large infrastructure projects, especially hydropower dams, which have been the focus of research since the start of development-induced displacement studies. In Chapter 7, Jane Singer, Pham Huu Ty and Thi Kinh Kieu explore both the livelihood-related benefits and the non-economic costs (particularly losses of social and cultural capital) associated with resettlement in peri-urban areas for displaced ethnic minority communities. The authors compare two communities resettled in peri-urban sites in central Vietnam with a dam-displaced village in a remote upland location. Their research suggests that, while non-farm livelihood adaptations (including manual and industrial labor, plantation labor and domestic migration) may be more accessible for peri-urban resettlees, the benefits conferred for rural villages by their robust social networks, strong ethnic identity and practices, and culturally significant structures can promote greater community resilience. In Chapter 8, through her analysis of economic restoration of communities affected by the Son La hydropower plant, Nga Dao aims to understand how people's resilience and adaptation – conditioned by access to land and resources as well as by particular social, cultural, and economic relations – have contributed to shaping their livelihood outcomes. She also explores the villagers' lives before resettlement, their livelihood diversification, and how coping and adaptation strategies in resettled villages have unfolded. She finds that affected households diversified their incomes and adjusted their livelihoods to compensate for the limited land in their new villages. With the resulting income, they could purchase more land from the host communities. In Chapter 9, based on their experience in project implementation, Nguyen Quy Nghi and Phan Huyen Dan identify the elements needed to promote an effective resettlement program that can contribute to the sustainability of hydropower projects. They conclude that models for sustainability should have the following characteristics: compliance with the project's policy; being people-centered; avoidance of potential risks/social impacts; suitability for the community context; and gender and cultural sensitivity (FAO 2013; Nguyen et al. 2020). In the last chapter of Part 3, the authors (Nguyen Quy Nghi, Nguyen Thi Minh Phuong, and Do Thi Le Hang) analyze the integration of relocated families into host communities. They conclude that resettlement requires efforts by the displaced people; robust preparedness; and facilitation from other stakeholders during the entire process. Attention to cultural, psychological, and social dimensions are equally important for successful resettlement: resettlement programs need to achieve a better balance between tangible aspects (such as land, buildings/structures, and crops) and intangible elements (such as culture, lifestyle, customs, and social capital). The authors of this chapter call for a change in paradigm, so as to place affected people at the center of resettlement processes. The resettlement program should consider resettlees as potential beneficiaries and provide them with opportunities for development and shared prosperity.

Part 4 of the book deals with emerging issues related to land acquisition, compensation, and resettlement in Vietnam. In Chapter 11, Dinh Thi Ngoc Bich explores the collaboration between public and private actors in compulsory land conversion in Vietnam, emphasizing good practice. Experience from a mining-induced resettlement project shows that public-private partnerships can produce results, solutions and processes that would not have been possible with single, hierarchical organizations. This type of PPP shares features with the corporate social responsibility model of PPP. In Chapter 12, Do Thi Le Hang, Nguyen

Quy Nghi and Nguyen Thi Minh Phuong present the psychological experiences of resettlees who involuntarily cede their lands and structures to infrastructure projects. They argue that current land acquisition practices primarily focus on the "hard" components of compensation: resettlement sites and physical infrastructure; compensation packages for affected people (in cash or in-kind); and livelihood restoration and income-generation activities. The "soft" aspects of the relocation process, such as psychological and social support programs, are currently poorly developed or non-existent in mitigation programs. This neglect may allow affected people to suffer severe mental health impacts. Action from resettlement planners is needed to incorporate these soft aspects, making resettlement more comprehensive and building resilience for affected people who settle in the new site. In the final chapter, Pham Thi Dieu My presents the experience of an NGO in conducting gender impact assessment (GIA) in hydropower development in the Central and Central Highland regions of Vietnam. In her view, GIA allows us to better understand how hydropower development affects women and men differently. Gaps in understanding could be bridged if the GIA process was applied correctly. It would also be helpful if various stakeholders, especially hydropower developers, included gender-sensitive measures to mitigate adverse impacts. GIA can validate the lived experiences of women and men and provide the evidence needed to persuade the government, as well as hydropower developers, that they ought to act more responsively. Her research has suggested that participation in a GIA process may also empower women to speak up about their issues.

There is a wide consensus among researchers about the adverse resettlement impacts caused by land acquisition for development projects. From initial studies of hydropower dam resettlement (Scudder 2005), scholars have expanded their scope to other types of infrastructure such as transmission lines, urban development infrastructure, irrigation, water supply, mining, and extractive industries (Stanley 2004). The assessment of impacts and associated risks has also broadened, from single elements (land, buildings, assets, crops); to inter-related factors (gender, social networks, participation, consultation, indigenous people); impacts on destination communities (Hay et al. 2019); cultural factors (Downing 2009); and mental health effects (Xi 2016). A comprehensive resettlement program is multi-layered, consisting of national policy, resettlement arrangements for a particular project, and the dynamics of each household.

There has been only scant literature in Vietnam on this subject, despite the growing number of large-scale infrastructure and urban development projects. This poses difficulties for many different groups. Researchers, for example, lack a general perspective across the issues involved, from legal aspects to specific interventions at the household level. Lawmakers and policymakers lack concrete evidence for their legal reforms or corrections. Practitioners, in turn, will find that critical information on resettlement impacts overall is missing. This book is an opportunity for the authors to present the latest evidence and research findings and to introduce practical experience, based on study of specific projects.

This may also be considered the first book that systematically and comprehensively approaches the issue of development-induced displacement and resettlement in Vietnam. It explores how a single-party state like Vietnam can protect the perceived interests of the state while still satisfying the demands of international financial institutions and other investors – and of civil society and the media for protection of human rights principles including free, prior, and informed consent (FPIC); stakeholder participation in decision-making; transparency; impartial adjudication of grievances; and benefit sharing.

Perhaps the greatest contribution of this book is the inclusiveness and completeness of its content, moving from the evolution of the legal framework to specific issues in rehabilitation and resettlement in hydropower projects; livelihood issues in agricultural land conversion; and post-resettlement issues such as resettlees' integration into host communities, psychological impacts, and cultural factors. We hope that the book will be a valuable and authoritative reference covering research and analysis of involuntary resettlement in Vietnam.

Notes

1 This report (based on the data of 34/63 provinces) indicated that, in 2014 alone, about 2,190 projects were implemented, leading to the acquisition of 7,882 hectares of land and affecting nearly 81,000 organizations/individuals/households.

2 https://vneconomy.vn/day-nhanh-du-an-dau-tu-cong-go-diem-nghen-giai-phong-mat-bang.htm. [accessed December 5, 2021].

3 https://monre.gov.vn/Pages/giai-quyet-tranh-chap-ve-dat-dai;-giai-quyet-khieu-nai,-to-cao-trong-quan-ly-va-su-dung-dat-dai.aspx. [accessed December 17, 2021].

References

Cernea, M.M. (1997). The risks and reconstruction model for resettling displaced populations. *World Development*, Vol. 25, Issue 10: 1569–1587. https://doi.org/10.1016/S0305-750X(97)00054-5.

Cernea, M.M. (2006). Development-induced and conflict-induced IDPs: Bridging the research divide. *Forced Migration Review* (Special Issue): 25–27.

Dang Hung Vo. (2017). Vietnamese laws on land acquisition, resettlement and gender mainstreaming. Presentation at the international conference on "Gender and Resettlement: Evidence and Policy Implications", Ha Long April 2017.

Downing, T.E., and Garcia-Downing, C. (2009). Routine and dissonant culture: A theory about the psycho-socio-cultural disruptions of involuntary displacement and ways to mitigate them without inflicting even more damage. In: Oliver-Smith, A. (Ed.), *Development & Dispossession*. School for Advanced Research Press, Santa Fe, pp. 225–320.

FAO (Food and Agriculture Organization). (2013). Good practices at FAO: Experience capitalization for continuous learning. Available at www.fao.org/3/a-ap784e.pdf.

Fish, C. (2011). *Land Acquisition for Special Economic Zones in India (M.A. 1488780)*. Temple University, PA. Available at https://scholarshare.temple.edu/bitstream/handle/20.500.12613/1220/Fish_temple_0225M_10580.pdf?sequence=1&isAllowed=y. [accessed December 20, 2021].

Ha-Duong, M., Lan, A.N., Strange, T., and Truong, A.H. (2015). Social acceptability of large infrastructure projects in Vietnam. Field Actions Science Reports. FACTS Report.

Hay, M., Skinner, J., and Norton, A. (2019). Dam-induced displacement and resettlement: A literature review. FutureDAMS Working Paper 004. The University of Manchester, Manchester.

Ministry of Natural Resources and Environment. (2015). Report on state management of land in 2014 and first half of 2015, Land Law execution and issues to be solved, Ha Noi 20 July 2015.

Nguyen Quy Nghi, Martin H. Lenihan, Saint-Pierre Claude, Nguyen Thi Minh Phuong, and Phan Huyen Dan. (2020). *Managing Social Risks and Impacts from Hydropower Development: Sharing Experience from a Medium-Sized Dam Project in Vietnam*. World Bank, Washington, DC. https://openknowledge.worldbank.org/handle/10986/34442 License: CC BY 3.0 IGO. [accessed May 31, 2021].

Nguyen Quang Phuc, Annelies Zoomers, and A.C.M. vanWesten. (2015). Compulsory land acquisition for urban expansion: A study of farmer's protest in peri-urban Hue, Central Vietnam. In: *Land Grabbing, Conflict and Agrarian-Environmental Transformations: Perspectives from East and Southeast Asia*. Chiang Mai University, Chiangmai.

Scudder, T. (2005). *The Future of Large Dams: Dealing with Social, Environmental, Institutional and Political Costs*. Earthscan, London.

Stanley, J. (2004). *Development-induced Displacement and Resettlement*. Forced Migration Online Research Guide, Refugee Studies Centre, University of Oxford, Oxford.

World Bank. (2011). *Compulsory Land Acquisition and Voluntary Land Conversion in Vietnam: The Conceptual Approach, Land Valuation and Grievance Redress Mechanisms*. World Bank, Hanoi. https://openknowledge.worldbank.org/handle/10986/26886 License: CC BY 3.0 IGO.

Xi, J. (2016). Types of integration and depressive symptoms: A latent class analysis on the resettled population for the Three Gorges dam project, China. *Social Science & Medicine*. Vol. 157: 78–86. ISSN 0277–9536. https://doi.org/10.1016/j.socscimed.2016.03.045.

Part 1

Legal framework on land acquisition and resettlement in Vietnam

1 Land acquisition legal framework in Vietnam

Balancing public and private interests

Phan Trung Hien

Introduction

In Vietnam, the involuntary conversion of land for public purposes (also known as "land acquisition") is practically inevitable, due to the growing demand for infrastructure development. The Government of Vietnam has introduced many policies to improve land acquisition practices and to regain people's confidence in law enforcement. Significant financial resources have been allocated to improving the *Land Law* through four amendments (in 1987, 1993, 2003, and 2013). Those policies and solutions have proven effective in pushing construction projects forward, keeping to the schedule, and saving costs.

Although Vietnam has a relatively good legal framework in general, its enforcement is far from flawless. Acquiring land for development projects is always challenging and rarely implemented on schedule. Site clearance usually takes a long time, which causes inordinate delays to construction projects (Thu Ha 2021). The compulsory acquisition of land – ostensibly for public purposes – has been the source of many complaints. According to the Ministry of Natural Resources and the Environment (MONRE), 98 percent of received complaints are related to land use, land acquisition decisions, or the dissatisfaction of land users with the offered compensation rates. These complaints or disputes, which are on the rise, tend to be increasingly prolonged and to harm national security and social order (Khanh Thi 2019). Land-related complaint and dispute cases reported by the media indicate a failure in negotiations between the land users and the acquiring authorities, which has led to a widespread perception of a malfunctioning system (Dang 2021).

Land-related complaints have partly stemmed from the country's inadequate system of policies and laws on land and from their poor application. The existing policies on land management, changed many times, have not been fully synchronized. There are legal provisions that lack specificity and are not contextually relevant. The land price for compensation calculation issued by the government is very far from the market price in many places, and the land acquisition process is often not transparent (Bui 2020). In addition, the mechanism of compulsory land acquisition has been used for some projects under the banner of "socioeconomic development" – while actually serving the interests of corporations and

DOI: 10.4324/9781003165774-3

companies. There is evidence that Vietnamese law has not been applied uniformly in all provinces and cities (Xuan Hung 2016). Many local authorities are only interested in attracting investment without paying attention to the legitimate interests of land users.

This chapter focuses on resolving conflict and balancing public and private interests in land that is subject to development plans or proposals. Its theme is the conflict between land-acquiring authorities and the affected individuals involved in the process. It examines the extent to which the law provides an effective medium to resolve existing issues, with an aim to limit compulsory land acquisition purposes; identify clear procedures for compulsory land acquisition; and guarantee fair compensation for land holders.

Ideologies of public and private ownership

In general, the Vietnamese land situation can be better understood in the context of global approaches to land ownership.

Private ownership is widely recognized in almost all countries. There is a connection between private property development and social development. A review of recent literature reveals the existence of three distinct ideologies.

Private ownership-based ideology

In most countries around the world, the state acquires land from property owners for public uses only. Property rights now constitute a fundamental human right in capitalist countries, where stringent conditions govern land acquisition by the state – but allow the state to infringe property rights if it is for the common good (Clarke 1992). The philosopher John Locke, one of the most influential thinkers of the seventeenth century, added the idea that natural rights include the right to property.

Under "natural law," every individual can enjoy their "natural rights" to land and other properties. However, individuals may enter into a form of social contract: they may agree to transfer some of their rights to a legitimate government, in order to protect their property and to live in safety and security. As Locke (1986) argued:

> The great and chief end, therefore, of men uniting into Commonwealths, and putting themselves under government, is the preservation of their property; to which in the state of Nature there are many things wanting.

Likewise, the English jurist Sir William Blackstone saw the right to property as a natural one, that could not be violated. In 1765, in his *Commentaries on the laws of England* (Blackstone 1966:135), Blackstone argued that:

> So great moreover is the regard of the law for private property, that it will not authorise the least violation of it; no, not even for the general good of the whole community.

While the aforementioned authors had different perspectives on how and why private property must be strictly respected, they both asserted some critical principles. First, private ownership is a natural right. The inference is that it is natural because it obviously arises from the natural order of life. In other words, when human beings were aware of the role of property, they knew how to acquire, keep, and dispose of it. Therefore, the right to possess property is closely related to human nature (Finnis 1980). Second, it is an absolute right. This means that private property is inviolate and cannot be forcibly acquired.

Recognition and codification of private ownership rights have been achieved by human beings over a long historical span (De Soto 2000). However, conceiving of unilateral private land rights as "natural" and "absolute" might cause challenges for society in economic, social, and political terms: should development be needed for the public interest, the government would face difficulties in persuading private owners to give up their rights, even with fair compensation (Phan 2009).

Public (or collective) interests-based ideology

At its most extreme, this ideology supports the extinction of private ownership. Karl Marx, the most influential proponent of this view, wrote about the "harmfulness of private property" (Marx 1977:87). He asserted (1977:99–100) that "further development of productive forces would lead to the disappearance of private capitalist ownership and the appearance of collective socialist ownership." Marx also declared (1977:134) that "all of people's sufferings originate from the establishment of private ownership, and landed property."

English philosopher Jeremy Bentham had a different political stance. He objected to Locke's ideology of a "natural right" to property, arguing that property rights could not exist in a state of nature. They can only exist under a government.

Bentham proclaimed that:

> The interest of the community is one of the most general expressions that can occur in the phraseology of morals: no wonder that the meaning of it is often lost. The community is a fictitious body, composed of the individual persons who are considered as constituting as it were its members. The interest of the community then is what? – the sum of the interests of the several members who compose it.
>
> (Bentham 1948:3)

Although Marx and Bentham looked at "property" from very different perspectives, they shared a viewpoint about public and private interests. With Marx, "the public interest" is the primary goal of a socialist regime, so everything needs to start and proceed from this point. For Bentham, "the greatest happiness of the greatest number" is the rationale when individual interests need to be subsumed within the wider whole.

In other words, one could see the views of Marx and Bentham as follows:

Bentham: Public interests are indispensable in a community, in a society.
Marx: Collective ownership – socialist ownership – must be the primary ownership in a society. The state should have full authority to acquire land from private property owners as far as that is for the public need.

There are a few ways to interpret and implement Marx and Bentham's point of view. In some socialist countries, including Vietnam, it was first considered that all major properties for society, which are productive materials, must belong to the state (McAuslan 2003:24). Certainly, besides its advantages, the predominance of "public property" may also imply disadvantages, as explored in the following scenario:

> Imagine a country where nobody can identify who owns what, addresses cannot be easily verified, people cannot be made to pay their debts, resources cannot conveniently be turned into money, ownership cannot be divided into shares, descriptions of assets are not standardized and vary from neighborhood to neighborhood or even from street to street.
>
> (De Soto 2000:15)

Thus, at its extreme, "public ownership" would give the state the role of an absolute owner, and this may not be suitable for development. What De Soto claims is that because there was no private ownership, no one would care about the property or be willing to invest in the factors of production. It is necessary to have an ideology that harmonizes both public and private interests.

Ideology of keeping a balance between private and public interests

This ideology respects private ownership as one of the fundamental rights to improve freedom and human dignity. It also respects public rights or interests. Therefore, balancing public and private rights becomes essential.

In 1765, Sir William Blackstone reinforced the principle that public interest could only prevail over private ownership with the consent of the owner:

> If a road, for instance, were to be made through the grounds of a private person, it might perhaps be extensively beneficial to the public; but the law permits no man, or set of man, to do this without consent to the owner of the land.
>
> (Blackstone 1966:135)

In *The rights of man*, Thomas Paine also stressed that a property right is man's natural right except for public necessity (Paine 1969:97). Of course, where expropriation is necessary, there should be compensation. Baron Bramwell advocated such an approach in 1862 in the United Kingdom:

> That law to my mind is a bad one which, for the public benefit, inflicts loss on an individual without compensation . . . I deny that it is for the public benefit he should do what he has done; if they are, he ought to compensate.
>
> (Bramwell, cited in Brubaker 1995:188)

This principle originated in the *Magna Carta*, the "Great Charter of Liberties" signed in 1215, that forbade the King's agents from taking a man's timber and horses without his agreement and without providing compensation in the event of expropriation.

> Expropriations are fair only if, through compensation, they leave all affected parties as well off as they were before. Just compensation could, for example, enable people to purchase properties and rights similar to those which have been taken.
>
> (Brubaker 1995)

Clearly, private property is seen as a subject of mutual interest and tension between the state and individual citizens. There must be some overlap between public and private interests in land use management. Hence, balancing these two is one of the most important challenges for state and society.

In a democratic society, both public needs and private interests are emphasized and must be protected by law. On the one hand, public needs for development, redevelopment, or regeneration are indispensable to every country's growth – so compulsory land acquisition in the public interest must be possible under the law. On the other hand, private property must be respected, and property rights must also be guaranteed by law. Therefore, when land is acquired for public needs, it must satisfy certain conditions such as serving the public interest, following strict procedures, and providing full compensation. In other words, compulsory acquisition of land is an interrelationship between public and private interests.

Key themes in the analysis of land acquisition law in Vietnam

Since Vietnam's Constitution of 1980 was promulgated, all land in Vietnam has been treated as belonging to the entire people, as represented by the state. Through constitutional provision (*Constitution of the Socialist Republic of Vietnam*, Article 19), no one in Vietnam can own land as private property. Clearly, the ideologies and philosophies of recognizing land ownership and land acquisition in Vietnam are quite different from those of most developed countries. Land in Vietnam only became the subject of compulsory acquisition, with compensation, after the *Land Law* was promulgated in 1993. However, the 1992 Constitution regulated nothing on land acquisition. It can be said that land acquisition in this period in Vietnam was only recognized by law, not constitutionally. The 2013 Constitution is the first constitution of Vietnam that mentions compulsory land acquisition. Clause 3, Article 54 of the 2013 Constitution states:

> The State shall recover land used by organizations and individuals in imperative cases provided by the law for the purposes of national defence, national security, and socioeconomic developments for national and public interests. The recovery of land must be public and transparent, and compensations must be provided in concordance with the law.

The existing legislation of Vietnam still uses the terminology "land recovery" rather than "land acquisition" (*Land Law 2013*, Article 146, Clause 1). However, the 2013 Constitution guarantees that land is only to be compulsorily acquired "for the purposes of national defence, national security, and socioeconomic developments for national and public interests"; that "the recovery of land must be public and transparent"; and that "compensations must be provided in concordance with the law" (*Constitution of the Socialist Republic of Vietnam*).

Therefore, given the contrasting underlying ideologies of balancing public and private interests, the constitutional grounds for land recovery in Vietnam can be analyzed and compared. Several key principles emerge for further discussion, including:

(i) limiting the purposes of compulsory land acquisition;
(ii) clearly identifying the procedures for compulsory land acquisition; and
(iii) guaranteeing fair compensation for land holders.

"Limiting the purposes of compulsory land acquisition"

As noted earlier, Vietnam's Constitution of 2013 stipulates land recovery "for the purposes of national defense, national security and socioeconomic development in the national and public interests" (*Constitution of the Socialist Republic of Vietnam*, Article 54, Clause 3). However, at present, even determining what is encompassed by "land acquisition for the purpose of socioeconomic development for national and public interests" poses challenges.

First, the *Land Law* and other legal documents in Vietnam mention the recovery of land for "urban embellishment" (*Land Law 2013*, Article 146, Clause 1) – but these documents have not fully explained the concept of "urban embellishment." Other concepts relating to "economic development purposes" have not been explained for land used to develop urban and rural residential areas. This kind of development is not clearly defined and may include projects related to graveyards, funeral homes, cremation sites, and residential facilities, and to concentrated production and processing areas for agriculture, forest products, aquatic products, and seafood.

In addition, the *Land Law* stipulates that, when implementing well-planned infrastructure projects, the state can proactively acquire land (including land for construction of infrastructure and its surrounding area) according to land use planning and master plans – but without detailed guidelines for these cases (*Land Law 2013*, Article 146, Clause 3). In fact, when the state acquires land for socioeconomic development, economic benefits will prevail:

> The emergence of economic factors makes it much more difficult to assess the public benefits. The state conducts land acquisition compulsorily, then transfers it to investors. The value of land after it is acquired and built upon is increased and it is traded on the real estate market. So, first of all, the benefits are in the hands of the investors.
>
> (Dinh 2016)

In some cases, "land acquisition for the purpose of socioeconomic development" shares the benefits with cases of transferring land to implement production and business projects (Phan 2021). In fact, when it comes to satisfying both economic and social interests, the determination of these production and business goals can be difficult (Oyez 2005). For example, projects related to high-tech industrial zones, economic zones, new urban areas, and the like do not only serve public interests but also bring more profits to investors.

> Therefore, the purpose of land acquisition must be for the community. The provincial government should not be allowed to expand the purpose of land acquisition, especially for commercial purposes, such as in urban areas. In fact, urban areas carry commercial purposes more than public purposes.
>
> (Nguyen 2016:75)

According to some experts, the scope of application of land acquisition methods in Vietnam is too wide, and for many projects it is difficult to prove whether they are for national interests or for public interests (Tien Long 2017).

Second, for many reasons, local government agencies arbitrarily designate land acquisition cases as being for "socioeconomic development." For example, in some localities, land acquisition for eco-tourism in urban areas is considered as being for socioeconomic development (Xuan Hung 2016). In fact, the construction of an eco-urban area is a profitable private investment project that does not serve public interests. Other examples include projects that use less than 10 percent of the project land for social housing and resettlement and more than 90 percent for condominiums, commercial buildings, gardens, and villas – but to justify land acquisition, this is still considered as serving "socioeconomic development" purposes (Nguyen and Hai Duong 2017).

Third, some provincial governments have acquired land for private commercial benefits but in the name of "public interest investment" (Tien Long 2017). This is cause for concern, particularly when they use public resources (staff, budget) to acquire the land compulsorily (V. Huy 2021). The offered compensation price is often lower than the actual market prices (Hoang 2017).

Indeed, in this situation the local government has compulsorily acquired land from the poor and reallocated it to private companies and wealthy corporations – so the principle of acquiring land for national and public interests has been violated. This suggests the need for clearer and more specific guidance in the country's relevant statutes. In addition, there is a need for the government's guiding documents to explain the application of the *Land Law*'s provisions on the ground.

"Clearly identifying procedures for compulsory land acquisition"

The 2013 *Constitution of Vietnam* (Article 54, Clause 3) requires that "the land acquisition must be public, transparent and compensated in accordance with law." "Public" means full information access for all interested parties, and "transparency" means clarity. When discussing these themes, researchers often refer to "opportunities," "equal access to information," "reliability," "consistency of information," "predictability," and to the "openness" of the agency that provides the information (Pham 2015).

In the process of land acquisition, access to information and transparency are key implementation principles to ensure broad public participation. Indeed, "citizens have the right to themselves or through representative organizations to exercise the right to supervise and report violations of land management and use" (*Land Law 2013*, Article 199, and Article 200). This includes supervision of activities such as land recovery, compensation, assistance, and resettlement.

However, the law does not specify how these principles should be implemented. Its application on the ground to date has not strictly followed legal requirements. For example, the Provincial People's Committee rarely consults the public when determining and approving compensation rates. The Council of Land Price Evaluation, which bears responsibility for appraising compensation rate proposals, is made up of administrative staff and generally consults with organizational leadership. Due to the lack of any participatory monitoring mechanism, land valuation organizations (under the pressure of local authorities as customers) cannot provide a practical and objective estimation that reflects actual market transactions. Because land prices are often fixed substantially below market levels, disagreements and complaints frequently occur.

Moreover, people are not informed about resettlement sites, infrastructure, and living conditions in new residential areas (Phan 2019). The law requires resettlement areas to conform with "each region and area's conditions, customs, and practices" (*Land Law 2013*, Article 85, Clause 3). In reality, many resettlement areas do not meet those requirements (Thai and Dao 2017). In addition, the timeline for the handover of resettlement plots is often not well defined, and it could happen much later, after the physical relocation of the affected people (Hoàng 2019). In many cases, resettlees could not move to their new places on time, due to incomplete resettlement sites and associated infrastructure (Le 2020).

Finally, although land users in Vietnam have the right to choose between filing administrative complaints or court lawsuits, these rights have certain limitations (Phan 2018):

(i) To file an administrative complaint, the complainant must go through two steps. The first step is to appeal to the District People's Committee. If the complainant disagrees with the decision at the district level, they can send a second complaint to the Provincial People's Committee. This second complaint marks the end of the administrative process.

Since provincial people's committees are responsible for many critical decisions in the land acquisition process (for example, for land prices and project implementation), there may be some bias (because the people responsible for determining land prices are the very governmental officials who are pursuing the development project in the first place).

(ii) In the case of a lawsuit, the people's right to sue over compensation prices is not accepted by courts in Vietnam (although the *Administrative Procedure Law 2015* does not restrict this right). According to the guidance of the Chief Justice of the Supreme People's Court, when resolving a case of compulsory land acquisition, revaluation of the land value is not to be conducted (Supreme People's Court 2016).

There are many reasons to explain this guidance. One of the Court's most serious concerns is that the judicial revaluation of a household's parcel of land could give rise to many subsequent parallel lawsuits (Phan 2018). For instance, if a litigant successfully obtained a land price higher than initially determined at the administrative level, other affected households who had already received lower compensation might return and ask for the revised land price.

"Guaranteeing fair compensation for landholders"

As stated in the Constitution, "Land acquisition must be public, transparent and compensated according to the provisions of law" (art. 54, cl. 3). In practice, the vague indication of "according to the provisions of law" creates certain difficulties in how land compensation is assessed. The local government only pays compensation according to specific provisions embedded in the letter of the law. Therefore, if the land user's property is damaged but not acquired, *and that kind of damage is not prescribed in the law*, the land user will not receive any compensation. For example, compensation for animal breeding affected by land acquisition only applies to aquatic animals, not other types. People who use the land for the latter will only receive support, not compensation (*Land Law 2013*, Article 90). This omission obviously creates inequality in compensation.

Vietnam's laws and judicial practices show a significant distinction in handling damages under the civil code and administrative law. When people suffer damage to their property or property rights, the first thing responsible state agencies have to do is to determine who has caused the damage. If individuals or non-state organizations have caused the damage, it will be considered for settlement according to civil compensation procedures and civil procedures. If the damage is caused by a competent state agency or a civil servant, it will be considered for settlement according to administrative or judicial procedures.

As a result, much of the damage caused by land acquisition cannot be adequately compensated (Phan 2016). For example, many development projects in Vietnam have been pending for a long period of time after the land has been acquired, leaving clusters of homes isolated with unfinished drainage systems or unpaved roads and causing hardships for local residents in their daily lives. As a result, the affected people may have had to sell their homes and leave, or they may have become enmired in an ongoing process of filing complaints that their local authorities are not able to settle (Hung Long 2015).

In general, there is a potential issue with the assets that can be compensated by the government. The law in developed countries defines interests as either "tangible" or "intangible" (Phan 2009). "Tangible" losses might include loss of land and of other properties connected to the land (such as dwellings, trees, ponds, fish, and so forth) while "intangible" losses might include such things as home loss; injuries from noise, fumes, vibration; loss of view; and so forth. However, for purposes of compulsory acquisition, Vietnamese law recognizes only "tangible" interests (except such intangible interests as home loss payment, grave replacement, and consideration of high voltage electricity lines). Other "intangible" interests that affect people or private properties are not recognized.

Assets acquired in Vietnam also include rights to use land but not land ownership in the forms common in developed countries. Certainly, the accepted definition of the acquired interests could affect the policies and compensation methods. To improve the Vietnamese system, the definitions of interests that can be compensated must be recognized in a broader sense. Based on the idea of keeping a balance between public and private interests in compulsory acquisitions, all damage to the "private interests" caused by "public work" (for public purposes) should be taken into account. Besides the interests involved in acquisition, other interests, even when not acquired, can be damaged or severely affected.

The compensation process in Vietnam exhibits significant variations in outcomes as well. The forms of compensation for land may be another piece of land with the same land use purpose, or the equivalent value of the acquired land plot may be paid in cash (*Land Law 2013*, Article 74). In practice, because there is not enough land available for land-for-land compensation, compensation is mainly paid in cash. In addition to the cash compensation, people whose land has been recovered also receive support for resettlement, production, and (for farmers who no longer have their productive land) training for job change. However, most types of support are received in cash (HP 2019). Compensation should not only provide a fair amount of money but also safeguard the affected people through financial assistance, job transition, and acceptance into a new community. This would help working-class residents who may not have enough resources to resettle, after their lives have been disrupted by the loss of property for public purposes.

All of those real-life examples show that there is an urgent need to fully address land acquisition issues in Vietnamese law, in line with international best practice. This reform could be combined with other issues related to compulsory acquisition, within one updated statute, to guarantee that fair compensation and private interests are safeguarded.

A call for legal framework reform in Vietnam

The topic of "compulsory acquisition" can comprise many issues, such as acquiring properties compulsorily, paying compensation fairly, and settling affected families in new places. However, the fundamental analytical issue is the need to balance state interests in acquiring land with individuals' interests in the land acquired. Therefore, the system for compulsory acquisition of land only works if it satisfies both individuals' aspirations and those of the state. In a broader sense, this section identifies some key issues for reforming the Vietnamese legal system.

Issues of land ownership

Land ownership, promulgated in the national constitution, is a fundamentally political institution in any country. Proposing a change in land ownership often requires extensive consideration based on each country's historical and legal traditions. In Vietnam's case, through amendments, Vietnam could make its current *Land Law* more flexible and responsive to its socioeconomic development.

First, if public ownership of land is still to be maintained, the real owner of the land should be identified. If the "landowner" is the people as a whole, the rights and obligations of the owner must be more clearly defined. Among those rights is the right to decide whether the state, as representative of the public land ownership, is subject to accountability. State agencies, such as the National Assembly, the government, people's councils, and people's committees, would be responsible for answering to the people about the land use and management activities within the scope of each agency's tasks. In short, to ensure the notion of the entire people's ownership of land where the state is their public representative, the working accountability of each relevant state agency should be established. In parallel, some fundamental processes or protections should be guaranteed under the land management responsibilities of the state (as representative of the entire people): democratic and just processes; open and transparent state actions; and outcomes that are both legally based and reasonable.

Second, Vietnam should develop regulations on dual ownership. Land belongs to the whole people: "primary ownership." When the owner's representative has assigned land to the users, they should be given secondary ownership. In fact, land use rights in Vietnam really have the characteristics of property ownership in a real estate market. This regulation of secondary ownership creates leverage in production motivation; guarantees the landowners' rights; and creates social stability. Strictly speaking, primary ownership would have priority over secondary ownership. Once the state needs land for public purposes, it can completely buy secondary ownership rights. Such regimes have been developed in countries where the land originally or formally belongs to the monarch or head of state. For instance, originally and officially, in British law, there is no absolute title. The reason was that the rights to the land were established through the Queen's tenancy. However, landholders are now treated like landowners (Riddall 1993).

Third, there are currently a number of land users in Vietnam who, for various reasons, have been using the land without holding a lawful certificate. In addition to the cases of illegal users (such as land trespassers), there are some cases that are not obviously illegal but lack the clarity to be considered lawful. How can we improve these situations and transform the Vietnamese system into a system that implements clearer property titling and registry?

Beyond clear titling, there is the issue of title security. In Vietnam, a "certificate of use" (on which lawfulness of use depends in this country) could be taken away or not renewed. Vietnam can learn from developed countries where a certificate of use, in the form of planning permission, is regarded as permanent and can only be withdrawn upon compensation.

The need to limit the purposes of compulsory land acquisition

There is a need to clarify and limit the state's rights in compulsory land acquisition to legitimate "public" purposes (that is, excluding private commercial interests disguised as "public" interests). The law needs to provide specific criteria delineating the types of projects expected to generate public benefit, and the justifications for acquiring land must be made clearer. In particular, land acquisition for "socioeconomic development in accordance with national and public interests" ought to be determined using clearer and more specific guidance, stipulated in the relevant statutes. There is a strong need to clarify certain operative terms used in the provisions of the Vietnamese *Land Law*, including "new urban areas," "urban embellishment," and "rural embellishment."

This will make the legal provisions clear and no longer ambiguous. It will also create the conditions to clearly distinguish two scenarios:

(i) Compulsory land acquisition for defense and security purposes and socioeconomic development for the national and public interests, according to Articles 61 and 62 of *Land Law 2013*; and
(ii) Transfer and lease of land use rights in case investors agree to carry out production and business projects according to Article 73 of the *Land Law*.

It is important that Article 73 cases be based on the principles of consensus and negotiation, avoiding any coercive measures.

According to De Soto, the individual rights relating to land not only express a fundamental right but could also be used as a lever either to stimulate the economy (if the policies are appropriate) or to depress development in the long term (if the policies are inappropriate; Ricketts 2005). To attract investment and stimulate the economy in a developing country such as Vietnam, the process of – and compensation for – compulsory acquisition of land needs to be clear and transparent. It would be useful to explore the ideas of Hernando De Soto in terms of respecting private property rights and lifting the economy, as follows:

> The key to unlock the development potential of the country was to drain the swamp, reduce the regulatory burden and give legal recognition to the already existing property claims of hundreds of thousands of poor people.
>
> (De Soto, quoted in Ricketts 2005)

Transparent processes with independent advice

Individuals must know about decisions before they are made and should participate in the decision-making process. And to be compatible with the rule of law, the process as a whole must be subject to review by a judicial body.

The experience of other countries shows that, when a significant number of properties are involved, it is useful to conduct surveys (that is, to get opinions from affected people) before land acquisition. These survey results will inform the construction of resettlement areas in terms of the number of people displaced, their lifestyles, and cultures. However, the most important principle of compulsory land acquisition for public purposes is based on reaching a consensus (of at least 70 to 80 percent) of the people who are using the land (Dang 2012). In addition, to ensure transparency and openness in compulsory land acquisition in Vietnam, the land acquisition laws should be more specific and should guarantee the people's participation. In particular, communication of information, transparency, and accountability in determining compensation prices and land prices must be implemented and information made available to the public. At the same time, it is necessary to ensure the principles of fairness, democracy, and objectivity in the process of acquiring land and of settling complaints.

Purposes, procedures, resettlement, and compensation in compulsory acquisition of land can only be "fair" when a balance between public interests and private interests is struck. If the "public part" – the acquiring authorities – hold the power to acquire land for public purposes and actively "offer" to acquire land and manage all the compulsory acquisition processes, the landholders (the private part) are thus consigned to a "passive" part. They can only know whether their land is under "a proposal" if they are informed. If the process is to be fair, it is necessary (but not sufficient) that these individuals be given the opportunity for more active involvement and can draw on "independent advice" rather than (as at present) being left to the mercy of public authorities who have an apparent conflict of interest.

It is suggested that Vietnam should learn from developed countries, where individuals being subject to a compulsory acquisition of land proposal have access to legal advice, which is paid for by the state. An example of an independent advisory service of this kind is the United Kingdom's Royal Institution of Chartered Surveyors (RICS), which provides independent valuation advice. In Vietnam, where the open market is still absent, such objective legal advice is even more essential.

In conclusion, Vietnam needs to adjust its compulsory land acquisition law, take into account the approaches adopted by other countries, and establish a consistent procedure for implementing land acquisition. That procedure would begin with an initial inquiry process, followed by adequate safeguards for land users. A nationwide consolidated, transparent, and harmonized procedure for land acquisition could bring about a number of major benefits: consistency in the system for dealing with compulsory land acquisition; harmonization and increased fairness in every province; encouragement for people to participate in government processes (which would also align those processes with the principles of administrative law as defined by the Constitution); and establishment of common ground for residents to voice their objections.

Fair compensation

In Vietnam, the compensation rate (to be determined when taking land) is based on the market price in normal conditions (*Land Law 2013*, Article 74). However, several factors may lead to price volatility, including the informal real estate market and price speculation leading to "land fevers." These issues will be revisited when the issue of compulsory land acquisition is explored, both in theory and practice. It can be argued that the notion of "fair compensation" is stretched to the limit when the concept of a "market" is not well developed and inflationary pressures are significant, as in Vietnam. Compensation packages may include cash compensation, a resettlement plot, or even a new dwelling. The latter could help the poor to stabilize their lives in the long term, more effectively than a one-time payment of a large compensation amount.

Conclusion

In whatever direction legal theory and the law in Vietnam is to proceed, it will be beneficial to balance private needs and public demands. By studying the theoretical foundations and the current laws on compulsory land acquisition, one can identify potential future improvements to the laws.

(i) First, land use and other property rights must be secured, including improved protection of existing land rights.
(ii) Second, the justifications for acquiring land must be clearer.
(iii) Third, those rights could be better reflected in the Constitution as firm principles for the legal system.
(iv) Fourth, the legal procedures dealing with property rights should be transparent throughout the entire process.
(v) Last, fair compensation in "conformity with the conditions, customs and practices of each region and area" for the resettlement should be adequately enforced. These changes would help improve the existing systems in Vietnam so that Vietnam – a regime with the state as the only landowner – can better develop fundamental rights for individual land users.

Other developing countries can also learn by appreciating the experiences and problems that have emerged in Vietnam.

References

Bentham, J., 1948. *An Introduction to the Principle of Morals and Legislation*, Hafner Pub. Co., New York.

Blackstone, W., 1966. *Commentaries on the Laws of England, Vol. 1: Of the Rights of Persons*, Oxford University Press, London.

Brubaker, E., 1995. *Property Rights in the Defence of Nature*, Earthscan, Toronto.

Bui, X. L., 2020. Improving effectiveness of handling land-related complaints as a solution to reduce administrative cases in courts, Quang Nam Provincial People's Court website, viewed 26 December 2021, <https://toaanquangnam.gov.vn/nang-cao-hieu-qua-giai-quyet-khieu-nai-hanh-chinh-ve-dat-dai-la-giai-phap-han-che-khieu-kien-cac-vu-an-hanh-chinh-tai-toa-an>.

Clarke, P. H., 1992. The law of compensation under the lands clause acts for land taken by compulsory purchase 1845-1919, Unpublished MPhil thesis, University of London.

Constitution of the Socialist Republic of Vietnam of 1980. Adopted 19 December.

Constitution of the Socialist Republic of Vietnam of 1992. Adopted 15 April.

Constitution of the Socialist Republic of Vietnam of 2013. Adopted 28 November.

Dang, H. V., 2012. *Experience in Land Acquisition of Several Countries in the World*, Information Centre, Library and Scientific Research, National Assembly Office, Hanoi.

Dang, V. C., 2021. What are the shortcomings of the current land law? *Vietnam Law Newspaper*, 2 June, viewed 1 September 2021, <https://baophapluat.vn/bds/luat-dat-dai-hien-hanh-co-nhung-bat-cap-nao-post396595.html>.

De Soto, H., 2000. *The Mystery of Capital: Why Capitalism Triumphs in the West and Fails Everywhere Else*, Basic Books, New York.

Dinh, V. M., 2016. *Nature and Principles of Land Acquisition and Compensation in Land Acquisition*, Inspection Science Institute, viewed 8 May 2019, <http://giri.ac.vn/ban-chat-va-nguyen-tac-cua-viec-thu-hoi-dat-va-boi-thuong-trong-thu-hoi dat_t104c2715n2228 tn.aspx>.

Finnis, J., 1980. *Natural Law and Natural Rights*, Clarendon Press, Oxford.

H.P., 2019. Creating jobs for people whose land is acquired – There are still many limitations, *Quangngai Newspaper*, 23 December, viewed 16 September 2021, <http://baoquangngai.vn/channel/2024/201912/tao-viec-lam-cho-nguoi-dan-co-dat-bi-thu-hoi-con-nhieu-han-che-2979915/>.

Hoang, H. L., 2017. Need to reconsider land acquisition to subdivide plots for sale, *People's Army Newspaper*, 2 December, viewed 16 September 2021, <www.qdnd.vn/phong-su-dieu-tra/dieu-tra/can-xem-xet-lai-viec-thu-hoi-dat-de-phan-lo-ban-nen-525272>.

Hoàng, P., 2019. Tired of waiting to be resettled, *Nguoi Lao Dong Newspaper*, 13 August, viewed 16 September 2021, <https://nld.com.vn/ban-doc/moi-mon-cho-duoc-tai-dinh-cu-20190812212409227.htm>.

Hung Long, 2015. Many damages arise after and beyond the decision on land acquisition, *Natural Resources and Environment Newspaper*, 2 July, viewed 27 July 2021, <https://baotainguyenmoitruong.vn/nhieu-thiet-hai-phat-sinh-sau-va-ngoai-quyet-dinh-thu-hoi-dat-230262.html>.

Khanh Thi, 2019. Complaints in land-related issues occupy for 98%, *Communist Party of Viet Nam Newspaper*, 26 July, viewed 1 September 2021, <https://dangcongsan.vn/y-te/khieu-nai-trong-linh-vuc-dat-dai -chiem-98–529832.html>.

Land Law of the Socialist Republic of Vietnam of 2013. No. 45/2013/QH13. Adopted 29 November.

Le, V., 2020. Resettlement must be one step ahead, *Dongnai Newspaper*, 14 September, viewed 16 September 2021, <www.baodongnai.com.vn/chuyenmuc/sotayphongvien/202009/tai-dinh-cu-phai-di-truoc-mot-buoc-3021864/>.

Locke, J., 1986. *The Second Treatise on Civil Government*, Prometheus Books, New York.

Marx, K., 1977. *Selected Writings*, D. McLellan (ed.), Oxford University Press, London.

McAuslan, P., 2003. Bringing the law back. In *Essays in Land, Law, and Development*, Routledge, Oxford.

Nguyen, L. H., 2016. Some limitations of the current land law relate to the safety of farmers' agricultural land use rights during the period of strong industrialization and modernization in our country. In T. H. Phan (ed.), *Law on Land Management and Use in Vietnam*, Cantho University Publishing House, Can Tho.

Nguyen, L. H. and Hai Duong, 2017. Gaps in Land Law (Dong Nai) – Lesson 6: Are people suffering? *Thuong hieu & Cong luan Online*, viewed 20 May 2019, <http://thuonghieu-congluan.com.vn/ke-ho-trong-lua-t-da -t-dai-do-ng-nai-ba-i-6-dan-la-nguoi-chiu-thiet-a41696.html>.

Oyez, 2005. Kelo v. New London, *Oyez*, viewed 31 May 2019, <www.oyez.org/cases/2004/04-108>.

Paine, T., 1969. *The Rights of Man*, Everyman's Library, Lincoln.

Pham, D. N., 2015. *A Viewpoint on Accountability in the Implementation of Public Tasks*, Inspectorate Strategy & Science Institute (ISSI), Hanoi.

Phan, T. H., 2009. The Law of compulsory acquisition of land – Striking a balance between public and private interests in the United Kingdom and Vietnam, PhD thesis.

Phan, T. H., 2016. *Determination of Damages and Compensation for Damages When the State Recovers Land*, Can Tho University Publishing House, Can Tho.

Phan, T. H., 2018. A legal mechanism to ensure enforcement complaints and administrative complaints in Vietnam, Ho Chi Minh City University of Law, *Journal of Legal Science*, 6 (9, 10).

Phan, T. H., 2019. Right of access to information in land acquisition, compensation, support and resettlement – A practical view of Can Tho City, *Legislative Research Journal*, 23 (399), December.

Phan, T. H., 2021. *Frequently Asked About Compensation, Support and Resettlement When the State Recovers Land*, National Political Publisher, Ha Noi, p. 102.

Ricketts, M., 2005. Poverty, institutions and economics: Hernando de Soto on property rights and economic development, *Economic Affairs*, 25 (2): 49–51.

Riddall, J. G., 1993. *Introduction to Land Law*, Butterworth, London, Dublin and Edinburgh.

Thai Oanh and Dao Phuong, 2017. Over 10 years still have not completed the infrastructure of the resettlement area in Phu Ly City, *Nhan Dan Online*, 7 August, viewed 16 September 2021, <https://nhandan.vn/dieu-tra-qua-thu-ban-doc/hon-10-nam-van-chua-hoan-thien-ha-tang-khu-tai-dinh-cu-o-tp-phu-ly-300353/>.

Thu Ha, 2021. Hanoi: 350 projects are delayed in implementation, violating the Land Law, *Communist Party of Vietnam Newspaper*, 12 August, <https://dangcongsan.vn/phap-luat/ha-noi-350-du-an-cham-trien-khai-vi-pham-luat-dat-dai-587936.html>.

Tien Long, 2017. Current land acquisition regime is 'arbitrary, *Tuoi Tre News*, 24 August, viewed 25 August 2921, <https://tuoitre.vn/che-do-thu-hoi-dat-hien-nay-dang-vo-toi-va-1374133.htm>.

V. Huy, 2021. Mobilizing nearly 1,000 people to participate in the enforcement of infringing works on defence land, *Public Security News*, 21 June, viewed 16 September 2021, <https://cand.com.vn/dia-oc/Huy-dong-gan-1 -ngin-people-participating-cuong-che-cong-trinh-vi-pham-tren-dat-quoc-phong-i617577/>.

Vietnam Chief Justice of the Supreme People's Court, 2016. Answering a Number of Issues About Administrative and Civil Proceedings, No. 02/GD-TANDTC, 19 September.

Xuan Hung, 2016. Relocating people, giving land to firm to build villas, *Lao Dong Online*, viewed 14 June 2019, <https://laodong.vn/xa-hoi/di-doi-nha-dan-danh-dat-cho-doanh-nghiep-lam-biet-thu-532951.bld>.

2 Local governments as catalysts for enhancing resettlement outcomes in infrastructure development

Le Anh Tuan

Introduction

Over the past three decades, Vietnam has made spectacular socioeconomic progress. Once a country marked by chronic poverty and poor infrastructure, Vietnam has largely eradicated hunger and eliminated severe poverty. These results were due to the government's multi-front development effort – to which rural transport infrastructure development made a large contribution, as it has facilitated agricultural production by the smallholder farmers who make up 75 percent of the population. The modernization of rural transport infrastructure has been a government priority since the early 1990s, when the country was in its infancy in terms of development. This infrastructure not only improves transport connectivity between rural and urban areas, but it also provides economic development opportunities for the rural population by promoting commodity exchange; increasing income; enhancing public service access; and improving the living standards of millions of rural people.

Infrastructure development in Vietnam has soared, particularly over the past ten years. Land acquisition for infrastructure development has increased commensurately, notably in fast-growing sectors such as transport, urban development, and industrialization. The magnitude of land acquisition – and its impact on people who are affected – vary from project to project. (At the household level, for instance, the impact may range from the loss of a small strip of land in front of one's house to allow road widening, to significant impacts – such as the loss of an entire house, cropland, or businesses dependent on land – which affect a family's livelihood.) These impacts do not just fall upon the household heads: they affect other household members as well, including extended family members who may share the house and farmland.

Social impact assessments (SIAs) have long been conducted for projects that involve land acquisition, in line with international good practice. An SIA is useful in this context in many ways. It helps to quantify the extent to which land acquisition may affect those whose land is expropriated, based on which mitigation measures are proposed.

In Vietnam, an SIA is not always conducted under projects using governmental finance. SIAs are not yet a mandatory part of the environmental impact assessment

DOI: 10.4324/9781003165774-4

procedure that is typically required. As a result, impacts due to land acquisition often go unnoticed for projects where an SIA is not required. Where large-scale land acquisition is expected (such as in urban development, industrialization, and hydropower development projects) an SIA may be commissioned. However, the capacity of local governmental agencies to carry out land acquisition is rarely assessed – even though it is an important factor affecting resettlement outcomes.

In Vietnam, as the entities that grant land-use rights, local governments are responsible for acquiring land for projects developed for national defense, public security, and socioeconomic benefit for communities – regardless of financing sources (government, private companies, or multilateral organizations). At the local level, governmental agencies called Land Fund Development Centers (LFDCs) are tasked with carrying out acquisition of land. LFDCs are established as an initiative of the Provincial People's Committees and are housed within the Department of Environmental and Natural Resources at provincial and district levels. Recently, in some provinces, LFDCs have been moved into People's Committees at the district level to work more closely with the People's Committee on resettlement activities that take place within district boundaries.

As a governmental agency, an LFDC observes governmental regulations related to land acquisition. If a project is financed by a multilateral organization that has specific requirements or standards related to land acquisition, an LFDC may not be able to identify gaps in terms of legal requirements and implementation practices. Since the capacity of LFDCs in resettlement implementation directly affects the quality and outcomes of the resettlement process, it is important to assess their capacity during project preparation. As an integral part of an SIA exercise, assessing LFDC capacity will help identify implementation risks.

In the following sections, I will briefly discuss the legal background that shapes how resettlement is carried out in Vietnam. I will then discuss key issues that usually arise with development projects with major resettlement components and how these issues could be addressed by enhancing the capacity of LFDCs as key actors in resettlement implementation. Finally, I will discuss how to bolster the capacity of LFDCs, both to improve resettlement outcomes in infrastructure development projects and to promote policy change as a long-term objective.

Background

In many countries, including Vietnam, the state exercises its power in expropriating land and natural resource rights in the public interest under what is known as "eminent domain" (Cotula 2021). Vietnam's *Land Law* is the legal document that governs how land is used, managed, and acquired for the purposes of socioeconomic development and national security. Under the current *Land Law 2013*, a number of decrees were issued to guide implementation of the law. These decrees contain provisions articulating principles, requirements, and procedures that govern issues such as compensation prices; support for livelihood restoration; and arrangements for resettlement – to name a few. A number of circulars (legal documents below the level of a decree) have been issued by the Ministry of

Environment and Natural Resources to guide how resettlement should be carried out under the *Land Law*. In addition to the *Land Law*, relevant legal documents such as the *Law on Complaints* will also be applied when affected people wish to file a complaint related to land acquisition. Compliance with pertinent laws in permanent land acquisition is mandatory for projects that use government financing, including projects funded by the private sector.

When land acquisition occurs under a project financed by bilateral institutions (such as the World Bank, Asian Development Bank, or International Finance Cooperation), the environmental and social policies of international donors are usually applied in a manner that harmonizes with Vietnam's national laws. Although Vietnam's *Land Law* and the environmental and social policies of these international institutions share the same objective (that is, to assist the resettled people to improve their livelihoods to the pre-project level or better), gaps exist in both policy and implementation practices:

- At the policy level, the gaps are typically found in technical requirements, guiding principles, and procedures that guide project implementation.
- In implementation practice, gaps exist in the capacity of LFDCs which, in some instances, exacerbates the gaps at policy level and affects the likelihood of achieving the ultimate resettlement objectives.

In Vietnam, when land acquisition is required for socioeconomic development or national security purposes, local LFDCs lead the process of land expropriation. In cases where a project is carried out across various districts or provinces, such as in a provincial or national highway rehabilitation project, several district LFDCs will be involved and lead the land acquisition process that takes place within their own district's administrative area. When land expropriation is required under a government-financed project, LFDCs take the lead and national laws and provincial regulations are observed.

However, when land acquisition is carried under a project using bilateral financing, LFDCs still typically observe Vietnamese national legislation on land acquisition, rather than complying with the Resettlement Policy Framework (RPF) which is prepared for project use. In this case, little attention is given to principles, social requirements, and standards set out in the RPF prepared by the project implementation agency to align resettlement requirements with Vietnamese national laws and those of bilateral institutions. Failure to assess the capacity of involved LFDCs raises the chance that pitfalls may be encountered during the resettlement implementation process. This, in turn, may alter the course of the intended resettlement process (included in the project's RPF) and thus affect resettlement results.

Common issues in resettlement implementation

In this section, I discuss common issues that may occur in projects financed by international donors. My discussion is from a risk- and impact-management perspective.

Legal requirements

LFDCs are government agencies. Thus, when it comes to consultation, compensation, and resettlement, they are disposed to follow domestic laws and provincial regulations. With a project that is financed by an international donor, the government and the donor typically agree on how resettlement in this project will be implemented. Such agreements should be reflected in the project's RPF, which is prepared by the project owner.

Through this preparation process, gaps that normally exist between national laws and a donor's policies should be identified in the project RPF. Based on these gaps, specific measures would be proposed to harmonize the resettlement requirements and standards of both sides. In the project's RPF, national regulations that deviate from the agreed requirements and standards are typically waived in favor of the donor's requirements. For this reason, the Vietnamese Prime Minister has to approve the project's RPF (i) to confirm its legal validity and (ii) to indicate that agreements set out in the RPF are applied in lieu of existing legal provisions that were not consistent with the principles, requirements, and standards prescribed by the agreed-upon RPF.

LFDC's resettlement implementation capacity

During project preparation, an SIA may be carried out as required by a bilateral institution. An SIA is typically conducted at project level, covering key social risks and potential impacts of project activities and proposing mitigation measures. Because they are the agencies that directly carry out land acquisition, the capacity of the LFDC is key to achieving expected resettlement results. LFDC staff awareness of RPF requirements, their willingness to adopt the RPF, and their ability to fulfill such requirements are fundamental to meeting the RPF objective. A project SIA occasionally attempts to assess local capacity to carry out resettlement, but these assessments are cursory. LFDCs involved in land acquisition are rarely examined in a depth sufficient to determine how ready they are to take on tasks and comply with the resettlement requirements that government and international donors agreed to in the project's RPF.

Experience in Vietnam shows that not all LFDC staff are aware of RPF requirements. Even when the LFDC and local governments are aware of RPF requirements, in most cases they are reluctant to fully adopt them, particularly those that are different from existing regulations. (One constraint that is most frequently cited is government concerns over potential grievances that may arise when two resettlement policies are applied in the same area that may result in two different compensation rates for the same type and scope of impact.)

Assessment of LFDC capacity during the project preparation stage helps anticipate if these implementation risks are likely to occur, so that mitigation measures can be proposed (such as budget allocations, design of training curriculum, and early delivery of training of LFDC staff) to avoid anticipated pitfalls and delays during project construction. This is particularly useful for a transport project that traverses several districts and, as such, involves LFDCs of varying resettlement capacity.

Technical factors

During project implementation for a project financed by international donors (such as the World Bank, Asian Development Bank, or the Green Climate Fund), various technical requirements help to ensure that the resettlement process remains on track to achieve the intended outcome. The intended results of the resettlement are directly affected by the capacity of LFDCs (and provincial government support for the LFDCs) in applying the principles, requirements, and standards set out in the project's RPF. However, in many instances, LFDCs are not ready to apply them, or they apply them ineffectively.

The consultation process

Consultations with relevant stakeholders are key to negotiation with people affected by a development project (WB 2013a; IFC 2009). Good consultation promotes participation, which is a necessary condition for successful resettlement (WB 2014). Consultation allows both district LFDCs and PMUs to understand the concerns of the affected households. This enables them to adjust compensation packages as well as to consider customizing support for the affected households – particularly for those who are severely affected due to loss of land-based income and ethnic minorities.

The following sections discuss key requirements that are not consistently applied by LFDCs in Vietnam.

Socioeconomic surveys

Socioeconomic surveys have been widely used internationally as a way of consulting with people whose land is affected. In Vietnam, *Land Law 2013* has not yet required the use of surveys to target households affected by land acquisition – particularly for government projects involving small-scale land acquisition. Projects using bilateral financing may conduct socioeconomic surveys and present survey findings in the Resettlement Plan – but such results are rarely used by LFDCs to inform their consultation strategy and/or the design of compensation and support packages. As a result, most affected households (though different in type, magnitude of impact and, in some cases, ethnicity) are only consulted through the most common consultation format: the community meeting.

Information disclosure

Disclosing key project information, early, to affected people facilitates meaningful consultation. When people are affected by loss of their land and/or land-based income, they are concerned about how to avoid or minimize the potential impacts. If they know about the project's purpose; activities; risks and potential impacts; and other aspects before coming to a consultation meeting, they can ask questions of greatest concern and make suggestions. These questions and suggestions may enable the project staff to consider and reflect on project design and implementation and to avoid or minimize possible adverse impacts.

Timely disclosure

My experience from several projects in Vietnam has indicated that timely disclosure of project information is not always delivered as required by a project's RPF. For instance, information is typically disclosed on the website of the Project Management Unit (PMU) and posted on bulletin boards at the commune's People's Committee. However, relevant information, as summarized in a project information booklet, is not always provided to affected people in enough time before they meet project stakeholders at a consultation meeting. Without prior information and enough time to process it, affected people may find it difficult to understand how the project will be executed and how local people will be affected. This is especially important considering the sociocultural diversity of the affected people (such as the majority Kinh as compared to ethnic minorities); vulnerable versus better-off people; the magnitude of impact at the household level; and other factors.

Consultation based on full and timely disclosure of project information fosters open discussion. This shows respect for the affected households (and thus impacts how affected people react to and/or support a project's proposed measures). This typically shortens the time spent on land acquisition. Experience shows that when questions raised by affected people are considered seriously and they receive timely and complete responses, the LFDC can build the trust of affected households.

This positively correlates to consultation outcomes. In past projects where there were significant delays in the consultation process, affected people have indicated they did not have a good level of trust in the local land acquisition agency: they did not think those who ran the consultation were truly listening to their concerns. Building trust throughout the consultation process actually changes the attitude of affected households, from doubt, objections, and resistance to open discussions, support, and cooperation.

Experience shows that subprojects[1] that do not disclose project compensation policies well in advance tend to spend more time later achieving consensus among affected people on proposed compensation and resettlement support packages. When this is the case, LFDCs are more likely to need to conduct additional consultations to negotiate compensation prices with affected households. Such a long process of consultation is likely to erode the trust of affected people – a trust that LFDCs may have spent considerable time building from the start of the consultation process. When project information (including procedures for adjudicating grievances) is clearly disclosed ahead of planned consultation, LFDCs are likely to spend less time obtaining the consensus of affected people on their proposed compensation prices.

Information leaflets

During the consultation process, there are a number of ways that communication of project risks and impacts can be further improved. For example, leaflets could be prepared to reach affected groups, particularly the elderly and ethnic minority households who may wish to clarify the information provided in meetings at home. Leaflets may also help household heads to communicate better with family members. This helps avoid confusion and supports consensus-building efforts. However, use of project information booklets as a supplementary means of communicating with ethnic minorities is still rare.

Ethnic minority languages

Ethnic minority languages should be used in meetings with affected ethnic minority households. Even though nearly all ethnic minority people understand Vietnamese, discussions in Vietnamese may be inconvenient for them, particularly for those who prefer to speak in the ethnic minority language. If a written language exists, it should be used in project information leaflets to encourage affected ethic minority people to read them and use them as reference material.

Communicating back to stakeholders

As part of the consultation process, communicating back to stakeholders to provide tangible responses to questions raised is essential to maintaining their continued participation throughout the project cycle. Feedback and grievances raised by affected parties should be processed and resolved within a required timeframe and reported back to the affected people by the agencies directly responsible for grievance resolution. (For example, a grievance related to compensation rates which is submitted through a commune People's Committee would be resolved and reported back by the responsible district-level LFDC.)

Setting compensation rates

When a compensation package is designed, LFDCs typically apply a set of compensation rates which were first developed by provincial offices of the Department of Environment and Natural Resources and approved by provincial People's Committees for use as reference rates for a period of five years. Depending on the location of affected lands, LFDCs may propose adjustments to the five-year reference rate. Although an independent land-price appraising firm can be engaged by LFDCs to conduct a market survey and to update compensation rates based on current market prices, use of such external services is rare. Experience has shown that when market surveys are conducted by external services to update compensation prices, there are always differences between provincial reference rates and market rates.

The differences in land prices are generally small for areas of low land value but tend to become larger where land is of higher value, such as in densely populated areas. The difference between provincial rates and market rates are typically small for agricultural land and residential land in rural areas. The differences become larger for residential land and (generally) for most types of land in commercial districts located in rural areas and in urban areas.

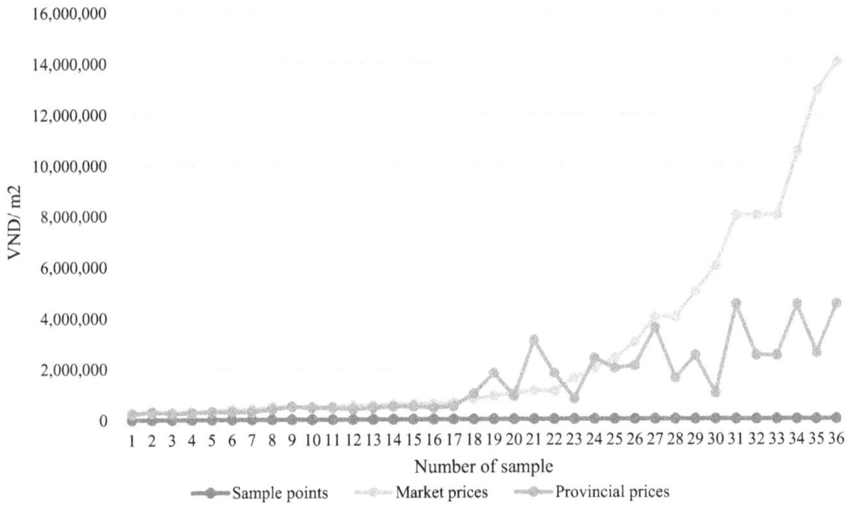

Figure 2.1 Provincial prices versus market prices (36 samples)

Figure 2.1 shows the differences between initially proposed provincial rates and market prices for a sample of 36 surveyed points from two randomly selected provinces.

Calculating land value and compensation

Grievances concerning compensation rates are common in Vietnam, most notably compensation rates for land, crops, and houses. In a survey of more than twenty PMUs across Vietnam, grievances relating to compensation rates for land were found to be the most common.[2]

Consultation with affected people indicated that they typically managed to learn about the market price for their affected land, based on actual land transactions that were successfully completed in nearby areas. Experience has shown that when compensation rates proposed by the LFDCs were notably low (compared to market prices), affected people refused the proposed compensation package and asked for a higher rate approaching their expected values. In most cases, compensation rates were adjusted upward.

It is noted that compensation prices initially proposed to affected peoples are typically low because such prices are established based on the land-price table that Provincial Peoples' Committees disclose for the purpose of charging land-use fees, land-use tax, and so forth for a period of five years. However, when a new project is implemented in a certain area (depending on the nature and scope of the project), land prices near the project area may increase. This widens the gap between the provincial land-price table and the land-market prices that increased as a result of the project, due to market demand in response to project development and/or to other factors.

LFDCs can engage land-price appraisal consultants to support them in the design of compensation packages. However, use of this service is still limited among LFDCs. In a survey conducted in 2020 with PMUs,[3] only 35 percent of PMUs said they always engage consultants to conduct land value surveys to identify market prices, while 18 percent said they have never done such surveys to establish a basis for proposing compensation prices for the affected land under their project. Past experience suggests that projects that conduct land value surveys are more likely to reduce consultation time spent to negotiate compensation prices with affected households.

In fact, when planned and carried out in a timely manner, land value surveys contribute to the consultation process and consultation results in at least three ways. First, the survey results are site-specific, generating more accurate land values than provincial reference rates, which are general for larger areas. Second, they put LFDCs in a better position to discuss rates with the affected people. Third, they provide affected households with a comparative basis for land value, which facilitates their acceptance of proposed compensation rates.

Livelihood restoration

In Vietnam, monitoring of livelihood restoration outcomes has not been a common practice for government-financed projects (especially small-scale projects), and monitoring of livelihood restoration is not required under *Land Law 2013*. Accordingly, once the compensation payment has been made, the resettlement implementation plan is also deemed completed. No further action – such as monitoring of the livelihood restoration process of resettled people – is required by law.

Yet compensation payment alone does not always engender full restoration of livelihoods to the pre-project level. This is particularly true for severely affected households who may be affected disproportionately because of their socioeconomic status, including their health and physical conditions.[4] Without monitoring of the livelihood restoration process, officials may be unaware of ensuing impoverishment. Impoverishment does not happen only with affected household heads and direct family members. It happens also to their extended family, particularly in situations where affected people have experienced pre-existing vulnerability. These impacts may be intergenerational (Cernea 1997, 2021).

Discussion

In this section, I will discuss the roles of key stakeholders involved in resettlement implementation. I will then elaborate how the issues discussed can be addressed through improved institutional arrangements. I argue that, by developing the capacity of local LFDCs to adopt international good practice in resettlement implementation, multilateral projects can achieve resettlement objectives, while also creating spillover effects for other governmental resettlement projects. Enhancing the accountability of PMUs and LFDCs is critical to achieving these expected impacts.

Project Management Units (PMUs)

In infrastructure development projects that use bilateral financing, PMUs play a fundamental role in ensuring compliance with the agreed resettlement arrangements set forth in the project's Resettlement Policy Framework. As a unit entrusted by governmental project owners to manage day-to-day project implementation, PMUs have to ensure that requirements and standards described in a project's RPF are satisfactorily implemented. However, since PMUs are not involved directly in carrying out land acquisition activities, they have to engage local LFDCs to conduct resettlement activities on their behalf.

It should be noted that having LFDCs carry out land acquisition to support project construction does not release PMUs from the responsibility of ensuring compliance with a project's RPF. However, contracts with LFDCs usually do not clearly detail requirements and standards, including implementation methods, which are described in a project RPF. This often results in shortfalls in resettlement implementation carried out by the LFDCs.

- Since PMU contracts with LFDCs are legally binding, contracts should have provisions that hold LFDCs responsible for satisfactorily implementing resettlement and standards set out in a project's RPF. Without such provisions, LFDCs will only apply national and provincial regulations; measures proposed in a project's RPF to address gaps in policies of government and bilateral institutions would not be applied.
- Both provincial PMUs and LFDCs should be fully aware of resettlement requirements and standards prescribed in a project's RPF and should be able to follow such requirements, standards, and measures. Experience has shown that not every experienced PMU[5] can ensure that all safeguard requirements set out in a project's RPF are fully realized and implemented by LFDCs. Thus, it is important for PMUs to ensure that contracts with LFDCs contain sufficient safeguard requirements and that contracted LFDCs fully understand such safeguard requirements and are trained to be able to fully implement them.

Land Fund Development Centers (LFDCs)

As a government agency, an LFDC's mandate is to assist local government to carry out land acquisition for projects that use government financing. When the service of a LFDC is required for a multilateral project that involves land acquisition, an LFDC would be required, by the terms of its PMU contract, to rearrange staff work schedules and optimize their limited human resources to carry out these additional tasks.

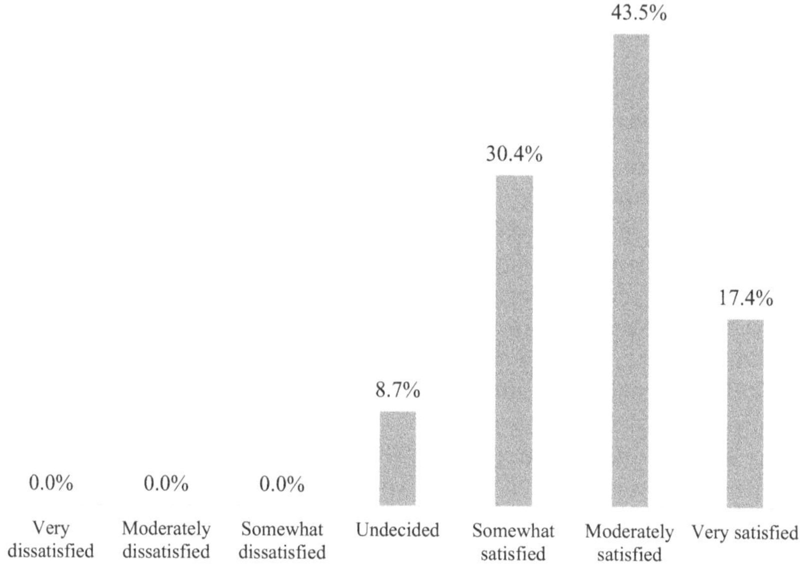

Figure 2.2 Satisfaction of PMUs with LFDC services

Because LFDCs are tasked to carry out all land acquisition that takes place within the district, irrespective of project financing sources (for example, government, bilateral, or private sector), LFDCs typically experience work overloads.[6] This can compromise the quality of land acquisition services being undertaken (see Figure 2.2). For instance, in a survey of PMUs using multilateral financing, the level of satisfaction of PMUs with LFDC services was varied.[7] Fewer than half of PMUs were "moderately" satisfied with LFDC's land acquisition services.

Building capacity for PMUs and LFDCs

While resettlement capacity development for PMUs is important, building safeguard capacity for district LFDCs is critical to ensure compliance with requirements and standards set forth in a project's RPF and, more importantly, to achieve resettlement objectives. LFDCs are mandated to apply national and provincial regulations for compensation and resettlement, including procedures on how resettlement is to be carried out. Although they are capable of conforming to local regulations, specific social requirements and standards (as set forth in a project RPF or a Resettlement Plan) may be new to them.

Inclusion of social requirements and standards in PMU contracts with LFDCs is the first step that PMUs should take to ensure that LFDCs are aware of these requirements and observe such requirements as part of contractual agreements. Training key staff at LFDCs on international good practice in involuntary resettlement is essential to ensure resettlement compliance – while also enabling LFDCs to realize the value of these practices and to slowly apply such practices in other projects, such as those that are financed by the government or private investors.

The following are key areas of improvement that should be addressed through targeted training for LFDC staff.

Consultation with affected people

LFDCs are contracted by PMUs to conduct project-related resettlement. Part of the contract responsibilities involve carrying out consultation with affected people on issues such as proposed compensation packages, resettlement options, and resettlement. Due to time pressures and heavy workloads in LFDCs, these consultations usually take the form of public meetings and hearings rather than consultation using focus-group discussions, key-informant interview techniques, and/or household surveys. (Experience also shows that LFDC staff who facilitate the consultation meetings are not trained on these consultation methods and that these methods are not yet consistently required under government-financed projects.)

In addition, the traditional public meeting format does not always encourage affected people, particularly those from vulnerable or marginalized groups, to raise their voices.

Consultation is a two-way communication process between affected people and the resettlement implementation agency. To get affected peoples' buy-in, it is important that affected households be engaged in the ongoing consultation process, through varied and appropriate techiques, to develop trust in LFDCs. This makes consultation meaningful.

Grievance redress mechanisms

In addition to public consultation, an effective grievance redress mechanism is important to provide affected people with channels that allow them to raise concerns and submit complaints about adverse impacts. Affected people may not raise individual concerns at public meetings – particularly when the project is at an early stage of project preparation, when adverse impacts are not yet clear to them. However, affected people will scrutinize potential risks and impacts – and the compensation and support to which they are entitled – when impacts become known to them. This is the time when affected people want to raise their concerns over compensation and support.

In Vietnam, grievance redress procedures for resettlement comply with the *Law of Complaints*. An effective grievance redress mechanism should be easy to apply and accessible to affected people (particularly for vulnerable groups such as ethnic minorities) so they can raise concerns. This helps prevent grievances from escalating into conflict – which, in some cases in Vietnam, has resulted in forced eviction. In a recent online survey in Vietnam, only 21 percent of PMU staff in the survey thought that "all" affected people have access to the project's grievance redress mechanism (GRM). Forty-nine percent thought "most" affected people in their projects have access to a GRM, and 52.1 percent of PMU staff thought that communication with affected households to inform them of the project purpose and its potential impacts is not as effective as expected.[8]

Conclusion

Although district LFDCs are contracted by PMUs to carry out resettlement implementation – and LFDCs directly affect the extent of safeguard compliance set forth in a project's RPF – there has been little organized effort to build the resettlement capacity of LFDC staff over the long-term. Since the capacity of LFDC staff can vary widely, assessment of LFDCs safeguard capacity as part of a project's SIA is important. It enables the project administrators to plan budgets and to develop training for relevant LFDCs and other stakeholders, thereby effectively managing the risk of impoverishing people economically and physically displaced by the project.

Successful development of safeguard capacity for LFDCs not only enhances safeguards compliance on the part of loan borrowers (which PMUs represent), but it also fosters a social-change process in which LFDCs serve as a catalyst to connect affected people and local governments involved in a development project. As resettlement-implementing agencies, LFDCs should develop trust and thereby promote participation by affected people throughout the resettlement process.

Enhanced safeguard capacity of LFDCs will increase the accountability of other local government stakeholders who join forces to achieve the desired resettlement outcomes. Investing in the development of safeguard capacity for LFDCs not only helps to achieve positive sustainable-development outcomes for the project, but may also create a spillover effect.

Lessons learned can be replicated and, over time, incorporated into a law-making process geared toward enhanced accountability and into legislation that fosters effective management of impoverishment risks and development outcomes. Positive outcomes of these efforts will benefit far more than the affected population in this project alone.

Notes

1 A transport infrastructure or urban development project may consist of various subprojects that are organized to facilitate bidding and construction purposes.

2 Tuan et al. (2020). Unpublished data.

3 A total of 23 PMUs participated in the survey. These PMUs are responsible for about 250 infrastructure subprojects that potentially affect 36,584 households, of which 54.5 percent will lose more than 20 percent of their total productive land, 33 percent will lose houses, and 20.3 percent will be physically displaced (Tuan et al. 2020, unpublished data).

4 34.8% of PMUs participating in a survey in 2020 (n=8) thought severely affected people did not have opportunities to provide their inputs to the design and implementation process of a livelihoods program that affects their livelihood restoration.

5 PMUs participating in this survey have a wide range of years of experience (min = 1, max = 23, mean = 9.86, SD = 5.91).

6 In a survey participated in by 23 PMUs from three regions in Vietnam, 73.9% of PMUs indicated that the workload of the LFDCs that they have contract with was too heavy to resolve grievances within their responsibility in a timely way. 69.1% of PMUs did not think the current capacity of LFDCs is sufficient to resolve grievances effectively.
7 An estimated 100 LFDCs were contracted by 23 PMUs (participating the survey) to deliver resettlement implementation service.
8 Tuan et al. (2020), unpublished report.

References

Cernea, M.M., 1997. The impoverishment risks and reconstruction model for resettling displaced populations. *World Development*, 25(10).

Cernea, M.M., 2021. The risks and reconstruction model for resettling displaced populations. In M. Koch-Weser, S. Guggenheim (eds.), *Social Development in the World Bank: Essays in Honor of Michael M. Cernea*. Cham, Switzerland, Springer Open, pp. 235–264.

Cotula, L., 2021. *Tenure Rights and Obligations – Towards a More Holistic Approach to Land Governance*. FAO Legal Papers No. 106. Rome, FAO.

International Finance Cooperation, 2009. *Good Practice Note Addressing Grievances from Project-Affected Communities*. Washington, DC, International Finance Cooperation.

Tuan, L.A., Win, N., Mehl, C., 2020. *Exploratory Assessment of Environmental and Social Knowledge for Training Curriculum Development – A Case in Myanmar* (unpublished report).

3 Noncompliance with land acquisition and resettlement in Vietnam

A policy tools approach

Nguyen Van Dang

Introduction

In the modern history of Vietnam, land access has not only been a driving force for political activity but also a central concern of the government (Toan & Quang 2014:280–285). Socio-political conflicts over land issues have not only occurred due to unequal access to land but have also been linked to differences between modern land administration and traditional perceptions regarding land ownership.

After the end of the Vietnam War, the 1980 Constitution formally abolished private land ownership in Vietnam. Since then, under the ruling of the Communist Party of Vietnam (CPV), Vietnam's Constitution and Land Laws in 1987, 1992, 2003, and 2013 consistently asserted the public ownership-based land regime: land is a public property owned by the Vietnamese people, and the "state" is the representative of the people's ownership (alternatively referred to as "public ownership" or "state ownership" in daily language). Individual citizens, households, and organizations are "land users" only (Pincus 2012). Resolution 100, issued in 1981 by the CPV, started the process of land policy reform characterized by "de-collectivization" of the land tenure system. In 1987, the security of land-use rights was ensured with the first *Land Law*, and Resolution 10 in 1988 allowed the privatization of land-use rights. Revisions of the *Land Law* in 1993, 2003, and 2013 further improved the security of land-use rights by addressing a wide range of issues, including threats from administrative reallocation; lack of transferability; and the short duration of land-use rights (Lodhi 2004; Deininger & Jin 2005; Ho & McPherson 2010; Wells-Dang 2013).

Since the early 1990s, the Vietnamese government has enacted "land-taking" (alternatively, "land acquisition") policy to meet the demands of rapid industrialization and urban expansion across the country (Butler 2009; Pincus 2012). Over the last three decades, open and easy access to land and cheap land rent have attracted investment projects from non-state and foreign investors who have played key role in Vietnam's economic growth. However, the land-taking policy has also generated negative outcomes. According to Lodhi (2004), from 1988 until the mid-1990s land users sent some 200,000 land-related grievances to the government at district, provincial, and central levels. In the early 2000s, land-linked confrontations became the most severe problem across the country. Around

DOI: 10.4324/9781003165774-5

50 percent of all civil disputes sent to the government in 2005 were about land conversion and compensation (World Bank 2011a:17). The Citizen Reception Office received more than 30,000 land petitions in 2006 – of which only 20 percent concerned boundary disputes or claims, while about 70 percent involved compensation for site clearance (Gillespie 2011). In 2020, the number of land-related complaints accounted for 61.5 percent of all complaints sent to the Government Inspectorate of Vietnam (Phuong Thuy 2020). Notably, reports of violent clashes over land-taking have significantly increased in recent years (Brown 2012; Economist 2017). The increase of land-taking disputes across the country not only indicates an economic problem but also suggests a socio-political threat to social cohesion, economic development, and political stability in Vietnam (Brown 2012; Economist 2017).

Policy noncompliance

From a public policy perspective, the widespread incidence of disputes and conflicts over land acquisition indicates policy noncompliance. According to Gofen (2015), "policy noncompliance" refers to behavior that is inconsistent with a given policy's goals and objectives. Noncompliance might be direct (for example, breaking the law); indirect (for example, failure to follow recommendations); active (for example, doing something different from what is expected in response to a policy); or passive (for example, refusing universal services). This raises the question of policy effectiveness (including policy acceptance and the achievement of desired policy outcomes). Noncompliant responses suggest that policy targets are willing to act in opposition to policy expectations. Policy noncompliance, thus, not only reflects target groups' disagreement with the government but also reveals an inconsistency between policy objectives and target group behavior (Cialdini & Goldstein 2004). In this study, noncompliance with land acquisition policy is defined as situational tensions and confrontations between local governments and land users. Disputes and conflicts between the two parties can take place prior to, during, or even after the enactment of a land-taking project. Because of unresolved disagreements, land users do not accept land-taking decisions, and government thus cannot acquire a piece of land as scheduled. Manifestations of land users' noncompliance vary, depending on the intensity of tensions, and they can range from resistant attitudes and claims of land-use rights, to peaceful demonstrations, and even violent acts.

According to policy researchers, noncompliance among target groups is often described as a problem of policy implementation and enforcement (Gofen 2015). Policy implementation is what develops between the government's intention and the ultimate impact in the real world – the process by which policies enacted by government are put into effect by relevant agencies (O'Toole 2000; Birkland 2016:332). When a policy is implemented, a variety of interests and desires are clearly manifested. Conflicting interests that have not been solved during policy formulation, design, and adoption might emerge again. As a complex political process, policy implementation involves various actors and stakeholders.

A world of multi-institutional actors – more than one government, agency, or sector – requires cooperation and coordination for implementation success (O'Toole 2000; Hill et al. 2002). Even a "good policy design," therefore, does not ensure a policy target's compliance. The ways local governments execute and enforce public polices in practice also play a critical role. In other words, the success of a policy not only requires "good policy design" but also "good policy implementation." Conversely, implementers might still obtain expected outcomes with a poorly formulated policy if they carefully and rightfully manage policy implementation (Pressman & Wildavsky 1973; Brinkerhoff & Crosby 2002; Salamon & Elliott 2002; Anderson 2014; Sandfort & Moulton 2015). Increased disputes and conflicts over land acquisition in Vietnam and the policy literature suggest a research problem: "Why don't land users comply with land-taking policy?" And "How do local governments respond to policy noncompliance to minimize public risks?"

Explanations of noncompliance with land acquisitions

A critical review of the literature on land-taking policy in Vietnam reveals the dominance of institutional and economic explanations, while governance and policy implementation approaches play a less influential role (ED et al. 2011; Kim 2011; McPherson 2011; Markussen et al. 2011; Marsh et al. 2007; Suu 2004; World Bank 2009, 2011a, 2011b, 2012, 2014; IRPLD 2013).

"Institutional settings" relating to the land sector encompass a wide array of issues, including the role of the state, the market, and the private sector – but "the ways in which property rights and land-use arrangements are structured and managed are widely accepted as being of the utmost importance" (Markussen et al. 2011:2). To explain land policy problems, institutional analysts are primarily concerned with the role of a nation's land regime and land tenure system (Ho 2005; Lipton 2009; Ingram & Hong 2009). Primary concerns of the institutional approach to land-taking challenges in Vietnam include problematic aspects of written norms such as laws, rules, legislation, and the organizational structure responsible for land administration. As in other developing nations, institutional ambiguities and inconsistencies of land legislation are among the most significant contributors to land-taking problems in Vietnam (Vo 2011; Ho & McPherson 2010; McPherson 2011; World Bank 2009, 2011a, 2012; Wells-Dang 2013). Another institutional cause of the rise of land-taking noncompliance relates to land pricing and valuation methods (Suu 2009; World Bank 2009, 2011a).

Despite having widespread influence, however, the "institutional" approach is unable to explain why local governments – even within the same commune and adopting the same procedures – may achieve different levels of implementation effectiveness. In other words, variations in the target group's resistance indicate that land-taking policy noncompliance is not only related to institutional settings. Policy literature also suggests that, both in Vietnam and globally, land institutions are not the only factors affecting policy compliance or noncompliance. Therefore, reforms of land institutions alone are not enough for governments to effectively deal with land-taking problems (Wehrmann 2008; Fu & Gillespie 2014).

The economic explanation of noncompliance with land-taking policy correctly ascribes conflicts between land users and government to (first and foremost) unfair land prices and low compensation. Acquiring land in a compulsory manner for economic development often causes unfairness in benefit sharing between beneficiaries (investors and local governments) and the affected people (land users). "Who loses" and "who wins" in terms of economic gains is a key cause of land-taking policy problems (Suu 2009; World Bank 2012; Bell 2014). However, while the economic assumption is applicable to market situations, it could be challenged in non-market contexts. As argued by Simon (1955), Williamson (1979), Mintz (2005), and Denhardt (2011), rational economic approaches do not take into consideration the influence of non-economic constraints (such as psychological factors and social meanings) for policy target groups when they have to make decisions in non-market situations. In non-market settings, the concepts of "cost" and "benefit" are not only linked to economic interests: they also include time and resources devoted to establishing and maintaining relationships or to an individual's reputation for being reliable and trustworthy. As a result, non-economic factors might motivate actions that do not generate optimal outcomes. Therefore, dealing with target groups' noncompliance is not simply a matter of offering them the best economic benefits. As argued by Brinkerhoff and Crosby (2002:6) and Stone (2012), policymaking and implementation are conducted in political communities (for example, by a country or state/province). Each community has its own standards to apply in setting goals, defining problems, and justifying policy solutions. As each policy is being implemented, it is affected by the unique contextual characteristics of the political community.

From a governance approach, studies of land-taking policy problems in Vietnam often focus on land administration systems and key principles of good land governance, such as accountability, transparency, control of corruption, public participation and so forth. Accordingly, Vietnam's current land governance system is described by researchers and international observers as a "bad system" – a system that is corrupt and willing to abuse public authority to seize land from landholders (FAO 2007; World Bank 2011b; Brown 2013). The governance approach to land acquisition problems advocates for market factors and modern democratic elements. Considering the current context of Vietnam, however, democratic governance-based recommendations face great barriers. Vietnam is now led by the CPV as the only constitutionally recognized political party; the governing-structure is unitary and hierarchical in nature; and the Leninist model-based Party-State system continues to control fundamental sectors of Vietnam's economy and society (London 2014). Over the last three decades, the reform process (Doi Moi policy) has mainly resulted in the de-centralization of the Vietnam's administrative system while decision-making power remains centralized (De Wit et al. 2012). This maintains the CPV and state agencies as the most powerful actors in public governance, while nongovernment actors and other underdeveloped civil society forces still play a limited role. The state's control over society and government intervention in the economy; the immaturity of civil society; and the lack of representative and participatory institutions, therefore, make recommended movement toward a democratic governance system unrealistic (Beresford 2008; De Wit et al. 2012; London 2014; World Bank & MPI 2016; Kerkvliet 2006).

Policy tool-based approaches

Theoretically, a policy cannot succeed in changing target groups' behaviors without "policy legitimacy" – a belief by all the actors and stakeholders that the policy is necessary, vital, and worth pursuing (Brinkerhoff & Crosby 2002). "Policy legitimacy" is not only contingent on how a policy is made and for what purposes – but also on how it is executed (Birkland 2016:331–361). This requires attention to interactions and relationships defined by policy tools between government and nongovernment actors in the policy implementation process (Lascoumes & Gales 2007).

This suggests a research opportunity regarding land-taking problems in Vietnam: looking at tools used in land acquisition and resettlement to generate new insights and to develop an additional explanation of land users' noncompliance with land acquisitions. Instead of looking at land-taking problems through traditional lenses (for example, institutional, economic, or governance), policy researchers can develop a new line of inquiry: a tool-based theoretical framework that can be used to explore the link between implementation tools and policy noncompliance. The "tool-based" approach, therefore, can motivate Vietnamese researchers to develop new theories about the role of policy tools and to seek new ways to use tools that are relevant within Vietnam's contexts.

Over the last two decades, the rise of new policy instruments has resulted from the emergence of new public governance perspectives (Salamon 2002). "Policy tools" as a theoretical approach was initiated by researchers such as Anderson (1971) and Salamon (1981). The original theoretical framework was primarily concerned with "what government uses rather than what happens inside government systems or what government does" (Hood 1983). As an alternative approach to dealing with public problems more specifically, the "policy tools" approach emphasizes the "how" question (Brinkerhoff & Crosby 2002; Agranoff & McGuire 2003; Gales 2011; Sandfort & Moulton 2015; Cooper 2018). Instead of focusing on an individual program or even a collection of programs and government agencies, policy researchers concentrate on the tools of governments, and on the techniques of social intervention.

Salamon and Lund (1989:29) defined "tools" as "a method through which government seeks a policy objective." Bemelmans-Videc et al. (1998:3) conceptualized policy instruments as "the set of techniques by which governmental authorities wield their power in attempting to ensure support and to effect or prevent social change." Howlett et al. (2009) and Mintrom (2012) viewed actual means or devices used by governments to address problems and to implement solutions as "policy tools." From a sociological perspective, Lascoumes and Le Gales (2007:4) argued that:

> a policy instrument constitutes a device that is both technical and social, that organizes specific social relations between the state and those it is addressed to, according to the representations and meanings it carries. It is a particular type of institution, a technical device with the generic purpose of carrying out a concrete concept of the politics/society relationship and sustained by a concept of regulation.

We need to differentiate "policy mechanisms" from "policy tools." A "policy mechanism" answers the question of how to put a policy into practice, while "policy tools" answer the question "By what methods/techniques or means?" Policy mechanisms (such as coercive regulations, direct and indirect government) will determine how or the ways in which policy tools work. Policy instruments (such as executive orders, rules, or contracts) will determine what legal devices will be used to put those mechanisms into operation (Cooper 2018:4).

In the 1990s and early 2000s, the "tools" argument became more powerful, due to the proliferation of public actions used to address public problems (Salamon & Elliot 2002:1–3). In the contemporary world, public services or goods are not only directly provided by government bureaucrats: a wide range of third parties such as commercial banks, private universities, private corporations, and firms also get involved in public actions. A variety of new government tools have emerged and are increasingly playing an important role in public goods delivery. As a result, public officials are required to develop collaborative relationships and to share public authority with nongovernment actors in order to implement public policies and programs. The "tools" approach to policy implementation problems, therefore, advocates for a shift in the "unit of analysis," from public programs, policies, and public agencies, to governing instruments. The main function of policy tools is to coordinate various actors in a multi-level system of policy implementation and governance (Salamon & Elliot 2002; Gales 2011). The important role of policy instruments is that they can define the relationship between the government and the governed and greatly affect policy outcomes. Policy makers and implementers, therefore, need to develop policy mixes that can incorporate socio-political-institutional factors into technical policy options. Rather than selecting policy preferences among different alternatives, policy makers should consider the guiding role of tools in policy development and implementation.

Analysis of policy tools used in three cases of land-taking

This study explores implementation tools used in three cases of land-taking in Vietnam, in Tu Son (Bac Ninh Province), Dong Tam (Hanoi City), and Thu Thiem (Ho Chi Minh City). The three events vary in terms of locations; time scale; the causes of noncompliance; the number of affected landholders; the number of

Table 3.1 Facts about the three land-taking events

Facts	*Land-taking events*		
	Thu Thiem	*Dong Tam*	*Tu Son*
Land area acquired	930 ha	50.03 ha	86.9 ha
Main purposes	Economic development	Defense	Infrastructure development
Number of affected landholders	14,351	All villagers	323
Number noncompliant	115	All villagers	49
Time span	2005–2019	2015–2019	2015–2017
Types of noncompliance	Petition and dispute	Land occupation and violence	Daily resistance, dispute, and land occupation
Types of compensation	Cash and resettlement apartments	No	Cash

noncompliant landholders; and the level of intensity. A common feature shared by all three events is that the local governments took land by force after failing to convince landholders to give up their land (see Table 3.1).

Research method

The research method adopted in this study is the cross-case analysis. Individual events of land-taking serve as the evidentiary base for answering the general research question:

> When and how do the policy tools used in the implementation of land-taking policy in Vietnam help to explain noncompliance?

The multiple case analysis was guided by several sub-questions:

(i) What were the tool mixes used by local implementers to acquire land in Thu Thiem, Dong Tam, and Tu Son?
(ii) What were common patterns of tool-based responses to noncompliance?
(iii) What tools were used to settle disputes?
(iv) How (if at all) did tools' characteristics (for example, strengths, weaknesses, choice, use, and management) contribute to policy noncompliance?

Based on policy tools literature, the author developed a theoretical framework for a tools-focused analysis of the three events. The "tools" framework consists of four mechanisms that define a set of tools available for choice by implementers to execute land acquisition projects. The analysis, therefore, is grouped into four sub-themes: "organizational tools"; "authoritative tools"; "financial tools"; and "information-based tools."

Organizational tools

Organizational tools available to government, quasi-government, or nongovernmental organizations will be assessed in relation to interactions between the government and policy targets, and to the effectiveness, efficiency, and consequences of types of organizational tools used to change target behaviors and to achieve policy goals (Howlett 2011:63). According to Vietnam's land legislation, direct government is a required mechanism to implement land acquisition (Articles 61, 62, and 73 of the *Land Law 2013*). Currently, there are two types of organizations that can carry out land acquisition: at the provincial level, the Land Fund Development Center (LFDC) operates as a service unit that assists the Provincial People's Committee (PPC) in acquiring land in accordance with land-use planning or land being used by organizations. At the district level, a Board for Compensation and Ground Clearance (BCGC) is temporarily established by the district government to take land from households. Each BCGC is responsible for one land-taking project and is dissolved as soon as its task is completed.

All three land-taking events under study were carried out by district BCGCs: the District 2 BCGC executed the Thu Thiem project (Ho Chi Minh City), while land-taking in Dong Tam commune (Hanoi City) and Tu Son district (Bac Ninh Province) were conducted by the My Duc BCGC and Tu Son BCGC, respectively. To obtain more information about the working principles and membership of BCGCs, the instructions and rules used to establish the BCGC in Ho Chi Minh City (HCMC), and the list of BCGC members responsible for the Tu Son event were reviewed. In both cases, a vice-mayor of the district government served as the head of the BCGC, while other members included heads of technical offices and units such as the Office of Finance, Office of Urban Management, Office of Agriculture, and district LFDC. Leaders and officials of the commune government, a head of a residential unit, representatives of investors, and affected landholders also participated in the district BCGC.

Document review showed that BCGCs were heavily government-based. Given that most members of BCGCs were government officials, the organization operated as an administrative unit. This was evident in the HCMC's instructions on establishing a BCGC: majority rule was the principle for making land-taking decisions. This rule allowed government officials (who outnumbered nongovernment actors) to effect their desired decisions. In addition, the process for land-taking (as described by land officials) suggested that affected land users could only engage in policy implementation once a land-taking project was enacted. Given this context, a BCGC functioned as a short-term and task-based administrative unit of the government.

Since the sole role of government organizations in executing land-taking is clearly stated in land legislation (Article 66, *Land Law 2013*), field interviews and focus groups with land officials and local leaders aimed to identify weaknesses, strengths, and organizational preferences. Policy implementers preferred government organizations: they believed that the government is the only legitimate actor able to take land in Vietnam's current context. A Deputy Director of the LFDC (Bac Ninh Province) asserted that:

> We must first follow legal procedures, as required by the Land Law, that emphasize the role of the government. . . . We conform to Articles 61, 62, 63, and 66 of the 2013 Land Law.

Local managers and leaders in both Vinh Phuc and Bac Ninh provinces also believed that, without the direct involvement of the government, investors and landholders are rarely able to achieve agreements for land recovery. Several of them explained that, since the land is owned by the state, government agencies have legitimate authority to take land for public purposes. In case of disputes, the government can apply compulsory forms of land acquisition. Land management agencies and government officials also have technical expertise and experience in the local land sector. They know the history of even small plots of land under their jurisdiction. By contrast, many landholders preferred nongovernment actors that operate in accordance with market mechanisms. When asked why they preferred non-state actors, some land users in Tu Son (Bac Ninh Province) and Vinh Yen (Vinh Phuc province) said they did not resist the government, but they wanted fairer land prices and higher compensation. That was why they requested that they should be able to deal directly with investors for land conversion.

Corruption was another common worry that emerged in discussions with affected land users. Since the unrealistic land prices resulted in very low compensation, landholders suspected that government officials could abuse land-taking for their private interests. According to some affected landholders, both local businesses and government greatly benefited by exploiting the cheap land price system. This made some affected landholders lose trust in the local government. The author also interviewed government managers and leaders working in the land sector in the provinces of Vinh Phuc and Bac Ninh concerning "indirect government" as an alternative land-taking mechanism. Currently, as they reported, there is no legal provision for land-taking policy implementation by nongovernmental organizations – in other words, land conversion is solely the function of the government. Article 115 of *Land Law 2013* allows eligible and qualified nongovernment actors to provide land valuation services. These kinds of organizations, however, do not represent the "indirect government" mechanism, because nongovernmental organizations are not offered funding for service provision.

Authoritative tools

A unique characteristic of authoritative tools is the "threat of state-enforced sanctions" (Howlett 2011:83). This is because authoritative tools – such as regulations and executive orders – are "backed by the legitimate authority of government that grants permission, prohibit, or require action under designated circumstances" (Schneider & Ingram 1990:514). Target groups will be punished if they violate regulations or disobey policy decisions as stated in executive orders. The use of authoritative tools thus involves significant coercion. To explore the use of authoritative tools, the researcher reviewed the history of the three events and discussed the choice and use of authority-based tools with land officials at the research sites. Interviews and focus groups revealed that policy implementers largely relied on authoritative tools to achieve land-taking goals. While executive orders were used to legalize the government's land-taking decisions, implementers' activities in specific situations were guided by rules and regulations issued by both the central government and the provincial/city government.

The *Land Law*, land price systems, and regulations regarding land valuation, compensation, support, and resettlement were the first authoritative tools mentioned by land-taking executers. The most disputed authoritative tool regarding land acquisition is the land price system. As a policy tool, the land price system is a "regulation" that guides the behavior of both implementers and landholders. Policy implementers are required to determine a land price equal to prevailing market land prices at the time of compensation. However, how to determine a "market price" is still unclear. The common method of price calculation has resulted in large differences between land prices controlled by the state and land prices in the market (World Bank 2009, 2011a). In Bac Ninh Province, implementers adopted Executive Order no. 522/2014/QD-UBND about land prices and Executive Order no. 528/2014/QD-UBND about compensation, support, and resettlement. Based on these two executive orders, which had been valid from 2015 to 2019, the district government of Tu Son issued an administrative document notifying landholders about levels of compensation that they would receive. According to land officials involved in the Tu Son event, to compensate landholders, the BCGC first had to value land and land-embedded properties such as houses and trees. Though the Tu Son government adopted the highest land price, the real compensation was much lower than land values on the market. In Ho Chi Minh City, where the value of land has changed radically over time, land officials had to deal with a complex system of authority-based rules and orders directing land valuation and compensation. Before 2003, Ho Chi Minh City government applied the *Land Law* of 1993, amendments of the *Land Law* (1998 and 2001), and the PPC's Executive Order no. 135/2002/QĐ-UB (2002) regulating compensation and support for residents affected by the Thu Thiem project. After 2003, the city government enforced compensation rules based on Executive Order no. 123/2006/QĐ-UBND (2006) and then Executive Order no. 06/2009/QĐ-UBND (CGI 2018).

Analysis of government documents and field experience suggested that land acquisition in Vietnam was a highly regulated process in which implementers were required to strictly follow land legislation, administrative rules, and executive orders. This was evident in the three land-taking events of Thu Thiem, Dong Tam, and Tu Son. Executive orders were a common tool used by local governments to execute land-taking projects. In Tu Son, each affected landholder received a package of documents (proclamation) from the district government.

Of those documents, two executive orders issued by the PPC and District People's Committee (DPC) informed landholders about the land-taking project and noted that they were required to collaborate with the district BCGC to enforce the orders. In the Dong Tam event, the district government of My Duc responded to villagers' land claims by issuing an executive order to take the disputed land. Regarding the Thu Thiem event, the city government issued multiple executive orders to undertake land-taking projects and to modify land-taking plans (Huu Nguyen 2018; CGI 2018).

To figure out how the city government's acts had resulted in land users' disobedience, the author reviewed case profiles and found serious abuses of the authority-based tool of executive orders (Zing 2018b; Truong Minh 2019). Visits to research sites also suggested that BT (Build Transfer) and BOT (Build Operate Transfer) constructions and land acquisition often started at the same time. This put time pressure on local governments that led to forced acquisition. In the inspection report released in 2018, the central government's inspectorate pointed out the Ho Chi Minh City government's violations:

> The city government, especially the 2nd district government, did not follow legal procedures and requirements regarding land-taking enactment. The government did not develop a compensation proposal.
>
> (CGI 2018)

The use of numerous executive orders changed land planning in Thu Thiem and enabled effective land acquisitions. However, the coerciveness of executive orders also increased land users' resistance, which led to long-lasting tensions.

Financial tools

A key feature of financial tools is the use of financial or financial-equivalent incentives to alter target groups' behaviors (Howlett 2011:101). These tools, however, are not the same as "political economy" or "economics," because they represent the actions rather than the economic conditions. (In theoretical terms, they are the implemented financial and economic compensation rather than the economic valuations.) Currently, as stated in the *Land Law 2013*, cash, land, and apartments are three forms of compensation. From a "tools" perspective, those forms of compensation are three finance-based tools used by government to convince policy target groups to give up their land. According to Articles 74, 75, and 79 of the *Land Law 2013*, "land and resettlement apartments" are the first financial-equivalent tools used for land acquisition. Implementers in HCMC, more specifically, were required to compensate affected landholders with the same type of land: cash is only the second option if the government is unable to provide a similar piece of land for landholders (HCMC 2018). Similar situations also occur in other provinces. However, local implementers rarely adopt land-based compensation due to their inability to find equivalent areas of land. The head of the land management agency in Bac Ninh Province reported that many affected landholders preferred compensation in land. However, he added, land-based compensation was unrealistic (though in the past, the Bac Ninh government could offer compensation in land. Regarding the option of new apartments, the local governments only constructed resettlement apartments if land acquisition affected a large number of households). In Thu Thiem, the city government offered land and apartments to encourage land users to accept land-taking decisions. However, as regulated by the city government, affected landholders only received financial support for 30 m^2 of the new apartment and 45 m^2 of the new plot of land. Landholders were responsible for paying for additional costs if they accepted compensation in the form of land or an apartment (HCMC 2018). These regulations made land and apartments less attractive because many affected people could not pay for their new apartments.

As a result, cash was the most common financial tool used to compensate landholders across the three land-taking events. In Ho Chi Minh City, implementers adopted land-taking legislation and rules (for example, Articles 75 and 114 of the *Land Law 2013*; Article 18 of Circular no.44/2014/ND-CP; and Articles 31 and 32 of Directive no.36/TT-BTNMT). Accordingly, landholders subjected to land acquisition in Thu Thiem were compensated for affected land, properties on land, and moving fees. Compliant landholders also received financial support in cash prior to the execution of a land-taking project. If landholders did not comply with land acquisition, compensation funding was transferred into a bank account managed by the government, and landholders were still required to give up their land. Landholders only received compensation based on the latest land price system if a payment was delayed due to the government. However, in disputed situations, violations were always the sole responsibility of noncompliant landholders. In Thu Thiem, for example, since landholders disputed with the city government, they had to accept compensation at the same rate as the first installment (Zing 2018b). Land officials in Bac Ninh shared that the government often made installments based on the progress of land acquisition. Since a landholder could own several small land parcels, he thus would receive multiple installments because his land was not acquired at one time. Another reason is that the government cannot arrange enough funding, which might result in late compensation.

Information-based tools

"Information-based tools" refer to devices used by the government to communicate information or knowledge to policy target groups (Howlett 2011:115). Unlike authoritative tools that involve coercion, a key feature of information-based tools is persuasion. Implementers provide information to influence target groups' thinking and attitudes that might result in behavioral changes. To identify information-based tools, the researcher reviewed the administrative and legal procedures required to implement a land acquisition project at the research sites. There were no differences regarding the procedural enactment of a land-taking project between the two provinces (Bac Ninh and Vinh Phuc) where the researcher examined policy implementation. Land officials in both provinces were required to follow the same procedures.

Proclamation was the first information-based tool used by BCGCs to inform landholders about a land-taking project. In the Tu Son event, each affected landholder received a document package that consisted of all official information regarding the land acquisition plan. Those documents included the "PPC executive order" approving the DPC's land-taking request; the "DPC executive order" establishing the BCGC – a list of affected households accompanied by a map; and compensation rules approved by the Provincial People's Council. After receiving the "land-taking proclamation," landholders subjected to land acquisition had the right to ask the BCGC for further clarifications on any issues of concern. Interviewed landholders, however, said they were only concerned about compensation, acquired land area, and the deadline for handing over their land. Land officials in Tu Son district also noted that landholders often did not really care about the land-taking proclamation until the government began listing properties on land and measuring their acquired land areas.

A "public poster" is a tool displaying all information regarding land-taking plans. According to land officials involved in the Tu Son event, public posters showed details of the land acquisition project, such as names and addresses of affected landholders, the land-taking purpose, the land area to be acquired; the types and origin of land; the basis for calculating compensation; and the timeframe for land acquisition. Such a public poster was required to be publicly displayed at communal committee offices or in public places, such as a village's community house. Communal authorities, community representatives, affected landholders, and investors were also required to confirm the availability of public posters. All public posters showing a land-taking project remained in public places for at least 20 days. (The author, however, did not find any public posters in Dong Ky and Trang Ha wards. As reported by local land officials, someone removed them because the land-taking project had been in operation for a long time and people did not care about public posters.)

As a policy tool, "government information portal" was an official device that affected landholders could access for information about three events. The researcher, however, was not able to find any information about the land-taking projects in Dong Tam and Tu Son. Some news regarding the two projects was posted on information portals of Hanoi City government and the Bac Ninh provincial government. When asked about the role of the government's information portal as an implementation tool, a land manager in Tu Son district explained that online sources of information such as government websites were not a useful tool because most people did not habitually search for information online. The Ho Chi Minh City government was the only entity to create a separate section for the Thu Thiem project on its information portal. The availability of an online source of information, however, was not necessarily associated with transparency. This was because all land-taking information was controlled by the government: only the government could decide what type of information to make available to the public. (In Thu Thiem, for example, landholders were most concerned with the original map, but such a map was never found on the city's websites.)

According to Article 69 of *Land Law 2013*, a "public dialogue" is a required information session where policy implementers and target groups can exchange information. As a tool, public dialogue was used to clarify affected land areas and compensation with landholders in all three land-taking events. According to the head of the LFDC in Tu Son district: "the district BCGC is required to conduct at least one public dialogue to inform affected land users about details of the land-taking plan." Additional public meetings and dialogues could be organized if disputes took place. However, it depended on the situation, he added. In reality, BCGC members did not prefer public meetings and dialogues, because such information sessions were often related to complicated situations. In the Thu Thiem event, for example, public dialogues became a nightmare for government leaders because they not only received forceful criticism but also were unable to clearly answer landholders' questions regarding land-taking.

Moral suasion, exhortation, and intrusive propaganda are persuasion tools that convey messages (which may or may not contain factual information) designed to motivate target groups to change their behaviors (Howlett 2011:117). All three means relied on persuasion schemes to convey messages designed to motivate target audiences and modify their behaviors (Adler & Pittle 1984:160). Discussions with local implementers in Bac Ninh and Vinh Phuc suggested that these tools emerged as the key information-based tools. Both moral suasion and exhortation were unofficially conducted by individual government officials, who could employ any means, at any time, and anywhere, to persuade landholders, urging them to follow the government's decisions. Intrusive propaganda was also an official means by which government authorized agencies and officials to formally conduct persuasive communication with landholders. The emphasis on moral suasion, exhortation, and propaganda was evident in Tu Son DPC's land acquisition documents. Once an executive order for land-taking was issued, landholders were expected to accept the government's executive orders. Persuasion, thus, was the most important communication strategy required of BCGC members. The Tu Son district government asked individual members of the BCGC and the propaganda unit to expend efforts to persuade landholders. However, the researcher's experience at research sites suggested that the heavy reliance on propaganda, exhortation, and moral suasion resulted in negative attitudes among landholders. This was because, instead of providing clear information, the government tried to convince landholders to acquiesce.

Conclusion

What arises from the three land-taking events analyzed in this study is a confirmation of the role of government organizations as the only organizational tool used in executing land acquisition policy in Vietnam. Utilizing the government can save budget funding because the policy implementation relies on available employees and resources. The direct involvement of government organizations also allows the exercise of legitimate force when implementers confront resistance. This ensures that the execution of a land-taking project is not left to chance. The government, therefore, can reach desired land-taking objectives as scheduled. However, the fact that public officials dominate BCGCs makes them less responsive to emerging needs. This is because BCGCs are not independent organizations that operate based on market mechanisms. As a temporary task-focused unit, BCGCs represent the state's interests, which might conflict with the interests of target groups. Due to the limited participation of non-state actors (such as landholders, legal experts, and land policy professionals), BCGCs can make decisions that do not meet the demands of affected landholders. Government organizations, thus, are not an appropriate choice, especially when the acquired land is then offered to private investors.

This case study also reveals an authority-intensive tool mix used in land-taking in Vietnam. Since a key feature of authoritative tools is the threat of sanctions backed by the state, the use of authoritative tools involves significant coercion. Certainly, the coercive nature of authoritative tools might result in greater implementation efficiency and effectiveness. However, a heavy reliance on authoritative tools might increase resistance over land acquisition. Landholders disobey government actions because – from their point of view – those coercive actions are not legitimate. The use of executive orders makes land-taking legal, but it is not necessarily a legitimate action by government. Citizens may doubt whether they should follow rules by governing authorities. This might derive from insufficiently expressed legal authority or unclear information regarding land acquisition plans. In addition, landholders express non-consent by refusing compensation or causing coercive land acquisition to be conducted. Without their consent, landholders might act against the government, often resulting in long-lasting disputes.

This study shows the inappropriate choice of land price regulation as an implementation tool. Regardless of land price calculation formulas, there is no possibility for local implementers to offer landholders land prices and compensation that are equal to market-based values. Regulations are agency-made laws, backed by legislation and judicial decisions. Government relies on regulations to govern private behaviors or to set a price ceiling (as in land acquisition). In practice, by using land price regulations, local governments can control compensation in a desired way. This, however, conflicts with a requirement (as stated in the *Land Law*) that land price and compensation should be close to market land values. This research finding demonstrates that unrealistic land prices and compensation are essentially the consequences of an inappropriate tool choice. In other words, the fixed land price regulation is the main factor causing disputed compensation, thus leading to policy noncompliance.

Field interviews and observations also indicate implementers' tool preferences over information-based tools such as moral suasion and propaganda. BCGC members mainly rely on ideological and moral justifications to persuade landholders giving up their land. Public media controlled by the state is used as the key propaganda device to create public opinion that encourages landholders' acceptance over land acquisition. Public dialogues between BCGC members and disobedient landholders are situationally organized when disputes last a long time;

landholders' grievances and tensions increase. However, information-based tools are not helpful in noncompliant situations. This is because implementers are not required to provide clear and exact information. They can inform landholders anything that might alter target groups' thinking and behaviors.

It becomes clear that "coercion," "instrumentality," and "routinization" are common patterns of tool choice and use in land acquisition in Vietnam. By instrumentality, as argued by Capano and Lippi (2017:10), implementers select tools to "keep with the policy makers' pursued goals." Routinization is a pattern whereby those implementers adopt "the same policy instruments in the same way." Previously adopted instruments are preserved by implementers, without any change. These patterns of tool choice and use ensure implementation effectiveness but do not necessarily result in a shared sense and a common acceptance that construct policy legitimacy. From a tool perspective, three features of coercion, instrumentality, and routinization might help government achieve policy effectiveness and efficiency. However, such a model of tool choice and use is not necessarily responsive to policy target groups' demands. Current tool mixes and tool preferences instead would be associated with two negative consequences: (i) low responsiveness and (ii) direct confrontation between the government and citizens.

The tools approach used in this study further explains landholders' noncompliance, because current tool mixes are not really associated with legitimate actions. Available tool preferences include formal government organizations, authoritative tools, and information-based tools – while financial incentives are underestimated. Current tools not only create a one-way relationship between government and target groups, but also legitimate coercive actions in land acquisition. This motivates implementers to take land regardless of the legitimacy of the government's actions. A policy tools approach, therefore, suggests that policy implementers can increase landholders' compliance with land acquisition if they remove inappropriate tools, change tool-use toward more collaborative interactions, and consider the legitimacy of the government's actions in practice.

References

Adler, Robert S., & Pittle, R. David. (1984). Cajolery or command: Are education campaigns an adequate substitute for regulations? *Yale Journal on Regulation*, *1*(2), 159–193.

Agranoff, Robert, & McGuire, Michael. (2003). *Collaborative Public management: New strategies for local governments*. Washington, DC: Georgetown University Press.

Anderson, C. (1971). Comparative policy analysis: The design of measures. *Comparative Politics*, *4*(1), 117–131.

Anderson, J. (2014). *Public policymaking* (8th Ed.). Australia: Wadsworth.

Bell, C. K. (2014). A review of the land sector in East Asia: Lessons for land governance and the spatial enablement of government and societies. *Paper presented at the "2014 World Bank conference on land and poverty"*. Retrieved from http://www.oicrf.org/document.asp?ID=13517

Bemelmans-Videc, M., Rist, Ray C., & Vedung, Evert. (1998). *Carrots, sticks & sermons: Policy instruments and their evaluation* (Comparative policy analysis series). New Brunswick, NJ: Transaction.

Beresford, M. (2008). Doi Moi in review: The challenges of building market socialism in Vietnam. *Journal of Contemporary Asia, 38*(2), 221–243.
Birkland, T. (2016). *An introduction to the policy process: Theories, concepts, and models of public policy making* (4th Ed.). New York: Routledge.
Brinkerhoff, W., & Crosby, B. (2002). *Managing policy reform: Concepts and tools for decision-makers in developing and transitioning countries*. Bloomfield, CT: Kumarian Press.
Brown, D. (2012, February 2). Vietnam's contentious Land Law. *Asia Sentinel*. Retrieved from www.asiasentinel.com/society/vietnams-contentious-land-law-part-2/.
Brown, D. (2013, February 6). Vietnam's contentious Land Law. *Asia Sentinel*. Retrieved from http://www.asiasentinel.com/society/vietnams-land-law-reform-is-it-enough/
Butler, B. S. (2009). Developing Land Markets within the constraint of state ownership in Vietnam. In Ingram, G. K., & Hung Hong, Y. *Property rights and land policies* (pp. 137–175). Cambridge, MA: Lincoln Institute of Land Policy.
Capano, G., & Lippi, A. (2017). How policy instruments are chosen: Patterns of decision makers' choices. *Policy Sciences, 50*(2), 269–293.
CGI (Central Government's Inspectorate). (2018, September 7). Ket luan thanh tra khu do thi moi Thu Thiem. Retrieved from https://vietnamfinance.vn/toan-van-ket-luan-thanh-tra-khu-do-thi-moi-thu-thiem-20180504224212652.htm.
Cialdini, R., & Goldstein, N. (2004). Social influence: Compliance and conformity. *Annual Review of Psychology, 55*, 591–621.
Cooper, P. (2018). *Policy tools in policy design*. Irvine, CA: Melvin & Leigh.
De Wit, J. W., Sang, L. V., Chien, L. V., Hien, L. T., Hung, H. V., Tuyet, D. T., & Bau, D. N. (2012). Assessing decentralized policy implementation in Vietnam: The case of land recovery and resettlement in the Vung Ang Economic Zone. *International Institute of Social Studies*. Netherlands. ISS *Working Paper Series/General Series* (Vol. 546, pp. 1–55). Erasmus University Rotterdam. Retrieved from https://repub.eur.nl/pub/32910/.
Deininger, K., & Jin, S. (2005). Land sales and rental markets in Transition: Evidence from rural Vietnam. Paper presented at the American Agricultural Economics Association Meeting, Rhode Island.
Denhardt, R. (2011). *Theories of public organization* (6th Ed.). Boston, MA: Wadsworth/Cengage Learning.
The Economist. (2017, June 15). No man's land. *The Economist*. Retrieved from www.economist.com/news/asia/21723423-communist-party-does-not-know-how-handle-them-property-disputes-are-vietnams-biggest.
ED, WB, and ES (Embassy of Denmark, World Bank, and Embassy of Sweden). (2011). *Recognizing and reducing corruption risks in land management in Vietnam*. Hanoi: National Political Publishing House.
FAO-UN. (2007). *Good governance in land tenure and administration*. FAO Land Tenure Studies. Rome: Food and Agriculture Organization of the United Nations.
Fu, H., & Gillespie, J. (2014). *Resolving land disputes in East Asia: Exploring the limits of law*. Cambridge: Cambridge University Press.
Gales, P. (2011). Policy instruments and governance. In Bevir, M. *The SAGE handbook of governance*. Los Angeles and Thousand Oaks, CA: SAGE Publications.
Gillespie, J. (2011). Exploring the limits of the judicialization of urban land disputes in Vietnam. *Law & Society Review, 45*(2), 241–276.
Gofen, A. (2015). Reconciling policy dissonance: Patterns of governmental response to policy noncompliance. *Policy Sciences, 48*(1), 3–24.

Hill, M., & Hupe, Peter L. (2002). *Implementing public policy: Governance in theory and practice (Sage politics texts)*. London and Thousand Oaks, CA: Sage.
Ho, D. H., & McPherson, M. (2010). *Land Policy for socio-economic development in Vietnam*. ASH Centre for Democratic Governance and Innovation, Harvard Kennedy School and UNDP. Retrieved from http://ash.harvard.edu/files/vnm_landpolicypaper.pdf.
Ho, P. (2005). *Institutions in transition: Land ownership, property rights, and social conflict in China*. New York: Oxford University Press.
Ho Chi Minh City People's Committee. (2018). Executive order no. 28/QD-UBND about compensation, support, and resettlement regarding land acquisition. Retrieved from www.donre.hochiminhcity.gov.vn//Lists/vanbanmoi/Attachments/834/28_2018_Q%C4%90-UBND.pdf.
Hood, C. (1983). *The tools of government*. London: Macmillan.
Howlett, M. (2011). *Designing public policies: Principles and instruments* (Routledge textbooks in policy studies). Abingdon, Oxon and New York: Routledge.
Howlett, M., Ramesh, M., & Perl, A. (2009). *Studying public policy: Policy cycles & policy subsystems* (3rd Ed.). Don Mills and New York: Oxford University Press.
Huu Nguyen. (2018, May 5). Quy hoach Thu Thiem thay doi the nao sau 22 nam? Retrieved from https://vnexpress.net/thoi-su/quy-hoach-thu-thiem-thay-doi-the-nao-trong-22-nam-3745564.html.
IRPLD (Institute for Research on Policy, Law, and Development). (2013). Conciliation of land disputes in Vietnam: A critical analysis of current law and practice with recommendations for reform. *Research Report*. Retrieved from www.nytimes.com/2017/04/21/world/asia/vietnam-hostages-protest-land-dispute-eviction.html.
Ingram, G. K., & Hung Hong, Y. (2009). *Property rights and land policies*. Cambridge, MA: Lincoln Institute of Land Policy.
Kim, A. (2011). Talking back: The role of narrative in Vietnam's recent land compensation changes. *Urban Studies*, *48*(3), 493–508.
Lascoumes, P., & Le Gales, P. (2007). Introduction: Understanding public policy through its instruments – from the nature of instruments to the sociology of public policy instrumentation. *Governance*, *20*(1), 1–21.
Lipton, M. (2009). *Land reform in developing countries: Property rights and property wrongs*. New York: Routledge.
Lodhi, A. H. A. (2004). Are landlords taking back the land? An essay on the agrarian transition in Vietnam. *The European Journal of Development Research*, *16*(4), 757–789.
London, J. (Ed.). (2014). *Politics in contemporary Vietnam: Party, state, and authority relations*. New York: Palgrave Macmillan.
Markussen, T., Tarp, F., & Van Den Broeck, K. (2011). The forgotten property rights: Evidence on land use rights in Vietnam. *World Development*, *39*(5), 839–850.
Marsh, S. P., MacAulay, T. G., & Hung, P. V. (Eds.). (2007). Agricultural development and land policy in Vietnam. *Policy Briefs*. Retrieved from http://aciar.gov.au/publication/mn123.
McPherson, F. M. (2011). Land policy in Vietnam: Challenges and prospects for constructive changes. *Journal of Macro-Marketing*, 1–10.
Mintrom, M. (2012). *Contemporary policy analysis. New York*: Oxford University Press.
Mintz, Alex. (2005). Applied decision analysis: Utilizing poliheuristic theory to explaining and predicting foreign policy and national security decisions. *Special Symposium Papers in International Studies Perspectives*, *6*(1), 94–150.
O'Toole, L. (2000). Research on policy implementation: Assessment and prospects. *Journal of Public Administration Research and Theory*: *J-PART*, *10*(2), 263–288.

Phuong Thuy. (2020). Chat luong giai quyet khieu nai, to cao con thap. Retrieved from https://cand.com.vn/Su-kien-Binh-luan-thoi-su/Chat-luong-giai-quyet-khieu-nai-to-cao-con-thap-i580626/.

Pincus, R. J. (2012). *Vietnam's reforms: The road to market Leninism*. Legatum Institute Working Report. Retrieved from https://lif.blob.core.windows.net/lif/docs/default-source/country-growth-reports/prosperity-in-depth-vietnam-39-s-reforms – the-road-to-market-leninism.pdf?sfvrsn=0.

Pressman, J., & Wildavsky, Aaron B. (1973). *Implementation: How great expectations in Washington are dashed in Oakland*. Berkeley: University of California Press.

Salamon, L. (1981). Rethinking public management: Third-party government and the changing forms of government action. *Public Policy*, *29*(3), 255–275.

Salamon, L., & Elliott, Odus V. (2002). *The tools of government: A guide to the new governance*. Oxford and New York: Oxford University Press.

Salamon, L., & Lund, Michael S. (1989). The tools approach: Basic analytics. In *Beyond privatization: The tools of government action*. Washington, DC and Lanham, MD: Urban Institute Press; Distributed in the United States and Canada by University Press of America.

Sandfort, J., & Moulton, S. (2015). *Effective implementation in practice: Integrating public policy and management*. San Francisco: Jossey-Bass.

Schneider, A., & Ingram, H. (1990). Behavioral assumptions of policy tools. *The Journal of Politics*, *52*(2), 510–529.

Simon, H. (1955). A behavioral model of rational choice. *The Quarterly Journal of Economics*, *69*(1), 99–118.

Suu, N. V. (2004). The politics of land: Inequality in land access and local conflicts in the Red River delta since de-collectivization. In Taylor, P., & Institute of Southeast Asian Studies. *Social inequality in Vietnam and the challenges to reform (Vietnam update series)*. Singapore: Institute of Southeast Asian Studies.

Suu, N. V. (2009). Agricultural land conversion and its effects on farmers in contemporary Vietnam. *European Journal of Anthropology*, *54*, 106–113.

Stone, D. (2012). *Policy paradox: The art of political decision making* (3rd Ed.). New York: W.W. Norton & Company.

Toan, L., & Quang, N. (2014). An historical overview of Vietnamese land law and dispute resolution. In Fu, H., & Gillespie, J. *Resolving land disputes in East Asia: Exploring the limits of law*. Cambridge: Cambridge University Press.

Tria Kerkvliet, B. (2006). Agricultural land in Vietnam: Markets tempered by family, community and socialist practices. *Journal of Agrarian Change*, *6*(3), 285–305.

Truong Minh. (2019, April 11). Nhung phan doi luu lac o Thu Thiem. Viettimes.vn. Retrieved from https://viettimes.vn/ky-cuoi-nhung-phan-doi-luu-lac-o-thu-thiem-350229.html.

TSG – Tu Son People's Committee website. Retrieved from http://tuson.bacninh.gov.vn/-ieu-kien-tu-nhien-xa-hoi.

Vo, D. H. (2011, September 30). Story of land price in Vietnam. *English Vietnamnet.vn*. Retrieved from http://english.vietnamnet.vn/en/special-report/13610/story-of-land-price-in-vietnam.html

Wehrmann, B. (2008). *Land conflict: A practical guide to dealing with land disputes*. Eschborn, Germany: Deutsche Gesellschaff fur TechnischeZusammenarbeit (GTZ) GmbH.

Wells-Dang, A. (2013). Promoting land rights in Vietnam: A multi-sector advocacy coalition approach. Paper presented at the Annual World Bank Conference on land

and Poverty, Washington, DC. Retrieved from https://landportal.info/library/resources/promoting-land-rights-vietnam-multi-sector-advocacy-coalition-approach.

Williamson, O. (1979). Transaction-cost economics: The governance of contractual relations. *The Journal of Law and Economics*, *22*(2), 233–261.

World Bank. (2009). Improving land acquisition and voluntary land conversion in Vietnam. Policy Note. Retrieved from https://openknowledge.worldbank.org/handle/10986/18611.

World Bank. (2011a). Compulsory land acquisition and voluntary land conversion in Viet Nam: the conceptual approach, land valuation and grievance redress mechanisms. Policy Note. Retrieved from https://openknowledge.worldbank.org/handle/10986/26886.

World Bank. (2011b). Improving land governance: The land governance assessment frameworks. Research Report. Retrieved from https://openknowledge.worldbank.org/handle/10986/2376.

World Bank. (2012). Revising the land law to enable sustainable development in Vietnam: summary of priority policy recommendations drawn from World Bank studies. Policy Note. Retrieved from https://openknowledge.worldbank.org/handle/10986/26777.

World Bank. (2014). *Land transparency study: Synthesis report*. Hanoi: Hong Duc Publishing House. Retrieved from https://openknowledge.worldbank.org/handle/10986/20714.

World Bank and MPI (World Bank and the Ministry of Planning and Investment of Vietnam). (2016). Vietnam 2035: Toward prosperity, creativity, equity, and democracy. Research Report. Retrieved from https://openknowledge.worldbank.org/handle/10986/23724.

Zing. (2018b, May 9). Nuoc mat Thu Thiem. Zing.vn. Retrieved from https://news.zing.vn/nuoc-mat-thu-thiem-sau-20-nam-quy-hoach-do-thi-moi-post841311.html.

Part 2

Agricultural land conversion, urbanization, and farmers' responses

4 Urbanization and land acquisition in Hue's peri-urban areas

Challenges and the way forward

Nguyen Quang Phuc

Introduction

International experience suggests that the conversion of land from agricultural to urban use unavoidably accompanies rapid urbanization and economic growth. Vietnam is no exception. According to an official report of the General Statistics Office (GSO 2020), the country's annual GDP growth averaged 5.9 percent between 2016 and 2020. Foreign Direct Investment inflows alone increased from US$24.3 billion in 2016 to US$39 billion in 2019. This economic transformation has been accompanied by rapid urbanization, with urban areas expanding and the addition of at least one million people per year. In fact, the rate of urbanization is expected to increase from 35.7 percent in 2015 to 39.3 percent by 2020 (GSO 2020). As a result, there is increased demand for quality housing, infrastructure, and facilities to allow for both economic growth and urban development. This has placed tremendous pressure on land and its users, especially in peri-urban areas, where land traditionally used for agriculture is still available and is cheaper than urban land.

In response to the increasing scarcity of land, the state has used the mechanism of compulsory land acquisition to commit massive amounts of rural land in peri-urban areas to urban uses. While this is not a new phenomenon in Vietnam, its growing frequency and its adverse socioeconomic impacts on local development have drawn increasing scrutiny from the academic community, the media, and policy makers. It has been estimated that nearly one million hectares of agricultural land were acquired for non-agricultural activities between 2001 and 2010 (World Bank 2011), while 630,000 households (nearly 2.5 million people) have been affected by these processes (Mai Thanh 2009). Accordingly, central issues in land policy debates in recent years have dealt with the consequences of land loss as well as the principles and processes of equitable compensation for affected people.

The overall objective of this chapter is to provide a better understanding of the debate over land acquisition for urban development. An in-depth study of Hue's peri-urban areas will focus special attention on the challenges of land acquisition for urbanization, and the chapter will conclude with policy recommendations for institutional improvement in Vietnam's land governance.

DOI: 10.4324/9781003165774-7

The debate over land acquisition for urban development

The past few years have seen a large number of studies focusing on the acquisition of land for urban development in developing countries. Though many issues have been raised in recent research (for example, the scale and type of land; the actors; and local implications), special attention has been given to the impacts of land acquisition on local development; the role of compensation policy; and suggestions for suitable policy frameworks.

The positive and negative effects of land acquisition

It is widely acknowledged that land acquisition for local development generates both positive and negative effects. On the positive side, land acquisition makes land available for housing, infrastructure development, and other facilities to support economic growth and urban development. As an indirect result of socioeconomic development, many non-farm employment opportunities (for example, factory work, self-employment, and casual labor) are created for the local population. Such opportunities can enable farmers to diversify and to improve their livelihoods (Oduro 2010; Toufique and Turton 2002; Zhang and Lu 2011). In Hunan Province, China, for instance, construction of factories was shown to provide job opportunities for farmers, allowing them to adjust their livelihood strategies after land loss (Zhou 2012). In addition, the development of economic activities and improvement of infrastructure (particularly roads) in peri-urban areas has facilitated rural-urban migration in many developing countries, including the Philippines (Kelly 1999), Sub-Saharan Africa (Tacoli 2004), and Indonesia (Winarso et al. 2015). Finally, in many cases, financial compensation resulting from land loss has allowed residents to repair their houses, to improve living conditions, or to invest in activities to generate livelihoods (Zhou 2012).

On the negative side, the loss of traditional livelihoods is one of the direct consequences of land acquisition, especially the acquisition of agricultural land (Firman 2000; Zhang and Lu 2011). For instance, it is estimated that more than 5 million hectares of agricultural land in China were acquired for non-agricultural uses between 1978 and 2008. This process has directly impacted approximately 73 million farmers in both rural and peri-urban areas (Zhang and Lu 2011). Due to the loss of traditional livelihoods, the majority of affected households have been forced to transition from being net food-producers to net food-consumers.

A similar situation was also found by Fazal in India. He states that, due to the decline in the availability of arable land, finding jobs for rural laborers is a great challenge for the country. Approximately 67 percent of India's total workforce engages in the agricultural sector, and about two-thirds of the total population live in rural areas (Fazal 2001). A lack of sustainable livelihoods is also a serious consequence of land acquisition (Zhang and Lu 2011; Oduro 2010), and for many farmers, land loss equates to the loss of stable jobs and stable income. Although there may be more income sources after land loss, the stability of temporary non-agricultural jobs is relatively low because of the changing requirements of the labor market. Zhou (2012) also argues that the compensation policy (a one-time financial payment) has contributed to a loss of long-term livelihood security. For example, 51.1 percent of Dongfanghong Town respondents reported that, while their compensation payment would be depleted in two or three years following land loss, they believed they would be able to survive very well for the first four to five years after land acquisition. In reality, most faced many difficulties in the following years. Other negative impacts of land acquisition include food insecurity and the disappearance of rural identity (Kelly 1999), as well as the destruction of irrigation infrastructure (Firman 2000). Finally, farmer resistance to land loss has occurred in many parts of the world, largely due to inequitable compensation and to livelihood issues (Walker 2008; Kelly 1999; Schneider 2011).

Despite these adverse economic and social consequences, land continues to be acquired by governments to provide the public facilities and infrastructure that support development (FAO 2008; World Bank 2011; Tan et al. 2009; Firman 1997). The remaining challenge is how the acquisition of land can be planned and implemented (FAO 2008; Chan 2003; UNDP 2014; Zhang and Lu 2011) so as to minimize the impact on people's livelihoods. Some policy initiatives have been proposed in order to improve the performance and limit the negative impacts of land acquisition. UNDP (2014) has argued that development can be inclusive only if all groups, particularly non-state actors, contribute to creating opportunities and participate in decision-making. This approach is consistent with the people-centered development approach promoted by Korten (1984), who stressed inclusiveness in decision-making processes. It also supports the principle of "free, prior and informed consent" (FPIC), which emphasizes the rights of local people in negotiating with investors as well as their right to make decisions on development projects (Forest People Programme 2007). It became evident in many studies that multiple stakeholder participation in decision-making processes is necessary.

The determination of compensation

Including affected people in the determination of compensation amounts is equally important. In past studies on land tenure, the Food and Agriculture Organization of the United Nations (FAO 2008) emphasized the need for adequate compensation packages for people's losses. They noted that compensation should be based on the principles of equity and equivalence. The principle of equivalence is crucial to maintaining (if not improving) the living conditions of affected households, compared to pre-project levels. For this, the FAO (2008) and the Asian Development Bank (ADB 2007) suggest two models of valuation and compensation for the compulsory acquisition of land: market value and replacement cost. The "market value" is the amount that a willing buyer would pay a willing seller on the open market, where some choice exists. The "replacement cost" is based on the level of compensation that will be sufficient for project-affected persons to replace their lost land with land of equal value or comparable productivity. The latter approach is useful in countries where the land market is not fully established (FAO 2008).

From a cost-benefit perspective, the World Bank as well as the FAO acknowledge that, while land acquisition brings benefits to the city as a whole, at the same time it creates losses for affected communities (World Bank 2011; FAO 2008). To address this contradiction, the World Bank has suggested that the benefit-sharing principle should be adopted among the parties involved in projects. This principle not only focuses on monetary compensation but also on forms of non-monetary compensation such as support for life stabilization; vocational training; and jobs in project areas. To achieve the principle of benefit-sharing recommended by the World Bank, land-acquiring agencies (for example, government agencies and investors) should be responsible for supporting affected people in livelihood restoration after land loss (World Bank 2011). This, to some extent, is consistent with the policy initiatives of international donors that focus on affecting investor behavior through notions of corporate social responsibility (CSR) (Zoomers 2013). For instance, the World Bank (2010) has been working on a "code of conduct" (or "principles"), together with appropriate land policies.

It becomes clear that the policy initiatives mentioned above are geared toward the objectives of equitable and sustainable development. Land acquisition should seek to secure a balance between economic development and social sustainability (Schumann et al. 2010) and to ensure equitable access to certain resources or assets as well as to sharing development benefits among individuals (Sen 1981; Conway 1987; UNDP 2000). However, these objectives may be difficult to accomplish if governance mechanisms are not well-designed and effectively implemented in practice (Pham 2014).

Issues of governance

Governance, according to the United Nations Development Program (UNDP 1997), is the management of a country's affairs, at all levels, through the exercise of economic, political, and administrative authority through the mechanisms, processes, and institutions whereby citizens and groups convey their interests, exercise their rights, and satisfy their involvement. In other words, governance is the process of decision-making and the process by which decisions are implemented on the ground. If these processes are well-organized, good governance is achieved and can contribute significantly to equitable and sustainable development (UNDP 2014). Good governance stipulates the need for accountability, transparency, and justice as well as the participation of all stakeholders in decision-making processes, particularly civil society organizations. While good governance and sustainable development are two separate concepts, they are closely linked: good governance does not guarantee sustainable development, but its absence can, at worst, severely impede the sustainability of development (Karods 2012).

The policy initiatives discussed previously have become important frameworks for improving institutions and enhancing practical implementation in many countries. However, as they largely depend on political regimes, governance mechanisms, and the capacity of governments, the level of success of applying these on the ground varies from one country to another. Therefore, it is necessary to understand how the global principles and guidelines are put into practice in different countries – particularly in countries like Vietnam where power is controlled by a single party-state and where a process of institutional reform (especially in terms of land policies, urban development strategies and investment promotion) is rapidly occurring.

In the next section, we focus on a case study of Hue's peri-urban areas in order to improve understanding of land acquisition for urban development in a specific location.

Case study of Hue's peri-urban areas

Background: the research site

This study was conducted in Hue, a medium-sized city in central Vietnam. Hue is organized into 29 wards and 7 communes with a total area of 265,99 square kilometers. Due to the restrictions imposed by heritage conservation policy in the north of the city (the Citadel area), the core of Hue has mainly expanded to the south of city. The south has become the center of administrative bodies for the province and city, for tourism and for residential areas. This process has created pressure regarding land use, especially in the city's peri-urban areas.

Land acquisition in Hue's peri-urban areas has mainly been characterized by the acquisition of agricultural land (Nhung et al. 2020). The vast majority of affected households have remained in their original homes and have received compensation money, while a limited number of households who lost housing plots have resettled elsewhere within the same village or surrounding villages. It is estimated that 427 hectares of land in Hue's peri-urban areas (over 80 percent of which was agricultural land) were acquired between 2000 and 2018 (HSO 2018). Nearly 3,000 households have been impacted by land acquisition processes.

For this study, the author selected four peri-urban sites (see Table 4.1): Thuy Duong, Thuy Van, Phu Thuong, and Huong So, where most of the agricultural land has been acquired to build new urban developments such as An Cuu City, An Van Duong, Vicoland, Royal Park, and Eco Garden Hue (Phuc et al. 2017).

Table 4.1 Compulsory land acquisition in Hue's peri-urban zones (2000–18)

Localities	*Area (ha)*	*Affected households (#)*
Vy Da	21	175
Xuan Phu	23	180
An Hoa	10	225
Huong So	30	280
An Dong	18	169
An Tay	12	210
Phu Thuong	81	580
Thuy Van	105	515
Thuy Duong	127	496
Total	**427**	**2,830**

Source: Computed by author from the reports of local authorities.

Note: The figures for area of land acquisition in Thuy Bieu, Huong Long, and Thuy Xuan are not available.

Data collection and analysis

Various data collection techniques were used to gather information, including desktop research, household surveys, and in-depth interviews.

Desktop research

General socioeconomic information for research sites was collected from annual statistical data sets and commune reports. Documents and newspapers detailing land laws; decentralization over land management; decisions on land-use planning and land conversion; development projects; and urbanization processes were also examined to obtain information on land acquisition and its impacts in Vietnam in general and in Hue City in particular. Previous studies on land acquisition for urbanization were reviewed in order to gain understanding of the impacts of land acquisition on local development.

Household surveys

Household surveys were used to investigate the impacts of compulsory land acquisition on affected households. Responses were collected from 170 households who had lost their farmland for urban expansion without being displaced, in the four peri-urban communities of Thuy Duong, Thuy Van, Huong So, and Phu Thuong. Households were randomly selected based on the land acquisition decision lists provided by local authorities. These interviews were mostly conducted in 2014 with one or two household members (usually the husband and/or wife). However, other members of the household occasionally contributed as well, and since the questions involved information about additional household members, this proved to be very useful.

In-depth interviews

After primary household surveys were completed, ten in-depth interviews were conducted and analyzed. These interviews covered the nature of community participation in the land acquisition processes and respondents' perceptions about the impacts of land conversion on their livelihoods.

The data from the household surveys was coded and analyzed using SPSS 22 software. Both qualitative and quantitative methods were applied to investigate the impact of land acquisition for urban expansion on household livelihoods.

Findings

In accordance with socialist principles, all land in Vietnam belongs to "the entire people" (*Land Law 2013*). As the state is the representative owner, the government decides on provincial and city land-use zoning and planning for national defense, security, public interest, and economic development. Purposes related to the public interest and economic development are defined broadly and may include the construction of public infrastructure, establishing sites for state agencies and foreign organizations and other non-profit development projects, as well as the construction of commercial centers and new urban, resettlement, and residential areas. Households, communities, and other entities to which the state allocates land have no "ownership" rights, only "use" rights. (Such use rights include the rights to exchange, transfer, inherit, lease or mortgage land, as well as to use land as a capital contribution to investments.) However, as the representative owner, the state also has the legal ability to acquire land, in a compulsory manner, from current users for national and public interests, including industrialization and urbanization.

In theory, these types of land acquisitions are expected to bring societal benefits because the land is used to improve access to infrastructure and to the facilities necessary for development – a phenomenon which has taken place in many countries as part of socioeconomic development and population growth. Such government acquisitions are legal actions, based on Vietnam's existing laws and regulations. However, the case study of land acquisition for urban expansion in Hue City illustrates that the process is often unbalanced and unfair, especially for marginalized groups.

Allocation imbalances in terms of benefits and costs

The process of land acquisition for urban expansion has played a part in significantly improving Hue's infrastructure. It has also helped to create a modern urban image which could promote the development of local tourism and attract domestic and foreign investment. However, a look at the benefits and the costs incurred by various stakeholders – viewed as "gains" and "losses" – reveals that some groups have benefited while others have become more disadvantaged.

The first group of beneficiaries is the local government at three levels: the commune, the district/city, and the province. The local government benefits because the compensation payments allotted to those affected by land loss often fall significantly below prevailing land market rates. As a result, the margin that is created between acquisition costs and the prices paid by investors (which include state-owned companies, foreign and domestic private-sector actors, and government agencies) significantly contributes to local revenue. The second group of beneficiaries is the investors who pocket the largest share of the margin between compensation costs and market-price sales. The final group of beneficiaries includes the individuals and households who are able to take advantage of the opportunities (such as access to employment and information) that result from urban growth; these households are able to successfully reconstruct their livelihoods after land loss (Phuc et al. 2017). This group also consists of those who sell their residential land and subsequently benefit from the increase in land values brought about by acquisition and investment.

At the same time, urban expansion creates disadvantages due to high *social costs*, of which the first is the conversion of hundreds of hectares of agricultural land for urban uses. Having lost valuable productive land, the majority of affected households in the acquisition areas have been forced to transition from being net food-producers to net food-consumers. According to household surveys, after land loss only 46.2 percent of households could maintain food self-sufficiency throughout the year, compared with 87 percent before land loss. In addition, despite concerted efforts toward livelihood reconstruction after land loss, not all people have sufficient capacity to cope with – and recover from – the effects of urban expansion. Nearly 85 percent of survey respondents agreed that the elderly, the illiterate, and the physically challenged faced many more difficulties as a result of land loss. For this group, total income decreased considerably after land loss – either because of the decrease in rice cultivation land or because they were not able to access the new employment opportunities that resulted from urban growth. For them, land loss equated to the loss of a stable livelihood and income source.

> Quyen is a seventy-nine-year-old widow in Hamlet 1, Thuy Duong Commune, Huong Thuy District. She suffers from back problems and chronic stomach pain. In 2004, Quyen lost 50 percent of her farmland (800 m^2) to a new urban project, Dong Nam Thuy An Town. She was compensated with close to VND 1 million. All compensation money was spent on furniture, a rice cooker, an electric fan, and medicine. After land loss, rice cultivation on the remaining land is enough for her daily consumption. However, although she has medical insurance, she usually spends VND 200,000 to VND 300,000 on monthly medical examinations and medicine. At present, she faces numerous difficulties due to both a decrease in farm income and to an increase in healthcare expenditures.
>
> (In-depth interview, women, 79 years old, Hamlet 1, Thuy Duong Commune, Huong Thuy District)

Land acquisition and unequal participation

Three main groups of stakeholders are involved in the land acquisition process: the local government, the investors, and the affected people. However, the findings show that unequal levels of participation by these actors lead to unfair outcomes. For example, local governments usually play a dominant role in the decision-making process while the people who stand to lose land and livelihoods generally are not part of the decision-making process. The local governments control both compensation plans and resettlement arrangements for land loss-affected people. A coalition between the provincial government and land investors was discernible in the villages studied, often associated with low compensation rates. Investors want clearance land as soon as possible, while local governments want infrastructure improvement and taxes from land-use rights.

Conversely, the participation of land loss-affected people was relatively passive. Although people were allowed to attend all formal meetings organized by the local governments, their roles in practice were limited: listening to announcements and identifying land loss areas. They did not have the right to negotiate about compensation rates or additional support. For those who were elderly, widowed, or disabled, participation in the land acquisition process was more limited. They were especially likely to be left out of the consultation process altogether – and may not even have been informed at all of changes that would seriously affect their lives and livelihoods. In this sense, the governance principle of "*People know, people discuss, people do, and people check*" (Decree 34/2007), a popular political slogan of the Communist Party of Vietnam, is not fully implemented in practice.

> I am sixty-seven years old and live alone. I am not strong enough to go to the communal people's committee to get land acquisition information. I only know summary information provided by Mr. B (a neighbor) – that my family will lose 1,000 square meters of farmland for a new urban area to be built, Dong Nam Thuy An. However, I do not know anything about compensation rates and how to get compensation. The local authorities also do not invite me to attend the meetings.
>
> (In-depth interview, man, 67 years old, Hamlet 1, Thuy Duong Commune, Huong Thuy District)

Unfair pricing framework

In line with the socialist principles of the Vietnamese state, all land-related activities that occur between the state and land users (such as land allocation, acquisition, leasing, and taxation) are based on a land-price framework (see Figure 4.1) issued every five years by the provincial government (the *Land Law 2013*). The official price for land is usually set low in comparison with the market price (see Table 4.2). However, after being allocated land by the state, investors are often relatively free to decide on land prices in subsequent commercial exchanges. Accordingly, land transactions between investors and buyers tend to follow market principles, not the land-price frameworks applied for land acquisition processes. These transactions, in practice, only benefit the investors and land speculators, not the original holders of the land-use rights. As a result, the clash between these two pricing systems is the most significant driver of social tension and local resistance to compulsory land acquisition.

Limited compensation program effectiveness for livelihood reconstruction

Affected households are compensated for the loss of land-use rights and land assets. These households also receive financial support for occupational change and vocational training. This compensation is expected to improve – or at least restore – a household's livelihood options and standard of living. However, in practice, the effectiveness of the existing compensation program for livelihood reconstruction is very limited. The financial compensation and support packages are not strong determinants of household income after land loss.

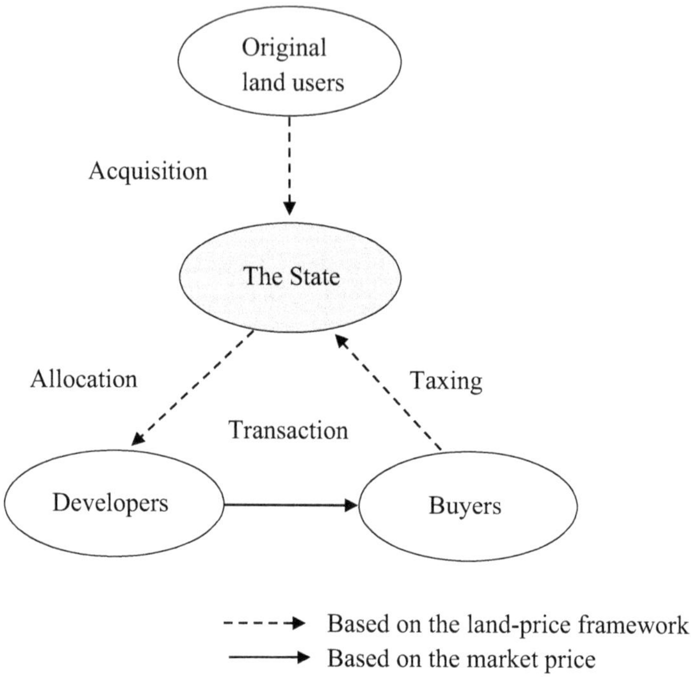

Figure 4.1 The dual-price system of land

Table 4.2 Increase in land prices following the completion of projects

Projects	*Localities*	*Compensation price (VND/m²)*	*Years*	*Market price (VND million/m²)*	*Increase level (%)*
An Van Duong	Thuy Van	19,000	2005	2–2.2	105–115
Resettlement Area	Huong So	38,000	2009	3–3.6	79–95
Dong Nam Thuy An	Thuy Duong	1,250	2004	7.5–8.3	6,000–6,640
My Thuong	Phu Thuong	21,000	2007	5.5–7.4	262–353

Source: Thua Thien Hue – People's Committee, 2018.

This implies a failure of government compensation methods employed in the process of compulsory land acquisition for urban development. The main reasons for this lack of effectiveness are not surprising. First, the existing policy of compensation and support is overly focused on a simple financial transaction that lacks sufficient consideration of the real objective: assisting people to reconstruct their livelihoods to at least the level they had before land loss. Second, people generally do not see

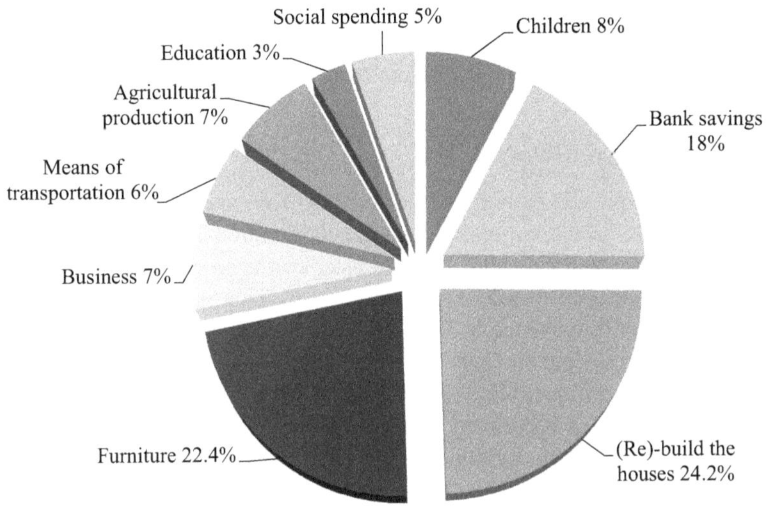

Figure 4.2 Use of compensation money

Source: Phuc et al. 2017.

how the often-modest amounts of compensation money can be effectively used to secure new livelihood sources. As a result, affected households are tempted to use compensation payments in ways that are less relevant to livelihood reconstruction, such as housing improvements and furniture purchases (see Figure 4.2).

Forces for change

The dynamics of strengthening institutions

The compulsory acquisition of farmland for urban expansion in Hue's peri-urban areas is leading to serious consequences: inequity in the distribution of benefits as well as increased social and economic marginalization, social tension, and contestation of land acquisition. International organizations, such as the World Bank, have asserted that these consequences can be explained by weak land governance (World Bank 2011), and thus it is necessary to improve the relevant policies, processes, and institutions.

However, this study argues that the problem is not necessarily a lack of rules, regulations, or international guidelines. It is instead the lack of stakeholder participation in decision-making processes, combined with a breach of decision-maker responsibility in policy implementation. This illustrates the need to first focus on practical policy implementation rather than on changing laws and regulations. The problem here is that more relevant changes, such as strengthening institutions or increasing the responsibility of policymakers and investors, are necessary but will not happen automatically nor through the willingness and efforts of the state, its agencies, and investors. It may, however, occur through the application of social pressure from various stakeholders, including the farmers involved in rural social movements, civil society organizations, and the media.

The role of collective resistance

Farmers in several places, including Hanoi, Hung Yen, and Ho Chi Minh City, have collectively resisted compulsory land acquisition in Vietnam through demonstrations, violence, and petitions. For instance, on the outskirts of Hanoi, Tho Da villagers resorted to violence to press for higher compensation (Han and Vu 2008). In Hung Yen, a province in the Red River Delta, hundreds of people in the Van Giang District, having lost their land to the new Eco-Park urban project, organized mass demonstrations in Hanoi and Hung Yen (Doan Trang 2012). Thousands of households affected by the Thu Thiem Peninsula Project in Ho Chi Minh City refused the compensation offered, as it was far below the speculative market price (Hoai Thu 2009).

To some extent, this resistance can be considered quite successful, since local government compensation frameworks have been positively adjusted in locations where collective action took place, so many farmers were paid higher compensation rates. This indicates that collective resistance has placed significant pressure on the government and other powerful actors to change the manner in which current institutions operate. In Hue, the resistance is mainly enacted by the elderly (who are affected by land losses more seriously than others), often through petitions and complaints. The resistance, in general, is not strong enough to fundamentally influence change in local government decisions. However, it might be assumed that resistance will become stronger and more effective if all affected individuals were to actively participate in collective resistance.

The role of civil society

In Vietnam, the party-state has formulated various legal frameworks to provide more space for the development of civil society organizations (CSOs), which currently number more than 2,000. In turn, CSOs create an arena for other non-governmental organizations (NGOs) to negotiate and debate with governments and other stakeholders over the equity and sustainability of development activities. One of the most successful campaigns is the anti-hydropower dam movement spearheaded by the Vietnam River Network, other Vietnamese NGOs, and many social and environmental activists (Pham 2014). As a result of the development and positive contributions of NGOs in recent years, similar positive results may be expected in relation to land acquisition for urbanization in many Vietnamese cities.

The role of the media

Over the past five to ten years, media groups such as *Tuoi Tre* (Youth News), *Lao Dong* (Trade Union), and *Thanh Nien* (Youth Union) have disclosed many scandals and corrupt acts, especially in relation to land management (World Bank 2011; Kim 2011). Among 5,000 respondents (including officials and leaders of enterprises), 83 percent agreed that "almost all" cases of corruption were detected by individual whistle-blowers and the media and not by the inspection or monitoring activities of state bodies (World Bank 2011). In addition to traditional media outlets, new forms of social media (including Facebook, blogs, Twitter, and Google+) have become important sources of public feedback and effective communication between the government and its population.

In Hue's peri-urban areas, we found only one example, in the case of Xuan Hoa Hamlet, Thuy Van Commune, Huong Thuy district, which was featured in Vietnamese mass media in 2014 such as VTV-Hue, *Bao Cong An Nhan Dan* (a police newspaper) and *Bao Giao Thong Van Tai* (a transport sector newspaper). It was reported that people in Xuan Hoa were forced to leave their farmland for a resettlement area without compensation, because they lacked legal documents related to land rights. This caused a land dispute between farmers and local governments. Although the media have not yet participated directly in recognizing corruption risks in land acquisition for urban expansion, their voices – channeled through newsletters, critical reports, and interviews – have influenced local government actions. Many meetings at the hamlet and commune level have been organized to assess the responsibility of all stakeholders, as well as to discuss suitable compensation solutions for affected people.

These positive contributions of the media, in combination with the emerging power of social networking forums, suggest that the media will be an important factor for strengthening institutions and implementing better policies. However, change will not result from singular and fragmented action: it requires the strategic cooperation of multiple stakeholders in society.

Conclusions and policy recommendations

Using Hue City as case study, this study has shown that compulsory land acquisition, driven by rapid urbanization, is an unbalanced and unfair process in terms of the distribution of both the benefits and the costs and in terms of equal participation and just compensation. These issues – along with the shirking of responsibility by decision-makers in policy implementation – are creating challenges that impede equitable and sustainable development.

Based on the findings, this study puts forth the following policy recommendations:

Recommendation 1*: *Urbanization and its related processes need to be fairer and more sustainable

Local governments often use a top-down approach, in which the political power of local leaders is at the core of the decision-making process. There is limited involvement of, and consultation with, other key stakeholders such as CSOs, the media, and the general population – especially with those affected.

As participation is both a right and a means to sustainable and inclusive development, urbanization and its related processes could be fairer and more sustainable if effective participation in decision-making and action could mitigate the emergence of "winners" and "losers." Affected people should be involved in the process of agreeing to proposed development projects, land-use planning, and deciding compensation levels. Policy makers should note that the notion of "fair urbanization" requires a consensus on the main agenda in development activities – namely, how urbanization should take place, how much land should be dedicated to urban landscapes and how to lessen the impacts and increase the development options of affected groups.

More specifically:

- *Fair urbanization* is a process that necessitates transparent communication, consultation, and consensus-building among the various stakeholders, particularly affected people and CSOs.
- *Fair urbanization* is also characterized by democratic processes, participation, transparency, access to relevant information, and gender equality.

Recommendation 2: To strengthen the effectiveness of the compensation programs, as well as to protect the rights of people whose land is to be acquired, a more suitable approach to compensation should be considered by the state

Toward this end, this study proposes two possible compensation models based on either the market value of land lost or the replacement cost of lost livelihoods:

Market value model

The valuation of land values should be carried out by independent organizations, not by government agencies that may benefit from cheap acquisition of land that can subsequently be allocated to investors at much higher rates. Compensation packages should consist of payment for the land lost per se; for buildings and other improvements realized on the land acquired; for the reduction in value of any land retained as a result of acquisition; and for any disturbances or other losses to the livelihoods of people caused by the acquisition (FAO 2008).

Under such conditions, when full compensation at market prices is given – enabling people to acquire alternative assets – the responsibility for livelihood reconstruction (including gaining skills training and other issues) can be laid on the shoulders of the affected people, releasing local authorities and those who use the appropriated land (investors) from further obligations.

Replacement cost model

Besides the general principles indicated, this study proposes that the assessment of land value should be done jointly by the acquiring organizations, independent agencies, and representatives of the affected people. This is to guarantee transparency and equity of the process – the results of which should be announced to the affected population.

Moreover, local authorities and investors should assume responsibility for reconstruction of the livelihoods of people involved. This implies that both consultative processes and programs enabling access to alternative sources of livelihood should be planned and implemented.

Recommendation 3: Sustainable urbanization requires that governments and investors be responsible for their decisions and actions while being responsive to the needs and expectations of the people

There is a critical need for the acquiring agencies to take into account differences among land-losing households in their capacity to adapt to the new conditions (particularly the elderly, widowed, and physically challenged). This may significantly contribute to limiting the vulnerability of these households.

- Before acquisition, a preliminary socioeconomic survey is necessary to clearly identify social differentiation among affected households (such as varying abilities to cope with land loss and livelihood reconstruction) as well as people's own ideas and initiatives (namely, what they plan to do after land loss). The survey will help local governments to design and implement practical compensation policies that are consistent with people's expectations.
- Toward this end, policy makers should consider the practice of "selective compensation." In other words, in addition to the amount of financial compensation, special attention should be given to the capacity of affected people to adapt to new conditions.
- Moreover, local authorities and investors should assume responsibility for livelihood reconstruction; this implies that both consultation processes and programs should be planned and implemented to improve access to alternative livelihood sources.

Recommendation 4: Defining the form of urban development is crucial to sustainable development

The debate on equitable and sustainable development not only raises questions about how land acquisition for urbanization should best be governed; it also raises concerns over which *form* of urban development is most sustainable. This is important because the form of urban development not only has a significant influence on the sustainability of a city; it also holds implications for the ecological, social, and economic systems of both peri-urban and rural areas. To define which urban form – sprawl, compact, or otherwise – is the best solution for Vietnam's urban future, there is a need for further research and action.

References

Asian Development Bank. (2007). *Compensation and Valuation in Resettlement: Cambodia, ADB, People's Republic of China and India*. The Philippines: The Asian Development Bank.

Chan, N. (2003). Land acquisition compensation in China – problems and answers. *International Real Estate Review*, 636–152.

Conway, G. (1987). The properties of agroecosystems. *Agricultural Systems*, 24(2): 95–117.

Doan Trang. (2012). *Vụ thu hồi đất ở Văn Giang tỉnh Hưng Yên*, viewed 20 June 2013, http://phapluattp.vn/20120507124723944p0c1015/vi-sao-nguoi-dan-quyet-liet-bam-giu-dat.htm.

FAO. (2008). *Compulsory Acquisition of Land and Compensation*. Rome: FAO Land Tenure Studies 10.

Fazal, S. (2001). The need for preserving farmland: A case study from a predominantly agrarian economy (India). *Landscape and Urban Planning*, 55: 1–13.

Firman, T. (1997). Land conversion and urban development in the Northern Region of West Java, Indonesia. *Urban Studies*, 34(7): 1027–1046.

Firman, T. (2000). Rural to urban land conversion in Indonesia during boom and bust periods. *Land Use Policy*, 17: 13–20.

Forest People Programme. (2007). Making FPIC – free, prior and informed consent – work: Challenges and prospects for indigenous people, viewed 26 May 2015, www.forestpeoples.org/guiding-principles/free-prior-and-informed-consent-fpic.

General Statistics Office (GSO). (2020). *Statistical Summary Book of Vietnam*. Hanoi: Statistical Publishing House.

Han, S.S. and Vu, K.T. (2008). Land acquisition in transitional Hanoi, Vietnam. *Urban Studies*, 45: 1097–1117.

Hoai Thu. (2009). *Tiền bồi thường Thủ Thiêm là bao nhiêu*, viewed 23 April 2015, http://vneconomy.vn/bat-dong-san/tien-boi-thuong-thu-thiem-la-bao-nhieu-2009070102074150.htm.

HSO (Hue Statistical Office). (2018). *Niên giám thống kê* [Statistical Yearbook]. Hue: Chi cục thống kê thành phố Huế [the Statistical Office of Hue City].

Karods, M. (2012). The reflection of good governance in sustainable development strategies. *Procedia-Social and Behavioral Sciences*, 58: 1166–1173.

Kelly, P.F. (1999). Everyday urbanization: The social dynamics of development in Manila's extend metropolitan region. *International Journal of Urban and Regional Research*, 23(2): 283–303.

Kim, A.M. (2011). Talking back: The role of narrative in Vietnam's recent land compensation changes. *Urban Studies*, 48(3): 493–508.

Korten, D.C. and Clauss, R. (Eds.). (1984). *People-Centered Development: Contributions Toward Theory and Planning Frameworks*. West Hartford, CT: Kumarian Press.

Land Law. (2013). *Luật đất đai*. Hà Nội: Nhà xuất bản Chính trị quốc gia.

Nhung Pham Thi, Martin Kappas and Daniel Wyss. (2020). Benefits and constraints of the agricultural land acquisition for urbanization for household gender equality in affected rural communes: A case study in Huong Thuy Town, Thua Thien Hue Province, Vietnam. *Land*, 9: 249.

Oduro, C.Y. (2010). Effects of rapid urbanization on livelihoods in the peri-urban areas of Accra, Ghana. PhD dissertation, Florida State of University, Tallahassee.

Pham, H.T. (2014). Dilemmas of hydropower development in Vietnam: Between dam-induced displacement and sustainable development. PhD dissertation, Utrecht University, Utrecht.

Phuc, N.Q., Westen, A.C.M. van, and Zoomers, A. (2017). Compulsory land acquisition for urban expansion: Livelihood reconstruction after land loss in Hue's peri-urban areas, Central Vietnam. *International Development Planning Review*, 39(2): 99–121.

Schneider, A.E. (2011). What shall we do without our land? Land grabs and resistance in Rural Cambodia. Paper presented at the International Conference on Global Land Grabbing I, Organized by the Land Deals Politics Initiative (LDPI), 6–8 April.

Schumann, K., Lau Saili, R.T. and Abdel-Malek, R. (2010). Hydropower and sustainable development: A journey, viewed 26 May 2015, www.indiaenergycongress.in/montreal/library/pdf/392.pdf.

Sen, A. (1981). *Poverty and Famines: An Essay on Entitlement and Deprivation*. Oxford and New York: Clarendon Press; Oxford University Press.

Tacoli, C. (2004). Rural-urban linkage and pro-poor agricultural growth: An overview. Paper presented at the Agriculture and Pro-Poor Growth Task Team, Hensiki Workshop 17–18 June 2004, viewed 9 April 2015, www.oecd.org/development/povertyreduction/36562896.pdf.

Tan, R., Beckmann, V., Berg, L. and Qu, F. (2009). Governing farmland conversion: Comparing China with the Netherlands and Germany. *Land use Policy*, 26: 961–974.

Thanh, M. (2009). Chuyển dịch cơ cấu lao động nông thôn sau thu hồi đất [Restructuring rural labour after land acquisition]. Tạp chí Cộng Sản [Journal of Communist], viewed 15 August 2017, www.tapchicongsan.org.vn/web/guest/nghien-cu/-/2018/1003/ve-chuyen-doi-co-cau-lao-dong-nong-thon-sau-thu-hoi-dat.aspx#.

Thua Thien Hue – People Committee. (2018). *Thông tin bất động sản*, viewed 10 October 2013, http://batdongsan.thuathienhue.gov.vn/bdsban/quy-dat-phan-lo.

Toufique, K.A. and Turton, C. (2002). *Hand Not Land: How Livelihoods Are Changing in Rural Bangladesh*. Dhaka, Bangladesh: Bangladesh Institute of Development Studies.

UNDP. (1997). Governance for sustainable human development. UNDP Policy Paper.

UNDP. (2000). *Human Development Report: Human Rights and Human Development. Summary 2000*. Oxford: Oxford University Press.

UNDP. (2014). Governance for sustainable development: Integrating governance in the post-2015 development framework. Discussion paper.

Walker, K. (2008). From covert to overt: Everyday peasant politics in China and the implications for transnational agrarian movements. *Journal of Agrarian Change*, 8(2): 462–488.

Winarso, H., Hudalah, D. and Firman, T. (2015). Peri-urban transformation in the Jakarta metropolitan area. *Habitat International*, 59: 221–229.

World Bank. (2010). *Rising Global Interest in Farmland: Can It Yield Sustainable and Equitable Benefits?* Washington, DC: World Bank.

World Bank. (2011). *Recognizing and Reducing Corruption Risks in Land Management in Vietnam*. Hanoi: The National Political Publishing House – Su That.

Zhang, X. and Lu, H. (2011). Compensation for compulsory land acquisition in China: To rebuild expropriated farmers' long-term Livelihoods. Working paper. Institute for Research on Labor and Employment (UCLA).

Zhou, M. (2012). Has farmers' livelihood improved? Case studies about the impacts of compulsory land acquisition on farmers' livelihood in China. MA thesis, Uppsala University.

Zoomers, A. (2013). A critical review of the policy debate on large-scale land acquisitions: Fighting the symptoms or killing the heart? In Evers, Sandra J.T.M., Seagle, Caroline and Krijtenburg, Froukje (eds.), *Africa for Sale? Positioning the State, Land and Society in Foreign Large-Scale Land Acquisition in Africa* (pp. 55–77). Leiden and Boston: BRILL.

5 Agricultural land appropriation for urban development

Villagers learn to cope with the state and adapt to the market

Nguyen Van Suu

Introduction

Since the 1990s, a new phase of industrialization and urbanization in the context of Vietnam's Đổi Mới [reforms] has led to the taking of large areas of land from people in numerous locations throughout the country. In order to obtain land for industrial and urban development and other non-agricultural purposes in the lowlands, rural and peri-urban areas, state authorities have strategically targeted agricultural rather than residential land, so as to avoid resettlement difficulties.

In the early 2000s I conducted research examining conflicts over agricultural land appropriation in villages located in the Red River delta (Suu 2004, 2007). In the second half of 2007 and early months of 2008, I began ethnographic fieldwork in Phú Điền village[1] to gain a better understanding of the livelihood strategies adopted by farmers after their agricultural land was appropriated. As Phú Điền was just a short distance from my home, I often visited the village by motorbike to participate in everyday life and to conduct informal conversations with villagers, tenants, and visitors who came to explore land and business opportunities. I also interviewed village, commune, and district officials and collected materials relating to village history, urban development projects, and agricultural land appropriation. In 2011, 2012, and later years I revisited the village to observe and update its numerous changes.

Drawing on ethnographic and secondary data, I will now use this as a case study to explore how villagers have responded to state authorities and to the market in the course of agricultural land loss and in the formation of new livelihood strategies. I argue that, while the resident farmers have been dissatisfied with the low land-compensation rate and simple vocational training packages offered by state authorities, many villagers have successfully adapted to new market opportunities by becoming landlords to tenants who come to study and work in the city. Although this involvement in rental housing and in non-agricultural work was unforeseen by state authorities, it has been the state's development of their home village that has enabled these former farmers to formulate new market-based livelihood strategies.

DOI: 10.4324/9781003165774-8

I have examined two processes in one single case study:

(i) the process by which the state appropriated agricultural land and offered farmers compensation and new vocational training packages and
(ii) the process by which farmers adapted to the market to establish their own new livelihood strategies.

This has enabled me to better understand why Phú Điền farmers have agreed to cede their agricultural land-use rights to the state authorities for urban development without engaging in violent protests. This case study also underscores the fact that conflicts over agricultural land appropriation in contemporary Vietnam are only one dimension of a phenomenon that has fundamentally changed many parts of rural and peri-urban areas in contemporary Vietnam.

The other dimension, as this case study demonstrates, concerns non-conflict behaviors and actions of the farm residents involved in agricultural land appropriation. It is possible to say that, of the hundreds of village communities affected, the majority have not engaged in violent protests over agricultural land appropriation since the 1990s. Therefore, understanding both dimensions – conflict and non-conflict (or conformity) – enables researchers and policy makers to achieve a more holistic understanding of state-society interactions and of farmers' behavior related to agricultural land appropriation in Vietnam.

Đổi Mới and agricultural land appropriation

Agricultural land appropriation in contemporary Vietnam

Vietnam officially declared its Đổi Mới policies in 1986, initiating radical changes in land tenure in Vietnam (Ravallion & Van de Walle 2008; Suu 2009). First, the state de-collectivized agricultural production and formulated land rights through a *Land Law* published in 1988 and its periodic revisions.[2] Through five rounds of revision thus far, the state has clarified three key rights to land: ownership rights (quyền sở hữu); controlling rights (quyền quản lý); and use rights (quyền sử dụng). "Ownership rights" (quyền sở hữu) refers to the right to own the land, which belongs to the entire people (toàn dân) represented by the state, in order to maintain the collective ownership of land. "Controlling rights" refer to the right of land administration, which has been given to the state. "Land-use rights" refers to the right to use the land for a certain period of time, based upon the type of land. The *Land Law 2013* divides land into four groups (nhóm), including agricultural land, non-agricultural land, non-use land, and coastal land.[3]

Second, the state has distributed agricultural land-use rights among villagers and other parties. Land rights are uniform throughout the country, and residential land experienced no redistribution. The first round of agricultural land-use rights was distributed on an equitable basis among family households in each village, beginning in 1988 and continuing over a period of between 5 and 15 years. In 1993, the state carried out a second round of agricultural land-use rights redistribution, allowing for a term of 20 years of land use for annual cropping and 50 years for perennial land.[4] In 2013, the holding of agricultural land-use rights was extended to 50 years without implementing the third round of redistribution by the state (Quốc hội Nước Cộng hòa Xã hội Chủ nghĩa Việt Nam 2013). The holding of land-use rights is legally recognized by the state through a certificate of land-use rights often called the "Red Book" (sổ đỏ). The holders of use rights to agricultural land and other types of land have further rights allowing transfer, exchange, lease, inheritance, and mortgage rights. However, the state limits the amount of agricultural land per household receiving use rights, and this amount varies from the north to the center and the south.

Third, since the 1990s, the state has appropriated many thousands of hectares of land throughout the country, especially around urban centers like Hanoi, Ho Chi Minh City, Danang, and Haiphong. Vietnam has promoted industrialization and modernization, which have engendered rapid economic, urban, and infrastructure development and has led to the appropriation of land-use rights in the country.

Today it is difficult to calculate the total area of land appropriation that has occurred in Vietnam over the course of the Đổi Mới years. However, available sources suggest that hundreds of thousands of hectares of agricultural land have been appropriated for non-agricultural purposes throughout Vietnam since the early 1990s. Between 1991 and 2013, an average of 58,000 hectares of farmland was appropriated annually for industrial zones, infrastructure construction, and other non-agricultural purposes. Agricultural land appropriation increased after the *Land Law* was revised in 2003, as the state loosened its regulations regarding land appropriation. Much of the appropriated agricultural land was in Hanoi and Ho Chi Minh City, where more than 1,000 hectares of agricultural land were taken annually between 2000 and 2013 (Vu & Kawashima 2017). Eventually, unused appropriated land; petitions and protests from farmers; and a global economic slow-down convinced state leaders to add restrictions on land appropriation to the revised *Land Law 2013*. Thereafter, the pace of land appropriation subsided.

Agricultural land is most often appropriated for development projects. The number of urban zones, industrial zones, economic zones, recreational areas, and the like that have been built since the 1990s in Vietnam points to the huge volume of appropriated agricultural land. According to the website of the Ministry of Planning and Investment, by February 2021 Vietnam had built 370 industrial zones in 61 provinces and cities throughout the country, occupying 115,200 hectares of land and 18 economic zones situated on 857,0000 hectares of land (Đức Trung 2021).[5] Vietnam's fast pace of urbanization is also a factor, with the urban share of the population growing from 19.6 percent in 1986 to 37.3 percent in 2020.[6] Numerous new urban zones have therefore been built in and adjacent to the country's big cities. In addition, a large number of projects for constructing golf courses,[7] ecotourism sites, highways, dams, and other infrastructure have also consumed agricultural land.[8]

Coping with the state

For small landholder farmers in rural Vietnam, especially in the north and center, such a large area of appropriated agricultural land has led to the dispossession of thousands of farmer households in hundreds of villages. For example, in one single new urban zone, Thủ Thiêm in Ho Chi Minh City, 14,000 households were displaced from their land (Harms 2013). Previous studies have revealed a number of critical cases of farmers in villages adopting resistance as a way to protest the actions of state authorities and land developers in the course of agricultural land-use rights appropriation. Farmers' resistance to state authorities has occurred because farmers blamed authorities for unfair compensation and corruption and because farm families were worried about their uncertain livelihoods. Land protests came to be among the most serious social conflicts in contemporary Vietnam (Suu 2004, 2007; Taylor 2014; Kerkvliet 2014).

Scholarly analysis on this topic has emphasized the dimension of violence and vocal contestation in a public manner in the course of agricultural land appropriation (Suu 2007; Taylor 2014; Kerkvliet 2014; Phuc et al. 2014; Labbé 2015a, 2015b; Binh 2017 among others).[9] Farmers' resistance over agricultural land-use rights and other types of land-use rights appropriation have often involved discussion, petitions, denunciations, gatherings, and sometimes violent resistance to voice their views and to make their demands. According to reports from state authorities, petitions relating to various land issues amounted to some 70 percent of the total number of petitions recorded nationwide in 2018 (Bảo Quyên 2018). Petitions and pressure from people involved in land conflicts throughout the country have also pushed the central state to periodically revise its *Land Law* and to increase its compensation rate for land-use rights (Kerkvliet 2006; Suu 2007).

Scholars have theorized about the nature and forms of resistance relating to land conflicts in Vietnam and other countries in Southeast Asia and East Asia. In the 1980s, Scott and Kerkvliet proposed the well-known concept of "everyday resistance" to explain how and why poor, weak, and marginalized people oppose the rich, powerful elites and the state in various social contexts in Southeast Asia (Scott & Kerkvliet 1986). Based on this concept, Kerkvliet (2005) has developed what he has called the "everyday politics" approach and used it to analyze and explain how the power of peasants pushed the Vietnamese state to change its central policy in agricultural production in the second half of the twentieth century. In the 1990s, in order to analyze farmers' popular resistance in China's post-reform rural areas and elsewhere, O'Brien (1996) identified a different form of peasants' resistance that he named "rightful resistance." As O'Brien (1996:33) writes, this is not simply another form of "everyday resistance":

> Rightful resistance is a form of popular contention that operates near the boundary of an authorised channel, employs the rhetoric and commitments of the powerful to curb political or economic power, and hinges on locating and exploiting divisions among the powerful. In particular, rightful resistance entails the innovative use of laws, policies, and other officially promoted

> values to defy disloyal political and economic elites; it is a kind of partially sanctioned resistance that uses influential advocates and recognized principles to apply pressure on those in power who have failed to live up to some professed ideal or who have not implemented some beneficial measure.

While "rightful resistance" can explain the phenomenon of popular protests in Chinese rural society and elsewhere, it cannot explain the cases of protests in which farmers stepped outside the officially approved channels and became involved in contestation and confrontation with state authorities.

Drawing on in-depth ethnographic data on land conflicts in the 1990s and 2000s from villages in Bac Ninh province, I have proposed the concept of "public resistance." This concept may be useful in helping to explain rural villagers' protests to the state authorities in the course of agricultural land appropriation (Suu 2007). I postulate that, in various cases of land conflict in contemporary Vietnam, villagers have dared to – and often do – step outside the state's officially approved channels to carry out contestation actions to claim their rights to land. In these cases, villagers engage in "public resistance," and contestation is very central to the behavior and actions of the protesting villagers, both within and outside their villages (for a detailed elaboration of this argument, see Suu 2007).

Other studies have enlarged and deepened our understanding of contestation in agricultural land appropriation in contemporary rural Vietnam (Taylor 2014; Kerkvliet 2014; Labbé 2015a; Binh 2017; et al.). Taylor (2014) has explained contests over land as a *process*, emphasizing that "land conflicts have become more visible, vocal and contentious" (Taylor 2014:2) and highlighting their political implications for understanding contemporary Vietnam. Kerkvliet (2014) has examined 60 cases of land conflict in contemporary rural Vietnam and asserts that "rightful resistance" is a useful concept for analyzing and explaining land conflicts – but the concept of rightful resistance fails to explain cases in which villagers became involved in confrontational reactions and moved beyond officially approved state channels. A consensus among scholars of land conflict in contemporary Vietnam is that land conflicts do not challenge the legitimacy of the state but force the state to revise its land policies in various aspects (Kerkvliet 2005; Suu 2007; Taylor 2014).

Adapting to the market

Vietnam has adopted a socialist-oriented market economy, pressuring farmers (and those who lose their agricultural land-use rights, in particular) to find ways to adapt to the market via alternative or diverse livelihood strategies (Kerkvliet 2006; Labbé & Musil 2014). As the state has gradually relinquished control of the household registration system in order to increase people's mobility,[10] the growth of the market economy, industrialization, and urbanization have resulted in increased flows of rural migrants to urban and industrial centers to seek new forms of livelihood (Vu & Kawashima 2017; Chau 2018). What may be a cause of concern is the fact that scholarly analysis tends to focus more on how farmers have confrontationally responded to the state. However, these analyses have failed to describe why farmers have chosen *not* to become involved in land disputes, in order to adaptively respond to the market. In the 1990s and early 2000s, several researchers highlighted how farmers in peri-urban Hanoi intensified and diversified their livelihoods to cope with agricultural land appropriation (Van den Berg et al. 2003) – while rarely engaging in non-agricultural production (Vien et al. 2005). The process in which agricultural land-lost farmers have adapted to the market needs to be examined critically and in greater depth, in order to illuminate the processes and nature of their choices.

In the next sections I will use a single case study to address the two processes mentioned earlier, in order to examine how farmers respond to the state and adapt to the market in the course of post-agricultural land appropriation. My analysis will explore the ways in which farmer villagers have chosen not to engage in disputes with the state authorities in agricultural land appropriation but to engage with the inchoate, emerging markets instead; in other words, how they have created economic opportunities for themselves.

Case study: agricultural land appropriation in Phú Điền village

The focus of this study is Phú Điền, a village west of Hanoi's peri-urban areas, which comprised 6,708 inhabitants in 2006. In just a few years, between 2000 and 2007, the village was the site of large-scale agricultural land appropriation to make way for urban development projects.[11] Having been established since at least the seventeenth century, Phú Điền was an agricultural community that, in comparison with other Red River delta villages, had a large area of agricultural land per farm household. In 1805, the village's land registry recorded that the entire village of Phú Điền had a total of 353 hectares of agricultural land. In 2000, Phú Điền had 147.7 hectares of agricultural land and 1,088 agricultural households: an average of 1,350 square meters per household. However, the village territory was subsequently rezoned as a central part of a designated urban extension area of the metropolis of Hanoi.

In the process, Phú Điền's agricultural land was appropriated for the construction of numerous buildings, offices, apartments, houses, schools, roads, commercial areas, and bus-station and parking areas. By the end of 2007, approximately 67 percent of the village's agricultural land (equivalent to over 100 hectares of the previous total of 147.7 hectares) had been appropriated and reallocated to more than 70 urban development projects. As a result, total agricultural land in the village decreased to 40 hectares, dispersed throughout 2 of its 4 hamlets (one has 27 hectares, and the other has over 10 hectares). Urbanization has embedded the village in an urban world and has meant that the remaining agricultural land areas in Phú Điền have also continued to change to non-agricultural land for urban development projects. These have resulted in critical changes in Phú Điền farmers' livelihood strategies, in their lives, and in the village landscape, without necessitating the displacement of their residential homes.

In return for the loss of agricultural land-use rights, Phú Điền farmers received compensation payments. According to state policy, when the state appropriates agricultural land-use rights, it pays economic compensation for use rights – which the state had previously allocated to the villagers to use for 20 years – and for crops that the villagers have cultivated on their fields. Academic research has often revealed that the low level of economic compensation for agricultural land-use rights has been the key cause of disputes between state authorities and farmers (Kerkvliet 2014). In the case of Phú Điền, like elsewhere in the country, the state authorities have increased economic compensation for villagers' agricultural land-use rights over the years. In 2000, the agricultural land-compensation (official) rate was 30 million Vietnamese đồng (VND) per sào.[12] This increased to 60 million VND per sào in 2003; to 171 million VND per sào in 2007; to 200 million VND per sào in 2008; and to 399 million VND per sào in 2009. However, the agricultural land-compensation rate has varied between administrative locations in peri-urban areas, as the authorities have applied their agricultural land-compensation rates in accordance with specific criteria. These criteria have included the administrative location of agricultural land appropriation; the time of appropriation; the purpose of appropriation; the forms of appropriation; and even the developers of appropriated agricultural land.

The compensation rate has even varied among different agricultural land appropriation projects within the village. In some projects, villagers were able to receive plots of land to use as residential land (called "service land" – đất dịch vụ). In a project of 13,879 square meters of agricultural land appropriation from 48 households, the compensation rate was a bit more than 204 million VND per sào, and 28 of the 48 households received additional plots of service land. However, in several other projects involving agricultural land appropriations around this time, no service land was given to farmers dispossessed of their land.

Overall, the agricultural land-compensation rate comprises several categories, in which compensation for non-land properties and payment in the name of rewards and livelihood assistance account for a good amount of the total. Table 5.1 displays these categories for Phú Điền's agricultural land-compensation rate in 2007.

Table 5.1 Compensation rate for agricultural land-use rights in Phú Điền in 2007

Items of compensation and assistance	*Amount (VND/m²)*
1 Agricultural land-use rights	108,000
2 Annual crops and perennial trees in the fields	35,000
3 Support for livelihood transformation	25,000
4 Reward for timely cooperation	3,000
Total	171,000

Source: The author's synthesis of ethnographic data.

In Phú Điền, a number of households received an even higher amount of compensation than other households because, upon learning of the coming agricultural land seizure, they acted to cultivate perennial trees such as willow and guava. This action made them eligible to receive additional compensation money, because the state's compensation policy distinguishes between the types of annual plants and perennial trees cultivated on seized land. One Phú Điền villager noted that the compensation for vegetables and other annual crops (such as rice and water spinach) cultivated on the land would have been 12,000 VND per square meter in 2004[13] while the compensation for perennial trees in the same year was 30,000 VND per square meter. Cultivating the latter added 60 percent to the compensation amount, relating to just one of the compensation criteria.[14]

The elevated pay-outs for tree crops notwithstanding, many Phú Điền farmers thought that the overall levels of monetary compensation were unfair, as they were lower than the "market prices" that they had expected. As has been true in Phú Điền and elsewhere in Vietnam, the state authorities decide land prices in adherence with administrative location, and this is often much lower than the local market price of land. This discrepancy makes land appropriation difficult, as farmers oppose the appropriation of their land to give to other parties at an inequitable compensation rate.[15]

Phú Điền farmers often complained about the state's compensation payments, especially when they learned that in several development projects their agricultural land, after having been seized, was sold for apartments, houses, and other structures at a price many times higher. Talking about the compensation price for their agricultural land-use rights, one Phú Điền farmer angrily noted:

> The compensation price for agricultural land is not reasonable. This is a peri-urban area, close to the urban district, but the compensation price for our agricultural land is much lower than that of the neighboring urban district. It's in the same project, with the same area of agricultural land, but the compensation price for us is just half of the amount for compensation money for agricultural land of those households that [administratively] belong to the urban district. For one sào, in 2007, we received only 62 million đồng, while in the neighboring communes the prices varied from 140 to 180 million đồng.
>
> More importantly, we supposed that they seized the land to build apartments to sell. While they paid us around 60 million đồng for one sào [in 2003], the land area has since been sold at the price of 40–60 million đồng per one square meter to build houses and villas. The villagers say that the state confiscates their property. Actually they [the entrepreneurs who use the appropriated land] are private, not the state. The private sector does this [appropriation] in the name of the state.
>
> The subsidies for converting to new livelihoods are also too low. Currently, one area of 300 square meters of agricultural land can be enough for one laborer farming water spinach to earn two million đồng a month. However, when the state seizes the land, they provide only 25,000 đồng for one square

> meter for changing livelihoods. This means that 300 square meters of agricultural land provides us with only 7.5 million đồng in subsidies. However, with such a small amount of money, how can we farmers change our work and business?
>
> (Interview with Mr. Q., 60 years old, 11 September 2007)

The loss of agricultural livelihoods

Wide-scale agricultural land appropriation has forced Phú Điền villagers to abandon their traditional agricultural production. In the 1990s, most Phú Điền farmers realized more than half of their annual income from agricultural farming and animal husbandry. This was supplemented by income from side employment in service industries in urban Hanoi or elsewhere. Due to agricultural land appropriation for various urban development projects, most agricultural farmers in Phú Điền no longer have land for farming. The irrigation systems supporting agricultural production have been destroyed in the course of a variety of construction projects, which has rendered farm work on the remaining plots of land virtually impossible.

Deciding what to do following appropriation

One of the greatest challenges facing Phú Điền villagers affected by agricultural land appropriation was the question of what to do after the acquisition of their land. Many farmers testified that they lost their agricultural land, and, because they had low levels of education, they found it difficult to acquire jobs outside their community. Although villagers had received economic compensation, the large-scale destruction of their rice fields critically transformed the village labor structure. Phú Điền farmers lost their peasant class designation, which previously offered them entitlements to agricultural land-use rights, because their residential location was reclassified as "urban"; and because they no longer farmed agricultural land but had to find alternative non-agricultural work. In practice, many villagers could not find stable salaried labor outside their village. In this sense, they felt they were forced to change from a more-or-less subsistence way of life to one that was greatly integrated into, and dependent on, the markets. Some villagers noted that in the past they produced most of the materials they needed for daily life, including food, and that they bought little in the market. This changed, as they now had to buy food and other necessities.

One woman described the local situation in this way:

> Many farmers in the village who are under 40 years of age now watch TV at home all day because, after the state seized land, they do not know what to do. Local farmers are mostly familiar with farmwork and [their] level of education is low, therefore it is difficult for them to apply for a job. We are ready to give land for the development of the city, but in return, the state must also show concern about jobs for us, the farmers, after agricultural land seizure.[16]

The question of work for farmers after agricultural land appropriation reflects a common phenomenon during the 1990s and 2000s in Vietnam that was also featured in national scholarly, media, and policy discourses, emphasizing the problem of farmers' low level of education and their difficulties in finding alternative livelihoods. Numerous mass media articles described cases and situations in which farmers faced the challenge of finding alternative jobs as they lost agricultural land – with titles such as "When the tiller is jobless" and "Finding a way out for land-lost farmers." Observing the Phú Điền area, one reporter wrote that, during the early years of agricultural land appropriation, he walked around the village, and "everywhere we go we see strong young villagers below the age of 40 sitting at home watching TV or hanging around bars."[17] A number of state officials were reportedly concerned that many farmers experiencing agricultural land appropriation faced difficulties in finding paid work: they lacked the skills required by employers due to low levels of education and to a lack of vocational training (Phong Lan 2005). In addition, there were worries that the scarcity of jobs could expose the farmers to "social evils," including HIV, prostitution, drug addiction, and theft.[18] Meanwhile, in line with recommendations made by Rigg and Nattapoolwat (2001) in another context,[19] some Vietnamese scholars endorsed state policies aiming to create non-agricultural jobs for farmers dispossessed of agricultural land. They urged the state to change its slogan of "người cày có ruộng" ("land to the tillers") to "người lao động có việc làm" ("jobs to workers") (Nguyễn Thế Nhã 1998:45), so the farmers could rely on small-scale industries in local communities for alternative incomes (Nguyễn Xuân Nguyên 1996:70).

Failure of government programs

Such trends and views put increased pressure on the state to adopt policies to assist farmers with appropriated land in finding work or launching new occupations. The state's assistance and support often included a financial subsidy to find or conceive alternative work; vocational training; and job creation for land-lost farmers.

The state's assistance and support for land-lost farmers have varied from location to location. Among the most promising state policies for land-lost farmers was vocational training for those who lost agricultural land. The concept of vocational training has been lauded by the state as an effective means to "rescue" the land-lost farmers, and responsibility for vocational programs has been allocated to government institutions and to those who use the appropriated land. State officials and state-controlled mass media sometimes depict an ideal scenario in which job training and job creation can help to change the "farmers" who work in the fields to "workers" who work in industry and the service sector. Vocational training is seen as helping land-lost farmers find alternative work outside the agricultural sector.

In practice, however, available training and retraining programs have not yet satisfied their targeted aims. In Phú Điền, a center for training and information development was established in 2003, under the authority of the Commune

People's Committee, to offer vocational training to land-lost farmers of the commune to help them find work in non-agricultural sectors. The center's training courses typically took five to six months to train farmers to do simple work like sewing, cooking, make-up, and hairdressing. (The training programs did not target industrial job opportunities for the land-lost farmers, because there were no industrial zones near the village.) At first, many farmers were eager to participate in such training programs, but they soon realized that the training was inadequate to ensure their success. Some villagers even accused local cadres and state officials of "cheating" them with respect to vocational training and job creation – while some local cadres blamed the villagers' low level of education for preventing them from obtaining paid non-agricultural work outside the village. Later, providing farmers with cash replaced this kind of support. (In Phú Điền, this amount came to 25,000 VND per square meter of agricultural land.)

Adapting to the market for new livelihood strategies

After agricultural land appropriation, many Phú Điền farmers gradually diversified their livelihood strategies through non-agricultural activities, including real estate, retail, and service provision.

Real estate

The major movement after loss of land has been into small-scale trade and services, specifically in constructing and in leasing rental houses (nhà trọ). Construction activities in new urban areas on former agricultural land have also forged new connections between Phú Điền and urban Hanoi and surrounding areas, which has produced a flow of people coming to the village to seek accommodations.

Many Phú Điền villagers took this opportunity to invest their compensation money in building new houses, both for their own use and for lease; many villagers even sold parts of their residential land to invest in this new business. The demolition of Phú Điền rice fields for urban buildings increased the market value of Phú Điền villagers' residential land.[20] In Phú Điền, many villagers experienced a rapid increase in residential land value after the late 1990s. In the early 1990s, transactions of residential land in the village were few and the price of residential land at that time rarely exceeded three million VND per square meter in such prime locations as those adjacent to entrance roads and commercial areas. However, since the late 1990s residential land prices have soared. The most expensive plots of residential land in the village in 2007 cost 60 million VND per square meter, equal to around USD 3,750 per square meter. The cheapest plots ranged from 13 to 15 million VND per square meter. As the village was incorporated into an urban district, residential land prices in the village have continued to increase. Today, residential land prices range from 40 to over 100 million VND per square meter depending upon the location. In the prime locations residential land prices are much higher. By the time of my ethnographic fieldwork, this had turned Phú Điền into a hotspot for land sales in Vietnam. Many households started to divide their residential land into two or more parcels for sale, mainly to people coming from the outside. It was estimated that up to about 80 percent of Phú Điền village households had sold part of their residential land to invest in rental housing, transforming themselves into landlords of rural tenants.[21]

Tenants during these early years included mostly students and immigrant laborers, who looked for accommodation in the village. The number of people taking up residence in Phú Điền increased rapidly. In order to rent a room, besides a financial arrangement with the landlords, tenants needed to register their "temporary residence"[22] with the village security officials and to pay a registration fee. By the second half of 2007, rental fees ranged from 300,000 to 400,000 VND per small room, per month, exclusive of water and electricity expenses. For a number of higher-standard rooms, rental fees varied between 500,000 to 600,000 VND per room per month. Rental housing and rental prices in the village have continued to increase in recent years, as will be described later.

Accommodation rental fees became a critical and stable source of income for many Phú Điền villagers. By 2007, many households could offer approximately five rooms for rent, bringing in a monthly income of over 1.5 million VND. More than 20 households who each possessed a large area of residential land could boast of possessing 20 to 50 rooms for rent; their income from room rentals alone added up to 30 million VND per month. At the same time, however, around 20 percent of households had no rooms available for rent.

Retail and service provision

Many villagers were also engaged in small-scale sales and services, including informal retailing, selling basic foodstuffs and household goods, and providing other services in the village residential area. The retail business took place both in the village's new market of 500 kiosks, built in 2003 to create a local trading site for Phú Điền's land-lost farmers and along the main village roads. Such sales and services include numerous small shops and bars, which often encroach on public space in the village. A small number of villagers have also successfully secured some non-agricultural jobs outside the village.

This experience of investment in accommodation and of engaging in various types of small-scale trade and services in the village shows how Phú Điền has adapted to the markets. While generally avoiding participation in the types of simple labor they might have accessed after joining the state's training programs, Phú Điền villagers successfully transformed themselves into accommodation hosts and have secured a higher level of income in comparison with what they earned while engaged in agricultural production. The villagers often said that they now appeared more robust and attractive, and they bought more new clothes than in the old days. One villager even noted that, in the old days, they bought only one set of new clothes per year, but now they purchased three or four; another noted that, in the old days, they had merely used salt but now they use soup powder as condiments in daily meals.

Empirical implications for policy and future research

This section discusses the empirical significance of this case study for policy and future research.

The implications of the villagers' move into real estate and rental

First, there is a need to delve into the policy implications of this case study of Phú Điền villagers' investment in rental housing, which illustrates the choices made by many Phú Điền residents. Certainly, in the early days of agricultural land appropriation, most farm households were concerned about the sustainability of the rental housing market. However, over a ten-year period, many Phú Điền residents were able to earn their living from rental housing. Rental housing draws flows of people into the village, and their residency also generates demand for services that supply employment for other people.

These developments have occurred even though central and local authorities had not adopted official policies to assist them in conceiving and sustaining this endogenous livelihood strategy. Yet local authorities benefit from the resulting tax revenues generated by the rental housing business.

The scale of change in Phú Điền village

In a follow-up visit to the village in 2011, it was clear that the volume of rental housing in the village has steadily grown. More families than before have built larger homes and even mini hotels and guesthouses. The local authorities reported that 530 households in the village possessed rental houses; of this number, 35 households operated guesthouses. The landlords continue to be mostly households living in the village (in addition to a few outside investors). The number of rental tenants totaled 11,000 persons, mostly young rural people and students who have moved close to Hanoi for work and education. These tenants have significantly contributed to the sustainability of many Phú Điền households' new livelihood strategies after agricultural land appropriation.

Income comparison

In the village residential area, the rental housing business continues to be a key livelihood strategy for Phú Điền villagers as well as for more recently arrived residents. Rental housing exists in various forms, ranging from single rooms to entire houses for rent; mini hotels; guesthouses; and offices. A single room of 15 square meters will rent for between 1.3 and 1.5 million VND per month, and a larger room measuring 25 square meters might be priced at 3.5 million VND per month. A mini studio apartment of 40 square meters or less that is fully furnished can reach up to five million VND per month. Some landlords even offer the rent of an entire house. For example, a small, fully equipped house of three floors on a 30 square meter site costs around 13 million VND per month. A bigger house will cost more.

Changes in context

In 2013, the government divided Từ Liêm rural district into two urban districts: Bắc Từ Liêm and Nam Từ Liêm. As result, Phú Điền village became a core component of a new ward in the Nam Từ Liêm urban district of Hanoi. The village today is surrounded by urban roads, placing the village's residential area in the midst of an aggregation of urban buildings such as apartment buildings, detached houses, schools, banks, and offices, which have been built on the former agricultural land areas of the village.

Growing use of online information and social media

One of the major developments in the rental housing business in the village is that it has moved online and is now strongly engaging with social media and professional services. The landlords have promoted their services through social media, including Facebook and local applications, as well as professional networks mediated by commercial companies. The top websites for real estate and housing services often publish information about rooms and houses for rent in the village. Tenants can easily access information on the location and size of rental properties and furnishings and of amenities such as internet access, parking space, security, local access to convenience shops and schools, and rental fees.

The choice between political action/contestation and engagement with the market

The existing literature on land conflict in Vietnam has significantly enlarged and deepened our understanding of contemporary Vietnamese society. Research and case studies, like that of Phú Điền village, show us that conflicts involving agricultural land appropriation in contemporary Vietnam are essentially a political dimension of the phenomenon of agrarian change. However, I believe that the Phú Điền case study reveals the empirical significance of another dimension of agrarian change: the economic dimension. Villagers in Phú Điền and in many other cases have chosen not to be involved in conflicts with state authorities but to engage with the market, both during and after the course of agricultural land appropriation. This dimension merits further examination and analysis.

The reason the Phú Điền villagers have been able to avoid conflict with the authorities concerning agricultural land appropriation was that they were able to adaptively respond to the emergence of a new rental housing market. When examining similar cases of agricultural land appropriation, it is clear that new market opportunities for local dispossessed farmers will vary from area to area. In peri-urban areas, urbanization can offer villagers a variety of non-agricultural livelihood opportunities, including rental housing and non-agricultural services. In industrialized areas, the development of industries might offer a variety of factory employment and services. In rural and ethnic minority areas, on the other hand, the appropriation of agricultural land (for recreation, ecotourism, and the like) might offer villagers some limited opportunities for diversifying their livelihoods. This diversity suggests that any examination of how and why villagers accept the state's appropriation of their agricultural land – both to avoid conflict and to formulate alternative livelihood strategies – should be locally contextualized for analysis.

Conclusion

In the wake of agricultural land appropriation, and in the course of urbanization, the rental housing sector has emerged as a core business for Phú Điền residents, particularly after the village became part of the new Nam Từ Liêm urban district of Hanoi in 2013. The village's landscape and the composition of its residential areas, as well as its social fabric, have transformed into something very different from the village where I conducted ethnographic field research in 2007 and 2008. During and after the experience of agricultural land appropriation for urban development (unlike other cases in which farmers have violently protested against state authorities), Phú Điền villagers purposely adapted to the taking of their agricultural land-use rights and responded positively to the market opportunities that urban development projects generated in their local areas, thus allowing them to adopt new livelihood strategies.

In this chapter, I have examined moments in this period of transition to illuminate how Phú Điền villagers interacted with state authorities and adapted to the market during and after agricultural land appropriation. Although state authorities failed to effectively conceive how these farmers could subsist on their compensation money and relied on offering vocational training for low skilled labor, Phú Điền villagers have been gradually and rationally adapting to the local market by investing in their residential land to supply rental accommodations. Their successful adaptation to the market has enabled them to overcome their earlier trauma due to agricultural land appropriation and the loss of agricultural employment and to formulate new non-agricultural livelihood strategies. Analysis of these processes of agricultural land loss and adaptation to the market also provides a better understanding of why these former farmers have generally accepted relinquishment of agricultural land-use rights to the state for urban development without violent protests, although the phenomenon of land conflicts has been richly documented elsewhere in contemporary Vietnam.

The empirical and conceptual significance of this analysis suggests that, to obtain a more holistic assessment of contemporary Vietnamese society, social scholars should consider more closely the economic dimension of the process of agrarian change, as driven by agricultural land appropriation during the Đổi Mới period. In this regard – and through case studies – ethnographic research might produce original empirical findings and enable new conceptual understandings of contemporary Vietnamese society.

Notes

1 The village name has been changed.
2 Revisions were made in 1993, 1998, 2001, 2003 and 2013. The *Land Law 2013* was revised in 2020, but its submission to the National Assembly was delayed. In

June 2021, the Prime Minister issued a decision to revise *Land Law 2013* to submit to the National Assembly in 2022. The proposed requirements for revision focus on six groups of issues, of which the efficiency of the state's land administration is the central focus.

3 My synthesis of various versions of the *Land Law*.

4 In various provinces, however, agricultural land-use rights remained unallocated because the local authorities simply extended farmers' agricultural land-use rights holding for 20 years after 1993.

5 These figures have been extracted from www.khucongnghiep.com.vn/tabid/65/articletype/ArticleView/articleId/1580/default.aspx.

6 Datacitedat:https://data.worldbank.org/indicator/SP.URB.TOTL.IN.ZS?locations=VN.

7 The Vietnamese central government aimed to build 140 golf courses in 2020 with an estimated area of over 38,000 hectares of land in 51 provinces and cities. It is estimated that there are around 40 golf courses currently in operation in Vietnam.

8 Dao (2015) has pointed out another form of land conversion from household farms to rubber plantations in northern parts of Vietnam, which is supported and promoted by the state authorities as a type of development in upland areas.

9 See Hall et al. (2015) for a recent discussion of political reactions involving land grabbing according to a broader context.

10 According to *Residential Law 2020*, the household registration system will be discontinued by the end of 2022.

11 In later years, agricultural land in the village continued to be appropriated for small-scale urban development projects.

12 One mẫu in the Red River delta is equal to 3,600 square meters, 1 sào is equal to 360 square meters, 1 thước is equal to 24 meters, and 1 tấc is equal to 2.4 square meters.

13 In 2007, compensation for these crops in Phú Điền was 35,000 đồng per square meter.

14 In addition, the village community as a whole received monetary assistance for local infrastructure improvement. In 2007, for example, the village purportedly received over 10 million VND from various projects, which the village used to renovate public infrastructure such as the community house, pagodas, cultural structures, kindergartens, clinics, and roads.

15 Truong Thien Thu and Ranjith Perera (2011) have argued that in Ho Chi Minh City, for example, the government is trapped between these two land-price structures, one based on the market and one created by the state that adheres to administrative location but is often much lower than the market price of land. The two prices make land appropriation difficult as farmers oppose the appropriation of their land to give to other parties with inequitable compensation.

16 Citing an article published in Báo Lao Động in 2003.

17 Citing an article published in Báo Lao Động in 2003.

18 Citing an interview of an official at the Ministry of Labour – Invalids and Social Affairs over the question of work for land-dispossessed farmers published by Thời báo Kinh tế Việt Nam, Issue 165, 19 August 2005.

19 Rigg and Nattapoolwat (2001) postulated that, in the context of increased interaction between rural and urban areas, commercialization, and the integration of local economies into the global economy, land is no longer a strategic resource for farmers.

20 Harms (2012) made a similar argument in his study on a land clearance project in Ho Chi Minh City.

21 In a study of land fever in Cổ Nhuế village, a few kilometers from Phú Điền, Huong (2007) described a revealing case of land value increasing as the village faced urbanization.

22 This form of temporary residence applies for those who do not have household registration in the area of current residence.

References

Bảo Quyên, 2018. 'Thủ tướng: Khiếu nại, tố cáo vẫn chủ yếu về đất đai.' VnEconomy: http://vneconomy.vn/thu-tuong-khieu-nai-to-cao-van-chu-yeu-ve-dat-dai-20180605063336344.htm (accessed 5 January 2019).

Binh, N.T.T., 2017. Multiple reactions to land confiscations in a Hanoi peri-urban village. *Southeast Asian Studies*, *6*(1), pp. 95–114. https://doi.org/10.20495/seas.6.1_95.

Chau, L.M., 2018. Actively cautious: Industrialization and rural livelihood choices in contemporary northern Vietnam. *South East Asia Research*, *26*(1), pp. 21–37. https://doi.org/10.1177%2F0967828X17752415.

Dao, N., 2015. Rubber plantations in the Northwest: Rethinking the concept of land grabs in Vietnam. *Journal of Peasant Studies*, *42*(2), pp. 347–369. https://doi.org/10.1080/03066150.2014.990445.

Hall, R., Edelman, M., Borras Jr, S.M., Scoones, I., White, B. and Wolford, W., 2015. Resistance, acquiescence or incorporation? An introduction to land grabbing and political reactions 'from below'. *Journal of Peasant Studies*, *42*(3–4), pp. 467–488. https://doi.org/10.1080/03066150.2015.1036746.

Harms, E., 2012. Social demolition: Creative destruction and the production of value in Vietnamese land clearance. In *State, Society and the Market in Contemporary Vietnam* (pp. 75–88). New York: Routledge.

Harms, E., 2013. Eviction time in the new Saigon: Temporalities of displacement in the rubble of development. *Cultural Anthropology*, *28*(2), pp. 344–368. https://doi.org/10.1111/cuan.12007.

Huong, N.L., 2007. 'Sot dat'(Land Fever). In *Hanoi: Ruralization of the urban space. Globalizing Cities: Inequality and Segregation in Developing Countries*, Ranvinder S. Sandhu & Jasmeet Sandhu (eds., pp. 206–229). India: Rawar Publication.

Kerkvliet, B.J.T., 2005. *The Power of Everyday Politics: How Vietnamese Peasants Transformed National Policy*. Ithaca, NY: Cornell University Press. https://doi.org/10.7591/9781501722011.

Kerkvliet, B.J.T., 2006. Agricultural land in Vietnam: Markets tempered by family, community and socialist practices. *Journal of Agrarian Change*, *6*(3), pp. 285–305. https://doi.org/10.1111/j.1469-7580.2007.00715.x-i1.

Kerkvliet, B.J.T., 2014. Protests over land in Vietnam: Rightful resistance and more. *Journal of Vietnamese Studies*, *9*(3), pp. 19–54. https://doi.org/10.1525/vs.2014.9.3.19.

Labbé, D., 2015a. Media dissent and peri-urban land struggles in Vietnam: The case of the Văn Giang incident. *Critical Asian Studies*, *47*(4), pp. 495–513. https://doi.org/10.1080/14672715.2015.1079993.

Labbé, D., 2015b. Critical reflections on land appropriation and alternative urbanization trajectories in periurban Vietnam. *Cities*, *53*, pp. 150–155. https://doi.org/10.1016/j.cities.2015.11.003.

Labbé, D. and Musil, C., 2014. Periurban land redevelopment in Vietnam under market Socialism. *Urban Studies*, *51*(6), pp. 1146–1161. doi:10.1177/0042098013495574.

Nguyễn Thế Nhã, 1998. Thực trạng sản xuất và đời sống của hộ nông dân không đất và thiếu đất ở vùng đồng bằng sông Cửu Long. *Nghiên cứu Kinh tế*, số 247, pp. 35–46.

Nguyễn Xuân Nguyên, 1996. *Khuynh hướng phân hóa hộ nông dân trong phát triển sản xuất hàng hóa*. Hà Nội: Nxb. Chính trị Quốc gia.

O'Brien, K.J., 1996. Rightful resistance. *World Politics*, *49*(1), pp. 31–55. https://doi.org/10.1353/wp.1996.0022.

Phong Lan, 2005. Việc làm cho nông dân khi thu hồi đất. *Thời báo Kinh tế Việt Nam*, số 138, ngày 13/7.

Phuc, N.Q., Van Westen, A.C.M. and Zoomers, A., 2014. Agricultural land for urban development: The process of land conversion in Central Vietnam. *Habitat International*, *41*, pp. 1–7. https://doi.org/10.1016/j.habitatint.2013.06.004.

Quốc hội Nước Cộng hòa Xã hội Chủ nghĩa Việt Nam, 2013. *Luật Đất đai*. Hà Nội: Nxb Chính trị Quốc gia.

Ravallion, M. and Van de Walle, D., 2008. *Land in Transition: Reform and Poverty in Rural Vietnam*. Washington DC: World Bank Publications.

Rigg, J. and Nattapoolwat, S., 2001. Embracing the global in Thailand: Activism and pragmatism in an era of deagrarianization. *World Development*, *29*(6), pp. 945–960. https://doi.org/10.1016/S0305-750X(01)00021-3.

Scott, J. and Kerkvliet, B. (edited), 1986. *Everyday Forms of Peasant Resistance in Southeast Asia*. London: Frank Class, Ltd.

Suu, N.V., 2004. The politics of land: Inequality in land access and local conflicts in the Red River delta since decollectivization. In *Social Inequality in Vietnam and the Challenges to Reform* (pp. 270–296). ISEAS Publishing. https://doi.org/10.1355/9789812305954-012.

Suu, N.V., 2007. Contending views and conflicts over land in Vietnam's Red River Delta. *Journal of Southeast Asian Studies*, *38*(2), pp. 309–334. https://doi.org/10.1017/S0022463407000069.

Suu, N.V., 2009. Agricultural land conversion and its effects on farmers in contemporary Vietnam. *Focaal*, *2009*(54), pp. 106–113. https://doi.org/10.3167/fcl.2009.540109.

Taylor, P., 2014. Introduction to the special issue: Contests over land in rural Vietnam. *Journal of Vietnamese Studies*, *9*(3), pp. 1–18. https://doi.org/10.1525/vs.2014.9.3.1.

Thu, T.T. and Perera, R., 2011. Consequences of the two-price system for land in the land and housing market in Ho Chi Minh City, Vietnam. *Habitat International*, *35*(1), pp. 30–39. https://doi.org/10.1016/j.habitatint.2010.03.005.

Trung Đức, 2021. 'Tình hình xây dựng và phát triển KCN, KKT đến tháng 02 năm 2021.' Bộ Kế hoạch và Đầu tư: www.mpi.gov.vn/Pages/tinbai.aspx?idTin=49041&idcm=188 (accessed 12 September 2021).

Van den Berg, L.M., Van Wijk, M.S. and Van Hoi, P., 2003. The transformation of agriculture and rural life downstream of Hanoi. *Environment and Urbanization*, *15*(1), pp. 35–52. https://doi.org/10.1177%2F095624780301500122.

Vien, T.D., Quang, N.V. and Van Dung, N., 2005. *Rural-urban land use changes in peri-urban Hanoi*. Hanoi, The Hague: Hanoi Agricultural University and Wageningen University and Research Centre.

Vu, M.H. and Kawashima, H., 2017. Effects of urban expansion on suburban farmers' livelihood in Vietnam: A comparative analysis of Ho Chi Minh City and Hanoi. *Habitat International*, *100*(65), pp. 49–58. http://dx.doi.org/10.1016%2Fj.habitatint.2017.05.001.

6 "Good" versus "bad" urbanization

Land appropriation impacts in two peri-urban villages in Hanoi

Nguyen Thi Thanh Binh

Over the last decade, land grabbing – which takes place in many parts of the developing world – has become an emerging topic of discussion, producing a large body of literature on developing countries in Latin America, Africa, and Asia. Scholars are paying increased attention to themes such as farmland conversion for large-scale processing and marketing agri-businesses; urban expansion in peri-urban areas; and infrastructure development (Edelman & Borras 2013; Nguyen Quang Phuc 2015).

In the case of Vietnam, a massive transfer of land is occurring in the context of urban expansion, rather than for land accumulation for agriculture. The country has experienced rapid industrialization and modernization ever since the 1986 economic reforms. Urban areas are continuously expanding, with the population living in urban areas increasing from just over 10 percent in 1950 to 34.4 percent in 2019; the total population in urban areas now is over 33 million people (United Nations 2014; Tổng cục thống kê 2019). Accompanying this rapid urbanization process is an extensive conversion of agricultural land. From 2001 to 2005, the state appropriated 366,400 hectares of agricultural land; rising to roughly 745,000 hectares by 2010 and affecting about 9 million people in farming households or about 10 percent of the country's population (Kerkvliet 2014: 20).

Since this urbanization process took off in the late 1980s, Hanoi, the capital city of Vietnam, has continuously expanded its administrative boundaries. In 2008, a merger with Ha Tay province enlarged Hanoi by more than 2,000 square kilometers, and its population increased by nearly three million people. This merger marked the highest-paced period of urbanization in the city's history (Trần Thị Hồng Yến 2013). From 2000 to 2004, Hanoi converted 5,496 hectares of land for 957 projects, and this has had critical consequences for the lives and work of 138,291 households, including 41,000 classified as agricultural households (Hồng Minh 2005). Despite the downturn in land transactions following the global economic recession in 2008, in recent years a large number of construction projects have been implemented. In its 2020 *Development plan*, the city of Hanoi proposed appropriating approximately 6,500 hectares for almost 2,000 projects; in 2021, these numbers will be 6,068.6 hectares and 1,738 projects, respectively (Nhĩ Anh 2021). In that context, rural communities, especially peri-urban villages, face both opportunities and challenges.

DOI: 10.4324/9781003165774-9

Research on urbanization in Vietnam has highlighted a set of problems that have arisen as the urbanization process extends into the peri-urban landscape. These problems include land degradation; chaotic land-use practices; growing income inequality; dispossessed farmers unable to find jobs in the urban economy; and land disputes (Nguyen Duy Thang 2004; Tran Duc Vien et al. 2005; Vu Hong Phong 2006; Labbé 2014; Nguyễn Văn Sửu 2014). Some researchers have focused on social and cultural changes in peri-urban communities that were transformed from rural to urban communes (Trần Thị Hồng Yến 2013; Nguyễn Thị Phương Châm & Đỗ Lan Phương 2016; Nguyễn Đình Tuấn 2013). Others have explored the drivers of land acquisition; processes and actors involved in land taking; livelihood transformation; and the reactions of farmers to land loss (Asia Foundation 2014; DiGregorio 2011; Labbé 2011, 2015; Nguyen Quang Phuc 2015). While those works identify the impact of land appropriation for urbanization, they do not capture all the experiences, emotions, and thoughts of local people in the affected communities. Some studies have shown how the differing impacts of land appropriation on rural groups have led to a range of different issues (Nguyen Thi Thanh Binh 2017; Nguyen Quang Phuc 2015). However, more can be said about the impacts of land expropriation in the last decade and the perceptions of people affected by this process.

This chapter explores the positive and negative impacts of urbanization and land appropriation on local people in two peri-urban villages in Hanoi since late 2000. Critical analytical themes include significant changes in livelihood and social life after land loss and villagers' viewpoints, feelings, and aspirations. This chapter argues that local people have turned the advantages of urbanization (for example, the increased value of residential land) into development opportunities, despite receiving unfair compensation packages. After some years of anxiety and turbulence, most households' lives in the two communities are gradually stabilizing, as many have transitioned from farming to join the urban working class. However, the remaining segment of the population is left behind, facing difficulties and pressures to better themselves. Evidence from the case studies shows that, to avoid social conflict and to ensure a sustainable future for peri-urban communities, more responsive policies are needed from the city government and from the state (including revision of the land appropriation process and of land compensation prices).

Research method and research sites

This chapter is drawn from field research conducted in La Ca village, Duong Noi ward, Ha Dong district and from La Tinh village, Dong La commune, Hoai Duc district, Hanoi city, between January and April in 2014 and a during a second short visit in September 2021.[1] In 2014, the research was carried out using both quantitative and qualitative research methodologies. For the quantitative component, 200 household questionnaire surveys were conducted in each village to determine household socioeconomic situations. Information was collected on land ownership and transfer; other personal and productive assets; income; and consumption expenditures. For the qualitative component (which represents the basis for this paper), 60 semi-structured interviews were conducted with individuals in each village. Half of these individuals were identified from the quantitative questionnaires, while the remainder were selected to ensure a broad representation of the village by age, gender, educational background, occupation, marital status, and economic status. The interviews included open-ended questions on the informants' personal information; family socioeconomic situation; occupational transformation; and living standards. More importantly, people were free to share their own opinions, feelings, and thoughts on urbanization and its impact on their lives and communities. Life-history interview methodology was used to understand experiences and emotions in a transitional society. During the researcher's short return visit in 2021, ten interviews were conducted in each village, focusing more on changes in the two communities since 2014.

Research site: La Ca village

Located in the west of Hanoi, La Ca village is about 16 km from the city's center. Before 2006, La Ca village belonged to Duong Noi commune, Hoai Duc district, Ha Tay province.[2] In 2014, the village population was approximately 3,400 households and 14,000 inhabitants. By 2020, it had increased to 4,914 households and 19,227 inhabitants. In this ancient village in the Ha Dong silk-producing area, rice cultivation and silk weaving were historically the two main livelihoods of villagers. Based on their handicraft traditions and aided by their close geographical position to Hanoi, La Ca people had always enjoyed diversified economic activities. Before 2008, approximately 70 percent of the over 2,000 households in the village were agricultural. Households also engaged in petty trade, manual labor, food processing, and small-scale service industries. Thirty percent of the households were non-agricultural households; the majority of these were traders and entrepreneurs who no longer cultivated rice. Of these, about 200 households had stalls at Dong Xuan market and at some other markets in Hanoi. Almost 100 households were owners of weaving and cloth-dying businesses in the village. The remainder ran different kinds of businesses, ranging from wood workshops and garment workshops to tobacco sales and managing food shops. In general, the 30 percent of households engaged in trading and craft could be regarded as the wealthiest people in the village. However, by intensifying their cash crops and petty trade, the other 70 percent of households also had relatively stable livelihoods. Compared with surrounding villages, La Ca village was considered one of the most prosperous villages in the region and one with the internal capacity to develop.

Research site: La Tinh village

La Tinh village is adjacent to La Ca village. It is a village in Dong La commune in Hoai Duc district, Hanoi city. The village is located about 18 km from Hanoi's city center, but there has been no direct road access to the village: from Ha Dong town, visitors have to pass by La Ca village or follow the Day River dike to get to the village. This is the reason La Tinh village has experienced a slower rate of urbanization than La Ca and other villages in the area.

The population of La Tinh village in 2014 comprised over 600 households and 2,300 inhabitants,[3] with a total agricultural area of over 65 hectares of land (655,200 m^2). Of this, more than 36 hectares were rice fields (367,200 m^2) (đất đồng), and the remainder (280,000 m^2) was riverside land (đất bãi). The area for housing and gardens was approximately 20 hectares. The economic activities of the village consisted mainly of agriculture, which employed 80 percent of the inhabitants. Most households in the village combined agriculture and livestock rearing with construction work; temporary manual labor; petty trade; and services. About 20 percent of the labor force was employed in the village bureaucracy and state sector. As most villagers were farmers, petty traders, and hired workers, socioeconomic disparities in La Tinh village were not as significant as in La Ca village. In 2014, about 15 percent of the households in the village were categorized as "high income" due to the incomes generated by their gardens or to salaries from their non-agricultural jobs, while most of the other households would have been considered "medium income" households.

Urbanization patterns and land appropriation in the two studied villages

As noted earlier, "global land grabbing" has become a popular term in academic literature and has been described as a "catch-all to describe and analyze the current explosion of large-scale (trans)national commercial land transactions" (Borras Jr. et al. 2011: 210). In practice, scholars on urbanization often use specific terms such as *land conversion*, *land acquisition*, or *land appropriation* to define the process of transforming agricultural land for urban use and for development projects. Although this process is mostly carried out by means of compulsory land acquisition by governments, it is implemented in different ways in different countries, depending on the land-tenure regime and land rights of each nation (FAO 2008). In developed countries where farmers own their land, the compensation rate will be at the market price, and the rights of holders are protected. Meanwhile, in countries without private land ownership, government agencies often determine land acquisition (Nguyen Quang Phuc 2015: 55). Given the pressure for economic development in developing countries, planners have played a dominant – and sometimes coercive – role in relocating lower-income families to make way for privately funded development (Kim 2009). In these cases, even in countries with private land ownership, like India, governments still play critical roles in land-taking through the ambiguous concept of "public purpose" and through combinations of compensation and coercion (Andreas et al. 2020: 1115–1116).

In the case of Vietnam, the term *land appropriation* (thu hồi đất) was officially used in the 2003 *Land Law* and was revised in *Land Law 2013* to refer to cases where the state appropriates land and allocates land-use rights to users (households, individuals or organizations) for "national defense, security, national interest, public interest, and economic development." According to this law, "economic development" projects include new urban and industrial parks; thus, local governments have reallocated agricultural land to developers by applying the state's right to allocate and appropriate land for the "public purpose" (Kerkvliet 2014). The government negotiates with farming households in project areas and compensates the households for the reallocated land on a fixed-rate basis. However, the compensation level set by the state often falls below the market rate; therefore, land acquisition has often disadvantaged farmers and given rise to social conflict (Nguyen Quang Phuc 2015: 57–58).

Land appropriation in Duong Noi commune

Appropriation and compensation in La Ca village

On March 1, 2006, under the national urban growth policy, Duong Noi commune was designated as belonging to Ha Dong town (Ha Tay province). In June 2009, soon after Ha Tay merged with Hanoi city, Duong Noi became an urban administrative unit in Ha Dong district. Although local residents were aware that land appropriation for urbanization of their communities was an inevitable process, many of them were quite shocked when it happened. In early 2008, after several months of rumors, meetings were held by the village authorities to announce the plans of the Ha Dong town authorities. More than 300 hectares (ha) of agricultural land of La Ca village and La Duong village in the same ward (more than 90 percent of the villages' total agricultural land) would be appropriated for 13 projects. The biggest project was the Duong Noi New Urban Centre, with an area of 197 ha.

According to the government's compensation policy, the project would give back 10 percent of the reclassified land as "service land"[4] (đất dịch vụ) for use or sale, plus 201.600 VND (Vietnamese đồng) per m^2 and financial compensation for crops that could no longer be cultivated. La Ca villagers received 86 million VND [about US$4,000] per *sào* (360 m^2) in compensation. In 1993, each inhabitant in La Ca village born before 1993 had been allocated 264 m^2 of agricultural land. According to the compensation policy, each of these residents received about 63 million VND [around US$3,000] and 17 m^2 of "service land."[5] However, people had to spend almost half of their compensation funds to build infrastructure on the new areas of service land (two million VND per m^2).

Local residents compared their situation with that of neighboring village La Khe where, for the same project, 97 million VND per *sào* was paid. La Khe was already a ward of Ha Dong town, while La Ca village, being part of Duong Noi commune, was still a rural village commune in a peri-urban environment. The land values of urban and rural areas were thus considered different. La Ca people objected to this difference in compensation, not only because their land was adjacent, but, as they pointed out, La Khe's rice land was less valuable than La Ca villagers' land: the village is known as the "peach tree village" for its peach trees and flowers (đào), which generate high incomes,[6] especially during the Tet season.

Another bone of contention was the fact that La Ca farmers could only retain 6.5 percent of the service land, instead of the higher amounts – up to 10 percent or more – that were being given elsewhere. The local government explained that the other 3.5 percent was to be used for opening roads and infrastructure for the new area of service land.

As with most complaints related to land clearance for development projects all over the country, the people of La Ca protested that the compensation was too low (Harms 2016: 211), that it did not conform to the situation of other projects in the area, and that the promise of providing jobs as a replacement for the loss of land was vague. The difference in compensation policy, together with many farmers' desire to keep land for cultivation, were two of the reasons La Ca villagers decided not to cede agricultural land to the project in return for compensation. In March 2008 a protest formed against land appropriation that lasted for over a year. Only toward the end of 2009, under various forms of pressure from the city government and tactics by property developers, did most villagers accept the compensation and cease protesting (Nguyen Thi Thanh Binh 2017). However, 36 households of La Ca had not yet received the money. These people, together with over 200 households in a neighboring village, continued their protest until 2021.

Appropriation and compensation in La Tinh village

In the case of La Tinh, from 2010 to 2021, about 5 ha of agricultural land have been appropriated for various purposes. In 2010, the commune had decided to use 2.9 ha of the cultivated land of 43 households in the village to build a new community house, sports stadium, and kindergarten (as facilities needed for urbanization). As the local government had no money to pay for compensation, these 43 households received "service land" as compensation. This meant that if a household lost one *sào* (360 m^2) for that project, it received in return 50 m^2 of service land. With land prices ranging from 14 million to 25 million VND per m^2 at that time, this exchange garnered a high compensation rate for village residents compared with what La Ca villagers and other urbanized villagers had received from megaprojects. People were happy with the compensation, and they regarded the project as being for their own benefit.

In 2017, Hoai Duc district took 7731.7 m^2 (0.77 ha) from 48 households in La Tinh village to develop land for auction. Having received compensation of only 400 million VND per *sào*, eight households voiced disagreement with the decision. They had transformed their paddy land into land for fruit growing, giving them quite a high income relative to the amount offered in compensation. The local government had to carry out compulsory acquisition of their land.

In 2019, 21.710 m^2 (about 2.1 ha) was taken from 53 households to expand the Le Trong Tan Road extension. The compensation was only 360 million VND per *sào*, but affected people did not oppose it, as they recognized that the development on that site would serve a needed public function: a main road. According to the local government's plan, in 2022, 12.3 ha of La Tinh village would be used for the construction of housing for low-income earners, to be carried out by Vietnam's

Construction Corporation (*Tập đoàn Xây dựng Việt Nam*). As Hoai Duc had been preparing to become an urban district of Hanoi, most of the village's agricultural land was envisioned as being subsumed under various projects.

Although the village has not yet been integrated into the urban area, the city's urbanization process has still impacted it. Since 2008, amid the "land fever" in the region, many households have sold their land (agricultural or residential) to external investors or buyers. In 2014, about 40 percent of the surveyed households had sold part of their residential or arable land to raise money to build a house. By 2021, about 60 percent of households in the village had sold part of their agricultural and/or residential land. This has caused considerable change in the physical appearance of the community and in the livelihoods of local people.

The impact of land appropriation on two communities

Infrastructure improvement

Research about the impact of land acquisition on local people often acknowledges that the acquisition process creates both positive and negative effects (Nguyen Quang Phuc 2015: 5–6). The initial positive impacts are the improvement of infrastructure in the peri-urban area and the chance for people to use compensation money to renovate homes, purchase furniture, or invest in business.

As soon as the merger of La Ca village with Ha Dong town occurred, two major roads (extended Le Van Luong and Le Trong Tan roads) were constructed, bisecting the village in 2006 and 2007. In the case of La Tinh village, according to the city plan, City Belt No 4 (Ring Road 4) will be built adjacent to a railway, which will cut the village in two. The extended Le Trong Tan Road will also be built to connect La Tinh village with Ha Dong town. In 2021, a bridge over the Dao River, connecting La Tinh village with To Huu Street, was under construction. The Day River dike running through the village was also expanded and paved with concrete in 2020.

In villages, roads and sewers are always built by the city when there is a decision to merge. The old main roads, which were 4 to 5 m wide in La Tinh village and 5 to 7 m wide in La Ca village, were repaired and upgraded, while many new roads were opened with widths of 7 to 15 m – greatly changing traffic conditions in the communities. In addition, community houses, kindergartens, schools, and other public infrastructure in the two villages were repaired and rebuilt to more spacious dimensions. Outside the old residential area of the two villages, new rows of multistoried houses were being built in an urban architectural style, creating an urban appearance (see Table 6.1). Inside the village, there was also an important change in the housing of families. As some studies have confirmed, since the 1990s (a few years after the 1986 economic reforms), the people of the Northern Delta have focused on investing in building houses, ranging from thatched-roof houses to tiled and flat-roofed houses, and even houses of two to three stories (Di Gregorio 2011). From the first decade of the twenty-first century onwards, high-rise buildings have been built at a greater rate, especially in urbanized areas.

Table 6.1 Types of houses in the two village communities in 2014 (%)

Types of houses	*La Ca Village*	*La Tinh Village*
House of 2 stories and above	67.3	47.1
Flat-roofed house	4.0	15.7
Tiled roofed house	2.0	4.9
Level 4 house (low tiled roof)	25.7	32.4
Temporary houses	1.0	0.0

Source: Survey result in 2014

As of 2021, the proportion of houses of two or more stories in La Ca village was about 90 percent and in La Tinh village about 80 percent. The proportion of high-rise buildings in La Ca village has increased sharply since the time of land acquisition in 2009 because 70 percent of the respondents used the compensation money to build houses and to spend on family needs. In La Tinh village, the number of households selling land to build a new house greatly increased from 2010 to 2021, reaching a peak in 2018, when some 50 out of 600 families in the village started to build a new house. Most families chose to build two- to three-story houses.

When asked to explain the desire to build spacious houses, people in both villages said that in the past, most of them had had to live in narrow, squat homes of poor quality, so everyone wanted to live in a large permanent house:

> Before land appropriation, most of our houses were small brick houses with low tiled roofs (nhà cấp 4). Living in that tiny space, we suffered the heat in summertime and worried whenever it was rainy and windy. In the 1990s, to have a one storied house with a flat roof was a dream of many people. I myself had to work very hard and accumulate for ten years to build a house like that in 1996. However, at the time, I had to rely on relatives for a helping hand. Nowadays, with compensation, we can live in a spacious house that's cooler in summertime and no longer worry about storms. At least, we feel more release from hardship.
>
> (Mr. Chan, 62 years old, La Ca village)

Villagers explained that the compensation money was akin to receiving cooked food (miếng ăn chín) when hungry. If they did not build new permanent houses, they might spend all their compensation on their daily needs and household items.

> If we just save our compensation in the bank and spend the monthly interest to buy rice and food every day, we might be fine for a long time. But life is not simple like that. The problem is it is impossible to keep it like that. If we cultivate crops, we will never have that amount of money. The children know that their parents have savings in the bank. Today they might ask us to buy

a bike, tomorrow they might ask for a motorbike. Thus, most people cannot save and properly manage the compensation.

(Mr. Oanh, 58 years old, La Ca village)

The two villages have also experienced an influx of new residents, who are buying land to build houses or are renting houses, mini apartment models, small row houses, and guesthouses (which have also appeared in the two villages). The new infrastructure and houses have given the two communities a more attractive appearance, especially La Ca village.

Livelihood transformation

The selling of service land: La Ca village

By 2014, half of all the households in La Ca village had sold their service land. Most of them were mainly reliant on agriculture. The interviews also showed that most people aged over 60 had sold their service land. These are people whose children are already grown up and independent. They no longer had to worry about building houses or organizing weddings for them. Instead, they might give their children or grandchildren some of their compensation or money from selling their service land, as a gift. The remainder was invested in the bank to receive monthly interest. With an amount ranging from 100 to 300 million VND, many older adults in La Ca village at least have enough money to cover daily expenditures. Meanwhile, one-third of the La Ca households also traded for a living and many traders did not sell their land; instead, they earned enough to buy land in their neighborhood. According to the survey results, by 2014 about 3 percent of the households in the village had bought land in other areas.

For the majority of La Ca villagers (70 percent of peasant households), after receiving a large amount of compensation, they moved from a state of anxiety to a feeling of "floating comfortably" (bồng bềnh). With their compensation funds, together with money from selling service land, La Ca villagers enjoyed some prosperous years. The village became a construction site as many families built their new multi-story houses around the same time. People could also spend more money on food and buy new items. However, since 2012, with Hanoi's city real estate market declining and their compensation funds gradually dwindling, local people began to face challenges in sustaining the changes they wanted to make in their livelihoods and family circumstances.

Rental accommodation, agriculture and trade: La Ca village

Research on peri-urban villages which are closer to the center of Hanoi discovered that most households there could earn money from rental accommodations, running shops, and providing services along the village roads (Nguyễn Văn Sửu 2014; Trần Thị Hồng Yến 2013). However, few households in La Ca village offered lodging services.[7] About 10 percent of households were engaged in trade and services along the village road, such as selling food, fruit, clothes, household items, pharmaceuticals, motorbike services, construction materials, or electronic goods. However, after land appropriation, almost half of the village households had to find a way to return to agriculture and continue their mobile vending and petty trade in the city and the village market.

Before 2000, about 50 percent of households in La Ca village had at least one member engaging in petty trade. After 2000, due to several official regulations on urban street trading, on urban order, and on pavement use in the city,[8] the number of La Ca mobile vendors has been reduced. Since then, street vendors and petty traders have to hang around markets or seek a site at markets. After the land acquisition, hundreds of La Ca women started selling goods at the village market and, along the village road, more than 100 vendors continued to "go to the market" in the city.

Women in these households, together with their husbands, grow vegetables and peaches to sell in the market or engage in small trade. These are primarily middle-aged women who work hard, bearing the main economic burden of their families and caring for children of school age. "Going to the market" became the main source of their family's livelihood instead of being a secondary source only mobilized during idle time between crops, as in the past.

As of 2014, about 45 percent of households in the village continued to cultivate the remaining agricultural land and land rented from surrounding villages, growing the peaches La Ca village is famous for and intercropping them with vegetables. Sales of peach blossoms by La Ca village residents improved when they were able to acquire 30 hectares of peachtree flowers in Nhat Tan (a famous flower village of Hanoi) that had been converted into urban projects in 2000 (Trần Thị Hồng Yến 2013: 135). Households usually rent between 5 and 7 *sào* to plant peaches, bringing an annual income of between 10 and 30 million VND per *sào*, depending on the weather and the market. (There are some successful peach growers with revenues of up to 300 million VND per year). Peach growers are usually middle-aged men who are accustomed to farm work and don't want wage-earning jobs in factories or the service sector. However, in recent years, land rental has been more challenging due to continued land acquisition in the village. At the same time, due to extreme weather and an unstable market, the number of peach-growing households has decreased to only about 20 percent of all the villagers.

Vocational training: La Ca village

When asked in 2014 why they had not invested the compensation money on expanding their businesses or acquiring new job skills, many villagers argued that opening a new business or service is difficult and risky. It also requires a significant capital investment. Meanwhile, investing in vocational training is not practical given the high rate of unemployment. Many young people who have certificates still cannot find a job. The local government organized several training courses every year, such as car driving, hairdressing, or cooking. Not many young people in the village attended these courses as what they learned was very basic, making it difficult for them to find a job based on these courses. As in many other localities, vocational training for farmers who lost their agricultural land has not been found to be a suitable solution in La Ca village (Nguyen Van Suu 2009: 38).

Low-wage manufacturing and service-sector work: La Ca village

Field research results in 2014 showed that, at that time, the number of people converting from agriculture to other occupations and services was very small. People claim that few jobs were created by the project that had acquired their land. However, since 2016, more factories and warehouses have been set up in La Ca village and surrounding suburban villages. New urban areas in the region are gradually filling with people, and a large shopping center (Aeon Mall) has sprung up next to La Ca village, creating more job opportunities. Therefore, most people have begun to think that their livelihoods have become more stable. Many young people work in small-scale industries or are selling goods at shopping centers and shops, while middle-aged people may work as security guards, janitors, or employees of landscaping companies in the area. These jobs usually pay income of about 6 million VND (less than US$300) per month. In these ways, the urban growth of the city has absorbed displaced rural labor into the low-wage manufacturing and service sectors (Andreas et al. 2020).

Urbanization and agriculture: La Tinh village

La Tinh village was a purely agricultural village and large-scale land acquisition has not been carried out. However, under the impact of urbanization since 2008, people's livelihoods have changed rapidly. The percentage of households engaged in agriculture is only 30 percent, mainly middle-aged and older adults.

Retail, manufacturing and service-sector work: La Tinh village

Of the 700 households in the village, about 50 have opened businesses and service shops. About 30 households have houses or guesthouses for rent. Many workshops are owned by local people and immigrants coming from elsewhere. Young people in the village work for factories and companies all over the city. As in La Ca village, middle-aged people also work as security guards, janitors, and employees of landscaping companies for urban areas. There are also urban services in both villages, such as taxi-driving, freight, babysitting, and taking children to school. The per capita income of La Tinh village reached 44.5 million VND per year in 2020.

Land protests and social conflict

Protest and division in La Ca village

The protest in La Ca in 2008 did not cause major consequences (other than the paralysis of local authorities for a short time and a woman in the village sentenced to a year in prison for resisting law enforcement officers during the protest). However, it did create division in the community and rifts in social relations. According to many interviewees, around 50 percent of villagers were very concerned from the beginning about their livelihoods if they were to lose their land rights; they did not want their land to be taken away. About 25 percent of the residents wanted their land to be appropriated, as they no longer practiced agriculture. The remaining 25 percent were unsure. They let the local government and the majority in the village make whatever decision they wanted regarding the land, and they kept quiet when most of the villagers expressed their uneasiness over the compensation scheme.

Villagers who had participated in the protest referred to what happened as a "movement to preserve land" (phong trào đấu tranh). Meanwhile, other villagers saw them as a "protesting faction" (phe đấu tranh). According to villagers who considered themselves in between these two sides, the "protesting faction" was formed right after the land-taking decision was announced. This went against the local government faction, which comprised local authorities and people who supported the land appropriation. The impetus of protest was stronger at the beginning, and about 60 percent of households looked favorably on it. (It is significant that this number included both villagers who participated directly in the protest activities and those who supported the protest but did not participate.) Only about 10 percent of households in the village were active protesters and these were enthusiastic about all activities of the movement.

During times of protest, the residents were divided, and rifts developed in relationships between villagers and cadres and among the villagers themselves. When attending weddings, funerals, formal meetings, or meeting socially in tea shops, people often argued over land appropriation. As the protest faction gained strength, anyone expressing a different opinion would be readily criticized by others: not only by protesters but by relatives of local cadres, who criticized or questioned them about corruption relating to their support for the land taking, either openly or behind their backs. This severed relationships, forcing some village residents to maintain a distance from each other.

These days, many years after the protest, villagers have normalized their relations, but the rift has not completely healed in all cases. Especially for those 36 households who continued their protest,[9] their current relationship with local authorities is not harmonious. Despite threatening these households with social exclusion, most of the other La Ca villagers have accepted their right to protest, and they still maintain social exchanges with them during weddings or funerals. However, the protesters themselves feel they are different, and they are frustrated.

Potential division in La Tinh village

In the case of La Tinh village, interview results in both 2014 and 2021 show that, so far, the views of villagers on land appropriation have been diverse. Interviewees said that if residents are asked whether or not they want their agricultural land to be taken over in return for compensation, 50 percent will agree and 50 percent will disagree. All respondents recently agreed to allow the Vietnam Construction Corporation to carry out a project to recover 12.3 hectares in agricultural land – if they paid more than 500 million VND per *sào*, the same amount the project had had to negotiate and pay to the neighboring village.

Because most people have abandoned rice cultivation, about 60 percent of the households have sold their land in that field. However, most villagers want to keep the remaining land close to the residential area, converting it to perennial crops, using it for intercropping, or raising livestock. Alternatively, they are willing to pay a fee to the state to convert the fields into service land, to have a source of capital and livelihood for their families in the future. Therefore, if these lands are taken, there may be conflicts and protests by local people.

Local residents' perceptions of urbanization and land appropriation

In 2014, when asked how urbanization had impacted their lives, La Ca residents felt they had had more advantages than La Tinh people. This is because La Ca villagers had already benefited from investment in the city after urbanization, while La Tinh villagers had not.

Since the district of Hoai Duc became a part of the greater city of Hanoi again, most La Tinh villagers report that the city invests more in rural transportation and sanitation, compared with when the village belonged to Ha Tay province – but at an unequal and sometimes slower rate. They expect more fundamental changes to their infrastructure in the future.

Some people complain about the negative consequences of rapid urbanization, including increased social problems (particularly gambling) and the presence of newcomers who were not part of the village or who had nothing in common with village residents.

When asked about perceived urbanization (see Table 6.2 and Table 6.3), a quarter of the respondents explained that they think urbanization is "good." A quarter stated that urbanization is "not good," but nearly half felt the development had brought both positive and negative results.

Table 6.2 Village residents' opinions on overall advantages/disadvantages of urbanization

Opinions on overall advantages/ disadvantages of urbanization	*Village*		*Combined percentage of the two villages*
	La Ca village	*La Tinh village*	
Primarily disadvantages	9.0%	36.8%	23.8%
Primarily advantages	77.6%	21.1%	47.6%
Both advantages and disadvantages	13.4%	42.1%	28.6%

Source: Survey results in 2014.

Table 6.3 Opinions of local people on recent urban expansion and development in their communities

Ideas on recent urban expansion and development in their communities	*Village*		*Combined percentage of the two villages*
	La Ca village	*La Tinh village*	
Good	18.2%	32.7%	25.9%
Not good	26.1%	21.8%	23.8%
Both good and not good	55.7%	45.0%	50.3%

Source: Survey result in 2014.

In general, nearly half of people in the survey thought that the recent urbanization in their villages was both "good" and "bad." The remainder were divided into two groups. The numbers above give us a broad view of people's ideas, while the qualitative results show that local people's thinking on the impact of urbanization is complex. As La Tinh village had not lost land entirely, La Tinh villagers were more concerned about their future rather than experiencing real impacts of urbanization like La Ca villagers.

> I would say urbanization is good but the authenticity of the countryside will not be the same. Personally, I am worried when I see urbanization happen. Some people might not take responsibility and start doing things that are done elsewhere, like drugs or gambling. They have money so they refuse to work, instead they spend their money, which is harmful.
>
> (Mr. Giang, 73 years old in La Tinh village)

> Over the past 10 years there have been so many changes. The quality of the road now is very different. The countryside is very beautiful. However, I am very concerned about the negative impact of urbanization. When land will be appropriated, people might have spent all their money, they will become broke. Because they do not have any other resources.
>
> (Mr. Tuan, 60 years old in La Tinh village)

> Urbanization brings more advantages in transportation. We felt happy as the national road came through the village, but the household economy is still the same.
>
> (Mr. Dzung, 55 years old in La Ca village)

> Life looks more urban but not sustainable. I prefer the life before. When we were farmers, after harvests we did petty trade for extra income. Now we do not have rice land, so life is harder.
>
> (Mrs. Nhan, 50 years old in La Ca village)

> If we still had the land, life would not be superficial at first appearance like this, but it would be stable and long lasting. It is incorrect to say that life is very hard, but many people have already used up their compensation funds.
>
> (Mr. Thoa, 60 years old in La Ca village)

> Urbanization is only good for those who know how to take the advantage of it. They are people who already had capital before or land middlemen during land fever. These people could buy more land and market stalls for themselves thanks to urbanization. Most villagers could only build a new house. Only the old people have some savings. Young couples who are paying for their children's education suffer the most challenges.
>
> (Mr. Quang, 40 years old in La Ca village)

> For me, urbanization or land appropriation had no impact on my life because I have been always striving for a better life. I always push myself to find ways to earn my livelihood.
>
> (Mr. Tinh, 44 years old in La Ca village)

These contrasting views show that villagers have different ideas on the impact of urbanization. In general, people think urbanization is basically "good" as it improves their infrastructure. Without land acquisition and urbanization, it is difficult for people who work only in agriculture to build large and beautiful houses, but they consider the lives of most local residents to be no more than "average" (bình bình). Those who are active – and able to adapt to livelihood transformation – think that life after urbanization is happier and "cooler" than with their previous agricultural work. Those who would have preferred to have kept the land think that life is leisurely with an urban lifestyle but that people have no money, no property assets for security.

In both communities today, between 20 and 30 percent of households are engaged in agriculture. Most of these are middle-aged and older people who feel they are only suitable for farming and who lack the confidence or energy to switch to another job. Many of them hold the view that they want to keep arable land as a valuable asset for their children – a stable source of livelihood as a backup for the family – as other studies on the persistence of agriculture in rural Vietnam have shown (Nguyen et al. 2019).

Conclusion

What happened in the two rural peri-urban villages communities of La Ca and La Tinh village shows the strong impact of urbanization and land acquisition. As a consequence of a policy of expanding administrative units and exchanging land for city infrastructure, the two communities have been able to invest in spacious infrastructure with an urban appearance. In addition, people have often used most of their compensation money for land acquisition, or they have used the sale of agricultural land and a part of the residential land to build bigger and more attractive houses and to enable a more comfortable material life.

One of the most important changes for communities is the transformation of livelihoods after land acquisition and urbanization. As with other communities that have gone through this process, the people of La Ca and La Tinh have transitioned from primary livelihoods in agriculture to income from off-farm activities. Similar to the general trend in urbanizing communities, residents in the two villages have engaged in newly popular livelihoods, such as providing services, trading along village roads, renting accommodations, and working as hired labor for small-scale industries, factories, and companies.

However, a separate trend rarely mentioned in previous studies is the return to agriculture, increased agricultural production, and the desire to maintain agriculture in both communities. Interestingly, both in the case of La Ca village that has lost land and in La Tinh village that has not lost land, between 20 and 30 percent of households continue to work in agriculture. This is the part of the population that urbanization studies say has the most difficulty transitioning, because of advanced age, lack of dynamism, and low self-confidence. This traditional livelihood is only completely lost when people no longer have land or can no longer rent productive land – and most of those with farmland are middle-aged or older than working age. New jobs have also been expanded, helping people work more comfortably than before, but their income and status remains low in society because most of them have become the city's low wage working class. Many people in La Ca village feel that their community's economy has slowed down, while the surrounding communities without land acquisition have had the opportunity to develop more actively.

Urbanization and land acquisition have caused a series of social impacts (such as a growing gap between rich and poor and an increase in social problems, especially gambling, football betting, and loan sharking) that are rarely noted in published research. It is notable that in the two villages, especially La Ca village, land acquisition has caused a strong reaction by residents. As in other localities, opponents of land acquisition in these two communities mainly disagree with the low compensation policy and the differences in compensation levels between projects. The reaction turned into a land protest, causing conflicts and cracks in community relations. After all the emotions accompanying the land acquisition process – from being stunned, worried, and concerned about the future, to "floating" along with a large amount of compensation – most people think that urbanization is "good" or "both good and bad."

In order to minimize the negative aspects of that process and to ensure stable and sustainable development for the community, people expect the city government to pay attention to their interests in applying land acquisition compensation policy and to create jobs. In recent years, the state and Hanoi authorities have adjusted land compensation policy, allowing the piloting of specific mechanisms and processes in compensation and in project site clearance. The local government has adjusted the land price every year and consulted with affected people whose land was recovered. Private projects in these two communities recently had to raise the level of compensation support for people higher than for public-works projects. However, residents confirmed that collecting people's opinions when implementing the project was not done in an open and transparent manner. Today the residents' greatest hope for these two communities is that the government will enact policy allowing the conversion of land in overlapping areas or adjacent to the residential area, to service land. This is a strategy to create capital development for the people while ensuring the common interests of the city and state.

Notes

1 During the lockdown in Hanoi due to the Covid-19 pandemic (August-September 2021), I interviewed acquainted informants by phone and online. After the relaxation of travel restrictions, I was able to visit some families.
2 In 2008, Ha Tay province was merged with Hanoi city after a period of 14 years of being an independent province.
3 In 2020, the village had about 700 households.
4 In addition to financial compensation, the province also allows farmers to retain 10 percent of the reclassified land, referred to as service land, for use or sale like residential land.
5 Given the land fever from 2010 to 2012, La Ca people could sell their service land for prices ranging from 10 to 40 million VND/m2. However, most villagers had already sold their land for prices from 10 to 20 million/m^2 during that time.
6 SGGP Special Report Urbanization "Runs after" Peach Villages. Sunday, Jan 27, 2008. Consulted on 15–04–14.
7 It is difficult to count exactly the number of households offering lodging services. Over 1,000 migrants stayed in the area in 2021; however, many of them live at construction sites. Interviews show that about 1 percent of households in the village offer this service.
8 For instance, Regulation No. 36/CP of the Government on 29 May 1995, ensuring order and safety for roads and urban transportation.
9 At the moment, 25 households continue protesting, while 11 households have already stopped. The protest's leader was arrested recently.

References

Andreas, J., Kale, S., Levien, M., & Zhang, Q. F., 2020. Rural land dispossession in China and India. *The Journal of Peasant Studies* 47: 1109–1142.

Asia Foundation Australian Aid and T&C Consulting, 2014. *Public Land Disputes in Vietnam: A Multi-Actor Analysis of Five Case Studies with an East Asian Comparative*. Hanoi.

Borras Jr. Saturnino, M., Hall, R., Scoones, I., White, B., & Wolford, W., 2011. Towards a Better Understanding of Global Land Grabbing: An Editorial Introduction. *The Journal of Peasant Studies* 38(2): 209–216, http://dx.doi.org/10.1080/03066150.2011.559005.

DiGregorio, R. Michael, 2011. Into the Land Rush: Facing the Urban Transition in Hanoi's Western Suburbs. *International Development Planning Review* 33(3): 293–319.

Edelman, M., Oya, C., & Borras JR, S. M., 2013. Global Land Grabs: Historical Processes, Theoretical and Methodological Implications and Current Trajectories. *Third World Quarterly* 34(9): 1517–1531.

FAO, 2008. *Compulsory Land Acquisition of Land and Compensation*, FAO Land Tenure Studies 10, Rome.

Harms, E., 2016. *Luxury and Rubble: Civility and Dispossession in the New Saigon*, University of California Press, Oakland, CA.

Hồng Minh, 2005. Hà Nội giải quyết việc làm cho lao động khu vực chuyển đổi mục đích sử dụng đất [Hanoi Solves the Problem of Jobs for Labor in the Area of Land Transformation]. *Lao động & Xã hội* 270: 2 23, 39.

Kerkvliet, B. J. T., 2014. Protests over Land in Vietnam: Rightful Resistance and More. *Journal of Vietnamese Studies* 9(3): 19–54.

Kim, A. M., 2009. Land Takings in the Private Interest: Comparisons of Urban Land Development Controversies in the United States, China, and Vietnam. *Cityscape: A Journal of Policy Development and Research* 11(1): 19–32.

Labbé, D., 2011. Urban Destruction and Land Disputes in Periurban Hanoi during the Late-Socialist Period. *Pacific Affairs* 84(3): 433–454.

Labbé, D., 2014. *Land Politics and Livelihoods on the Margins of Hanoi, 1920–2010*, UBC Press, Vancouver and Toronto.

Labbé, D., 2015. Critical Reflections on Land Appropriation and Alternative Urbanization Trajectories in Periurban Vietnam. *Cities*, viewed 28 November 2021 <http://dx.doi.org/10.1016/j.cities.2015.11.003>.

Nguyễn Đình Tuấn, 2013. Biến đổi văn hóa trong cộng đồng dân cư vùng đô thị hóa (nghiên cứu trường hợp tại phường Định Công và xã Minh Khai, Hà Nội) [Cultural changes in urbanized communities (case studies in Dinh Cong ward and Minh Khai commune, Hanoi)], Cultural Anthropological PhD Thesis, Academy of Social Sciences.

Nguyen Duy Thang, 2004. The Impact of Urbanization on Poverty and Social Stratification: A Case Study of Hanoi Suburban Areas. *Sociology* 3(87): 62–70.

Nguyen Quang Phuc, 2015. *Urban Land Grab or Fair Urbanization? Compulsory Land Acquisition and Sustainable Livelihoods in Hue*, Eburon Publishers, Vietnam.

Nguyễn Thị Phương Châm, Đỗ Lan Phương, 2016. *Làng ven đô và sự biến đổi văn hóa: Trường hợp làng Xuân Đỉnh, huyện Từ Liêm, thành phố Hà Nội [Peri-urban Village and Cultural Changes: Case Study of Xuan Dinh village, Tu Liem District, Hanoi City]*, Social Sciences Publishing House, Hanoi.

Nguyen Thi Thanh Binh, 2017. Multiple Reactions to Land Confiscations in a Hanoi Peri-urban Village. *Southeast Asian Studies* 6(1): 95–114.

Nguyen Tuan Anh, Jamie Gillen, & Jonathan Rigg, 2019. Economic Transition Without Agrarian Transformation: The Pivotal Place of Smallholder Rice Farming in Vietnam's Modernization. *Journal of Rural Studies* 74: 86–95, https://doi.org/10.1016/j.jrurstud.2019.12.008.

Nguyen Van Suu, 2009. *Industrialization and Urbanization in Vietnam: How Appropriation of Agricultural Land Use Rights Transformed Farmers' Livelihoods in a Peri-Urban Hanoi Village*, EADN Working Paper No. 38.

Nguyễn Văn Sửu, 2014. *Công nghiệp hóa, đô thị hóa và biến đổi sinh kế ở ven đô Hà Nội [Industrialization, Urbanization, and Livelihood Transformation in Peri-Urban Hanoi]*, Knowledge Publishing House, Hanoi.

Nhĩ Anh, 2021. Đông Anh sẽ thu hồi hơn 1.000 ha đất làm 136 dự án trong năm 2021 [Dong Anh District Will Appropriate Over 1000 Hectares of Land for 136 Projects in 2021], *VnEconomy*, 3 May 2021, viewed 28 November 2021 <https://vneconomy.vn/dong-anh-se-thu-hoi-hon-1-000-ha-dat-lam-136-du-an-trong-nam-2021-646987.htm>.

SGGP Special Report, 2008. Urbanization "Runs after" Peach Villages, Sunday, 27 January, viewed 15 April 2014 <www.saigon-gpdaily.com.vn/Special_report/2008/1/61262/>.

Tổng cục thống kê, 2019. Tổng điều tra dân số và nhà ở năm 2019 [The 2019 Vietnam Population and Housing Census], viewed 28 November 2021, http://tongdieutradanso.vn/cong-bo-ket-qua-tong-dieu-tra-dan-so-2019.html.

Tran Duc Vien, Nguyen Vinh Quang, & Nguyen Van Dung, 2005. Rural-Urban Land Use Changes in Periurban Hanoi. SEARUYN: EU 5th Framework INCO2 funded research project, contract no: ICA4-CT-2002–10025, viewed 28 November 2021, https://citeseerx.ist.psu.edu/viewdoc/download?doi=10.1.1.517.9930&rep=rep1&type=pdf.

Trần Thị Hồng Yến, 2013. *Biến đổi về xã hội và văn hóa ở các làng quê trong quá trình đô thị hóa tại Hà Nội [Social and Cultural Changes Among Rural Villages in Urbanization Process in Hanoi]*, National Political Publishing House, Hanoi.

United Nation, 2014. Department of Economic and Social Affairs, Population Division. World Urbanization Prospects [highlights], Revision 2014, viewed 28 November 2021, <https://population.un.org/wup/default.aspx?aspxerrorpath=/wup/Highlights/WUP2014-Highlights.pdf>.

Vu Hong Phong, 2006. Impacts of Urbanization in a Peri-Urban Area of Hanoi: The Voice of Affected People. *Social Sciences* 5: 51–60.

Part 3

Navigating resettlement practices in large infrastructure projects

7 Development-induced peri-urban resettlement

Livelihood opportunities, but at what cost?

Jane Singer, Pham Huu Ty and Thi Kinh Kieu

Introduction

Vietnam's rapid economic growth in recent years has driven burgeoning demand for electricity supplies and infrastructure, spurring a proliferation of hydropower and other large infrastructure projects. As discussed in other chapters, this trend has in turn led to increasing displacement and resettlement of those "in the way" of development. Much of this displacement is due to large hydropower dams, which numbered 306 in operation as of 2016, accounting for some 35 percent of energy production (EVN Annual Report 2018). It has been estimated that, by 2030, approximately 300,000 people – equivalent to 0.3 percent of the total population – will have been displaced by dam construction.

Most of those displaced by hydropower dams in Vietnam are farmers, practicing shifting cultivation, rice paddy cultivation, livestock husbandry, hunting, and some supplementary livelihoods such as aquaculture or manual labor. As is the case for dam-displaced resettlees in other developing countries (Scudder 2005), displaced Vietnamese households have typically suffered from impoverishment after resettlement. Research has shown that the loss of highly productive arable land, due to displacement and resettlement after dam construction, tends to have the greatest adverse impact on household income (Cernea 2003). The insufficiency of replacement land (in terms of both volume and productivity) has been cited by many researchers as the greatest challenge for successful resettlement in Vietnam as well (Bui et al. 2013; Ty et al. 2013; Dao 2016). Many resettled communities in Vietnam have also suffered from increased morbidity, loss of homes, economic marginalization, loss of access to common resources such as forests and rivers, and community disarticulation, including the loss of cultural traditions (Singer et al. 2014).

Up to 90 percent of the displaced are reported to be members of Vietnam's 53 indigenous ethnic minority groups, who predominantly live in the upland river catchments where most hydropower dams are sited and who are heavily dependent on forest- and farm-based livelihoods (Minority Rights Group 2018; Bui & Schreinemachers 2011; Dao 2010; Ty et al. 2013). The high percentage of ethnic minorities among those involuntarily resettled is of concern, because this population suffers from high poverty rates and has a poor overall capacity for coping

DOI: 10.4324/9781003165774-11

with the shocks of displacement. According to a World Bank report in 2020, while ethnic minority groups accounted for only 14 percent of the total population of Vietnam in 2016, 73 percent of those under the official government poverty line were from ethnic minority groups.

While poverty rates have declined rapidly among majority Kinh residents, residents from ethnic minority groups continue to lag for most development indicators, including nutrition and health; household income; education; and gender parity. In the upland south central coast region, in particular (which is one focus of this study), more than 90 percent of ethnic minorities were living below the poverty line in 2004, compared with 15 percent of Kinh and ethnic Chinese residents (Swinkels & Turk 2006). This inequality has increased in recent years, even as the government nears its goal of eliminating extreme poverty. According to the World Bank report cited earlier, "these minority groups are poor because they are facing unequal access to human capital development and jobs" (World Bank 2020:55).

According to Baulch et al. (2002), the minority groups whose living standards have risen fastest are those with more education and Vietnamese fluency who have attempted to assimilate with the Kinh majority. Conversely, poverty rates are highest among geographically and culturally remote residents of upland regions.

Resettlement outcomes and location

The government's approach to improving post-resettlement livelihoods and living conditions prioritizes financial compensation and agricultural support. This has not proven successful for affected households resettled in remote rural areas, where replacement land is poor or limited and where supplementary livelihood prospects are few (as has been noted in several other chapters of this book). Resettlement on the fringe of urban areas would seem to promise superior outcomes, because displaced households can diversify beyond traditional subsistence livelihoods. Urban proximity – and exposure to novel agricultural techniques practiced by ethnic Kinh residents – may enable adoption of a range of market- and migration-based strategies. However, these economic opportunities may come at a cost for ethnic minority communities: peri-urban resettlement in areas dominated by Kinh residents may also be accompanied by strained social networks, increased economic inequality, and weakening of traditional practices and of ethnic identity. These effects can lead to a decline in overall community resilience (Nguyen et al. 2017b).

Resettlement of development-displaced residents in peri-urban areas has been a popular strategy in countries like China (Wilmsen & Webber 2016; Li et al. 2018). Peri-urban zones have been defined by Nguyen et al. (2017a:100) as "the area where traditional farming comes into conflict with alternative economic activities." Agricultural land in peri-urban areas is more limited than in rural areas, yet less expensive to acquire than residential land, and perceived opportunities for off-farm employment may make peri-urban sites an attractive resettlement destination for local governments. Yet these assumptions not only disregard the non-economic factors needed for successful adaptation (such as social networks and cultural practices) but also overlook the difficulty of mastering the skills and competencies that would allow farmers to transition to non-farm employment. This is particularly true for middle-aged and older farmers: Wilmsen et al. (2011) found that many of those resettled to urban or peri-urban areas after displacement by the Three Gorges Dam in China were unable to secure full-time employment and reported greater economic insecurity in their new urbanized settings.

Benefits and challenges for peri-urban resettlement

The majority of large hydropower dam projects in developing nations are located in remote river watershed regions that may host a significant population of ethnic minority or indigenous residents. Compensation for rural displacement typically includes productive land to replace prior land holdings; however, the high costs (to the government or project investor) of securing sufficient peri-urban land and resettling rural farmers in distant urbanizing areas has often precluded consideration of peri-urban resettlement. In some cases, however, particularly when poverty alleviation was an integral project objective, peri-urban resettlement has been implemented (Nguyen et al. 2017a).

The potential benefits of peri-urban life listed previously are predominantly economic. However, application of a more comprehensive "community capitals" framework in this research reveals more far-reaching implications of resettlement, encompassing changes in financial, human, natural, physical, social, and cultural capital as well. Cernea's popular analytical framework, the "Impoverishment Risk and Reconstruction" model (2003), includes eight risks that project-affected populations may face in the process of displacement and resettlement, namely loss of land, jobs, and homes; marginalization; morbidity; food insecurity; loss of access to common property resources; and community disarticulation. All eight risks commonly affect development-displaced populations in Vietnam, but, as noted earlier, perhaps the most significant are the loss of adequate replacement land and the loss of access to natural resources. Access to common property resources, especially forests and river fisheries (formerly important sources of household income, food security, and nutrition), have been found to act as a crucial safety net for farmers in case of poor harvests, as well as a diversified source of income (Kibreab 2000). In addition, the high cost and difficulty of procuring replacement land in peri-urban areas may result in resettled farmers receiving paltry allotments of productive land, thus necessitating additional non-farm income.

Social and cultural challenges may be equally profound. In some projects, the displaced may be resettled in dispersed areas or among Kinh ethnic majority or other minority-dominated communities. This can result in conflict over jobs and land and in ethnic tensions – yet it may also foster assimilation into the dominant culture by formerly isolated minority groups, accompanied by attenuation of indigenous language skills, cultural practices and identity. Finally, this process may promote a fraying of previously established social networks, as communities become less physically and socially cohesive.

In a study of Greek refugees settled in an urban area, Herschon (2000) found that strong community ties, traditional practices, and ethnic identity promoted maintenance of stable communities, despite weak infrastructure and inadequate government-provided social services. When comparing peri-urban and rural community resettlement, some studies have observed mixed impacts. Research on peri-urban post-resettlement communities near the Saguling Dam in Java, Indonesia, for example, found that improved access to education facilitated higher levels of educational attainment for children – suggesting the potential for higher incomes for succeeding generations and decreased reliance on agricultural production (Sunardi et al. 2019). However, bonding social capital was much greater in rural areas, which fostered smoother social integration and subsequent livelihood reconstruction.

The research discussed in this chapter sought to compare the livelihood outcomes and human, social and cultural capital of three selected resettlements, in order to shed more light on the relative costs and benefits of resettling ethnic minority communities in peri-urban versus rural sites.

Research sites and methodology

Ethnic Cotu communities at three different sites in central Vietnam were studied over a three-year period, from 2015 to 2017. The Cotu are the 25th largest ethnic minority in Vietnam, with 74,000 people who mainly live in the vicinity of the Annamite Cordillera mountain range in Quang Nam and Thua Thien Hue provinces in central Vietnam (General Statistics Office Vietnam 2019). Because many Cotu have traditionally lived along major river systems in upland regions, in recent years a large number of Cotu communities have been inundated by dam impoundment and resettled. However, only 8,700 now live in what are officially characterized as "urban" areas (General Statistics Office Vietnam 2019).

The Cotu traditionally practiced swidden agriculture, fishing, and hunting, but recent deforestation and loss of river fisheries, bans on the hunting of large game, and the loss of access to protected forest have curtailed these livelihood sources (Arhem 2010). Traditional Cotu culture is patrilineal and patriarchal, with women primarily responsible for farming (mainly swidden cultivation) and men for hunting, fishing, and carrying out ritual activities such as the annual buffalo sacrifice ceremonies that mark harvests and other seasonal events. In the past Cotu villages frequently moved location within a particular watershed area due to a decline in game or natural resources; outbreaks of illness; or conflict with neighboring villages (Ta 2002). This tradition of residential mobility promoted acquisition of home and building construction skills.

The traditional rural Cotu village is an administrative unit akin to all recognized Vietnamese villages, administered at communal, district and provincial levels and presided over by an elected headman. According to Arhem (2010), however, it is also a cultural unit embodying unique Cotu traditions and identity, led by local elders whose knowledge and judgment is recognized by other villagers. The Cotu believe that each village is linked to a supernatural guardian spirit whose protection must be sought through holding rituals and the sacrifice of a buffalo (Ta 2002). These rituals are conducted in or beside the community house, which is called a *guol* in Cotu: a wooden building on stilts with a broad thatched roof. Meetings of village organizations or visiting officials take place at the community house, as do Tet celebrations and other village-wide events, and it is a popular gathering place for young villagers. The guol houses the ceremonial village drum, and skulls of hunted wildlife adorn its walls. The guol has been called the "soul" of the village (Luu 2007).

The three research sites

The three research sites are described briefly here:

1 Gian Bi village, Hoa Bac commune, Hoa Vang district, Danang
A total of 123 households (440 people). The site is located 15 km from a Danang industrial zone. Households were resettled in 1997 as a poverty alleviation measure.
2 Bo Hon village, Binh Thanh commune, Hung Ta district, Thien Thua Hue province
A total of 54 households (278 people). The site is located 25 km from Hue city. Residents were resettled in 2006 due to dam construction.
3 Cutchrun village, Ma Cooih commune, Dong Giang district, Quang Nam province
A total of 95 households (450 people). The site is located three hours' drive from Danang. Residents were resettled in 2006 due to dam construction.

Methodology and data

The data collected for this article augments resettlement study results previously collected by Singer in 2013 and 2015 in Quang Nam province and by Pham between 2010 and 2014 in Thien Thua Hue province. Information was newly collected for the Danang province site. In this project the original data was supplemented by household surveys, focus group interviews and semi-structured interviews in all three sites. Survey respondents totaled 51 in Danang, 46 in Hue and 56 in Quang Nam; the interviews were conducted with village residents and present and former village and commune leaders.

Data for forms of community capital – financial, human, social, physical, natural, and cultural – were collected at each site, supplemented by manual coding for qualitative data and comparison across sites. While economic and livelihood outcomes have been the main concern of other research on resettled communities, this chapter will primarily discuss perceived social and cultural changes by members of an ethnic minority group, compared across geographic locations.

Living conditions and livelihoods for three peri-urban and rural resettlement communities

Gian Bi village

The oldest resettled community under study was Gian Bi village outside Danang, where most residents reported income from a range of sources, including collection of non-timber forest products such as thatch and honey; forest cultivation and management for a plantation enterprise; manual labor for road construction; subsistence agriculture; some labor migration to other urban areas; and, for those with a high school degree, employment in an industrial zone located some 15 kilometers away. Eleven of the 51 households reported at least one family member as living outside the village and remitting income, mainly from industrial labor or from teaching positions. The average monthly income was 2.78 million VND (Vietnamese đồng).

The village was established in 2002 as part of a government sedentarization and poverty reduction policy discouraging shifting cultivation and residential mobility for ethnic minorities in order to consolidate political control, improve opportunities for income diversification, and enhance provision of education and social services (Le 2018).

As a former village head explained:

> Over time, the number of Cotu residents in the village increased but the amount of productive land for each household decreased. We first were provided with land use rights for forest cultivation, but those rights were later withdrawn when the local government determined that our income levels had risen. We grow crops but the volume is small, so it's not economical to market them ourselves in the city; we sell them cheaply to Kinh traders.

Bo Hon village

The village of Bo Hon in Thua Thien Hue province consists of 55 households, with each having been allocated 1 to 2 hectares of productive forest land after resettlement in 2006. The new location is some 15 kilometers from their original village, which was inundated due to construction of the Binh Dien hydropower dam. Earlier research revealed that total land area greatly declined after resettlement, from 618 hectares in 2004 to 94 hectares in 2009 – an 85 percent decrease (Nguyen et al. 2017a). Common pool resources such as fish and non-timber forest products also showed dramatic reductions.

The main sources of agricultural livelihood are from cassava cultivation in forest areas; acacia plantations at sites 2 to 3 kilometers from the village; and livestock husbandry, while some new crops, such as lemongrass and pineapples, are increasingly significant. In addition, 15 of the households sampled were receiving monthly pension or veterans' payments, while 12 households reported at least one member having migrated to Ho Chi Minh City or other urban areas for employment. A Binh Thanh commune official explained that several projects promoting crop diversification, forest allocation, and livestock husbandry had been implemented in the village by the World Bank and by Dutch and Japanese ODA (official development assistance) agencies, but that the villagers' low educational levels limited the programs' effectiveness (personal communication 2015).

Cutchrun village

The village of Cutchrun, comprising the two adjacent hamlets of A Den and Tro Gung, is located in remote upland Quang Nam province, along the A Vuong river, a tributary of the Vu Gia river system. In 2006, due to construction of the A Vuong hydropower dam by the national electricity utility Vietnam Electricity (EVN), the exclusively Cotu villagers were resettled from their original riverside site to their current location, which is within the same district. The resettled households were each allocated a residential plot measuring 400 square meters (Asian Development Bank 2007); 750 square meters of land for upland cultivation; and 500 square meters for wetland rice cultivation. The main livelihood sources are paddy rice and upland rice cultivation, cassava, livestock, and other agricultural subsistence practices. There is virtually no off-farm employment, except for occasional construction work and oft-delayed payments from EVN for forest protection as part of a Payments for Forest Environmental Services (PFES) benefit-sharing scheme.

Original research, conducted mainly in 2012 and 2013 in Cutchrun using the Sustainable Livelihoods framework (Scoones 2009), revealed acute post-resettlement livelihoods and living conditions that were substantially below the villagers' original living standards (Singer et al. 2015). Physical capital (including electricity, roads, a school and other infrastructure) promised improved opportunities for well-being, but a lack of arable land and poor financial and human capital constrained their ability to diversify crops, to acquire new skills and livelihoods, or to migrate outside the region to urban or industrial centers. In focus group meetings, the villagers identified a lack of productive land as their greatest challenge, followed by a lack of water for drinking and irrigation.

The main project investor, EVN, arranged for construction of similarly designed stilted concrete block houses for each family. However, many villagers complained of shoddy home construction and inappropriate design, which required them to repair storm-damaged stairways, add on kitchen facilities, and convert the ground floor into living space by erecting walls and installing flooring. They also collaborated to construct and maintain a traditional thatch-roofed *guol*, or community house, which became an important social and cultural hub for the community. The *guol* experienced frequent use by young people and adults alike, for weddings and rituals, village meetings, visits by government officials, and informal gatherings.

Comparing rural and peri-urban human and financial capital

A comparison of average monthly income between the three sites found that the highest reported monthly income was in Gian Bi, Danang, with an average of 2.78 million VND, compared to 2.18 million VND for Bon Ho in Hue and only 910,000 VND for Cutchrun in rural Quang Nam. It should be noted, however, that average monthly household expenditures for the two peri-urban sites, at 1.75 million for Gian Bi and 1.62 million for Bon Ho, were also much higher than for Cutchrun, which had an average monthly outlay of only 640,000 VND. Net income showed less variation, at 1.033 million VND, 566,000 VND and 270,000 VND, for Gian Bi, Bo Hon, and Cutchrun, respectively. The percentage of survey respondents under the poverty line was 28 percent for Bo Hon, 30 percent for Gian Bi, and 74 percent for Cutchrun in Quang Nam. This conforms to expectations of higher levels of poverty in upland areas, particularly those predominantly comprising ethnic minorities, compared with lowland and urban areas in Vietnam.

When asked to identify "main sources of income," the Quang Nam households selected agriculture, followed by acacia plantation, PFES payments and manual labor. In contrast, industrial and manual labor were selected by the largest proportion of respondents in both Hue (77 percent) and Danang (71 percent), followed by farming, acacia plantation, and livestock for Hue and by PFES payments, acacia, and livestock for Danang, respectively.

Non-farm employment was far more accessible in Hue and Danang than in Quang Nam. Jobs in an industrial zone in Gian Bi, Danang, and manual work such as construction and acacia plantation labor in Bo Hon, Hue were supplemented by labor migration by young residents and by a few well-educated teachers and doctors. The younger group went to textile factories or to other industrial work in major urban hubs like Hanoi or Ho Chi Minh City. Of the survey respondents, 22 percent of the Danang households, 26 percent of those in Hue, and only 7 percent of the Quang Nam households reported that at least one family member had engaged in labor migration, and, in the case of Quang Nam, most of those who did migrate stayed within the region.

In earlier interviews, Cutchrun residents cited the remoteness of urban centers; lack of education; need to care for children or elderly parents; and few contacts outside the villages as restricting their opportunities for labor migration (Singer 2014). Sociologists like Ali and Hartmann (2015) have reported that, in certain parts of the developing world (including in the Philippines, India and Vietnam), there is an expectation that young and able family members will migrate globally or domestically to secure a flow of needed remittances, thus creating a set of norms and values they call a "culture of migration."

Yet this migrant flow is dependent on access to migration networks; some level of education (typically high school or above); and initial financial assets to cover transportation and brokers' fees – all lacking for households in Cutchrun. Of the three sites, respondents in the long-established village of Gian Bi reported the highest percentage of children accessing secondary and tertiary education, with 21.6 percent graduating from high school compared with 13 percent in Hue and 10.7 percent in rural Quang Nam. University graduates accounted for 9.8 percent of adults in Gian Bi compared with 6.7 percent in Hue and 3.6 percent for the Quang Nam site. Until young people in Quang Nam can attain these minimal requirements, labor migration, a critical modern pathway for economic advancement, will remain largely beyond their reach.

Post-resettlement changes in social capital

The research also raised some possible concerns over social and cultural capital issues such as weakened post-resettlement community cohesion, social networks, cultural practices, and identity – all loosely identified by Cernea (2003) as "community disarticulation." For the most part, the peri-urban survey respondents did not experience the hostility that many resettled communities have encountered from host community residents (see the chapters by Nguyen Quy Nghi et al. and Do Thi Le Hang et al.). In fact, nearly all the respondents in Hue and Danang characterized relations between local Kinh and Cotu as "positive." As one 70-year-old Bo Hon man said, "We have close relations with the Kinh here. We meet all day, every day. We've learned from them about animal husbandry." However, integration into the ethnic Kinh-dominated local society in the two peri-urban sites has been accompanied by many social and cultural adaptations.

Table 7.1 displays some of the differences in social characteristics that have evolved in the three geographically diverse settlements. The two peri-urban communities (although comprised almost exclusively of Cotu residents) live adjacent to Kinh and some other ethnic minority residents. Cutchrun, in contrast, is in a district that is predominantly Cotu. Other researchers have found attenuated social capital resulting from community resettlement, especially as indicated by the level of intra-community exchange of financial resources and farm labor (Tilt & Gerkey 2016; Nguyen et al. 2017a).

Within the villages, most survey respondents reported that mutual assistance remained strong after resettlement (74 percent agreeing in Hue, 100 percent in Danang, 98.2 percent in Quang Nam), but significant differences were observed for responses to other questions. For example, when asked if they would borrow money from neighbors, if necessary, only 6.5 percent of those sampled in Hue responded affirmatively, compared with 11.8 percent in Danang and 14.3 percent in Quang Nam. Similarly, 41 percent of survey respondents in Hue and 49 percent in Danang responded that they would ask their neighbors to look after their homes if they were away, while a significantly higher proportion (60.7 percent) of those in Quang Nam said they would do the same.

A 61-year-old man living in Gian Bi village explained:

> Although we villagers worked together in the forest and paddy fields before resettlement, today most people are trying to generate livelihoods independently. We go to the forest to plant acacia or to the factories, so we don't get

Table 7.1 Selected household survey results: Human and social capital

Village	*Site 1: Peri-urban Hue (n=47)*		*Site 2: Peri-urban Danang (n=51)*		*Site 3: Rural Quang Nam (n=56)*	
Children's educational level (%)	Elem./below	69.4	Elem./below	54.9	Elem./below	62.5
	Jr. high school	10.9	Jr. high school	13.7	Jr. high school	23.2
	High school	13.0	High school	21.6	High school	10.7
	University	6.7	University	9.8	University	3.6
Strong mutual assistance	73.9% agree		100% agree		98.2% agree	
Would borrow money from neighbors	6.5% agree		11.8% agree		14.3% agree	
Ask neighbors to look after homes	41.3%		49%		60.7%	
Cantril life satisfaction median score (1–10)	4.9		5.8		6.2	

> together much in the village. We rarely ask help from neighbors to borrow money or ask if they're sick. As they say in Vietnamese, "Den nha ai nay sang, tran nhai ai nay gai" [can be roughly translated as "If you only know life in your own home you cannot know how others live"]. If I do need to borrow money, I would ask other Cotu people, not Kinh. Kinh people are just for talking or drinking together.

With the diversification of livelihoods and employment opportunities in Hue and Danang it would be expected that income inequality would increase for the two peri-urban villages. A Gian Bi resident noted that families with more working-age members could earn more than small families from manual labor, while veterans and others with monthly pension payments were regarded as more secure than those dependent on seasonal crops. Interestingly, however, even though nearly all Cutchrun residents are farmers, the perception of a widening gap between rich and poor was indicated by both peri-urban and rural survey respondents, with positive responses chosen by 74.5 percent for Danang and 76.1 percent for Hue, compared with 64.9 percent for Quang Nam. The similarity in responses may reflect the widespread perception that some households fared better than others after the wrenching process of displacement and resettlement, regardless of the extent of actual deviations in household income.

Finally, the respondents were asked to assess their overall life satisfaction according to the popular Cantril Self-Anchoring Scale, with "10" indicating their best possible life and "0" their worst possible life. The lowest mean score (of 4.9 for Bo Hon in Hue) was surpassed by a score of 5.8 for Danang and 6.2 for Quang Nam. This difference is notable in that higher income typically correlates with higher scores on this scale, while a low score of 4 or less is more commonly found in communities suffering from stress, poverty and unease (Gallup n.d.). In this case, the highest scoring community, Cutchrun, reported the lowest mean household income, suggesting the contribution of non-economic factors to reported life satisfaction.

When asked if the respondents felt that their Kinh neighbors exerted any influence on their lifestyles or practices, 30 in Hue agreed and 13 disagreed, with four unable to agree or disagree. Forty-five Danang respondents agreed and six did not, while in remote Quang Nam, 37 residents felt that Kinh influence could be felt while 19 disagreed – an unexpectedly high response given the low number of Kinh residents living nearby. However, thanks to electrification in rural Cutchrun, television and other media now provide rural villagers with a glimpse of urban Kinh lifestyles, norms and values independent of personal experience.

An official in Bo Hon explained:

> We learned a lot from the local Kinh people, such as how to cultivate lemongrass and acacia and livestock husbandry. We often socialize with Kinh communities and have drinking parties, and some people have erected Buddhist shrines in front of the house, which we learned from the Kinh.

Cultural capital: differing perceptions of identity and traditional practices

Significant differences could be found when comparing the three communities on their adherence to Cotu traditions, practices, and identity (see Table 7.2).

Traditional dress and weaving

When asked if they often wear traditional black hand-woven Cotu dress, 26 Hue respondents responded affirmatively, while 20 did not. Traditional attire seemed more popular in Danang, where 44 answered "Yes" and seven answered "No." The highest scores were for Quang Nam residents: 51 saying "Yes" and only 5 saying "No." This is not unexpected, since many of the Quang Nam villagers can be observed weaving the colorful cloth on hand looms. Traditional weaving is no longer practiced by any of the peri-urban residents, although one man in Hue practiced Cotu basketry.

Practice of religion

Residents were also asked which religion they professed, if any. In Hue, 31 identified themselves as practicing Cotu religious rites and beliefs as compared with 19 who self-identified as "non-religious" and two residents who were Christian. For Danang, 31 identified as Cotu, 19 as non-religious, and 1 as Buddhist, while for Quang Nam 52 residents identified as Cotu and only 4 as non-religious. This may reflect more opportunities to engage in Cotu rituals, such as the buffalo sacrifice for the Tet holiday and Cotu-style funerary and wedding traditions in Cutchrun. In Bo Hon, rituals like the harvest festival or hunting rituals were less common than before resettlement, reflecting economic constraints as well as lagging interest in large traditional gatherings (Nguyen et al. 2017a). According to a local official, the commune government provided some assistance for holding a buffalo sacrifice festival every 5 or 10 years.

Maintenance of language and cultural identity

Varying degrees of acculturation could be seen when the respondents were asked about use of the Cotu language at home and about children's identity issues. When asked to identify to what extent their children seem to have adopted the ways of the Kinh majority, 39 percent of those in Hue and 40 percent of those in Danang claimed they were "completely or somewhat like Kinh people." In contrast, only 26 percent of the Quang Nam respondents felt that way; 30 percent thought they were more like Cotu or that it was difficult to choose. According to a Cotu commune official in Hue, the local residents usually speak Cotu at home and are called by their Cotu names, but at school they are identified by their Kinh names, which all households adopted after resettlement. Gian Bi residents suffered the loss of their family registries by fire during the Vietnam War, so they chose Kinh names and now tend to practice Kinh rituals for Tet and other holidays.

Although ethnic minority communities have been prioritized for incorporation in government poverty alleviation programs like Programs 134 and 135, and targeted by many NGO and bilateral ODA projects supporting ecotourism or traditional handicrafts, the government's position toward the assimilation of ethnic minorities versus the retention of strong ethnic identities continues to be ambivalent at best. The desirability of ethnic minorities adopting majority Kinh values and practices was implicitly recognized by legislation, such as Decree No. 79/2003/ND-CP, which promoted village participation in "building a civilized lifestyle, maintenance of security and order, abolition of bad practices, superstition and social evils" (Article 7, No. 2). In recent years, however, many local governments have come to recognize the tourism and economic potential of distinctive ethnic dance and music, clothing and practices, and have subsidized the construction of culturally significant structures like the indigenous community house. Whether these are little more than "ethnic symbols" or more meaningful indicators of strong ethnic identity, however, is unclear.

Although all three studied communities have received assistance in erecting traditional community houses, or *guol*, only in Quang Nam was construction and maintenance completely left to the community. As Luu (2007) explains, Cotu traditionally built their village *guol* themselves, without hiring Kinh carpenters: "By looking at the guol, people can see whether the village is big or small, and measure the skills and strength of the villagers" (Luu 2007:51). In style, the *guol* in Danang is broadly representative of Cotu tradition. The community house in Bo Hong, Hue, however, was erected in the style of a different minority group by the local government. At the time of the field visits, the structure stood mainly locked and unused.

Table 7.2 Selected household survey results: Cultural capital

Village	*Site 1: Peri-urban Hue (n=47)*		*Site 2: Peri-urban Danang (n=51)*		*Site 3: Rural Quang Nam (n=56)*	
Influence from Kinh neighbors	Yes	30	Yes	45	Yes	37
	No	13	No	6	No	19
	Can't say	4				
Often wear Cotu attire	Yes	26	Yes	44	Yes	51
	No	20	No	7	No	5
Religious practices	Cotu	31	Cotu	32	Cotu	52
	Non-religious	19	Non-religious	13	Non-religious	4
	Buddhist	1				
Children's names	Kinh	48	Kinh	44	Kinh	27
	Cotu	3	Cotu	1	Cotu	29
			Unsure	2		
Effects from Kinh proximity	Yes	45	Yes	30	Yes	37
	No	6	No	13	No	19
Cotu practices	Lack funds for Cotu festivals; rarely use *guol*		Rarely sponsor Cotu festivals; speak Vietnamese at home		Continue buffalo sacrifice festival, frequent use of *guol*	

Residents of the three sites were asked about affective perceptions of their cultural identity. In semi-structured interviews in 2013, 17 Cutchrun villagers were asked which ethnic identity they would select if they had a choice, Cotu or Kinh. Nine of the 17 responded that they would choose to be Kinh, with most explaining that this would enable them to access greater financial and educational opportunities. Seven respondents preferred to be Cotu, stating that they were proud to be Cotu and that they were accustomed to their culture or that they "had no choice but to be Cotu." (One interviewee had "no preference".)

A man living in Gian Bi noted:

> Our young people want to marry other Cotu people. If no one is suitable they will look for a Dalai spouse [from anther ethnic minority]. Only one man here has taken a Kinh wife, although some Cotu women have married Kinh men. Other Cotus understand them better and can live here more successfully.

Conclusion

Previous research suggests that there are a number of economic and livelihood-linked benefits for development-displaced residents who are resettled in peri-urban rather than rural areas, including improved access to education and to non-farm employment. We found that the peri-urban ethnic minority residents in our survey also valued the employment opportunities provided by their Kinh neighbors, such as labor on farms and acacia plantations, as well as their exposure to Kinh work ethics and practices. We also found heightened access to labor migration as an adaptive response that increased employment options for peri-urban residents.

Nevertheless, these economic opportunities alone will not ensure a quality of life free of impoverishment but also rich in social cohesion and ethnic pride. The rural residents expressed greater engagement with their ethnic traditions, higher levels of social capital, and greater life satisfaction than did their peri-urban counterparts.

Improved economic prospects for ethnic minority communities resettled in peri-urban sites should not come at the cost of cultural dispossession and privation. Continued mutual assistance can help resettled rural households to improve living conditions and to succeed in livelihood diversification. Indigenous knowledge, practices, and competencies (such as the ability of the Cutchrun Cotu to construct sturdy homes and community houses) may prove extremely beneficial in fostering community resilience and place attachment after resettlement. It is critical that resettlement action plans for large infrastructure and development projects integrate support for social and cultural resilience, particularly in resettlement to urban or peri-urban sites.

References

Ali, S., & Hartmann, D. (2015). *Migration, incorporation and change in an interconnected world*. Oxon, UK: Routledge.

Arhem, K. (2010). *The Katu village: An interpretive ethnography of the A Vuong Katu in central Vietnam*. Goteborg, Sweden: University of Gothenburg Sans: Papers in Social Anthropology.

Asian Development Bank. (2007). *Benefit sharing mechanisms for people adversely affected by power generation projects in Viet Nam*. Final report. Appendix 1: Rapid appraisal report on the A' vuong project. www.adb.org/sites/default/files/projdocs/2007/39379-VIE-DPTA.pdf.

Baulch, B., Haughton, D., Haughton, J., & Chuyen, T. T. K. (2002). *Ethnic minority development in Vietnam: A socioeconomic perspective*. World Bank Research Working Paper No. 2836. http://papers.ssrn.com/sol3/papers.cfm?abstract_id=636183.

Bui, T. M. H., & Schreinemachers, P. (2011). Resettling farm households in northwestern Vietnam: Livelihood change and adaptation. *International Journal of Water Resources Development, 27*(4), 769–785.

Bui, T. M. H., Schreinemachers, P., & Berger, T. (2013). Hydropower development in Vietnam: Involuntary resettlement and factors enabling rehabilitation. *Land Use Policy, 31*, 536–544.

Cernea, M. (2003). For a new economics of resettlement: A sociological critique of the compensation principle. *International Social Science Journal, 55*(175), 37–45.

Dao, N. (2010). Dam development in Vietnam: The evolution of dam-induced resettlement policy. *Water Alternatives, 3*(2), 324–340.

Dao, N. (2016). Political responses to dam-induced resettlement in Northern Uplands Vietnam. *Journal of Agrarian Change, 16*(2), 291–317.

Gallup. (n.d.). *Understanding how Gallup uses the Cantril Scale*. https://news.gallup.com/poll/122453/understanding-gallup-uses-cantril-scale.aspx.

General Statistics Office Vietnam. (2019). *Completed results of the 2019 Vietnam population and housing census*. www.gso.gov.vn/wp-content/uploads/2019/12/Ket-qua-toan-bo-Tong-dieu-tra-dan-so-va-nha-o-2019.pdf.

Herschon, R. (2000). The creation of community. In M. M. Cernea & C. McDowell (Eds.), *Risks and reconstruction: experiences of resettlers and refugees*. Washington, DC: World Bank, 393–411.

Kibreab, G. (2000). Common property resources and resettlement. In M. M. Cernea & C. McDowell (Eds.), *Risks and reconstruction: Experiences of resettlers and refugees*. Washington, DC: World Bank, 283–331.

Le, N. P. Q. (2018). *State-making and local response in North Central Vietnam*. Ph.D. dissertation, Okayama University. https://ousar.lib.okayama-u.ac.jp/files/public/5/56295/20181212145413284575/K0005835_fulltext.pdf.

Li, C., Wang, M., & Song, Y. (2018). Vulnerability and livelihood restoration of landless households after land acquisition: Evidence from peri-urban China. *Habitat International, 79*, 109–115.

Luu, H. (2007). *A contribution to Katu ethnography*. Hanoi: The Gioi Publishers.

Minority Rights Group International. (2018). *World directory of minority and indigenous peoples: Vietnam*. https://minorityrights.org/country/vietnam/.

Nguyen, H. T., Pham, T. H., & de Bruyn, L. L. (2017a). Impact of hydropower dam development and resettlement on the natural and social capital of rural livelihoods in Bo Hon village in central Vietnam. *Sustainability, 9*. doi:10.3390/su9081422

Nguyen, P., van Westen, A., & Zoomers, A. (2017b). Compulsory land acquisition for urban expansion: livelihood reconstruction after land loss in Hue's peri-urban areas, Central Vietnam. *International Development Planning Review, 39*(2), 99–121. https://doi.org/10.3828/IDPR.2016.32.

Scoones, I. (2009). Livelihoods perspectives and rural development. *The Journal of Peasant Studies*, *36*(1), 171–196.

Scudder, T. (2005). *The future of large dams: Dealing with social, environmental, institutional and political costs*. London: Earthscan.

Singer, J. (2014). *Examining the roles of multiple stakeholders in dam-forced resettlement of ethnic minorities in Vietnam*. Doctoral thesis. Kyoto University Graduate School of Global Environmental Studies.

Singer, J., Hoang, H. & Ochiai, C. (2015). Post-displacement community resilience: Considering the contribution of indigenous skills and cultural capital. *Asia Pacific Viewpoint*, *56*(2), 208–222.

Singer, J., Pham, H. T., & Hoang, H. (2014). Broadening stakeholder participation to improve outcomes for dam-forced resettlement in Vietnam. *Water Resources and Rural Development*, *4*, 85–103.

Sunardi, Ariyani, M., Febriani R., Maharani, G. S., Fu, R. H. Y. F., & Fujikura, R. (2019). Rebuilding livelihoods of the rural and peri-urban resettlers in post-involuntary displacement of Saguling dam construction. *Journal of Asian Development*, *5*(1). file:///C:/Users/eel%20main/Downloads/JAD-Saguling2019.pdf.

Swinkels, R., & Turk, C. (2006). *Explaining ethnic minority poverty in Vietnam: A summary of recent trends and current challenges Hanoi–Vietnam. Background paper for CEM/MPI meeting on Ethnic Minority Report, 28 September 2006*. Hanoi: World Bank.

Ta, D. (2002). *Understanding Katu culture*. Hue: Thuan Hoa Publishing House.

Tilt, B., & Gerkey, D. (2016). Dams and population displacement on China's Upper Mekong River: Implications for social capital and social – ecological resilience. *Global Environmental Change*, *36*, 153–162.

Ty, P. H., Van Westen, A. C. M., & Zoomers, A. (2013). Compensation and resettlement policies after compulsory land acquisition for hydropower development in Vietnam: policy and practice. *Land*, *2*(4), 678–704.

Vietnam Electricity (EVN). (2018). *Annual report 2018*. https://en.evn.com.vn/d6/news/-Annual-Report-2018-6-13–2118.aspx.

Wilmsen, B., & Webber, M. (2016). Displacement and resettlement as a mode of capitalist transformation: Evidence from China. In S. Price & J. Singer (Eds.), *Global implications of development, disasters and climate change: Responses to displacement from asia pacific*. London: Routledge, 59–73.

Wilmsen, B., Webber, M., & Duan, Y. (2011). Development for whom? Rural to urban resettlement at the Three Gorges Dam, China. *Asian Studies Review*, *35*(1), 21–42. doi:10.1080/10357823.2011.552707.

World Bank. (2020). *Vibrant Vietnam: Forging the foundation of a high-income society*. Main Report. Washington, DC: World Bank.

8 How to deal with hunger? Household strategies and rural livelihood diversification at a dam-induced resettlement site

Nga Dao

Introduction

In late 2010, having requested compensation several times without receiving adequate responses, a group of resettled villagers from one village in Vietnam's Muong La district, Son La Province, went together to the district center and held captive an officer from its Resettlement Board and a deputy head of the board. The villagers took turns guarding the locked office while relaying demands for compensation to the district authority. The officials were released the next day when villagers received their compensation money (Dao 2016). Resettlees experienced other types of adversity, in other districts, during the first three years after resettlement was necessitated by construction of the Son La Dam. In Moc Chau, Mai Son, and Yen Chau districts of Son La Province, for example, many resettlees felt compelled to return to their old villages for farming and grazing purposes – in defiance of orders not to do so and despite the fact that the original villages were located as far as 170 kilometers away from their new homes. In some cases, accidents happened during such trips, causing death or permanent disability among these resettlees.

These incidents – and many others like them – reflect the struggles and sacrifices of villagers who were displaced "for the national interest" to enable development of the Son La hydropower dam in the northwest uplands of Vietnam. As the largest hydropower plant in Vietnam and Southeast Asia, the 2,400-megawatt (MW) Son La hydropower plant has long been a symbol of development and modernization in the Northwest (Dao 2011). However, alongside its benefits for the country's economy and development (including both electricity and irrigation), the dam and its construction have had significant impacts on local people and on the environment in its vicinity and in downstream areas. The Son La Dam – in particular – and dam development in Vietnam in general, continue to raise concerns regarding displacement, land shortages, livelihood loss, and food security at nearly all resettlement sites (Pham et al. 2013; Dao & Bui 2015; Pham 2016). Resettlees, while struggling to make their homes in a new place, have often had to deal with other matters, including hunger, the fraying of community bonds, and loss of cultural practices and identity (Dao 2011; Tran 2011).

DOI: 10.4324/9781003165774-12

Focusing on a pilot resettlement site in Tan Lap commune, Moc Chau district, Son La Province, this chapter examines the emergence of new livelihood strategies and diversification among resettlees and seeks answers to the following questions: How do resettlees reconstitute their lives in the context of being forced to move and the resulting lack of land for farming? How effective are these strategies, and why do the displaced choose to use these strategies over other alternatives?

The aim of this chapter is to understand how people's resilience and adaptation, conditioned by access to land and resources as well as by particular social, cultural, and economic relations, have contributed to shaping their livelihood outcomes. I will focus on livelihood strategies and diversification, agrarian change, and market integration among resettled communities. The chapter begins with a brief discussion of livelihood strategies and diversification literature and its relevance for dam-induced displaced communities in Son La Province. After describing the study's methods, I offer an overview of the Son La resettlement project, followed by an exploration of the villagers' lives before resettlement; livelihood diversification and how coping and adaptation strategies in resettled villages have unfolded.

Understanding livelihood strategies and diversification

Over the last few decades, the definition of "livelihood" has been extensively discussed among academics and development practitioners. Even though there are many different definitions of the concept, there has been a consensus that "livelihood" is about the ways and means of "making a living" (Ningshen & Primrose 2018). Wallman (1984) explained the concept as follows:

> Livelihood is never just a matter of finding or making shelter, transacting money, getting food to put on the family table or to exchange on the marketplace. It is equally a matter of ownership and circulation of information, the management of skills and relationships and the affirmation of personal significance . . . and group identity. The tasks of meeting obligations, of security, identity and status, and organizing time are as crucial to livelihood as bread and shelter.
>
> (As quoted in Appendini 2001:25)

Wallman's definition of "livelihood" can be seen as an umbrella concept, suggesting that there are many intertwined and overlapping layers in human social life. In a similar vein, Bebbington (1999) considers livelihood as not only a matter of material assets but as including non-material aspects of human well-being. In other words, our understanding of livelihood must go beyond the economic or material value of life:

> A person's assets, such as land, are not merely [the] means with which he or she makes a living: they also give meaning to that person's world. Assets are not simply resources that people use in building livelihoods: they are assets

> that give them the capability to be and to act. Assets should not be understood only as things that allow survival, adaptation and poverty alleviation: they are also the basis of agents' power to act and to reproduce, challenge or change the rules that govern the control, use and transformation of resources.
>
> (Bebbington 1999, 2022)

There is a rich body of research drawing on the "sustainable livelihoods" approach developed by Chambers and Conway (1991), which demonstrates how individuals and households negotiate and restlessly work to improve their living conditions (also discussed by Ellis 1998; Bonnin & Turner 2014). The central objective of the "livelihood" approach, according to Appendini, is "to search for more effective methods to support people and communities in ways that are more meaningful to their daily lives and needs" (2001:24). Chambers and Conway highlight the importance of paying attention to livelihood interactions with resources and to community relationships, well-being, capability, and poverty. They consider a "sustainable livelihood" as one that can:

> cope with and recover from stress and shocks, maintain or enhance its capabilities and assets, and provide sustainable livelihood opportunities for the next generation; and which contributes net benefits to other livelihoods at the local and global levels and in the short and long-term.
>
> (Chambers & Conway 1991:6)

In this context, diversification can be seen as central to individuals and households' efforts to form sustainable livelihoods (Ellis 1998; Moser 1998; Bonnin & Turner 2014).

"Livelihood diversification," as defined by Frank Ellis, is "the process by which rural families construct a diverse portfolio of activities and social support capabilities in order to survive and to improve their standards of living" (1998:1). Livelihood diversification, therefore, should not be understood just as income diversification. Diversification can be motivated by livelihood distress over deteriorating conditions caused by displacement and disaster or can be considered as opportunities to achieve livelihood security under improving economic conditions (Ellis 1998; Collier 1988; Preston 1989; Bonnin & Turner 2014). Batterbury sees the process as a form of productive "bricolage": the ways in which villagers have constructed a livelihood system in response to local constraints and opportunities, and to broader patterns of income generating possibilities (2001). The term "plural activity" is often used to describe a situation in which agricultural activities are combined within and outside the production unit (household) – or where a combination of agricultural activities are carried out within the production unit, with non-agricultural activities carried out in industry, commerce, and/or services (Schneider & Niederle 2010).

In general, rural people are "combining livelihoods in new ways across sectors and developmental spaces, they embody new desires and aspirations, and their values are often different from those of past peasant generations" (Rigg &

Vandergeest 2012:7). Key determinants of diversification and adaptation include seasonality, differentiated labor markets, coping behaviors, migration, and accumulation (Ellis 1998). If we consider one or only a few determinants of livelihood diversification, we risk adopting a one-dimensional view of the forces shaping resettlees' livelihoods – because all of these determinants may be conceptually distinct but are rarely separable in practice. They are mediated through social norms and relations – including community and kinship (Berry 1989, 1993) – and gender relations within the household (Hart 1995), as we will see in the case of resettlees in Tan Lap commune. For resettlees in Tan Lap (as for resettlees from the Son La project and other dams), livelihood diversification is born of adversity (including displacement, poverty, hunger, lack of land, community breakdown, and separation). Their diversification was first for survival, but later some turned to "diversification for accumulation" when resettlees could purchase more land and expand their production (Hart 1994).

Study site and methods

This chapter draws on fieldwork in two villages (Doi and Long Coc) in Tan Lap commune, Moc Chau district, Son La Province in the northwest of Vietnam. The dominant population in the commune is the Thai ethnic minority (both Black and White Thai) (51 percent), followed by Hmong (22 percent), Kinh (16 percent), and others (Moc Chau Division of Statistics 2020). Tea and plums are two key agricultural products, along with rice, maize, and other subsidiary crops like beans, squash, groundnuts, and so forth. (See Table 8.1.)

Resettlees moved here from Trang and Dang villages of It Ong commune, Muong La district, Son La Province. In 2003, 49 households arrived in Doi village, but only 40 remained in February 2021; 9 returned to their old village or went elsewhere. Long Coc has 20 households, all of which belong to one clan that arrived in 2004.[1]

My first trip to Tan Lap was in April 2005, and I returned in May 2016 and June 2018 to learn how the resettlees have navigated their lives and recovered

Table 8.1 Land use and agricultural structure in Tân Lập commune

Total area (hectares)	*9,386.01*
Agricultural land	**7,926.35**
Rice	314.40
Subsidiary crops	2,784.14
Perennial trees	665.79
– Tea	(292.50)
– Fruit trees	(373.29)
Protected forest	2,911.79
Production forest	1,156.08
Ponds for aquaculture	13.15
Other agricultural land	81.00

Source: Tân Lập commune's 2020 socioeconomic annual report (Tan Lap Commune 2020)

their livelihoods after their displacement. The COVID-19 pandemic thwarted my plans to return in mid-2020. In early 2021, my research assistant helped me to carry out a survey with 30 households in the 2 villages and to interview 12 villagers. Over the span of almost 16 years since my initial visit, my research assistant and I have conducted 28 in-depth interviews with villagers from the resettled groups and from the host communities. I interviewed five resettlement officers at the provincial and district levels about Tan Lap pilot resettlement sites; seven representatives from the Women's Union, Farmers Association, and Youth Union at village and commune levels during my trip in 2018; and in 2016 we also conducted two focus group discussions to gauge villagers' views on adaptation and diversification in 2016 (Doi village) and 2021 (Long Coc village). Most of the interviews and discussions were conducted in Vietnamese, and I had the assistance of the Doi village headman for translation of the few Thai language interviews. For secondary information, I reviewed government policies on resettlement, compensation, and livelihood recovery. Books, national newspapers, professional reports, and relevant scholarly works were also used to provide a broader view on resettlement, livelihoods strategies, and diversification in Vietnam in general and at Son La resettlement sites in particular.

The Son La Dam

The National Assembly of the Socialist Republic of Vietnam (Decision No. 44/2001-QH10) formally approved the construction of the Son La hydropower project on the Đà River on 29 June 2001. It became the most controversial infrastructure project in modern Vietnam and required the largest resettlement of people in the country's history.

The dam itself was built in It Ong town, Mường La district, Son La Province, 350 kilometers northwest of the Vietnamese capital of Hanoi. The plant's designed power generating capacity is 2,400 MW, and the electricity generated per annum is expected to reach 9,429 billion kilowatt hours (kWh). According to the Vietnamese government, the Son La hydropower project was approved in the "national interest" and its construction had the following key objectives:

1 To provide electricity for socioeconomic development, industrialization, and modernization of the nation state;
2 To contribute to flood control in the rainy season and irrigation in the dry season in the Red River Delta; and
3 To contribute to promoting socioeconomic development in the northwest uplands and narrowing the development gap between the upland and lowland regions (Son La People's Committee 2006).

As the dam is located in the Northwest region, which is ranked as one of the poorest areas in Vietnam and is inhabited mostly by marginalized ethnic minorities, the government has particularly highlighted the project's first and third objectives in the northwest provinces where the affected people reside: Sơn La, Lai Châu, and Điện Biên.

Organizing resettlement and policy

The Son La hydropower project has displaced more than 100,000 people in the provinces of Son La, Lai Chau, and Đien Bien. In Son La Province alone, portions of three districts (Quynh Nhai, Thuan Chau, and Mương La), the whole of Quynh Nhai town, and a large part of Mương La district are in the submerged area, which includes 31 communes and 248 villages comprising 14,993 households (Son La People's Committee 2006). The most challenging task for the project was to organize resettlement.

During the dam's construction, displacement was divided into three main stages:

1 Preparation of the dam construction site (2003);
2 Resettlement of people who lived below the 140-meter water level of the dam (2005–06); and
3 Resettlement of people who lived above the 140-meter water level but below the 218-meter water level (2007–09).

There are 78 resettlement areas with 285 sites for 20,477 households. For Son La Province, 37,207 hectares were allocated for resettlement (both housing and farmland), 12,004 hectares in Đien Bien province and 9,278.3 hectares in Lai Chau province. The resettlement component of the project cost more than 26,457 billion VND (Vietnamese đồng), of which more than 17,417 billion was allocated in the government budget, and almost 9,040 billion VND was paid by the national utility Electricity of Vietnam (EVN).[2]

Due to the scope of the project, Prime Minister Nguyen Tan Dung issued extra legal documents specifically for the Son La project resettlement, in addition to general government decrees on resettlement and compensation. The key legal documents for the Son La resettlement program are Decision No. 196/2004/QĐ-TTg and Decree 197/2004/ND-CP. Supplementary policies include Decision No. 459/QĐ-TTg and Decision No. 02/2007/QĐ-TTG. Decision No. 196 elaborates on the resettlement budget, while Decision No. 459 offers detailed instructions on resettlement and assigning compensation. However, the first supplementary document, Decision No. 459 (dated 12 May 2004), encountered a series of obstacles in application (that is, land measurement and compensation) after a few years, and was later replaced by Decision No. 02/2007/QĐ-TTg. This second decision gave more detailed instructions for compensation, assistance, and resettlement for the Son La project. It included amendments and supplements relating to management practices and benefits for both resettlees and host communities. Since the project's resettlement component was assigned to local governments, the provinces of Sơn La, Lai Châu, and Điện Biên were entirely responsible for implementing resettlement within their constituencies. Therefore, each provincial government also issued a number of decisions to offer instructions for carrying out the national government's decisions in their own locales.

The government's guiding principle for dam-associated resettlement in Vietnam is that resettlees' lives must be better or at least equal to those in their home villages. The government probably adopted this principle from World Bank policies released in the mid-1990s. The government, assuming villagers were homogenous upland peasants, has pursued an egalitarian policy in resettlement, which means that all affected people receive the same level of support and subsidies related to displacement – regardless of differences in their employment, access to capital, social networks, resilience capability, and other characteristics.

In terms of compensation, each family resettled because of the dam project received 400 m^2 of residential land and 2,500 m^2 of farmland for each family member. Therefore, a family of four people would have received only one hectare of farmland – much less than the amount of land they had had access to before resettlement (Dao 2016). To support livelihood recovery after resettlement, the first resettlement policy in 2004 for the Son La project (459/QĐ-TTg) stated that each resettlee would receive 10 million VND[3] for livelihood recovery after resettlement and that data on land measured using a measuring tape in the source villages before resettlement was acceptable for valuing compensation for lost land. In the early stages of implementation, project officers used regular measuring tapes to measure the area of land lost, instead of land-survey equipment. However, a national decision issued in 2007 (02/2007/QĐ-TTG) affirms that only the first person in each family would receive 7 million VND for livelihood recovery support and that each of the other family members would receive 3 million VND for the same purpose. The policy also stated that only land data measured by land-survey equipment are acceptable for compensation of lost land; other types of measurement (such as by measuring tape) would now be invalid. These changes in policy caused quite a lot of controversy among resettlees and resettlement officials, especially for people who were moved in Stage 1 and early in Stage 2.

Tan Lap resettlement site

In the pilot resettlement project in Tan Lap, as I mentioned earlier, people were moved from It Ong commune, Muong La district. That was the first stage of the resettlement project, and villagers were moved in preparation for the construction of the dam site. During this period, unlike with the "land for land" policy that was applied in other resettlement sites after 2004 (Pham et al. 2013; Dao 2010), the government resettlement policy referred to "land for infrastructure," meaning that host communities had to give up a portion of their own land to resettlees in order to gain improved infrastructure (roads, electricity, and so forth.). At first, the resettlees did not receive complete compensation for land losses, since there were no detailed measurements of the land that they had lost in their old villages. Villagers in host communities also did not receive compensation for the land that they were forced to share with resettlees. People on both sides were very unhappy and complained to the local authorities, who considered these complaints before referring them to the central authorities. As a result, the compensation policy for resettlement was changed: resettlees received cash compensation for the difference between the area of land that they lost in their home villages and land received in resettlement sites. Host communities later received cash for the land that they gave up to resettlees.

For people in Tan Lap, the provincial government finally proposed a solution to compensate both resettlees and host communities: each resettlee received VND 10 million (equivalent to about US$670) regardless of how much land he or she lost, and host communities received 70 percent of the total amount granted to resettlees. Similar changes were made to the original housing policy. In the pilot sites in Tan Lap, people had to move into pre-built brick/concrete houses, which were very different from their traditional homes built from wood and raised off the ground. These concrete houses exacerbated the loss of ethnic identity. The resettlees were very unhappy and complained to the local authorities. The result was another policy change,[4] but it only applied to resettlees who moved in Stage 2 and Stage 3, which are not covered in this chapter.

Farming and livelihood before resettlement

Before being relocated, villagers from It Ong (like the majority of the population in the Northwest) were largely self-provisioning, with cash-generating activities such as cash crops and provision of water transportation along the river. In general, land for farming was not an issue, as every household had enough land to grow their crops. For people who lived near the water (river or stream) and had wet rice fields, methods of growing wet rice were passed down from generation to generation: how to move water from the river or stream into their fields; how to raise fish in the rice fields; and so forth.

Since the villagers had plenty of land for farming and their plots were scattered, people usually practiced extensive rotational farming. One year they would grow maize, soybeans, cassava, peanuts, and rainfed rice in some plots, and use others for grazing. A few years later, when the land was becoming eroded and infertile, they would burn the grazing plots in order to grow crops on them, leaving the former cropland for grazing. Usually after burning the field, they planted the seeds. They waited for the plants to grow, weeded two or three times per crop, and then harvested. They rotated farmland and grazing land. In the fields of the old villages, since they incorporated animal manure from grazing and then burned all of the grass and bushes on that patch before growing their crops, they did not need to use fertilizers. Their plots of land could periodically lie fallow and regain fertility. Because of this, they also did not use pesticides on their maize or soybeans. In terms of livestock management, people did not have to worry about learning intensive husbandry techniques in their old villages – they let their cattle (normally at least five to seven head per household) graze freely and needed only to keep an eye on them occasionally. One hundred percent of villagers who we surveyed said that cattle in the old villages were considered to be like household savings. They only sold the cattle when they needed money for important family expenses.

In addition, in the old villages, daily activities were organized in quite simple patterns of labor division, and gender played a very clear role. Only men engaged in outside work, which required going beyond the village boundaries. They also dealt with outsiders and did the heavy work such as chopping trees in the woods, carrying logs, and so forth. Women were in charge of work inside the house, including cooking, taking care of the family's daily meals, washing clothes, and cleaning. When they worked in the field, husband and wife always went together. They shared daily farming work based on individual family arrangements (Dao 2018). The connections and sense of tight community in the villages were strong, as one Doi villager shared with me:

> My family used to live in Trang village (It Ong commune, Muong La district, Son La Province). We had about five hectares of land, where we mostly grew rice and maize. Land never was an issue as we could work on as much land as our health permitted. Our life was quite stable because we always had enough food. Fish were abundant in the river, and we never had to spend a penny for food. I did not have to work as a paid laborer. Indeed, nobody in our village did. In our old village, no one worked for anyone for money, we only helped each other when needed. The family who got help only needed to invite everyone who helped them to join a meal or help others in return when asked.
>
> (Interview, 20 May 2016)

Farming land shortages and resettlement challenges

As in most other parts of the country and in Southeast Asia in general, land in the northwest uplands of Vietnam is a particularly important asset in social as well as economic terms. As land is not only a means of livelihood but also an indicator of security and happiness, the government has made a significant effort to address resettlement, rehabilitation, and livelihood issues in its laws and policies (Dao 2010, 2011; Pham et al. 2013). The legal framework for land acquisition in Vietnam has seen significant improvements since 1993 (Pham et al. 2013). *Land Law 2003* granted land users more rights, especially the right to compensation. More recently, Vietnam's *Constitution* (2014) and *Land Law 2013* have strengthened legal protections for people affected by development displacement, with provisions to identify them, inform them, and consult with them prior to any acquisition; to recognize certain customary land-tenure rights; to recognize and compensate for loss of economic activity on land; to provide replacement land as a compensation option; to compensate before possession; and to pay a relocation allowance when people must relocate.[5]

However, despite the government's efforts in improving its land policies, for a large number of dams and development projects that have required land acquisition and displacement over the last three decades, the prevailing issue in resettlement areas has been a shortage of land for farming. The majority of both the host (receiving) communities and the resettled communities were farmers. They had no other choice but to rely on land for farming. Only a large area of land for growing a variety of crops could help them sustain their lives without hunger. Land acquisition and displacement in these cases has caused many adverse impacts, as resettlees often lost their incomes and job opportunities – both farm and non-farm (Ding 2007; Zaman 1996). In general, according to the resettlement plan of the Son La project, the majority of resettled villages did not receive wet rice farming land; they were only allocated hilly subsidiary crop lands (NIAPP 2005). In my research site, 100 percent of resettlees to Tan Lap from It Ong commune used to have wet rice land; none of them received suitable land as part of their resettlement compensation. Generations of wet rice farming experience became virtually useless in the new locations.

The most vivid change, that all of the resettlees to whom we spoke recognized and rued in the new villages, was the need to purchase everything, from rice to foodstuffs (such as eggs, fish, and even vegetables). One woman from Doi village said:

> The worst thing [that has] happened to us here is to think about how much money we need. Money, money, money – that [is] what I had to worry about from morning when I woke up until midnight. In the old village, we did not really use much money. We grew our rice, vegetables, maize, and beans. We raised our pigs, cattle, and chicken to sell and for our own consumption. The forest was nearby where we could collect bamboo shoots and fuelwood. We caught fish in the river and ponds. We did not have to buy food every day. At the end of each working day, we were at ease and could sleep well at night without having to worry about what to eat the next day. But when we moved here, we had to buy everything in the market.
>
> (Interview, 15 June 2018)

Since it was a pilot site, Tan Lap resettlees received their farmland quickly, within one month of their arrival. All resettlees did not experience problems with land issues in the same way, even though they may have received a similar amount of land per person. In Doi village, each person received about 2,000 m^2 of both tea land (land with tea trees on it (1,500 m^2)), and of upland farmland (500 m^2).[6] The farmland in Doi is located near to the village, so villagers are not too inconvenienced by traveling to work on their land every day. But they did face many other problems in recovering their livelihoods, and the most obvious of these were land shortages and a lack of skills for tea cultivation (see Box 8.1).

Box 8.1 The story of Doi Village

> It was very hard to persuade our villagers to move. It took at least five to six meetings with each family. At the end, about 15 to 16 households did not want to move, but they were forced onto trucks at the last minute. When we came here, we were very nervous. We did not know how we would continue our lives in the new place. I had bad dreams every night for a very long time. My brothers and sisters did not move here. We were assigned different locations. So, my family has been separated. Almost 17 years have passed, but every time I dream, I dream about

my old village. Never about the life here. The resettlement houses are very small. We did not have enough space for the kids, no gardens. We used to live in wooden houses on stilts, but everything here is brick and cement. It took many years for us to get used to it, but we still don't like it, even now. We had running water and electricity when we came, but only got three months free; after the first three months, we have to pay the fee. Land shortage was a serious issue. We were given land for tea growing, but we know nothing about tea, so many of us abandoned the tea trees and grew maize on our plot of only 500 m^2. We were hungry and we needed money. In the old village, we never had to worry about land, never experienced any conflicts related to land. But here, in the early stage, there were quite a number of complaints and grievances as people felt it was not fair in land allocation and compensation. There were even grievances made to the district and province. It took a while for problems to be solved. We had 49 households at first, but nine of them could not stand the life here. They left. They returned to the old village, but right now, we don't even know where two of them are. People were devastated at being uprooted.

(A Doi villager, 17 February 2021)

The story for Long Coc village is different (see Box 8.2). In the old village of Dang, they had 60 households. Due to land shortages in the resettlement sites, they were asked to move to three separate villages: Na Phay, Long Coc, and Nam Khao. The three main clans automatically divided themselves and settled in the abovementioned three villages, all located in Tan Lap commune. They all had to integrate with host communities (*ở xen ghép*). They did not receive any paddy rice land, either, even though these three villages are located in a valley with a large area of paddy rice land.

Box 8.2 The story of Long Coc Village

The Project Management Board let some of us come to see the resettlement site before we moved here. A cadre showed us the village. We saw a large area of paddy rice surrounding the village and thought "Oh, that's great. We won't be hungry if we could have some paddy rice land." So, we agreed to move and came back to persuade other villagers to move as well.

However, when we arrived, it turned out that all of the paddy rice land belong to the host communities and the host communities did not agree to share with us. We did not have tea land either because tea land was already assigned to those who moved in before us. The cadre showed us an area deep in the forest, which was very far from the village, and told us to clear that forest patch for farming. Initially, they measured and planned to allocate about 2,500 m^2 per person, as set out in the province's resettlement policy, but when we learned that the area was designated for us 20 households only, we took the initiative to ask them if we could divide the land ourselves. As a result, we got a bit more – about 3,000 m^2 per person.

We then worked very hard to clear that forest land. Since the land was deep in the forest, very steep, and there was no road, we were, at the same time, chopping trees, burning bushes to build our field, and creating a road to lead to the field. The field location made it very difficult for us all. If we left the house at 6 a.m., we reached to the field at 10 a.m. We worked in the field from 10 a.m. to 3 p.m., then walked back to get home by around 7 p.m. During that time, we filed so many complaints to the commune, district, and province, but had no response until the fourth year. The Project Management Board brought a bulldozer to make a road for us to the field. After that we could ride motorbikes to the field. However, because the road was steep and there was only rocks and dirt, after a few heavy rains, we could not use the road as we would like to. Sometimes, we left our field untended, other times, even during maize harvest time, we could not come to collect the maize as it cost even more to come and bring out the maize than the money we could get from selling the maize.

We were all very miserable because we did not have enough to eat, and compensation money took forever to come. We only received a subsidy for rice and crops once every three months for two years. In the first two years, we all suffered from hunger for two to five months a year.

(Focus group discussion, February 2021)

As a consequence, resettlees in Long Coc had to borrow money more frequently. Our survey revealed that all of the villagers were in debt, yet no one reported being in debt before the move. They borrowed from the Vietnam Bank for Social Policies, a government-owned bank that lends money to poor people at low interest rates. Each household was allowed to borrow 10 to 20 million VND, which was not enough to support their daily needs and production inputs in one year. Most of the villagers turned to the informal sector and borrowed at a 20 percent annual interest rate to pay for their food and other necessities. They often paid back the debt in May when they harvested their maize, but most of the time it was only enough to pay off the incurred interest, not the principal.

Conflicts between resettled and host communities are another challenge for resettlees. According to our interviewees, young people (under 25) fought regularly in the first five years after the move. Host communities considered resettlees as outsiders who came to take their land and competed with them for water resources. Host communities were also very upset to see resettlees clear common land and turn it into private plum orchards. Both communities and their headmen had to meet monthly to reconcile various conflicts. Doi village's headman recalls:

> Every month I told the other headman that, because of the country's industrialization and modernization, we left our homeland to come here. You shared some land with us so we can recover our life. We did not steal land or anything from anyone.

But Doi villagers who are members of the host community had different opinions:

> We had no problem at first, but when construction workers came here to build resettlement sites, they caused chaos and disturbed our peaceful life. Then, we realized that the government was not fair in compensation. Project officers came to promise many things but did nothing. Local authorities have always been on the resettlers' side, saying that they had to sacrifice so much so we had to compromise. We began to hate the resettlers. But we had to admit that they [the resettlees] work so hard to recover their lives. We can't compare ourselves to them. Now a number of them are even wealthier than us.
>
> (Interview, June 2018)

Learning new ways of living in resettlement sites

When the resettlees moved to Tan Lap, there were three different models of household economies that the province and the Resettlement Management Board imposed on the resettlees, based on tea, dairy cows, and special types of bamboo shoots (*măng tre Bát Độ* and *trúc*). This was despite the fact that commune authorities were strongly against the latter two, arguing that they were not appropriate for local conditions. Project officers brought 50 cows and released them at the edge of the village. Stronger animals ran farther so households at the end of the village captured and kept them. Households near where the animals were released kept the weaker ones. In general, resettlees had no experience in raising dairy cattle, so most of the cows died within months. Villagers returned the five surviving animals to the project office. Bamboo was given to villagers to grow in rocky topography areas where they could not grow tea. The bamboo shoots also died after a few months. Tea was the only remaining option.[7]

A woman in Doi village shared her thoughts on tea growing in May 2005:

> Oh, we only know how to grow rice and maize. Tea is a foreign tree to us. Growing maize, you only need to weed twice or three times and you can harvest. Tea needs more care and techniques.

Moving from a paddy rice growing area to an area with a different micro-climate and farming practices, where tea was the dominant crop, was a great challenge for resettlees in Doi village, who had already suffered so much from loss of income and community networks. But as Ellis (2000) points out, of all people, the poor tend to be engaged in complex, plural activities or livelihood diversification for their survival. Resettlees in Doi and Long Coc villages were no different.

As cash became the most urgent need in their new home, villagers developed different strategies to raise the money needed for their families' survival. For resettlees here, the first three years were probably the most difficult. Each family had their own arrangements for survival, and gender played a very important role. Villagers started to diversify their activities, combining agricultural with non-agricultural activities, focusing on paid labor. Most villagers, both women and men, had to sell their labor every day in order to earn a living. They maintained their subsistence through their integration into wider social divisions of labor and markets. As their families' livelihoods no longer depend entirely on farming activities, many villagers are now part-time farmers or "marginal farmers" – the term that Hazell et al. (2007) use for farmers who cultivate small tracts of land and have livelihoods that depend on various activities beside farming.

In Doi village, as every household received tea land, they had to learn how to grow and nurture tea trees. In the first two years, only about 20 percent of households devoted their time to learning how to grow tea, even though they all received land that already had young tea trees.[8] Other households only focused on maize as this was a familiar crop. Moc Chau district and Tan Lap commune sent agricultural extension workers to the village to guide villagers in how to grow tea. Villagers learned to plant, weed, apply fertilizers, and other planting techniques like grafting and extracting. Indeed, even though tea needs more care when compared to maize, it is not a very time-consuming crop. Villagers only need to dedicate about one week per month to tending the trees, including weeding and applying fertilizers. For those who started working with the tea trees when they received their land, their first crop was ready to harvest by late 2007. Tea leaves are harvested five times annually (averaging one harvest every 90 days). However, in the first three years after they moved in, it was quite common for the wife to receive training in tea cultivation and take care of the children and the elderly, while the husband returned to their old village to work. The distance between the old and new villages is almost 170 kilometers, but in the period immediately after the move, all of the resettled men in Doi village returned to their old village.

One man told me:

> Oh my, for two years, I was unable to do anything here. I missed my old village so dearly, so I walked to the bus station and took the bus back. It was a four-hour ride. I went back to see how other families in my old village were doing, I wandered around and checked my old land and crops. After I received my compensation money, I bought a motorbike, just like everyone else in the village. I rode my motorbike to the old village and worked as a motorbike driver (xe ôm) for workers who worked at the construction site of

> the Son La Dam for three years. I came home to see my family once every three or four weeks.
>
> (Interview, 27 June 2018)

For the women, their struggle was not the same. One woman from Doi village recalled:

> My husband bought a motorbike and returned to the old village to work as xe ôm. I had to stay home and take care of everything. It was similar for most of other families here back then. Every day I got up at 6 a.m. to cook for three children, then I went to plant tea. We had 7,000 m^2 of tea land and I worked on it all by myself. I had to ask people to learn how to do it step by step because I did not understand much during the training. I had to learn by doing it. I came back at 11a.m. to have lunch. The two big kids went to school, the little one was four years old staying home all by himself. At 2 p.m. I left for work again until dark. It was the same routine every day. When I did not work on my tea farm, I went around to ask if anyone needed labor. I tended cows, I did weeding, applying fertilizers, planting, and picking plums for other families who hired me. Each day I got about 150,000 VND (about US$12). I was not used to that type of life. Some days I was too tired and did not know what to do, so I cried. I cried because I missed my home village, because I never thought my life would be that hard, because I worried if I did not work that much, my children would go hungry. I missed my husband. We used to do everything together. . . . Time went on and things started to get better when we had the first tea harvest. We got a bit more money from the tea, and my husband came back here for good, so I spent less time working for other people.
>
> (Interview, 27 June 2018)

After seeing other families starting to collect income from tea trees, the rest of the villagers also started to grow tea. At first, tea was sold to the Tan Lap Tea Cooperative, but after one year, the cooperative stopped operating due to human resource issues, and villagers had to bring their tea 20 kilometers from home to sell it on the roadside. If they couldn't sell all of their tea each day, they had to throw it away. Fortunately, in 2010, the Tan Lap Tea Cooperative restarted operations and once again purchased the villagers' tea, which offered them a more stable income. In 2006, a Taiwanese tea company arrived in the commune to build a tea processing factory. In 2010 they started to organize trainings for villagers on how to plant, care for and pick tea leaves by the company's standards. After the villagers followed all of their instructions for three years, the company started to buy their tea at a good price in 2013. But the company stopped doing so in 2017 when villagers began to interplant plum trees on tea land.

With additional income from tea and paid labor, some households began to purchase paddy rice land and other farmland from members of the host communities. They also collectively decided to claim common land in the forest as their own. As a result, about 75 percent of the resettlees in Doi village are ranked as "medium" or "wealthy" by the commune's standard. However, for families without members who can provide manual labor, things are much more difficult. Mrs. Tang's household is one example. As the family could not rely on the 6,000 m^2 of tea land allocated to them, for ten years she and her husband returned to the old village to work, leaving their children on their own in the new village. In 2015, her husband suffered a stroke and was paralyzed, so they returned to Doi village. Without money, they could not afford to buy any farmland there. Her family suffers from food shortages at least one month each year. Four households have family members who are drug users and have also struggled to recover their lives and livelihoods.

Since their income has stabilized (thanks to tea production), the number of young people leaving Doi village to work in other provinces in the Red River Delta has declined. By January 2021, none of them were far away from home. They focus on tea, plum, and mango cultivation, occasionally working for nearby people or businesses for cash. The situation is not rosy for everyone. A middle-aged woman complained:

> We only have 8,000 m^2. Now the tea trees are mature and don't need a lot of care. My husband used to work hard when we had more land. Now he doesn't work much. I go to pick the tea and he just stays home. Very lazy.

Lo Van Lang is the village's success story (see Box 8.3). He was the headman when I first visited his village in 2005. When I returned in 2018, I was surprised to see how many changes Lang and his family had experienced.

Box 8.3 Lang's story

> When we had just arrived here, my wife and I worked like crazy. We both left the house at dawn to go to Co Do state farm (about 20 kilometers from home) to work. We did whatever they hired us to do to get money. The first year we did not have any income from tea, maize, or anything yet. We knew nothing about tea trees, so when we got the land, we abandoned the tea and only grew maize on the tiny plot we received. I was consumed by the thought of working to get money. Once you had money, you wouldn't have to worry about going hungry. Then I was consumed by the thought that if I had land, it would provide a safety net for me. So, we saved. We ate as little as possible and saved money to buy land. Nobody showed me. I did it because I had no other way. First, I bought cattle whenever I saved enough, one and then two, three . . . then I sold them altogether to get a bigger lump sum to buy land. I bought a total of about 6,000 m^2 of paddy rice land from host communities.

Because the life here was extremely difficult, some households could not stand it. They returned to the old village for good. They sold their houses. I bought one with 80 million VND (about US$6,100). Seeing that I was working as paid labor and could save enough to buy land and a house, other households followed me, and about ten households were able to buy paddy rice land. I also started to clear common land to grow plums. Of course, the authorities did not like it. Growing your trees on common land was not allowed. They summoned me to the office and asked me to stop. But I told them that I was hungry. My children were hungry, and we were miserable. If I did not do it, what was my family going to eat? So, they let me do it. Most of my neighbors saw me doing it, and they followed as well.

Since I moved here, I worked on so many jobs. But I've also learned so much. When agricultural extension workers came to do training on tea growing, I took note very carefully. When I worked in people's plum orchards, I paid very close attention to how they planted and tended the trees. I've learned that fruit trees like plums could provide a good income without much work like growing maize. So, when I went to the forest to clear land, I planted plums. Now I have more than 6,000 m^2 with a few hundred plum trees. I also experimented with a special variety of pomelo, the green-skinned ones (bưởi da xanh) that are very juicy and can be sold at a higher price compared to other varieties. And because I took any type of work available, I've also learned to do a bit of everything, such as construction work, carpentry, plumbing, so now I can fix my house if there are problems.

(Interview, June 2018)

In Long Coc village, the men did not return to their old village but worked to clear the forest area that was assigned to them and grew maize. Families who had strong teenage sons often did better in getting extra income. Most village boys dropped out of school at age 13 to work as paid labor outside the village. The boys worked as helpers in stores making doors and roofs, or on host communities' farms during the farming season. Others worked as porters or seasonal construction workers in Moc Chau town. While none of the villagers were in debt in the old village, at the resettlement site all of the households have borrowed from the Bank for Social Policies and from informal sources, at high interest rates, to buy maize seed, fertilizer, daily food, materials for house repairs, or sometimes, to purchase small paddy rice fields. One woman told us:

> I still cry thinking about the first few years after we moved here. No one could imagine how hard it was. Every day all of us worked from early morning until late afternoon to clear the land for farming. We had to move huge rocks to

> clear a path so we could walk to the field. Back then, every day, we cried to think about the land we lost in the old village. The good thing was, in the first few years, the land we cleared was fertile, and we could harvest up to 50 million VND per year only from maize. We also did all kinds of work we could find to get more money. But we couldn't save as everything needed money. Seven years ago, I borrowed 50 million VND to buy six small plots of paddy rice land. We harvest about 0.8 tons each year for family consumption. We haven't been able to pay the debt until now.
>
> (Interview, 17 February 2021)

Unlike in Doi village, where young people have stayed home to work in the tea fields and plum orchards, in Long Coc all of the young people, both female and male, have left the village to obtain work elsewhere – leaving middle-aged family members and the elderly to take care of the farmland. The young people often travel as far as Hai Duong, Hung Yen, and Bac Ninh provinces in the Red River Delta, which is over 200 kilometers away. If a family is able to save enough, they buy farmland from the host community so the parents can work these lands while the children continue working away from home and send remittances back to the village to help pay off debts.

One man (age 55) explained:

> I saved my money from compensation and from my sons working to buy 500 m^2 of paddy fields at the cost of 30 million VND so we can grow rice. For each crop (one crop per year) we harvest ten bags (each bag is 40 kilograms) and it's marginally enough for six people. We still have to borrow with a high interest rate for many other expenses, including food and agricultural inputs such as fertilizers (cắm quán). My sons work hard to send money home, but mostly it's only enough to meet our daily needs and pay for the interest. We don't know when we are going to be debt-free. My wife and I have never felt at home here. We tolerate this life. We are so tired of sending complaints to the authorities for so many years, but we don't have a choice.
>
> (Interview, May 2016)

Since the farmland for Long Coc village is very steep, after about ten years of growing maize, the soil degraded to the point that it could no longer produce good crops. Since late 2017, the villagers have replaced maize with plum and mango trees. In 2020, the trees bore their first fruits. However, with the road to the field only accessible on sunny days, their harvests were badly affected, and they received a poor price for their crops. Middlemen only bought the plums if their trucks could access the orchards. Long Coc villagers had to carry their plums in baskets a long distance to trucks waiting on the main road; as a result, their plums always received a lower price (10,000VND/kilogram) compared to crops that could be conveniently accessed with trucks (15,000 to 25,000VND/kilogram). It has been the same for other produce like tapioca and cassava. Villagers complained constantly to the authorities and received the promise of a concrete road to their orchards and fields before 2021, but *Tết* (Vietnamese New Year) came and went without any construction. When the authorities heard that the villagers were planning to pool their money and build the road themselves, they came to the village again and promised to have the road completed by March 2021. As of May 2021, there was still no sign that the road would be built anytime soon. According to the villagers, a proper road would offer them a stable income from their fruit trees, which would change their lives for the better. This is why they continue to fight for the road – for 17 years and counting – and will continue to do so until the government delivers on its promise.

As one man said:

> We went back and forth to the province and district so many times to ask for a proper road. It cost us to go there. Every time we went, we had to take days off from work. But they (the authorities) don't lose anything, so they just let us do it until we get so tired and stop. But we can't stop. We don't mind working hard. We have been working our whole lives. What we want is to have the authorities understand our difficulties, keep their promise, and help us with the road. We don't ask for anything else.
>
> (Interview, 17 February 2021)

As we see from Doi and Long Coc villages, despite all the hardships that the resettlees have endured, they have never been passive victims of their circumstances. They have actively engaged in responding to and making changes, even though their choices and actions have not always been considered as strategic or intentional by the authorities, experts, or even the villagers themselves (de Haan & Zoomers 2005). The villagers have played an active role in achieving their financial successes by continuously exploiting opportunities. Multiple motives prompted households and individuals to diversify assets, incomes, and activities. In these cases, poverty was the driver that intensified their need to generate income, using whatever resources were available and to the full extent possible. The experiences of the resettlees in Doi and Long Coc villages attest to the hardships – but also to the eventual rewards of the will to rise to life's challenges, rather than submit to its difficulties. These families did not sit and wait for government subsidies, but exploited their own potential and took advantage of their strengths. Using the resources available to them, each family developed its own strategy for efficient economic development in their new place, even though it was never easy.

Conclusion

My research shows that in the almost two decades since their forced displacement, the resettlees have been working very hard to recover their livelihoods. Even though their lives and production are more stable for many villagers, not all resettlees have fared the same. The process of implementing resettlement policy has focused on moving people out of the flooded area, not on effectively and efficiently supporting them to recover their lives and livelihoods in their new locales. Problems such as lack of land and poor infrastructure have negatively affected people's ability to deal with post-displacement stresses and shocks.

Diversification happens all the time and in all communities – for host or resettled, upland or lowland, minority or majority ethnic people. Casual consideration might suggest that resettlees all had the same experience: they were all moved to a strange environment and received the same amount of land (per person) and other government subsidies. In their new homes, they all suffered from land scarcity (compared with the situation in their old villages) and from changes in control over and access to surrounding resources. In the new places, the host communities and the authorities mediated the resettlees' access to resources.

However, their starting points and their outcomes have not all been the same. Resettlees started with different capacities and with different resources and networks. They have all had to work hard to diversify their livelihoods, and in that context, they have sometimes challenged the dominant power through everyday resistance and by (re)negotiating power relations as they have adapted and formed strategies.

My research shows how the circumstances of the resettlement experience shape the process of livelihood diversification. Key determinants of diversification and adaptation are basically in line with what Ellis highlights, including seasonality, differentiated labor markets, coping behaviors, migration, and accumulation (Ellis 1998). However, these determinants are rarely separable in practice, as we have seen in the case of resettlees in Tan Lap commune.

A variety of factors has led to differences in the dynamics of diversification in upland resettlement sites and influenced resettlees' choices – including their social networks, the availability of labor and capital, and sometimes of expertise and experience (as with the dairy cattle and bamboo shoots). Their strategies were not always effective, but they also learned to adjust them, depending on available resources. Their individual cases show that changes in the nature and intensity of market integration have played an important role in diversification. Instead of self-provisioning and being partly engaged in markets with their cash crops, they shifted to a state where they were totally dependent on the market because the amount of land that they received was insufficient to sustain their lives. Labor mobility/availability enabled some families to earn their living without too much reliance on the land they had received as compensation. People with good social networks also tended to recover faster as they received support from people in their network (as was the case with Lang and his close neighbors).

In summary, these families diversified their incomes and adjusted their livelihoods to compensate for the limited land that they received in their new villages. This diversification took many forms, including different farming activities (from growing tea, rice, maize, vegetables, plums, peaches, and mangoes to raising cattle, pigs, and chickens) as well as engaging in laboring work near to or far from home. With the resulting income, they were able to purchase more land from the host communities. Perhaps for some families, they have simply been luckier in their diversification activities than their neighbors. Others have benefited from hard work or strong labor. After 17 years of resettlement, Lo Van Lang told me:

> I still missed my old village so much. I missed the river, the pond, the wooden house on stilts, the peace of mind each day after work. We can't reverse what has happened. We came here and laid the foundation. Now it's time for my children and grandchildren to make their homes on this very land.

Notes

1 When they moved in there were about 200 households in the original Doi village. First, resettlers refused to be merged into the host village, so they separated themselves and named their hamlet Doi 2, but they were required by the local authorities to merge with the original one in 2019. There were approximately 100 households in the original Long Coc village. Twenty resettled households later arrived and lived in already-built brick houses in a separate area in the village.
2 www.pvpower.vn/bo-sung-von-di-dan-tai-dinh-cu-thuy-dien-son-la/.
3 VND 10 million was valued at about US$750 in 2009. It was about half of an annual average income of an upland family at that time.
4 A new policy allowed resettlers to dismantle the old house and transport it to be rebuilt in the resettlement sites. This policy has helped people retain their customary forms of housing. Support for house moving, according to most of the resettlers interviewed, has been very useful and even necessary.
5 *Land Law 2013*, Chapter 6, Article 69. https://thuvienphapluat.vn/van-ban/Bat-dong-san/Luat-dat-dai-2013-215836.aspx. The most recent Constitution was approved in November 2013 but took effect on 1st January 2014.
6 As they received land that already has tea trees on it as part of their compensation, the government allocated them less than the average of 2,500 m^2 per person.
7 Interviews with the Chairman of Tan Lap commune, June 2005.
8 Before the resettlers moved in, the Resettlement Management Board had workers come to prepare the land and planted tea trees on these lands.

References

Appendini, K. 2001. Land and livelihood: What do we know, and what are the issues? In A. Zoomers (ed.), *Land and Sustainable Livelihood in Latin America*. Royal Tropical Institute/Vervuert Verlag, Amsterdam, The Netherlands, pp. 23–38.

Batterbury, S. 2001. Landscapes of diversity: A local political ecology of livelihood diversification in South-Western Niger. *Progress in Human Geography* (35): 843–50.

Bebbington, A. 1999. Capitals and capabilities: A framework for analyzing peasant viability, rural livelihoods and poverty. *World Development* 27(12): 2021–44.

Berry, S. 1989. Social institutions and access to resources. *Africa* 59(1): 41–55.

Berry, S. 1993. *No Condition is Permanent: The Social Dynamics of Agrarian Change in Sub- Saharan Africa*. University of Wisconsin Press, Madison.

Bonnin, C., and Turner, S. 2014. 'A good wife stays home': Gendered negotiations over state agricultural programmes, upland Vietnam. *Gender, Place & Culture: A Journal of Feminist Geography* 21(10): 1302–20.

Chambers, R., and Conway, G. 1991. *Sustainable rural livelihoods: Practical concepts for the 21st century*. IDS Discussion Paper 296. Institute of Development Studies, Brighton, UK.

Collier, W. L. 1988. *A Preliminary Study of Employment Trends in Lowland Javanese Villages*. Agency for Agricultural Research and Development, Bogor.

Constitution of Vietnam. 2014. [Hiến Pháp nước cộng hoà xã hội chủ nghĩa Việt Nam]. CÔNG BÁO/Số 1003 + 1004/Ngày 29–12–2013. https://vbpl.vn/FileData/TW/Lists/vbpq/Attachments/32801/VanBanGoc_Hien%20phap%202013.pdf

Dao, N. 2010. Dam development in Vietnam: The evolution of dam-induced resettlement policy. *Water Alternatives* 3(2): 324–40.

Dao, N. 2011. Damming rivers in Vietnam: A lesson learned in the Tây Bắc (Northwest) region. *Journal for Vietnamese Studies* 6(2): 106–40.

Dao, N. 2016. Political responses to dam-induced resettlement in northern uplands Vietnam. *Journal of Agrarian Change* 16(2): 291–317.

Dao, N. 2018. Rubber plantations and their implications on gender roles and relations in northern uplands Vietnam. *Gender, Place and Culture: A Journal of Feminist Geography* 25(11): 1579–600.

Dao, N., and Bui, P. 2015. Rethinking development narratives of hydropower in Vietnam. In Nathanial Matthews and Kim Geheb (eds.), *Hydropower Development in the Mekong Region: Political, Socio-economic and Environmental Perspectives*. Earthscan, London, UK, pp. 17, 197.

De Haan, L. and Zoomers, A. 2005. Exploring the frontier of livelihoods research. *Development and Change* 36 (1): 2 47.

Ding, C. 2007. Policy and praxis of land acquisition in China. *Land Use Policy* 24: 1–13.

Ellis, F. 1998. Household strategies and rural livelihood diversification. *The Journal of Development Studies* 35(1): 1–38.

Ellis, F. 2000. *Rural Livelihoods and Diversity in Developing Countries*. Oxford University Press, Oxford, UK.

Hart, G. 1994. The dynamics of diversification in an Asian Rice Region. In B. Koppel, J. Hawkins, and W. James (eds.), *Development or Deterioration? Work in Rural Asia*. Lynne Reinner, Boulder, pp. 47–71.

Hart, G. 1995. Gender and household dynamics: Recent theories and their implications. In M. G. Quibria (ed.), *Critical Issues in Asian Development: Theories, Experiences and Policies*, Oxford University Press, Oxford and New York, pp. 3–74.

Hazell, P., Wiggins Poulton, S., and Doeward, A. 2007. *The Future of Small Farm for Poverty Reduction and Growth*. International Food Policy Research Institute, Washington.

Land Law. 2013. Chapter 6, article 69. https://thuvienphapluat.vn/van-ban/Bat-dong-san/Luat-dat-dai-2013-215836.aspx.

Moc Chau District's Division of Statistics. 2020. Moc Chau. Son La.

Moser, C. O. N. 1998. The asset vulnerability framework: Reassessing urban poverty reduction strategies. *World Development* 26(1): 1–19.

NIAPP (*Viện Quy hoạch và thiết kế nông nghiệp*). 2005. *Quy hoạch và thiết kế nông nghiệp: Phương án điều chuyển dân cư dự án thuỷ điện Sơn La tỉnh Sơn La*. Document prepared for the Son La Hydropower Project. Hanoi.

Ningshen, Athing, and Primrose, Ningson. 2018. *Urban Poverty and Livelihoods*. Lulu Publication and Solapur: Laxmi Book Publication, Raleigh.

Pham, H. T., Van Westen, A. C. M., and Zoomers, A. 2013. Compensation and resettlement policies after compulsory land acquisition for hydropower development in Vietnam: Policy and practice. *Land* 2: 678–704.

Pham, V. D. 2016. Responses to Compensation affected by the Son La Hydropower resettlement in Northwestern Vietnam. Presented at the International Conference on the

Mekong, Salween and Red Rivers: Sharing Knowledge and Perspectives Across Borders, Chulalongkorn University, Bangkok, Thailand, 12 November 2016.
Preston, D. A. 1989. Too busy to farm: Under-utilisation of farm land in Central Java. *The Journal of Development Studies* 26(1): 43–57.
Rigg, J., and Vandergeest, P. (eds.). 2012. *Revisiting Rural Places: Pathways to Poverty and Prosperity in Southeast Asia*. NUS Press, Singapore.
Schneider, S., and Niederle, P. A. 2010. Resistance strategies and diversification of rural livelihoods: The construction of autonomy among Brazilian family farmers. *The Journal of Peasant Studies* 37(2): 379–405.
Son La People's Committee. 2006. *Compiling of Policies on Resettlement for the* Son La *Hydropower Project*. Son La People's Committee, Son La Province, Vietnam.
Tan Lap commune. 2020. *Socio-Economic Annual Report*. Tan Lap commune, Son La Province, Vietnam.
Tran, Van Ha. 2011. Local people's participation in involuntary resettlement in Vietnam: A case study of the Son La Hydropower Project. In Kate Lazarus, Nathan Badenoch, Nga Dao, and Bernadette Resurreccion (eds.), *Water Rights and Social Justice in the Mekong Region*. Routledge Publishers, London and Washington, DC.
Wallmann, S. 1984. *Eight London Households*. Routledge, London.
Zaman, M. Q. 1996. Development and displacement in Bangladesh: Toward a resettlement policy. *Asian Survey* 36: 691–703.

9 Dam-induced resettlement in Vietnam

Proposing a socially sustainable model

Nguyen Quy Nghi and Phan Huyen Dan

Introduction

Hydroelectricity is still one of the main pillars of global and national energy security. The International Energy Agency (IEA 2021) estimates that the contribution made by hydroelectricity and other renewable energy sources will increase from 29 percent in 2020 to 70 percent by the middle of the twenty-first century, as hydroelectricity becomes the third largest power source worldwide. To prevent global temperatures from rising by 1.5° C or more, 2,600 GW from hydroelectricity must be produced by 2050; as of 2020, the installed capacity of hydropower plants worldwide came to 1,330 GW, an increase of 22 GW (1.68 percent) compared with 2019 (IHA 2021).

Hydropower dams deliver several benefits (including flood control, irrigation, and energy), yet they also have unavoidable socio-environmental impacts. The difficulty in balancing costs and benefits for sustainable hydropower development has long posed a challenge for project implementers.

The concept of "sustainable development" was first introduced in the 1987 Brundtland Commission's report *Our common future* (UN 1987:39):

> Sustainable development is development that meets the needs of the present without compromising the ability of future generations to meet their own needs.

However, this is an umbrella definition with varying interpretations. According to Meppem and Gill (1998), while the concept is widely used by governments, the lack of a common understanding of "sustainable development" has led to differences in formulating and implementing sustainable development policies.

"Sustainable development" should be understood as a process promoting social change. The emphasis should be on the quality of the development process (rather than on a specific output); on representativeness (the involvement of many different actors); and on the role of policymakers in identifying the underlying structure/institution/framework that will promote an integrated economic, social, and ecological approach (Meppem & Gill 1998).

DOI: 10.4324/9781003165774-13

What does sustainable development mean for the hydropower sector? In their sustainability guidelines, the International Hydropower Association (IHA 2020) provides specific implementation guidance for 26 topics, ranging from technical design, economic analysis, and communication to identifying and managing environmental and social impacts. The social impacts of hydropower projects have always been of particular interest, due to their characteristics and scale. Cernea (2004) divides them into four groups: boomtowns, downstream impacts, loss of cultural heritage, and forced displacement of people. These impacts (including changes in lifestyle, culture, displacement, and intangible cultural factors) require substantial time, knowledge, and budget for successful impact mitigation and remediation.

The approach a specific hydropower project adopts for handling environmental and social impacts may not be the same from one project to another. While technical, safety, and design factors are achievable with adequate resources, social impacts cannot as easily be identified (especially considering cumulative and indirect effects). Effective rehabilitation of affected communities is even more challenging to measure because it often has intangible aspects.

This chapter will address the mitigation and reversal of resettlement impacts – a critical component of environmental and social impact assessment and mitigation. After examining project implementation at the Trung Son hydropower dam in the Northwest region of Vietnam and analysis of secondary materials, we will identify the elements needed to promote a successful and sustainable resettlement program for hydropower projects. Improved resettlement will undoubtedly contribute to the goal of sustainability for the project.

Hydropower development in Vietnam and resettlement impacts

Sectoral context

The draft Power Plan VIII, released in 2021 by the Institute of Energy, indicated that hydropower has almost reached its maximum capacity in Vietnam (see Table 9.1). Its contribution to total national electricity supplies is forecast to decrease – from 37 percent in 2018, to 18 percent in 2030 and 9 percent in 2045. This decline is mainly because potential sites for large hydropower generation have been exhausted. Out of a total estimated at 20,000 MW nationwide, power plants generating approximately 17,930 MW (89.7 percent) have already been installed and commissioned. In addition, 40 percent of the projected capacity (4,000/10,000 MW) from small hydropower projects (under 30 MW) has been removed from the master plan, due to deforestation and other environmental concerns. The rapid development of small hydropower projects in the past decade has left little margin for expansion in the future: it is estimated that only 2,800 MW could be further developed (accounting for 46.7 percent of total potential capacity).

According to Vietnam Electricity (EVN), as of 2018 Vietnam had 385 hydropower projects (5 MW or more) under operation.[1] The northwest region hosts the

Table 9.1 Distribution of energy sources and projections (%)[2]

	2018	*2019*	*2020*	*2030*	*2045*
Hydroelectric power	37.0	35.7	35.3	18	9
Coal thermal power	37.4	36.5	36.0	27	18
Gas thermal power	24.7	23.6	23.2	21	24
Wind electric power	0.3	0.4	0.5	29	44
Solar power	0.1	3.3	4.4		
Other electric power sources	0.5	0.5	0.6	1	3
Imported power	n/a	n/a	n/a	4	2

Sources: MOIT (2020, 2021)

country's three biggest dams, built on the main stem of the Da River: Hoa Binh, Son La, and Lai Chau. The Son La hydropower dam project, constructed in 2005 and officially commissioned in 2012, is the largest hydropower plant in Southeast Asia. It generates an average electricity output of 10 billion kW per year, equivalent to nearly one-tenth of Vietnam's electricity output in 2012. However, the Central and Central Highland regions have the highest density of hydropower projects, thanks to their system of interlaced rivers with many short tributaries (Le Anh Tuan 2014:7).

The major trends for hydropower development to 2045 will feature three scenarios, including:

(i) implementing already approved projects;
(ii) expanding existing plants to increase capacity; and
(iii) exhausting the remaining small hydropower sources.

The last scenario can be achieved through 313 small hydropower projects in 34 provinces/cities, mainly in the northern region (22 provinces).

Another direction is developing pumped storage hydropower. According to the Ministry of Industry and Trade (2021), eight of these projects, generating 12,500 MW, have been proposed for Son La, Thanh Hoa, Lam Dong, Ninh Thuan, and Binh Thuan.

Resettlement impacts

Hydropower dam-induced land taking and resettlement impacts depend on many factors, including project location, dam size, applied technology, and ancillary facilities (access roads, transmission lines, and resettlement areas). The number of families affected may range from a few families to millions of people. The most significant impact observed to date is at the Three Gorges Dam in China, where the dam and its 632 km^2 reservoir have directly affected more than 1.1 million people (Wilmsen & van Hulten 2017). Many hydropower projects have been designed as multi-sectoral projects, consisting of the construction of a dam and ancillary works and socioeconomic development activities.

Table 9.2 Number of affected and relocated households due to the construction of some hydropower projects in Vietnam[3]

	Hydropower plant	*Number of relocated households*	*Number of relocated people*
1	Lai Chau[4]	2,009	8,467
2	Huoi Quang	722	4,333
3	Ban Chat	2,664	15,017
4	Son La	20,340	92,301
5	Ban Ve	3,022	n/a
6	Song Tranh 2	1,196	6,300
7	Song Bung 4	253	1,342
8	Dong Nai 3	500	800
9	Hoa Binh[5]	3,356	n/a

No official statistics have been issued on the number of households and individuals who lost their land and were relocated as a result of hydropower projects in Vietnam. Researchers have attempted to gather data based on individual project information, but such data can be incomplete. Nevertheless, it is undeniable that land taking and resettlement impacts in hydropower projects are concentrated and remarkable. Entire communities can be displaced from their original sites. Table 9.2 describes more clearly the impact of some large-scale hydropower projects in Vietnam.

As Table 9.2 shows, approximately 34,000 households (more than 130,000 people) have been displaced due to nine large hydropower projects. Small hydropower plants (under 30 MW) may cause a lower level of physical displacement, but the number of households losing their land is still high. The implementation completion report for the Vietnam Renewable Development Project (funded by the World Bank) indicated that 19 small hydropower schemes required resettling fewer than 50 households and taking the land of approximately 2,500 households (World Bank 2018).

All projects require land acquisition because of the flooding of the reservoir area, which results in a large number of resettled households. Since dam construction typically occurs in mountainous areas, the majority of affected people are members of ethnic minority groups. (For example, the Black River watershed in the Northwest region has been inhabited for generations by many different ethnic minority groups, including the Muong, Dao, Thai Trang, Thai Den, Kho Mu, Hmong, La Ha, Khang, Si La, Mang, and Giay (Dao 2011).)

As with many dam projects worldwide, the great majority of resettled households have experienced a sharp deterioration in living conditions and reduced income. The to-be-submerged lands along valley bottoms are usually the most fertile for agricultural production, while the replacement land in the destination area is usually far less productive. In the Son La hydropower project, people were not provided with arable land or adequate technical support for new farming practices when transitioning from wet rice cultivation to upland agricultural production. This made livelihood restoration more challenging, leading to greater food insecurity, a loss of income, and a decline in living standards (Nguyen Manh Cuong et al. 2006; Tran Van Ha 2008). Unemployment, infertile productive land, shortage of water, and unstable livelihood conditions are common in almost all dam projects in Thua Thien Hue province (Nguyen et al. 2018:56). Studies presented at the annual meeting of the Vietnam River Network in 2006 confirmed the inadequacy of dam projects' handling of social impacts, and, worse, their destructive impacts on local people (Dao 2011).

How are resettlement impacts being handled?

Land Law 2013 provides the main legal framework regulating land acquisition, compensation, and resettlement associated with development projects, including dams. As discussed in Chapter 10 of this book, compensation packages typically include the following sub-components: compensation for land (Articles 74–82); property/construction or land use restrictions (Articles 88–94); assistance (Articles 83–84); and resettlement (Articles 85–86).

Table 9.3 Regulations on compensation when the state acquires residential land[6]

Affected group	*Eligibility conditions*	*Compensation package*
Household, individual **Vietnamese people living abroad**	Using affected residential land and meeting other eligibility criteria for compensation under Article 75 Owning houses attached to land use rights	If affected households do not have other residential lands/houses elsewhere, residential land/house should be provided. Cash payments are available upon request. If affected households have other houses elsewhere, cash payments will be provided. Compensation by land is possible if the local authorities have available land.
Household, individual	Using land and houses to be affected by the project, not meeting eligibility criteria for compensation; and having no houses elsewhere.	Eligible to buy or rent houses; or be allocated with rental land.
Economic organizations **Vietnamese people living abroad** **Foreign Direct Investment enterprises**	Currently using land for housing projects when the state acquires the land	Compensation for land

Article 79 links compensation for acquired residential land to the resettlement arrangements and delineates the eligibility conditions and compensation package composition that apply when the state acquires residential land. Details of Article 79 are summarized in Table 9.3.

Decree No. 47/2014/ND-CP (May 15, 2014), on "Compensation, support, and resettlement when the state acquires land," guides implementation of *Land Law 2013*.

Its highlights are as follows:

- First, in order to receive compensation, households/individuals/Vietnamese citizens residing abroad need (or should be eligible to be granted) a land use right certificate.[7]
- Second, the decree assesses the viability of the leftover land and uses it to guide the compensation package. This package may include land-for-land (residential land), housing-for-land, or cash compensation, depending on the viability of leftover land and the ownership of land/house in the area. The latter group may still be eligible for compensation by land in localities where land is available.
- Third, for affected households that are not eligible for compensation and have no other accommodation, the Provincial People's Committee will set the rates for buying and renting houses and of residential land prices with land use fees.
- Fourth, in the parcel containing the acquired residential land, the decree allows for the conversion of agricultural land to residential land (within the land allocation limit), provided that:

  (i) affected households demand such a conversion;
  (ii) the conversion follows overall planning;
  (iii) affected households fulfill the accompanying financial obligations.

- Fifth, for housing development projects where the state acquires the land, the decree stipulates specific compensation packages for persons or enterprises using the land. Accordingly, the packages are specified as follows:

  (i) Cash compensation for the affected portion if the project can be implemented on the remaining land.
  (ii) Land-for-land or cash compensation if the whole land parcel is acquired or the remaining land is not sufficient for the project's continuation.
  (iii) Cash compensation if the project has been commercialized.

In the energy sector, in addition to the application of *Land Law 2013* and its associated decrees, land taking and resettlement impacts are also subject to the application of the *Electricity Law* and its decrees governing implementation (No. 51/2020/ND-CP (April 21, 2020), and No. 14/2014/ND-CP (February 26, 2014)). The Prime Minister's Decision No. 64/2014/QD-TTg, dated November 18, 2014, covers the particular policies regulating resettlement and land acquisition necessitated by construction of irrigation and hydropower dams. This decision was revised by the Prime Minister's Decision No. 06/2019/QD-TTg (February 1,

2019). All major dams (Hoa Binh, Son La, Lai Chau, Tuyen Quang, and so forth) have dedicated resettlement policies approved at the Prime Ministerial level. For projects using funds from international financial institutions (including the World Bank, the Asian Development Bank (ADB), the European Bank for Reconstruction and Development (ERBD), and the Asian Infrastructure Investment Bank (AIIB)), relevant policies of the funding agencies will also apply.

Elements of a successful resettlement program

As discussed earlier, addressing the environmental and social impacts of hydropower projects can be quite difficult – not unlike solving a math problem with too many unknowns. There are no standardized approaches or universal formulas for a successful resettlement program; it can only be achieved through the most effective combination of financial, human, and legal resources.

The following sections will clarify the specific elements of a successful resettlement program. Land acquisition, compensation, and resettlement are multi-stage processes, so the following sections focus exclusively on resettlement-related arrangements in hydropower development.

Legal framework

The legal framework is arguably the most critical factor in shaping the success of the resettlement program. Since *Doi Moi* (reforms) in 1986, Vietnam has made positive improvements through four versions of its *Land Law* (see Figure 9.1). This section emphasizes resettlement regulations and compensation amounts, as these are the most important determinants of compensation packages in cases of land acquisition.

There were no specific provisions on resettlement in *Land Law 1987* and *Land Law 1993*. *Land Law 2003* stipulated that the Provincial People's Committee would be responsible for implementing the resettlement project before land acquisition and that the resettlement area should be in the same locality and have developmental conditions equal to or better than the former residence (Article 42, Clause 3). *Land Law 2013* stipulated that the District People's Committee would be responsible for completing the resettlement site before acquiring people's lands and that the resettlement area must ensure synchronous infrastructure according to the standards and customs of each region (Article 85). *Land Law 2003* was distinguished by requiring the new residence to be equal to or better than the original one, while *Land Law 2013* was more advanced because it emphasized the importance of conforming to local customs. Regarding the compensation rate, several improvements in land valuation were introduced so that this rate could be brought closer to the market price.

Based on these laws, Vietnam's regulations and the World Bank's Environmental and Social Standard (ESS) 5 "land acquisition, restriction of land use and involuntary resettlement" have similar objectives and requirements in certain areas.

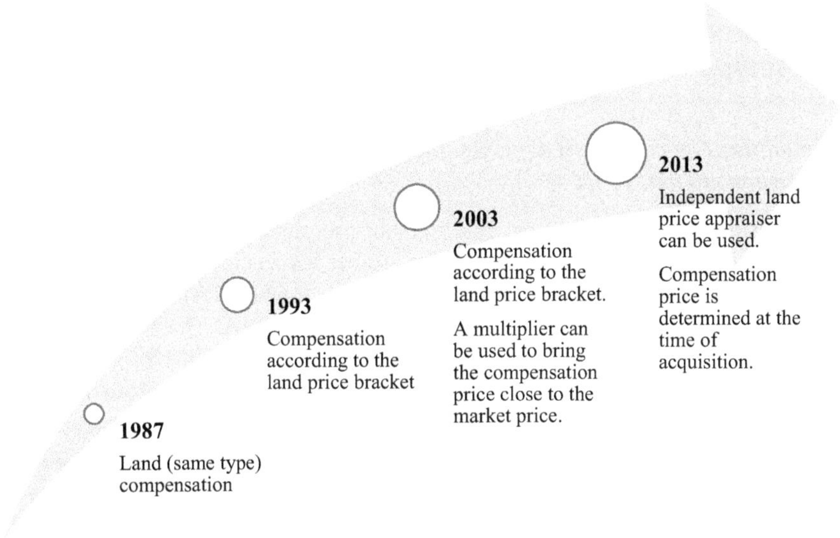

Figure 9.1 Changes in regulations on compensation in the *Land Laws* during the period 1987–2013

- First, the principle of land-for-land compensation was set out in *Land Law 2013* and guiding documents. In principle, affected households should be compensated by land for the land they lost, matching the type of land and purpose of use. Local authorities could consider cash compensation if replacement land was not available for compensation.
- Second, affected households could choose different compensation packages depending on their circumstances and on the magnitude of impact. These packages could include cash, land/house, or a combination of both. Affected households who were not eligible for compensation and who had no place to live would also be offered an opportunity to buy, to rent a house, or to be allocated a land parcel with a land use fee. This arrangement was to ensure that all affected households could afford a new place to live after resettlement.
- Third, provisions on the usefulness of the remaining land and on the compensation/support packages were clearly defined.
- Finally, the principles of democracy, objectivity, and openness in land acquisition processes were also codified.

These principles align with the community engagement requirements of the World Bank's ESS 5. The umbrella regulations are relatively advanced and are compatible with similar requirements by other international financial institutions – but in reality, the lack of effective enforcement results in resettlement failures. In addition, the country safeguards framework assessment has found that significant gaps remain, including the application of compensation according to the full replacement cost principle; compensation for structures built on illegal lands; livelihood restoration; and the limited capacity of responsible agencies (Nguyen et al. 2019).

Commitment by competent agencies and Project Management Units (PMUs)

Notwithstanding good planning, resettlement programs cannot succeed without commitment by the local authority and the Project Management Unit (PMU). This statement is particularly true in the case of Vietnam, where district-level governments appraise and approve resettlement-related decisions. The PMU monitors and provides technical recommendations for implementing the project-related resettlement. The commitments entail adequate staffing, allocation of (financial) resources, and institutional arrangements (monitoring, supervision, and reporting). Since the local government has many competing demands, allocating adequate time, resources, and staff is essential for success. In a hydropower project, where most of its components need to be built in a certain order, the highest commitment by the government and the PMU is critical. In addition, the commitment underlies an approach in which the government and the PMU are willing to do more than legally required to benefit the affected communities. In fact, *Land Law 2013* cannot cover all cases, and substantive efforts by all parties (especially by local governments and PMUs) are required to apply the law in an optimal way for the affected people. This needed effort is sometimes multiplied in official development assistance (ODA) projects, because the borrower must comply with the relevant policies of the donor.

In one World Bank-funded project (Trung Son hydropower in Vietnam), the resettlement policies stipulated that affected people had the right to build their own houses in the new residential areas. A series of procedures have been carried out to enable this option, including six rounds of review and appraisal by the authorities. This process concluded after three years of discussion and negotiation (Nguyen et al. 2020). This had been a worthy effort, with which more than 95 percent of the affected households indicated satisfaction. This contributed to high levels of satisfaction expressed with the relocation and resettlement activities overall, as indicated in the final project assessment. At the outset, the borrower (represented by the utility Electricity of Vietnam) expressed a commitment to international standards on managing social and environmental impacts. Likewise, the Song Bung 4 Hydropower Project (financed by the ADB) adjusted its social and livelihood support program to match the project's progress and delivered on a commitment to promote women's participation and gender equality in compensation. By contrast, low commitment by local authorities and PMUs may have led to delayed compensation payments or budget allocations (Dang et al. 2018), which ultimately slowed progress in project implementation (Vu 2017).

The extent to which the commitment of stakeholders affects the success of resettlement programs is not a new topic. It has been an issue of contention for advocacy groups for years in most countries. In an evaluation of World Bank-funded projects in Africa, Cook and Ivarsdotter (1994) pointed out that only strong participation and commitment by local authorities at the project level would result in positive resettlement outcomes. Scudder (2005) also confirmed the role of implementation capacity, political will, and local institutions in his analysis of the failures and successes of resettlement programs in large hydropower projects (especially in Phase 4: transfer and integration). In large infrastructure projects, PMUs and local governments often under-value the importance of timely completion of resettlement activities in affirming and maintaining their commitment to benefit affected people and to the overall progress of the project.

Consultation, participation, and stakeholder engagement

Resettlement does not happen overnight. It constitutes a long negotiation process, and its success largely depends on the effectiveness of consultation and stakeholder engagement activities. Singer et al. (2014) indicated that one of the major sources of dissatisfaction is the lack of thorough communication with villagers, leading to mistrust of government-led resettlement programs. Unclear information always provokes unnecessary questions from the public, and unclear responses from project implementers may hinder the progress of the whole program. Consultation and information sharing activities allay fears, anxiety and concerns. In our recent survey, 84.3 percent of households (Nguyen et al. 2018) reported at least one negative perception when learning about resettlement impacts. Policies of all major international financial institutions include consultation requirements in the impacts assessment processes. In Vietnam, the existing legal framework (*Land Law 2013*; *Environment Protection Law*) requires that public consultation be conducted at pivotal moments throughout project cycles. Consultation constitutes an excellent opportunity to collect the community's feedback on project design, including the resettlement program.

What made the Trung Son Hydropower Project stand out was a consultation strategy (see Table 9.4) that included three aspects: timing and frequency; usage of appropriate local languages; and targeting correct audiences. The local people first heard about this project in 2004, when an initial geological survey team arrived in the project area. Consultation activities since that time were conducted frequently until the project ended in 2019 with modified, updated, and customized content following project advances. Local languages (Thai, Muong, H'Mong) were used to maximize the participation of ethnic minority women and other vulnerable groups. The main themes covered in major consultation events in Trung Son Hydropower Project included overall social and environmental impacts; options for resettlement houses; resettlement options (project-built or self-constructed resettlement houses); resettlement plots (typically decided by lottery); and a livelihood restoration program.

Previous studies confirmed that proper consultation with – and meaningful participation by – resettlees might strongly support positive resettlement outcomes (Scudder 2005; Singer & Hoang 2014:15). Nevertheless, limited participation by

Table 9.4 Consultation activities during project preparation

Date	*Areas and participants*	*Purpose*
2008 (January and April)	• 5 communes affected by access road, 12 villages	Prepare resettlement plan for access roads
2008 (March)	• 5 communes affected by the reservoir, 10 villages • Household sample (1 household out of 7) and focus group discussions, 3 meetings (102 farmers), local leaders and agencies, and local mass organizations	Prepare CLIP: analysis of livelihood challenges and opportunities
2008 (April–June)	• 5 communes affected by the reservoir and 1 commune affected by access road, 11 villages • 440 people, of which 190 people were from resettled households; leaders and health workers	Health impact assessment
2008 (May–August)	• 6 communes affected by the reservoir, 3 communes affected by access roads • 499 participants in meetings, 30 in-depth interviews with households, 57 with district and commune official	Social assessment
2008 (June)	• 14 villages to be relocated in the reservoir area	Resettlement consultation
2008 (October)	• Relocated and host communities	Consultation on resettlement and livelihood restoration
2008–2009 (December–January)	• 34 villages affected by access road, construction sites, reservoir, and downstream impacts. Including villages with loss of land but no relocation	Consultation on environmental and social impacts
2010 (January–March)	• Consultation on all project mitigation measures, including communities, commune and district authorities • National consultation with civil society organizations	Consultation on the design of RLDP and environmental management plan

Source: World Bank (2011), reused in Nguyen et al. (2020).

local people is not uncommon in hydropower sector development in Vietnam. Dang et al. (2018), through analysis of 5-scale questions, revealed that participation by local people during the Buon Kop hydropower project was limited to receiving information and meeting attendance only. Most dam projects are under pressure to ensure progress because the costs of delay are high, and this pressure puts local people in an unequal negotiating position (Aronsson Inga-Lill 2009). Ideally, resettlees should "be aware or be made aware" of their lives and social relations, culture, and economic livelihood, to help in formulating priorities for what they would like to save and change: what they identify as core traditions and what may be allowed to lapse. Since many affected people are not prepared to negotiate, they become passive participants via relevant decision-making bodies (Skinner et al. 2014:6). Although they are real "shareholders," as Cernea describes them, they often do not share in the benefits from the projects (Cernea 2003, 2008).

Communication gaps have hindered people's voices and decision-making capacity. Without the proper use of laws, project documents, and action plans, communication might become one of the biggest barriers to active participation for local people (Dang et al. 2018). It will take time for them to improve their ability to challenge the government's decisions, to ask for their rights, and to hold competent agencies accountable. Affected households are often not considered as "project stakeholders" – and so people have not seen participation as an "empowerment" process. Meaningful participation rarely exists with the prevalence of "one-size-fits-all" models or the traditional top-down approach. Often participation by villagers in the program cycles of government-supported programs has been superficial or absent (especially by the ethnic minority poor) (CEMA & UN 2009).

The lack of cultural appropriateness and the presence of inherent prejudice toward ethnic minority people may worsen the situation. The belief that minority residents are uneducated, are less developed, and need assistance to make decisions is widespread among government officials, health professionals, and teachers, who are often from the ethnic majority (the Kinh) (World Bank 2019a). Although international and national regulations have formally recognized participation requirements in environmental and social standards, achieving them fully remains challenging for dam projects in Vietnam.

Adaptative management of the resettlement program

In hydropower projects, displaced households often have the right to either self-arranged relocation or moving to pre-determined resettlement sites. The latter option is widely used. Project Management Units will develop these sites with sound basic infrastructure systems (electricity, roads, water supply, and drainage); social service infrastructure (schools, medical stations, community cultural houses); and individual homes. Resettlement houses may be of various sizes; often follow a standard design (concrete structure, iron roofs); and often have attached works (for example, water tanks, toilets). Families affected by the Son La Hydropower Plant have relocated to new residential sites – newly developed or integrated into existing villages – in 82 communes and 99 local sites in three provinces of Son La, Dien Bien, and Lai Chau (Government of Vietnam 2018). Resettlement for the Lai Chau hydropower project has been arranged in 28 rural locations, four urban sites in six communes and one town in Dien Bien province (Government of Vietnam 2011). Depending on the location, the size of each plot may have a maximum area equivalent to the rural land allocation quota (300 m^2), with resettlement houses constructed within the larger plot.

Such an arrangement is favorable in terms of project management (especially in terms of construction progress control). However, it limits the ability of people to reuse materials from their original houses, to make further investments to improve their houses, or to maintain the cultural characteristics found in former homes. Conserving traditional housing styles is also a principle specified in the *Law on Housing 2014*, Article 20, Item 1 – but it is one that is rarely applied in practice. The sense of ownership is low for project-provided homes because people do not see resettled houses built by the project as being "their homes." The World Bank (2004:261) has communicated the following as good practice during the formulation and implementation of resettlement programs:

> Where new housing is being constructed under the resettlement program, house layouts and designs, as well as the location of community infrastructure, should be determined with resettlees' participation and approval. DPs [displaced persons] can help make the design meet their specific needs, such as space for livestock, gardens, and other activities not obvious to others. They should have a range of housing options, and these options should not be overly standardized. One option should allow DPs to add their own resources so that they can obtain larger or better houses. Housing options should include a cash option, which would allow DPs to build their own houses or move elsewhere. This option can include a voucher applicable to a range of housing alternatives. Housing options should not exceed the financial means of DPs: mortgages, rent, utilities, and other costs should be manageable.

Housing concerns, combined with choice of an unsuitable location, may cause the resettlement program to fail. For the Ban Ve Hydropower Plant, resettling more than 2,000 households from Tuong Duong district to Thanh Chuong district (a distance of more than 150 km) has proven ineffective. Poorly developed infrastructure and a lack of arable land and livelihood resources have driven many households to return to their old residences (in a reservoir area) after only a short time.[8] After 15 years of construction, the resettlement site for the Dak Rtih Hydropower Plant project was occupied by only one household. The dissatisfaction of affected households is partly due to such factors as the lack of water supplies; the deterioration of infrastructure; and urban dwellers' opposition to relocation to rural areas.[9] In the Trung Son Hydropower Project, flexibility in implementing the resettlement program, coupled with regular consultation with the affected people, has brought about positive results. Figure 9.2 reveals households' overall satisfaction with project activities. More than three-quarters of the respondents

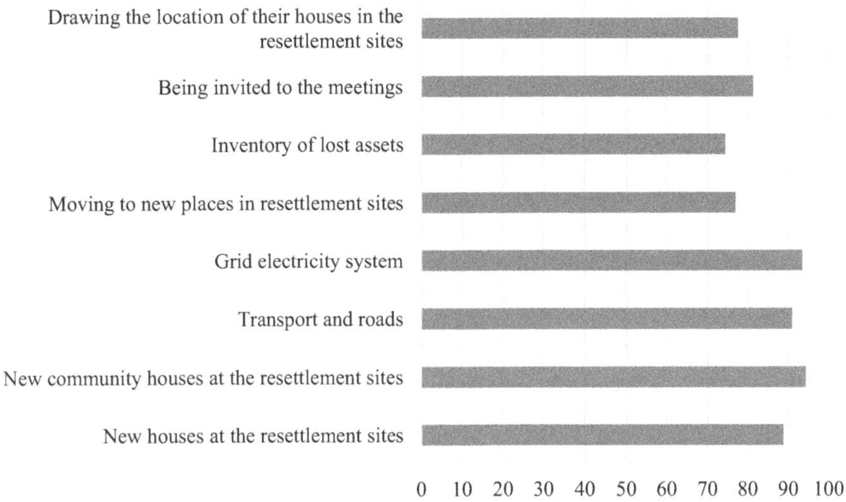

Figure 9.2 Percentage of satisfaction with project implementation (NIAPP & ASEC 2018)

were satisfied with the plot drawing (77.4 percent) and with new residential areas (76.8 percent). The satisfaction rate with their new houses was 88.7 percent and more than 90 percent were happy with infrastructure conditions (electricity, road, community house).

These encouraging resettlement outcomes for the Trung Son Hydropower Project result from a combination of factors, including planning; self-construction of houses; and payment for the construction of houses (Nguyen et al. 2020).

Site selection that draws on local people's knowledge

First, in the consultation process, local people used indigenous knowledge to inform their selection of new resettlement sites. It turned out that the sites pre-selected by the project – flat areas, convenient for the land and house arrangements – were not the choice of local people. People's knowledge of the ecosystems in the region helped them to choose suitable alternatives that are a manageable distance from the old villages.

Allowing resettlees to construct their own houses

Second, resettlees had complete flexibility in constructing their new houses, as long as they complied with technical parameters defined by the resettlement policy. This construction option was revitalized through consultation meetings, where it was the preferred option for most affected households. Allowing resettlees to build their own houses can engage their proactivity and sense of ownership and encourage additional financial investment to achieve a better house that satisfies different preferences for style, decor, and view.

Farmers will need a large residential area, a characteristic that project-built houses often cannot satisfy, due to the rigid application of technical standards. An option offered to affected households allowed them to use the compensation and resettlement packages more effectively in design, labor mobilization, construction, timing, and decor. It also helped preserve the popular style of Thai stilt houses, while improving housing quality and living conditions. New, comfortable homes have proven to have facilitated resettlees' attachment to their new location and helped to allay the shock of moving from their old village.

Sufficient allocation of land (residential and garden)

Third, as required under the project's Resettlement Policy Framework (RPF), significant efforts were made to ensure sufficient allocation of land (residential and garden) for affected households. Technical solutions alone have been unable to overcome the limits of geological and terrace conditions – but thanks to significant effort and to on-site adjustments during construction, most land-related issues have been resolved to the satisfaction of affected households.

Disbursement tied to compliance and satisfactory progress in self-construction

Fourth, as mentioned earlier, opting for self-construction still means that the households must comply with pre-determined technical parameters (including housing area; safety standards; hygiene and environmental conditions; kitchen; water tank; and toilet). Compliance and satisfactory progress trigger the disbursement, which is divided into three installments. As a result, relocation timelines have been achieved in line with the pace of construction.

The project has taken steps to empower people, to listen to their feedback, and to let them participate in the decision-making process.

Appropriate livelihood restoration planning in the post-resettlement period

In development projects in general and hydropower projects in particular, livelihood restoration is acknowledged as the most difficult task in mitigating the impacts of land acquisition and resettlement. Lack of investment in rebuilding livelihood assets may impact the long-term ability of the resettled households to sustain their livelihoods (Bui & Schreinemachers 2011; Luu Chinh et al. 2015).

- First, changes in livelihoods (and ultimately in incomes) require enough time for interventions to produce measurable effects. Hay et al. (2019) summarize existing studies and suggest that the "reasonable" amount of time needed can range from 10 to 20 years. However, this time span is not included in most hydropower projects, especially when profitability is emphasized over environmental and social impacts.

- Second, specific activities are often not designed based on the skills of the displaced people; on their experience with livelihood activities in their previous location; or on the livelihood opportunities in the new place. Livelihood programs are likely to fall into a one-size-fits-all trap as the same formula is proposed, regardless of people's situations and of local socioeconomic conditions.
- Third, the funding committed for livelihood activities is always lower than actual needs. The total funding to stabilize affected people's lives in Son La hydropower project was VND (Vietnamese đồng) 6,945 billion, of which livelihood-related support accounted for 36.3 percent (Government of Vietnam 2018).
- Fourth, displaced people and communities are not well-prepared for maximizing livelihood opportunities in a new place. This point is particularly critical for projects in which the livelihood base in the new place is completely different from the original site.

The income restoration program of the Trung Son Hydropower Project is not a perfect example. Its implementation timeframe followed the project cycles, and its impacts have not been fully verified. However, some experience may be suitable for consideration in other projects.

- First, restoring the livelihoods of affected households to the pre-project level is a requirement reflected in all project documents (including the loan agreement signed with the World Bank). This strategy ensures an upfront commitment by all stakeholders and requires proper follow-up throughout the project cycle.
- Second, technical assistance for livelihood restoration activities is performed by a third-party entity selected through competitive bidding, who must demonstrate the experience and capacity to carry out similar activities.
- Third, households benefiting from this program are organized into common interest groups, a model proven to be fairly successful in community-driven development projects. This model requires resettlees' proactive behavior and sense of responsibility for the support that they receive. In-kind livelihood support was provided based on people's prioritization of income-generating activities.
- Fourth, livelihood support activities resulted from several consultation rounds at the village and household levels. Three rounds occurred between 2016 and 2017, with more than 2,600 participants, of whom about 22 percent were women (Nguyen et al. 2020).

- Finally, coordinating local socioeconomic development plans throughout the project cycles was critical for the sustainability of livelihood activities.
    - Successful models should be integrated into the local socioeconomic development plans, so that they will be scaled up and maintained after project closure. The project team kept district authorities informed of livelihood activities through a reporting process.
    - Part of the project's funding was used to finance extra work by commune livelihood boards (consisting of commune leaders, agricultural extension or veterinary staff, Women's Union representatives, and village heads) to plan, implement, and monitor local activities.
    - In terms of field operations, frequent exchange and communication was strengthened among technical assistants (individual consultants contracted by the project); field coordinators (commune agricultural extension staff, veterinary staff, or other local people); village heads; and interest-group leaders.

Satisfaction with livelihood improvement activities in the Trung Son project scored positively, and indicators of the quality of life in the new villages were also assessed favorably. These included monthly income; number of permanent residents in resettlement areas; school infrastructure; healthcare facilities; cultural structures; roads; schooling status of children; and number of household members with employment.

Although it is included in the existing legal framework, the effectiveness of livelihood support remains questionable. Only a few infrastructure projects in Vietnam have successfully implemented livelihood restoration activities (Nguyen et al. 2020:44). Livelihood and life stabilization support are generally converted into cash payments and often lack follow-up activities. Farmers may also face difficulties in managing a large compensation amount without instructions on how to save and invest it effectively (Nguyen et al. 2014:24; Bui & Schreinemachers 2011).[10]

In many cases, the vocational training programs that are offered do not align with people's interests or market demands. The job replacement program may not work for ethnic minority farmers because of their limited educational level and unfamiliarity with wage-based work, which makes them feel hesitant about training for new jobs (Pham et al. 2014:149). Trainees' demands and their actual production situation are often not fully considered in designing proper training materials and in selecting demonstration sites (Oxfam 2017:32). These factors, coupled with insufficient and unproductive replacement land, can contribute to the deterioration of food security once project support ends. Therefore, households need assistance that supports their strategic planning activities (Bui et al. 2013) to help them rebuild their livelihood assets over time.

While livelihood restoration remains challenging, it is promising to see a program – like that of Trung Son – implementing empowerment, participation, demand-driven, responsibility, and accountability principles. Such a program will likely succeed. Active participation and technical assistance have once again proven to be critical factors in achieving positive results.

Attention to vulnerable groups (women, ethnic minorities) and local culture

Like many countries globally, hydropower development in Vietnam occurs mainly in remote upland areas, where conditions for socioeconomic development are far less developed than in lowland areas. These areas are also home to many ethnic minority groups with different cultural characteristics, customs, and practices. Therefore, for development projects (including hydropower), understanding the local culture becomes more and more critical for the project to meet the needs of culturally diverse populations living in the area.

Implementing agencies should equip themselves with adequate information and skills to interact, communicate, build relationships, and work effectively with people from diverse cultures and ethnic groups. Failure to adequately address cultural differences potentially causes mistrust and conflicts between project implementation teams and local communities, which can compromise resettlement results. Therefore, delivering culturally appropriate interventions and projects should become a principle in achieving positive outcomes among ethnically diverse groups. This approach is recognized in the United Nations Declaration on the Rights of Indigenous Peoples (United Nations 2007); the Equator Principles (Equator Principles Financial Institutions 2020); and the operating policies of major financial institutions such as the World Bank, the ADB, the ERDB, the Inter-American Development Bank (IADB), and the African Development Bank (AfDB).

Besides cultural appropriateness, implementing development projects requires attention to vulnerable groups such as women and ethnic minority groups. These groups need attention due to their unequal access to project benefits, while suffering disproportionate impacts. They are often more exposed to external shocks that impact their lives and may lack the capacity to cope with such shocks or other external changes (such as those created by development projects).

Economic wealth is an important resource for families coping with external shocks, but this is a resource seldom available for many ethnic minority groups. Although Vietnam has achieved remarkable income growth overall – with the proportion of people living in extreme poverty falling from 20.9 percent in 2010 to 9.8 percent in 2016 – the majority of those who remain poor are ethnic minorities. Ethnic minorities account for only 14 percent of the country's population but for 73 percent of its total poor (World Bank 2019). Similarly, female-headed households will be more disadvantaged than male-led households when dealing with project impact. They may have difficulty adapting to new places because the compensation package does not take into account their contributions (Thukral 1996; Perera 2011; Asthana 2012; Hay et al. 2019; Mathur 2009); livelihoods in new places may not be suitable; support networks may be disrupted (Ganguly 1996; Mathur 2009); and/or they may lack access to paid work (Mathur 2009; Young Ooi Lin 2001). In Vietnam, the under-participation of women in the resettlement process can lead to gender inequalities in determining the use of compensation money; property titling; and household decision-making processes (Nguyen et al. 2021).

Such outcomes are often the result of a combination of different factors, including inadequate impact assessment; poor consultation and planning; deficiencies in the formulation of mitigation measures; and a lack of effective implementation and monitoring mechanisms. Aronsson (2009) suggests that local people should be engaged to help the PMU to understand what is important in their culture and to identify the economic framework necessary for them to rebuild their society. Unfortunately, however, opportunities for participation are lacking in many hydropower projects. Indigenous communities have suffered the most from the impact of resettlement projects on their culture, which has resulted in culturally inappropriate housing styles; inappropriate choice of resettlement sites; and even the loss of century-old cultures. The relocated residents at A Vuong Hydropower Plant suffered the loss of many elements of their traditional indigenous culture (Nho 2013). The relocated site of K'la village people was too close to Ka Liec village, which is considered "taboo"[11] in Cotu traditional thought, causing objections to be raised by the affected communities (CSRD 2018:43–44). In another project in Dak Lak province, affected ethnic minority residents voiced displeasure with urban-style areas with inadequate garden space and the short distance between kitchen, well, and toilet (Dang et al. 2018:123–124).

Luu and Von Meding (2014) state that environmental impact assessments for hydroelectric power plants in Vietnam have not been thoroughly implemented and have focused mainly on measurable physical impacts (waste, noise, dust) without paying attention to significant changes in water balance, deforestation, and cultural impacts. These issues in ODA-funded projects are better addressed by environmental impact assessments that include community consultation, biodiversity, and traditional culture. The Song Bung 4 Hydropower Project, financed by the ADB, (ADB 2014) has demonstrated efforts to incorporate gender into project activities such as consultation; implementation of compensation; restoration of livelihoods; and capacity building. This project introduced a relatively comprehensive and systematic approach, from gender impact assessment to developing and implementing action plans. Embedding gender in assessment and implementation processes complies with ADB requirements but requires the commitment and continuous support of PMUs and locally based experts.

The World Bank-funded Trung Son Hydropower Project boasts similar activities that incorporated gender into livelihood, compensation, and consultation activities (Nguyen et al. 2020). Gender issues were also taken into account in impact assessment, in support activities, and in monitoring indicators. In addition, the project mobilized gender experts to strengthen its capacity and provided District-level Women's Union groups in the project area with support by communicating project activities and associated risks. Communication activities for women (including ethnic minority women) have also been implemented and monitored. The Trung Son Hydropower Project has also committed to addressing environmental and social impacts in a culturally appropriate way. For example, the project was notable for allowing people to build housing that preserved architectural traditions; listening to people's opinions in choosing resettlement sites; and persuading them to relocate more than 2,300 affected graves. On this last point, it is worth emphasizing that, in Thai culture in the reservoir area, people consider touching graves taboo – fearing that it will bring bad luck to their families. This underscores the fact that resettlement cannot proceed smoothly if people are not empowered and involved in decision-making and in monitoring its implementation.

Conclusions

Despite several recent efforts made by development researchers and practitioners, the resettlement impact of hydropower is still a complex problem to deal with thoroughly. Notwithstanding significant improvements, compensation for loss or damage to physical/tangible assets is still far from approximating the market price. Short-term livelihood support activities have never achieved the desired effect, due to their short duration and limited relevance. In addition, there is often little attention paid to intangible psychological, cultural, lifestyle, and community impacts. Analysis by Colson (1971) of the Kariba hydroelectric dam project revealed the social consequences of not considering ethnographic and religious factors in the resettlement process. These points are especially important in the post-resettlement period and in supporting integration into the host community. Mehta (2009) emphasizes the importance of gender and social justice dimensions in resettlement and participation in decision-making throughout project cycles.

Although there are different understandings of developing and implementing a sustainable resettlement model in hydropower projects, we believe that the measures described in this chapter may share some common features. From our experience, we believe that resettlement models should have the following characteristics: compliant with the project's policy; people-centered; no potential risks/social impacts; appropriate for the community context; and gender and culturally sensitive (FAO 2013; Nguyen et al. 2020).

In the long run, the share of hydropower in the national power system may decline, given that most medium-large hydropower projects have been constructed and operationalized. However, lessons learned from completed projects can inform ongoing and upcoming development projects in general and dam operations in particular. Resettlement should be a process in which the views and concerns of all actors involved – despite their different interests – are equally important and merit consideration. This process should fully address the physical, socioeconomic, and psychological challenges posed by resettlement, allowing the voices of all the stakeholders to be heard via discussion and/or consultation. Resettlement projects should also operationalize all actionable mitigation/compensation measures (with appropriate monitoring and evaluation arrangement), healing the harms inflicted throughout the resettlement cycle.

Notes

1 www.evn.com.vn/d6/news/385-cong-trinh-thuy-dien-dang-van-hanh-tren-ca-nuoc-6–12–22154.aspx (accessed 6 November 2021).
2 Data for 2018–2020 were collected from http://dieutrananglucsanxuat.moit.gov.vn/Bieudo01.aspx (accessed 1 September 2021). Other data were retrieved from the 3rd draft of Master Plan for National Power Development in the 2021–2030 period with vision to 2045, Institute of Energy (MOIT). Available for public consultation at https://

moit.gov.vn/phat-trien-ben-vung/quy-hoach-dien-viii-dinh-huong-phat-trien-nganh-dien-viet-na2.html (accessed 1 September 2021)

3 Unless otherwise indicated, information presented in this table was taken from table 16.5 (page 754), Master Plan for National Power Development in the 2021–2030 period with vision to 2045 (3rd draft).

4 Information retrieved from decision No. 1782/QĐ-TTg dated November 12, 2017 to supplement decision No. 193/QĐ-TTg dated January 30, 2011 of Prime Minister, approving Master Plan for Relocation and Resettlement of Lai Chau Hydropower.

5 http://baohoabinh.com.vn/220/149425/Thuy-dien-Hoa-Binh-cong-trinh-xuyen-the-ky.htm (accessed 30 August 2021). Excluded the resettlement impacts associated with the on-going expansion of this hydropower plant.

6 Summary of Article 79, *Land Law* No. 45/2013/QH13

7 The *Land Law 2003* stipulates land use right certificate is a document issued by a competent agency to a land user, confirming their legitimate rights and interests.

8 https://bnews.vn/dan-tai-dinh-cu-thuy-dien-ban-ve-van-quay-ve-noi-o-cu/117654.html and https://vietnamnet.vn/vn/thoi-su/hoang-lanh-khu-tai-dinh-cu-thuy-dien-lon-nhat-nghe-an-chi-3-ho-sinh-song-610354.html (accessed 8 September 2021).

9 http://m.baodaknong.org.vn/trat-tu/15-nam-khu-tai-dinh-cu-thuy-dien-dak-r-tih-chi-co-mot-ho-den-o-87250.html (accessed 8 September 2021).

10 In the survey, the resettled households spent most of it (43.9 percent) on building a large new house. Another large share (26.8 percent) was spent buying furniture, television sets, motorbikes, mobile phones, and CD-players. Respondents saved only 12.5 percent and invested 6 percent in production activities.

11 In Cotu culture, two villages are not built close to each other to avoid conflicts, especially conflict over productive land (CSRD, 2018:43–44).

References

Aronsson Inga-Lill, 2009. The paradox of local participation in forced displacement and resettlement caused by the development process. *Revista Română de Sociologie*, serie nouă, anul XX, nr. 1–2, pp. 37–59, Bucureşti.

Asian Development Bank, 2014. *Navigating gender-inclusive resettlement: The experience of the Song Bung 4 hydropower project in Viet Nam*. Asian Development Bank, Mandaluyong City, Philippines.

Asthana, V., 2012. Forced displacement: A gendered analysis of the Tehri dam project. *Economic and Political Weekly* 47 (47/48), 96–102.

Bui Thi Minh Hang and Schreinemachers Pepijn, 2011. Resettling farm households in northwestern Vietnam: Livelihood change and adaptation. *International Journal of Water Resources Development* 27 (4), pp. 769–785. DOI: 10.1080/07900627.2011.593116.

Bui Thi Minh Hang, Schreinemachers Pepijn, and Berger Thomas, 2013. Hydropower development in Vietnam: Involuntary resettlement and factors enabling rehabilitation. *Land Use Policy* 31, pp. 536–544, Elsevier.

Committee for Ethnic Minority Affaris (CEMA) and United Nations in Vietnam, 2009. *Reviewing the past, responding to new challenges: A mid-term review of the national targeted programme for poverty reduction and progamme 135-II, 2006–2008*. Hanoi, Vietnam.

Centre for Social Research and Development (CSRD), 2018. *Hydropower impacts: From environmental, social and gender perspectives – Evidence from the central and central highlands, Vietnam*. Thuan Hoa Publishing House, Hue.

Cernea, M.M., 2003. For a new economics of resettlement: A sociological critique of the compensation principle. *International Social Science Journal* 55 (175), pp. 37–45.

Cernea, M.M., 2004. *Social impacts and social risks in hydropower programs: Preemptive planning and counter-risk measures*. Keynote address: Session on Social Aspects of Hydropower Development United Nations Symposium on Hydropower and Sustainable Development Beijing, China 27–29 October 2004.

Cernea, M.M., 2008. Compensation and benefit sharing: Why resettlement policies and practices must be reformed. *Water Science and Engineering* 1 (1), pp. 89–120. https://doi.org/10.1016/S1674-2370(15)30021-1.

Colson, 1971. *The social consequences of resettlement: The impact of the Kariba resettlement upon the Gweme Tonga*. Published on behalf The Institute for African Studies, University of Zambia by Manchester University Press, Manchester.

Cook C. Cynthia and Ivarsdotter Kristine, 1994. *Development and displacement: Resettlement review for the Africa region*. AFTES Working Paper No. 5, Environmentally Sustainable Development Division, Africa Technical Department. The World Bank. https://documents1.worldbank.org/curated/en/709501468914745358/pdf/Development-and-displacement-resettlement-review-for-the-African-region.pdf (accessed 20 September 2021).

Dang Ngoc Quang, Tran Mai Huong, Tran Thi Thanh Tam, 2018. Hydropower impacts and community responses: An analysis of barriers. In *Centre for social research and development (CSRD), 2018. Hydropower impacts: From environmental, social and gender perspectives – Evidence from the central and central highlands, Vietnam*. Thuan Hoa Publishing House, Hue.

Dao Nga, 2011. Damming rivers in Vietnam: A lesson learned in the Tây Bắc Region. *Journal of Vietnamese Studies* 6 (2), pp. 106–140.

Equator Principles Financial Institutions, 2020. The equator principles. https://equator-principles.com/wp-content/uploads/2020/05/The-Equator-Principles-July-2020-v2.pdf (accessed 20 September 2021).

Food and Agriculture Organization (FAO), 2013. *Good practices at FAO: Experience capitalization for continuous learning*. http://www.fao.org/3/a-ap784e.pdf (accessed 20 September 2021).

Hay, M., Skinner, J., and Norton, A., 2019. *Dam-induced displacement and resettlement: A literature review*. FutureDAMS Working Paper 004. The University of Manchester, Manchester.

International Energy Agency, 2021. *Net zero by 2050 a roadmap for the global energy sector*. https://iea.blob.core.windows.net/assets/beceb956-0dcf-4d73-89fe-1310e3046d68/NetZeroby2050-ARoadmapfortheGlobalEnergySector_CORR.pdf (accessed 31 August 2021).

International Hydropower Association, 2020. *Hydropower sustainability guidelines on good international industry practice*. https://assets-global.website-files.com/5f749e4b9399c80b5e421384/604b7d2381cf9d101f68472c_hydropower_sustainability_guidelines_feb_2021.pdf (accessed 1 September 2021).

International Hydropower Association, 2021. *Hydropower status report: Sector trends and insights*. International Hydropower Association. https://assets-global.website-files.com/5f749e4b9399c80b5e421384/60c37321987070812596e26a_IHA20212405-status-report-02_LR.pdf (accessed 30 August 2021).

Le Anh Tuan, 2014. Rivers in the central – Central highlands and hydropower planning. In CSRD (ed.), *Hydropower in the central, central highlands: People's concerns and stakeholders' responsibilities*. Vietnam Rivers Network, Thuan Hoa Publishing House.

Luu Chinh, Meding J. V., Kanjanabootra, S., and Pham Doanh, 2015. *Resettlement in Vietnam's hydropower industry: Policies and social impact assessment*. The Construction,

Building and Real Estate Research Conference of the Royal Institution of Chartered Surveyors, The Australasian Universities' Building Educators Association Conference, RICS COBRA AUBEA 2015.

Luu, T. D. C., and Von Meding, J., 2014. *Hydropower development and environmental impact assessments in Vietnam: Current practice and shortcomings Vietnam*. 37th WEDC International Conference, Hanoi, Vietnam.

Mathur, H. M., 2009. Gender biasses in resettlement planning. In L. Mehta (ed.), *Displaced by development: Confronting marginalisation and gender injustice*. pp. 166–195. India: SAGE Publications India.

Mehta, L. (ed.), 2009. *Displaced by development: Confronting marginalization and gender injustice*. SAGE Publications India Pvt Ltd, New Delhi, India.

Meppem, T., and Gill, R., 1998. Planning for sustainability as a learning concept. *Ecological Economics* 26, pp. 121–137.

Ministry of Industry and Trade, 2020. *Investigation on production capacity of industrial products*. http://dieutrananglucsanxuat.moit.gov.vn/Bieudo01.aspx (accessed 1 September 2021).

Ministry of Industry and Trade, 2021. *Master plan for national power development in the 2021–2030 period with vision to 2045* (3rd draft). Available for public consultation at https://moit.gov.vn/phat-trien-ben-vung/quy-hoach-dien-viii-dinh-huong-phat-trien-nganh-dien-viet-na2.html (accessed 1 September 2021).

Nguyen Manh Cuong, Dao Thi Viet Nga, Le Kim Sa, Nguyen Thu Phuong, Tran Van Ha, Nguyen Hong Anh, Le Thi Thanh Huong, Nguyen Huu Thang, Nguyen Ngoc Sinh, and Nguyen Danh Truong, 2006. *A work in progress: Study on the impacts of Vietnam's Son La Hydropower project*. Vietnam Union of Science and Technology Association (VUSTA), Hanoi. https://archive.internationalrivers.org/sites/default/files/attached-files/sonla2006.pdf (accessed 31 May 2021).

Nguyen Quy Hanh, Le Thi Nguyen, Bui Phuoc Chuong, Nguyen Van Que, and Nguyen Le Van Phuong, 2018. Social impacts of A Luoi Hydropower on local communities. In CSRD (ed.), *Hydropower in the central, central highlands: People's concerns and stakeholders' responsibilities*. Vietnam Rivers Network, Thuan Hoa Publishing House, Hanoi.

Nguyen Quy Nghi, Lenihan Martin H., Saint-Pierre Claude, Nguyen Thi Minh Phuong, and Phan Huyen Dan, 2020. *Managing social risks and impacts from hydropower development: sharing experience from a medium-sized dam project in Vietnam*. World Bank, Washington, DC. https://openknowledge.worldbank.org/handle/10986/34442 License: CC BY 3.0 IGO (accessed 31 May 2021).

Nguyen Quy Nghi, Nguyen Thi Minh Phuong, and Do Le Hang, 2018. *Social Readiness of Resettlement Programs in Vietnam: Gender Sensitivity, Participation and Community Cohesion*. World Bank Office in Vietnam, Hanoi.

Nguyen Quy Nghi, Nguyen Thi Minh Phuong and Do Thi Le Hang, 2021. Gender biases in resettlement processes in Vietnam: Examining women's participation and implications for impact assessment. *Impact Assessment and Project Appraisal* 39 (3), pp. 206–217. DOI: 10.1080/14615517.2021.1904376.

Nguyen Van Son, Martin H. Lenihan, Nguyen Duy Thang, David Annandale, Claude Saint-Pierre, Nguyen Thanh Duong, and Le Anh Tuan, 2019. *Vietnam: Environmental and social country safeguards framework assessment – Phase I*. World Bank Australia Safeguards Partnership. https://thedocs.worldbank.org/en/doc/788801595006256885-0070022020/original/VNCSFAReport2019.pdf (accessed 2 September 2021).

Nho, T., 2013. What do people in resettlement sites of hydropower need? *The People's Forum in Quang Nam Province* 29, pp. 28–30.

NIAPP and ASEC, 2018. *Final evaluation report – Resettlement livelihoods and ethnic minorities development program (RLDP)*. Trung Son Hydropower Project, Trung Son Hydropower One-Member Limited Company, Hanoi.

Oxfam, 2017. Enhancing the effectiveness of vocational training in ethnic minority areas – Summary of surveys. In *Lao Cai, Hoa Binh, Nghe An, Quang Tri, Dak Nong, Ninh Thuan and Tra Vinh Provinces*. Pro Poor Policy Monitoring, Hong Duc Publishing House, Vietnam.

Perera, Jayantha, 2011. The limitations of current approches to resettlement. In Hari Mohan Mathur (ed.), *Resettling displaced people: Policy and practice in India* (1st ed.). Routledge, India and London.

Pham Huu Ty, Nguyen Quang Phuc, and Guus van Westen, 2014. Vietnam in the debate on land grabbing: Conversion of agricultural land for urban expansion and hydropower development. In Mayke Kaag and Annelies Zoomers (eds.), *The global land grab: Beyond the hype*. ZED Books, Bloomsbury Publishing, London.

Scudder, T., 2005. *The future of large dams: Dealing with social, environmental, institutional and political costs*. Earthscan, London.

Singer, J., and Hoang, H., 2014. Participation in resettlement decision-making by dam-displaced villagers in central Vietnam. *Asia Journal of Global Studies* 6 (1), pp. 16–29.

Singer, J., Pham, H. T., and Hoang, H., 2014. Broadening stakeholder participation to improve outcomes for dam-forced resettlement in Vietnam. *Water Resources and Rural Development* 4, pp. 85–103. http://dx.doi.org/10.1016/j.wrr.2014.07.001.

Skinner, J., Krauss, J., and Newborne, P., 2014. *Redistribution of revenues from hydropower dams: Review of benefit-sharing mechanisms and local control*. International Institute for Environment and Development, London.

Thukral E. Ganguly, 1996. Development, displacement and rehabilitation: Locating gender. *Economic and Political Weekly* 31 (24), 1500–1503.

Tran Van Ha, 2008. *Follow-up study on impacts of resettlement of Son La Hydropower plant*. Vietnam Union of Science and Technology Association (VUSTA), Hanoi. https://archive.internationalrivers.org/sites/default/files/attached-files/vusta_son_la_report_2008.pdf (accessed 31 May 2021).

United Nations, 1987. *Report of the world commission on environment and development: Our common future*. https://sustainabledevelopment.un.org/content/documents/5987-our-common-future.pdf (accessed 30 August 2021).

United Nations, 2007. *United Nations declaration on the rights of indigenous people*. Resolution adopted by the General Assembly on 13 September 2007, www.un.org/development/desa/indigenouspeoples/wp-content/uploads/sites/19/2018/11/UNDRIP_E_web.pdf (accessed 20 September 2021).

Vu Thu Hang, 2017. *Equity issues in land acquisition: A source of delays in large construction project in Vietnam*. PHD thesis, School of Civil Engineering and Built Environment Science and Engineering Faculty, Queensland University of Technology.

Wilmsen, Brooke, and van Hulten, Andrew, 2017. Following resettled people over time: The value of longitudinal data collection for understanding the livelihood impacts of the three gorges dam. *China, Impact Assessment and Project Appraisal* 35 (1), pp. 94–105. DOI: 10.1080/14615517.2016.1271542.

World Bank, 2004. *Involuntary resettlement sourcebook*. World Bank Publications, Washington, DC. https://documents1.worldbank.org/curated/en/206671468782373680/pdf/301180v110PAPE1ettlement0sourcebook.pdf (accessed 31 May 2021).

World Bank, 2011. *Vietnam – Trung son hydropower project* (English). World Bank, Washington, DC. http://documents.worldbank.org/curated/en/104781468134093713/Vietnam-Trung-Son-Hydropower-Project (31 accessed May 2021).

World Bank, 2018. *Vietnam – Renewable energy development project* (English). World Bank Group, Washington, DC. http://documents.worldbank.org/curated/en/380731546007839041/Vietnam-Renewable-Energy-Development-Project (accessed 30 August 2021).

World Bank, 2019a. *Drivers of socio-economic development among ethnic minority groups in Vietnam*. World Bank, Washington, DC. https://openknowledge.worldbank.org/handle/10986/32307 License: CC BY 3.0 IGO.

World Bank, 2019b. *Better opportunities for all: Vietnam poverty and shared prosperity update*. World Bank, Hanoi. https://openknowledge.worldbank.org/handle/10986/33545 License: CC BY 3.0 IGO.

Young Ooi Lin, C., 2001. Gender impact of resettlement: The case of babagon dam in Sabah, Maylaysia. *Gender, Technology and Development* 5 (2), 223–244.

Legal documents

Government of Vietnam, 2011. Decision No. 193/QD-TTg of the Prime Minister dated January 30, 2011 approving the Master Plan on Migration and Resettlement of Lai Chau Hydropower Project.

Government of Vietnam, 2014. Decree No. 47/2014/ND-CP dated May 15, 2014, regulating compensation, support1- and resettlement when the State acquires land.

Government of Vietnam, 2017. Decision No. 1782/QD-TTg dated November 12, 2017 on Adjustment and Supplementation of Decision No. 193/QD-TTg dated January 30, 2011 of the Prime Minister approving the Master Plan on Migration and Resettlement of Lai Chau Hydropower Project.

Government of Vietnam, 2018. Decision No. 666/QD-TTg of the Prime Minister dated May 31, 2018 approving the project on population stabilization and socio-economic development in the resettlement area of Son La hydropower plant.

National Assembly, 1993. *Land Law No. 24-L/CTN*. National Assembly (NA), Vietnam.

National Assembly, 2003. *Land Law No. 13/2013/QH11*. National Assembly (NA), Vietnam.

National Assembly, 2013. *Land Law No. 45/2013/QH13*. National Assembly (NA), Vietnam.

National Assembly, 2014. *Law on Housing. Law No. 65/2014/QH13*. National Assembly (NA), Vietnam.

10 Post-resettlement integration into host communities

Evidence from a cross-sectional survey of large infrastructure projects in Vietnam

Nguyen Quy Nghi, Nguyen Thi Minh Phuong and Do Thi Le Hang

Introduction

Integration into host communities constitutes a central problem in resettlement processes, yet this issue rarely receives adequate attention from resettlement planners (Cernea 1995). Besides being seen as a direct impact of land-taking, resettlement is also seen as a process in which each actor, whether involved voluntarily or involuntarily, has different interests. Affected people want to maintain the status quo (or delay relocation) and to negotiate the highest possible compensation package. Local authorities, in turn, seek the fastest possible land acquisition progress and the lowest rates of compensation. Investors wish to rapidly kick off project implementation without having land acquisition headaches. Other stakeholders, including social scientists, NGOs, and human rights activists, often recommend that resettlement occurs according to international standards, minimizing harm to affected people and communities.

Resettlement processes, in many cases, end when households accept the offered compensation/relocation package and cede the affected land to the project owner. However, surrendering their land to the project is the easiest part of what will be a long, winding road for relocated households integrating into new communities. Achieving successful relocation will depend on factors beyond their control.

Social integration is a sociological term that has been widely used in refugee and migration research to refer to how individuals find their way to acceptance in host communities and vice versa (Laurentsyeva & Venturini 2017). This multi-dimensional term refers to "the conditions for, and actual participation in, all aspects of the economic, social, cultural, civil and political life" (UNHCR 2002:12). This term perfectly suits the case of refugees and migrants as they arrive in their living areas. The integration strategy for each group would be significantly different, depending on their understanding of their new communities. In addition, how refugees, international/internal migrants, and development-induced relocated households adapt to the new context varies enormously. However, the integration mechanism for these diverse groups follows similar principles. In our

DOI: 10.4324/9781003165774-14

view, critical success factors include the resilience and coping capacity of individuals; their social capital and networks; how accepting host communities are; and policy and other support modalities at the macro level.

The abundant literature on international migration and refugees includes detailed theoretical frameworks covering the original and host communities. Ager and Strang (2008) have argued that integration can be supported through the achievement of four elements: markers and means (employment, housing, health, and education); social connection (social bridges, bonds, and links); facilitators (language, culture knowledge, safety, and stability); and foundations (rights and citizenship). However, measuring integration for internal migrants in the case of households affected by development-induced resettlement is slightly different. This contextual factor requires us to adapt an analytical framework. For us, the "success" of the integration process refers to the resilience and coping capacity of relocated households and to the capacity of receiving communities to absorb them.

This chapter will present key aspects of the integration process, using a portion of a cross-sectional survey conducted in Vietnam. Participants in the survey were households affected by the construction of large infrastructure projects, including hydropower, expressway, urban development, and industrial conversion (Nguyen et al. 2018).

Methodology and research locations

We undertook the survey in four provinces or cities, including Son La, Quang Ngai, Binh Duong, and Hanoi, with data collection missions completed in July 2016 (Son La), August 2016 (Quang Ngai and Binh Duong), and October 2016 (Hanoi).

Son La

The survey was conducted in Thuan Chau in Son La province, a district heavily affected by the Son La hydropower project[1] with more than 1,000 affected households. Most of them are Thai ethnic families, one of the ethnic minority groups affected by this project. Thuan Chau is also the host community for families relocated from Muong La and Quynh Nhai districts.

Quang Ngai

In Quang Ngai province, the survey was conducted in Binh Trung and Tinh Ha communes (Son Tinh district) as they both hosted a section of a national expressway under construction at the time of conducting this research.

Binh Duong

Most of the surveyed respondents in Binh Duong province were residents of Di An Town (Di An, Tan Binh, and Dong Hoa wards). This province has witnessed rapid urbanization in the last 20 years, with the conversion of agricultural land for industrial development. Although residents ceded land for regional development, the surveyed households did not necessarily require physical relocation.

Hanoi

In Hanoi, our primary target group was households relocated due to urban development projects. Hence, the survey was conducted in three wards of Nam Tu Liem district (Xuan Canh, Phuong Canh, and My Dinh[2]) and three of Hoang Mai district (Hoang Liet, Hoang Van Thu, and Thinh Liet). These were rural districts of Hanoi until their conversion into urban districts in 2003 (Hoang Mai)[2] and 2013 (Nam Tu Liem).[3]

In total, 876 households that lost land for development projects (with or without physical displacement) participated in the survey. In addition, 35 in-depth interviews and three focus group discussions were conducted with resettlees, community heads, Women's Union representatives, local authorities, and project management boards. Household survey data were analyzed using the Statistical Package for the Social Sciences (SPSS). Qualitative data were recorded, transcribed, and analyzed using content analysis. Findings from qualitative data were mainly used to validate survey findings.

Findings

Since integration is a multi-faceted process, as noted earlier, we are not aiming to describe it in its totality. Instead, we will only focus on a few aspects that are crucial for integration success. These include indirect factors contributing to integration (distance to communities of origin and frequency of vising parents/relatives); barriers for social integration; and reestablishment of community cohesion.

Being uprooted from the communities of origin

Most families displaced by hydropower and urban development (mainly in Hanoi) had to move to a location different from their home communes or wards, while most of the families in Quang Ngai relocated within their original locations.

Distance

The average distance between the old and new places of residence was 27.3 km, but this varied considerably across project types. The farthest observed distance was associated with the hydropower project in Son La[4] (55.4 km), followed by the urban development project in Hanoi (2.45 km) and the transport project in Quang Ngai (850 m).

Travel time

Travel time between old and new residential places typically correlates with distance (see Table 10.1). Those affected by the hydropower project take an average

Table 10.1 Distance and travel time between the new and old places of residence

	Moving to another commune/ ward? (Yes)	*Distance (km)*			*Travel time (minutes)*		
		Mean	*N*	*Std*	*Mean*	*N*	*Std*
Hydropower projects	85.5	55.36	237	32.165	112.34	234	62.259
Transportation projects	1.1	0.85	88	1.109	7.12	88	5.152
Urban development projects	71.4	2.45	174	2.117	11.87	174	7.839
Total	65.7	27.30	499	34.731	58.43	496	66.744

Table 10.2 Distance to parents' houses after relocation in Son La province (km)

	Increased distance from parents after relocation (km)		*Increased distance from parents-in-law after relocation (km)*	
	Number	*Mean*	*Number*	*Mean*
Male	106	11.0	109	24.3
Female	54	25.5	43	12.1
Total	160	15.9	152	20.9

of approximately two hours (by motorbike) to commute between the two locations. This travel time is much longer than the ten minutes recorded for transport and urban development projects. The relatively large standard deviation reflects the more extended area involved in a hydropower project (32.2 km by distance and 62 minutes in time), compared with transport and urban development projects.[5]

Distance from parents and parents-in-law

The results show that Thai resettled households now live far from their parents and parents-in-law in the post-relocation area for the Son La hydropower project (see Table 10.2).

After the relocation, respondents in Son La reported that they have to travel a greater distance to reach their parents' (an average of 16 km) or their parents-in-laws' (an average of 21 km) houses. The distance increased more for females than for males, because women's living locations change following marriage.

Frequency of family visits

The increased distance may affect the frequency of visiting family members and relatives of relocated households (see Table 10.3). The findings revealed that the farther the distance, the fewer the visits to parents ($r = -.515, p < .001$). In delta areas (Hanoi, Quang Ngai, and Binh Duong), relocation within the same commune or ward (meaning a relatively close distance) would increase the frequency of visiting parents (including in-laws) and relatives.

Table 10.3 Frequency of visiting parents before and after relocation (%)

	Almost everyday		*Several times a week*		*Once a week*		*Once a month*		*Once a year*		*<=1 visit/year*	
	Before	*After*	*Before*	*After*	*Before*	*After*	*Before*	*After*	*Before*	*After*	*Before*	*After*
Province												
Son La	66.7	53.0	13.2	8.2	8.5	4.5	3.1	3.7	4.7	22.4	3.9	8.2
Quang Ngai	23.4	24.3	20.3	22.9	18.8	17.1	20.3	15.7	15.6	18.6	1.6	1.4
Binh Duong	26.8	21.4	12.2	14.3	17.1	19.0	14.6	19.0	9.8	9.5	19.5	16.7
Hanoi	13.5	18.9	25.0	18.9	21.2	22.6	11.5	13.2	28.8	26.4		
Gender												
Male	57.8	49.3	15.6	14.3	8.6	8.6	7.0	5.0	6.3	17.9	4.7	5.0
Female	28.5	23.9	17.7	14.5	19.0	16.4	12.7	15.1	17.1	22.6	5.1	7.5
Average	**41.6**	**35.8**	**16.8**	**14.4**	**14.3**	**12.7**	**10.1**	**10.4**	**12.2**	**20.4**	**4.9**	**6.4**

In the pre-relocation period, 57.8 percent of male respondents reported visiting their parents daily, and we observed a sharp decline to 49.3 percent after relocation. The number of respondents reporting weekly visits also decreased slightly, from 25 percent to 18.9 percent among resettlees in Hanoi.

Barriers to the integration process

Stigma and discrimination

The success of the integration process depends on many factors, particularly the openness or acceptance shown by the host communities. "*Ma cũ bắt nạt ma mới*" (to bully newcomers) is a popular idiom in Vietnamese culture, describing the situation that a person may face when they live or work in a new place. This idiom is also relevant for resettled people, as they may suffer various forms of bullying from original residents, especially if they belong to different ethnic groups.

The most obvious is using language to distinguish "we" (local people) from "they" (resettlees). The newcomers felt stigmatized when the hosts addressed them with phrases such as "resettled people" and "immigrants." This stigmatization was experienced by everyone, including children, young people, women, and men. In Son La, local children called Thai children "displaced persons."

In Hanoi, the move from single houses or townhouses in the city center to an apartment in resettlement buildings on the periphery was considered disadvantageous by many households. These relocated households reported a sense of loss and sacrifice and a perception of being disparaged by others as displaced people, settlers, or migrants.

> For example, in that apartment complex, people from other provinces or other places come to buy resettlement houses and show disdain: "Wow, those resettled people." You see, people despise us resettled people . . . it means dirty, stupid, not classy. Actually, we sacrificed the most for the countryside people to move here. People in Hanoi, who have money, will never buy resettlement houses and apartments. In my case, I worked and retired. My pension is not enough to buy a house. But in the countryside, people sell land and come here to buy a house. . . .
>
> Now I don't understand what class I belong to, I'm neither a merchant nor a worker. . . . I'm not even a farmer because I don't have land. Now there emerges a new class, which is resettled people . . . that is, having nothing. That's why I'm saying that I don't know which class I belong to, not a peasant, not a worker, not an intellectual.
>
> (IDI No. 117, Female, 70-year-old, Exchange city building, Hanoi)

Conflict and fighting

Another manifestation of host community acceptance is the sharing of natural resources – a collective good – with resettlees. This sharing has become a flashpoint, and it is where conflicts are most likely to arise. Mahaptra and Mahapatra (2000) found that potential clashes between migrants and host communities are likely to occur in the collective sharing of resources such as irrigation canals, forests, grasslands, and burial sites.

In the Son La hydropower project, relocated Thai households have moved far away from their old village into an area where other ethnic groups reside. The host community of Mong people claimed that the incoming Thai people had taken their land.

> When dividing the land, they [resettlement officials] pointed out that our land ran to the top of the hill. But the people in Cao San said they had not received compensation money so they did not give land to us. They said that if we did not receive compensation, we were just like them, we were all the same. Finally, we had to give up. That caused disputes.
>
> (In-depth interview, Thai female, Son La, relocated in 2008)

> There were also conflicts between Meo locals and the newcomers. Meo people had more land. They also said: "You are here to take our land. Why didn't you just stay where you were?" Displaced Thai people responded: "We did not want to come here. We came because the party and the government told us to come." Such arguments went on for some time.
>
> (In-depth interview, Mong male, Sơn La)

In Hanoi, differential treatment sometimes comes from the local authority when different requirements are applied to resettlement groups. For instance, even though resettled children were admitted to school, they still encountered some difficulties. Children of relocated families were classified as "non-resident" students, and their parents had to pay fees to enroll their children in school.

To maintain their traditional livelihoods in a location far away from their homes, the incoming Thai community had no choice but to use natural resources alongside local (Mong) people. The latter, who have been there for a long time, warned that they would arrest any Thai resettlees entering their forest.

From stigmatized language to physical assault is only a short step. It was not uncommon for respondents to have witnessed fighting between local residents and resettlees.

> At the beginning, Mong locals were fighting with Thai relocated people because they believed that Thais took their farming land. They chased us away. Children were fighting at school, too. Later, when a Thai was beaten, we called people from 5–6 Thai resettlement communities to come together. Only then did they stop because they were afraid. That happened because, at that time, we were unfamiliar with this place. However, now we are afraid no more. Dare them to beat any one of us, we'd have our people from 3–4 villages pulled together right away.
>
> (In-depth interview, Thai female, Son La, relocated in 2008)

A woman shared her story of 12 years ago with many laughs, tears, and changing emotions. She and a few other Thai women had been detained by Mong people, who accused them of illegally gathering firewood in the forest. They demanded a fine of VND 5 million (equivalent to US$ 217) per person. It was lucky that the story had a happy ending, as these women were released and returned safely, but it became a source of unease for female resettlees. The respondent believed that a rumor of Thai communities receiving abundant compensation money had motivated the Mong people to engage in such illegal behavior.

> Here, we have Kinh, Thai and Mong people in the same village, but we live in separate areas. The Kinh tend to live in a concentrated place. Thai people are here, and Mong people are over there. Although people live together in the same village, the living styles are different. No one wants to go to another area. We live in one village but rarely visit people of other ethnic groups.
>
> (Male of Thai ethnic group, Son La)

Obviously, resettled people in Son La had not anticipated or prepared for this situation when moving to a new living place. The first few years after relocation were punctuated with frequent disputes and conflict between Mong and Thai communities. It took some time for the resettlees to get along with people and familiarize themselves with local norms when exploring collective access to natural resources.

Absence of effective maintenance services for resettlement apartments

"Resettlement buildings" are the typical arrangement for relocated people in a mega-urban center like Hanoi, providing homes for many households affected by development projects throughout the city. City authorities started using this modality 20 years ago, and it still constitutes a large share of resettlement options in Hanoi. During 1996–2000, most resettlement housing comprised old-fashioned, low-rise buildings with stairs – and without a fund for management and collective services such as cleaning in common areas or pruning trees and plants. In the first decade of the twenty-first century, this old-fashioned condominium model was replaced by modern high-rise buildings. When receiving their apartments, many households had to make repairs and adjustments (electricity, water, layout) to maximize utility and space to meet their needs. However, the management and maintenance of resettlement buildings remains problematic, causing challenges for the stabilization of resettlees in post-resettlement life. Living in apartments also forces them to share common spaces and utilities, where conflicts or tensions may arise.

Critical maintenance and management issues

A summary of critical problems and concerns is provided in the following sections.

ELEVATORS

In Hanoi, there have been cases of elevator incidents causing injury and death to users. Moreover, the media has repeatedly covered the issue, warning of poor elevator quality and safety in resettlement buildings. Households reported feeling insecure when using elevators. Elevator maintenance is often delayed, sometimes requiring households to arrange for repair or maintenance themselves.

NOISE

As another concern, many households complained about the limited sound insulation in the apartments, exposing them to noise from other apartments and nearby traffic.

GARBAGE

Apartment buildings have waste-disposal sites on each floor, but households noted that not everyone disposes of waste in the right place, which creates an unsanitary environment.

PETS

Some households keep animals in apartment buildings, angering other households. Owners may not clean up after their dogs and cats, and there have been incidences of biting. There are certain regulations against this, but the government does not sanction people.

PARKING

The residents' demand for motorbike parking consistently exceeds the planned capacity of parking lots. As a result, it is not uncommon for playgrounds and flower gardens to be used for parking as well.

COMMON SPACES

Finally, our assessment found that shared spaces (hallways, staircases) were often encroached upon for personal use. Some playgrounds and flower gardens were also converted into vegetable gardens and chicken coops. In addition to harming the building's appearance and usability, this practice may also block fire lanes and emergency exits.

Timely access to funding for maintenance

Part of the problem is the unclear mechanism for mobilizing funds and using them for maintenance purposes. According to regulations, maintenance activities could be financed from the building management funds (2 percent of an apartment's selling price). However, in our assessment, spending is constrained out of concern that generous spending could cause financial deficits for future activities. In addition, ongoing disagreements between some resettled households and the management board could prevent the fund's disbursement. Some resettled families think that maintenance funds should not be used when the post-construction warranty is still valid; in this case, maintenance work is the building owner's responsibility. The management board, in turn, emphasizes the residents' safety and convenience, citing the lengthy application procedure for triggering related provisions in the warranty document. They wish to use maintenance funds first and to be reimbursed afterward via warranties. Additional revenue sources (from outdoor advertising, parking, and banking interest) would give management boards some flexibility to fund joint activities or essential operations and maintenance; however, not every building has such diverse revenue streams.

Another reason for poor coordination and collaboration in resettlement sites lies in the weak cohesion of the resettlement communities of mixed populations. The deterioration of collective good in apartment buildings could only be reversed if a sense of community exists. The turnover rate of residents is relatively high, causing a constant change in the number of households. After 10 years, the resettled households still in residence accounted for only 30 to 40 percent of all residents in the studied resettlement apartment complexes. Given this constant change, it is difficult for internal linkages and resident norms to take form and develop – so it is not easy to call for residents' contributions to a common maintenance fund. Living in high-rise buildings requires a lifestyle in which safety, respect, and compliance with common standards are crucial. However, a diverse community faces challenges in adopting and establishing these fundamental standards.

Changes in livelihood pattern and strategies

Displacement has disrupted overall livelihood patterns for many respondents. Before relocation, the Thai community in Son La had abundant natural resources as a basis for their livelihoods and for maintaining a self-sufficient economy (see Table 10.4). However, they now have entirely different living environments full of difficulties (including unfavorable natural conditions and water shortages). They confronted numerous challenges: soil that was depleted after a few crops; unfamiliar livelihood models introduced by the project; and livestock/poultry farming failures due to an unfamiliar production environment. In addition, hillside farming, soil erosion, and climate change threaten agricultural productivity in the new area of residence.

The impacts of resettlement on households in Hanoi are unique. Land acquisition for urban development projects has disrupted their business significantly, in some cases even causing the loss of business. Many families had used their place of residence for small-scale commercial activities to generate their primary income. When moving to a new home, this source of income can be significantly affected (as the new location does not have easy access for running a small business). Young people might find new jobs, but the elderly, especially women, find it hard to secure new jobs.

Table 10.4 Description of livelihood activities in old and new places of residence among displaced Thai communities in Son La

Old place of residence	*New place of residence*
– Self-sufficient – Natural resource-based (fish, bamboo shoots, firewood) – Water supply available – Long-established patterns and deep knowledge of the ecosystem – Wet rice cultivation	– Mainly self-sufficient but with some new additional production activities such as tea cultivation – Limited water supply for daily use and irrigation – Unfamiliar farming/land conditions – Limited natural resources – Pressure from host communities – Terraced cultivation/hillside farming

In Binh Duong, many households ceded their agricultural land to construct the town's resettlement sites, but this construction has never been completed. Affected farmers are facing a dilemma: on one hand, they no longer have agricultural land for cultivation; on the other hand, the resettlement plot, which they are entitled to, is not yet available.

Meanwhile, in Hanoi, women living in the Nga Tu So area who had run small commercial businesses quickly became unemployed after relocating to a place distant from the city center, in part due to unfavorable conditions in the new living area (see Box 10.1).

Box 10.1 From Nga Tu So to Dong Tau: The occupational shift of resettled people

In most cases, the resettlement process brings displaced persons to a new residential site or environment that they must adapt to.

Dong Tau apartment building (in Hoang Mai district, Hanoi) accommodates households mostly relocated [due to] a traffic junction construction project in Nga Tu So (Dong Da district, Hanoi). At the time of the survey (late 2016, early 2017), these families had lived here [in Nga Tu So] for ten years. In their original location, they had been able to take advantage of their houses being located close to the road to run small shops in their old site.

Since moving to the current place and living in high-rise buildings, they could no longer conduct business, which severely affected their income. In the process of adaptation, women were more adversely affected. It was not easy for many women, especially those middle-aged and above, to switch to a new job without appropriate vocational training or a specific support mechanism. Therefore, years after relocation, most of them had not been able to find new jobs.

Table 10.5 Self-assessment of community engagement in the new residence

#	*Statements*	*N*	*Mean*	*STD*
1	I think this is a good place to live	821	3.05	.749
2	My neighbors and I have the same desire to join this neighborhood	817	3.03	.778
3	I can recognize most of the people here	819	3.35	.679
4	Things in this neighborhood are familiar to me	821	3.25	.712
5	I care about what my neighbors think about me	820	2.61	.859
6	If there is a problem in this neighborhood, people who live here can get it solved	814	2.94	.738
7	Living in this neighborhood is very important to me	819	3.12	.743
8	I like and expect to live here for a long time	820	3.18	.782
9	Very few of my neighbors know me*	820	3.31	.804
10	People here generally don't get along with each other*	816	3.35	.737
11	Neighbors here don't really care about each other*	817	3.23	.826

* *Statements with response options in reverse order and points have been converted accordingly.*

Community rebuilding

Self-assessment of community engagement in the new residence

A sense of belonging can play a crucial role in helping immigrants/resettlees achieve integration (UNHCR 2002; Wang et al. 2020). The stronger the feeling of belonging, the more motivated individuals became. We used 11 indicators (see Table 10.5) to examine resettlees' perceptions of various aspects of community engagement.

We asked respondents to rank these indicators from 1 ("fully disagree") to 4 ("fully agree"). Most items were rated around 3.0, indicating that resettled people positively assessed their community. Out of 11 items, there were 2 statements with mean values less than 3.0: Statement 5 (whether people care what the community thinks of them), and Statement 6 (regarding the likely success of community involvement in solving a problem). Table 10.6 shows that, for these two statements, women seem to be less positive about community engagement, as their disagreement rate is slightly higher than that of men. Likewise, people in Hanoi tended to be less confident in the community's ability to solve common problems than respondents in other provinces. We also found respondents in Hanoi had the highest percentage disagreeing with Statement 5: "I care about what my neighbors think about me."

For the sum of individual indicators of community engagement, the average score was 34.5/44 points. This result confirms our observation, stated earlier, about the generally positive attitude exhibited by resettled people.

We compared the means of two groups (T-tests) and between groups (ANOVA) to confirm if the differences were statistically significant (see Table 10.7). The results showed that the mean value for the female group was lower than

Table 10.6 Concern about other people's opinions

		I care about what my neighbors think about me		*If there is a problem in this neighborhood, people who live here can get it solved*	
		Disagree	*Agree*	*Disagree*	*Agree*
Gender	Female	39.8	60.2	16.2	83.8
	Male	34.2	65.8	8.3	91.7
Provinces	Son La	29.6	70.4	7.0	93.0
	Quang Ngai	30.0	70.0	5.6	94.4
	Binh Duong	40.7	59.3	5.4	94.6
	Ha Noi	54.3	45.7	40.0	60.0

Table 10.7 Average scores on community engagement

		Number	*Mean*
Gender of respondents***	Male	474	35.2
	Female	402	33.7
Respondents' age groups	<=35	115	35.0
	36–45	194	33.4
	46–55	245	34.3
	56–65	189	34.6
	>=66**	133	36.2
Level of education of respondents	Illiterate	71	34.6
	Primary education	214	35.4
	Lower secondary education	327	35.1
	Secondary education	192	33.7
	Post-secondary education **	59	30.6
Ethnic group*	Majority (Kinh)	626	34.3
	Minority	250	35.1
Age of respondents at the time of land acquisition	18–30 years old	158	34.4
	31–40 years old	199	33.2
	41–50 years old	223	34.6
	51–60 years old	160	35.2
	Above 60 years old ***	103	36.5
Household type	Farm household	146	35.5
	Mixed household	354	36.0
	Non-farm household***	373	32.8
Rural/urban***	Rural	4.98	35.8
	Urban	378	32.8
Province	Son La	246	35.0
	Quang Ngai	252	36.5
	Binh Duong	236	35.3
	Hanoi***	142	29.3
Project type***	Hydropower	246	35.0
	Road	252	36.5
	Urban development	378	32.8

(*Continued*)

Table 10.7 (Continued)

		Number	*Mean*
Resettlement community model***	Original non-displaced	362	36.4
	Displaced as the whole community	243	35.0
	Displaced but not separated from community	145	34.3
	Displaced with mixed population	125	29.1
Total		876	34.5

that for the male group (33.7 and 35.2, respectively). This difference was statistically significant ($p < .001$). This result confirms our preliminary observation in the preceding section of this chapter. Qualitative analysis also confirms that men appear more positive than women regarding community engagement. This difference may be explained by the fact that women have little chance to interact with people outside the home and that they still do not see themselves as a part of the new community even after a long period. Men who have greater opportunities to socialize appear to find it easier to get acquainted with the new place and with the local people.

> There are many Mong people around here. When we came here we didn't know each other. My family didn't know them either. My children and my wife did not speak the Mong language. I could speak some Mong language because when I was in my hometown I liked to make friends with Mong people. I could understand some words they said. Because I know the language, I visited and communicated with them often. We deal with each other more easily.
>
> (In-depth interview of a male, Son La)

For variables that more or less reflect differences in levels of socioeconomic development, we found that groups with a lower level of development had higher mean values compared with those with a higher level of development. The Kinh majority ethnic group had a lower score on community engagement than ethnic minority groups (34.3 and 35.1 points, respectively; $p < .1$). Non-farm households had the lowest score (32.8 points) compared with the other two groups (farm household – 35.5 and mixed household – 36.0 points, $p < .001$). Households in the rural group had a higher score than those living in urban areas (35.8 points and 33.8 points, respectively; $p < .001$).

Households affected by urban development projects had the lowest mean value (32.8), compared with those affected by road projects (36.5) and hydropower projects (35.0 points, $p < .001$). We also found that the resettlement modality may affect the way people assess community relationships. The more homogenous

Table 10.8 Means of scores for mutual support in pre- and post-relocation periods

Occasions/Events	*N*	*After relocation*		*Before relocation*		*Mean difference*
		Mean	*Std Dev*	*Mean*	*Std Dev*	
Funerals, weddings	765	3.18	0.941	3.33	0.887	-0.15
House construction/repair	765	2.02	1.621	2.23	1.654	-0.21
School pick up and drop off	763	1.89	1.448	2.02	1.466	-0.13
House monitoring	765	2.04	1.427	2.23	1.444	-0.19
Lending money	765	2.20	1.368	2.34	1.359	-0.14
Visiting the sick	765	3.14	0.917	3.27	0.898	-0.13
Experience sharing (farm)	763	1.77	1.608	2.07	1.633	-0.30
Experience sharing (business)	747	1.37	1.483	1.49	1.532	-0.12

the resettled communities, the higher the mean values they had. The original non-displaced community had the highest mean value on "community engagement" (36.4), while the lowest value (29.1) was from the community with mixed populations. For the non-displaced group, the unchanged pattern of their relations allowed them to maintain their social networks. The differences between displaced and non-displaced groups were statistically significant ($p < .001$).

Mutual support in the new communities

Community relations are characterized by reciprocal trust and support on a regular basis or during occasional events. Mutual aid creates and reinforces social bonds and linkages between community members. In this study, we used eight indicators to measure the levels of community cohesion. All items are scored from 0 to 4, with 4 being the highest score and 0 representing no relationship. Hence, the maximum combined score is 32, and the minimum is 0.

Overall, the low average score for each activity indicates a low level of reciprocity in the community (see Table 10.8). In the old community, 7 out of 8 activities had had an average score above 2.0/4.0, while after relocation, 3 out of 8 activities had an average score below 2.0. People tend to support each other when their presence is expected (such as attending funerals, weddings, or visiting the sick). These were the only two activities with an average score above 3.0 – but even these activities declined in the post-resettlement period.

As shown in Table 10.9, there was a decrease in mutual support activities among community members in the post-relocation period. The average score for support activities in the pre-relocation period was 2.37, which decreased to 2.20 after relocation. The most significant reductions were observed in three activities: sharing agricultural experience (decreased by 0.3 points); home construction/repair (decreased by 0.21 points); and house monitoring [*trông nhà* – asking someone to keep an eye on their homes when the owner is absent] (decreased by 0.19 points). At the aggregated level (Table 10.10), the average was reduced by

Table 10.9 Level of mutual community support in pre- and post-relocation periods

		N	*After relocation*	*Before relocation*	*Difference*
Gender	Male	474	18.4	19	-0.6
	Female	402	15.1	15.9	-0.8
Ethnic group	Majority (Kinh)	626	13.8	14.6	-0.8
	Minorities	250	24.5	24.9	-0.4
Household type	On-farm household	146	23.4	24.1	-0.7
	Mixed household	354	20.3	20.7	-0.4
	Off-farm household	373	11.1	12.1	-1.0
Project type	Hydropower	246	24.7	25.1	-0.4
	Road	252	18.7	19.1	-0.4
	Urban development	378	10.6	11.7	-1.1
Resettlement modalities	Original non-displaced	362	14.7	15	-0.3
	Displaced as the whole community	243	24.7	25.1	-0.4
	Displaced but not separated from community	145	15.1	16.5	-1.4
	Displaced with a mixed population	125	10.1	11.6	-1.5
Total		**876**	**16.9**	**17.6**	**-0.7**

Table 10.10 Current participation rates in social organizations and activities (%)

	After relocation	*Before relocation*
No participation	22.9	26.5
Participation in at least 1 activity/organization	77.1	73.5
Classmate/age mate reunion	7.7	6.7
Clubs	5.3	4.2
Cultural festivals	31.8	33.2
Neighborhood meeting	72.5	67.0
Women's Union	29.7	28.7
Other mass organizations	41.0	37.1
Local pagoda visiting group	13.9	13.3

0.7 to 16.9 points for the post-relocation period. The difference was statistically significant ($p < .001$).

We now proceed to analyze a composite variable determined by the average score of the sum of all individual indicators. We named this newly added variable "level of mutual community support."

The study revealed that men seemed to be more attached to the new community than women were: the rating for community engagement among men was 18.4 points, while that of women was 15.1 points. This difference was statistically significant ($p < .001$). This trend aligns with what we have identified elsewhere regarding the higher exposure of male groups to community activities, given their prescribed gender roles in Vietnamese society. Further analyses also confirmed the differences in level of community engagement between ethnic groups ($p < .001$); household types (ANOVA, $p < .001$); and resettlement modalities. In summary, community engagement was lower in the ethnic majority group (Kinh); in off-farm households; and in households in urban areas.

Although these groups represent different socioeconomic characteristics of respondents, they all have endogenous and exogenous factors that facilitate or reduce community engagement. For instance, in a resettlement complex in Hanoi, one of the factors explaining the low level of interest in community engagement among young people may be the complexity of life in an urban setting. Pressures and concerns in the workplace may preoccupy many urban residents: spending their daytime hours at work, they often return home when it gets dark. Hence, they may pay little attention to their surroundings. They may even find it troublesome when neighbors are close and they cannot enjoy quiet and privacy at night. On the contrary, it seems easier for people living in rural, mountainous areas to get acquainted and then to improve their level of community engagement. That may be why on-farm households had a relatively high average community engagement score (23.4), compared with off-farm households (10.8). This difference was highly statistically significant at $p < .001$.

Last, we considered how two inter-related factors – project types and resettlement modalities – may also affect community engagement. A project with concentrated resettlement impacts (for example, hydropower) will lead to the relocation of entire communities. In this case, the relocated people are likely to know each other, and hence the level of community engagement would be maintained if not improved. In our study, households displaced by hydropower projects had the highest level of engagement, compared with households displaced by road and urban development projects. Regarding resettlement modalities, the results show that those displaced as a whole community had the highest level of engagement (24.7 points). Households relocated to a mixed-population community had the lowest level of engagement (10.6 points).

Research results showed that relocation makes families less likely to participate in mutual support in the new community. Figure 10.1 shows that after relocation, a slightly increased percentage of households reported "no support"/"no relationship" for each activity. We believe that the nature of the new residential community – and of the resettlement modality in each project type – may have influenced the household level of community engagement.

Participation in social organizations and cultural events

Another indicator that can be used to assess the level of integration into host communities by resettled households is their participation in political and social organizations and activities. The survey revealed a slightly increased rate of participation in social organizations and cultural events in the period after relocation, and the 26.5 percent "No participation" rate before relocation declined to 22.9 percent after relocation. (The reduction in "No participation" also means

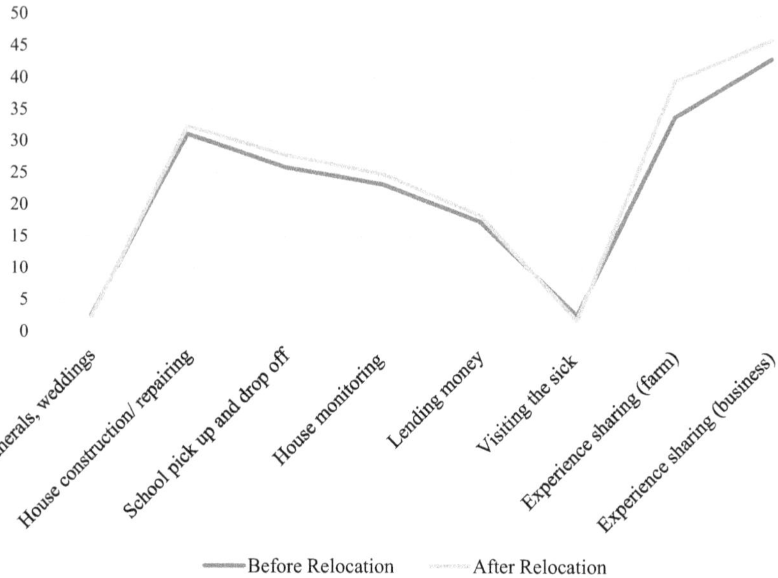

Figure 10.1 Percentages of households reporting no support/relationship in specific events/organization: before and after relocation (%)

an increased participation rate in at least one activity or organization by resettled households.)

The trend of participation in each activity/organization seemed to remain unchanged at two points in time. The activity with the highest level of participation, before and after relocation, was the neighborhood meeting. Participation in cultural activities declined slightly but still accounted for about a third of respondents. The participation rate in Women's Unions remained roughly unchanged, but the participation rate in other mass organizations increased by 3.9 percentage points, to 41.0 percent, in the post-relocation period.

Regarding the number of organizations and activities that households participated in, Table 10.11 shows that, on average, a household engaged in 1.6 activities/organizations before relocation and 1.7 activities/organizations after relocation. Both men and women participated in slightly more activities during the post-relocation period. The average number of activities was higher for male than for female respondents, but the gender difference was only statistically significant in the pre-relocation period. Ethnic minority households reported that they participate in more activities than Kinh households at both time points: pre- and post-relocation (2.4 versus 1.5 and 2.6 versus 1.6).

Analysis by household type shows that non-farm households participated in fewer activities than mixed-livelihood or farm households. The participation level of mixed households was unchanged, while it increased slightly for non-farm households. Among surveyed provinces, on average, households in Son La

Table 10.11 Average number of activities or organizations joined by relocated households

		After relocation		*Before relocation*	
		N	*Mean*	*N*	*Mean*
Gender	Male	452	1.9	452	1.8
	Female	337	1.8	337	1.7
Ethnic group	Majority (Kinh)	555	1.6	555	1.5
	Minorities	234	2.5	234	2.4
Household type	On-farm household	134	2.1	134	2.1
	Mixed household	331	2.2	331	2.1
	Off-farm household	322	1.4	322	1.3
Province	Son La	230	2.5	230	2.4
	Quang Ngai	228	1.9	228	1.9
	Binh Duong	201	1.3	201	1.2
	Ha Noi	130	1.6	130	1.3
Project type	Hydropower	230	2.5	230	2.4
	Road	228	1.9	228	1.9
	Urban development	331	1.4	331	1.2
Total		**876**	**1.7**	**876**	**1.6**

participated in more activities/organizations (2.4 before relocation and 2.5 after relocation) than households in the other research sites. Meanwhile, the participation level of households in Hanoi and Binh Duong was lower than the overall average. Comparing the mean values across provinces, we found that the differences between Son La, Quang Ngai, and Hanoi were highly statistically significant while differences between Hanoi and Binh Duong were not statistically significant. Hanoi and Binh Duong have more or less the same level of socio-economic development, as Binh Duong is an increasingly urbanized province. Therefore, there was little discernible difference between them. However, the last variable, "project type," revealed that the average number of activities joined by households affected by hydropower projects was much higher than that of households displaced by urban projects.

Discussion

These analyses show that many factors may hinder integration of resettled households into a new community. The land acquisition process may have ended, but the long journey of integration has only just begun for most. According to Vietnam's *Land Law 2013*, depending on the project impact, the resettlement plan usually includes the following sub-components: compensation for land (*Land Law 2013*, Articles 74–82); property/construction or land-use restriction (Articles 88–94); assistance (*Land Law 2013*, Articles 83–84); and resettlement (*Land Law 2013*, Articles 85–86).

However, in Vietnam, even the fundamental component "compensation" is still not as fully implemented as it should be. The offered package is often lower than the prevailing market price, which leads to persistent resistance and causes

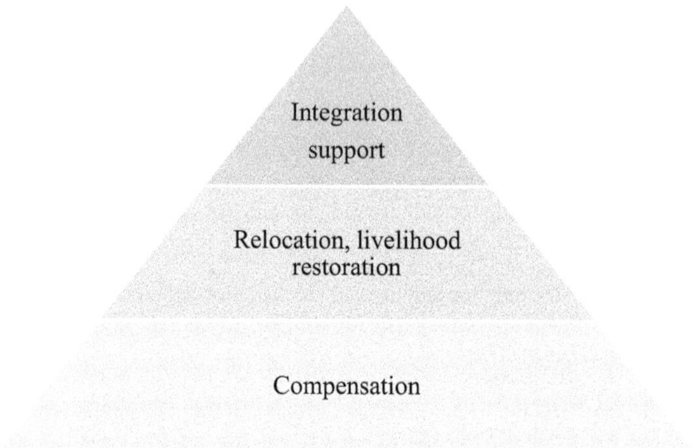

Figure 10.2 The structure of a three-tiered resettlement program

project implementation delays. Studies reveal that inadequate compensation is a common feature of development-induced resettlement – worldwide, not only in Vietnam. It is difficult to calculate and determine fair compensation packages for affected households (Cernea 2008; Fernandes & Thukral 1989; Drèze et al. 1997; Picciotto et al. 2001; World Bank 2011). Studies on resettlement in the late 1990s and early 2000s have demonstrated the causal relationship between poor resettlement planning and the legacy of impoverishment in the displaced communities, in a vast majority of cases (Mahaptra & Mahapatra 2000; Scudder 2005; de Wet 2006). Compensation is simply understood as reimbursement for what has been lost. This conception is far from the oft-stated goal of reconstituting resettlement as "development opportunities" for affected people. The sustainability of livelihood restoration activities is questionable, because affected households typically receive one-time payments under the "life stabilization" budget line.

What is missing in the formulations outlined in Vietnam's *Land Law 2013* is a support mechanism to help displaced people to better integrate into the community and enhanced preparation for the receiving community. In addition to filling gaps in compensation, resettlement, and livelihood restoration, it is time to review the composition of resettlement programs to ensure that tangible and intangible impacts are considered. With that in mind, as shown in Figure 10.2, we recommend a three-tiered resettlement program that covers compensation, rehabilitation/relocation, and integration support.

Such a program could be operationalized as follows.

Maintaining and developing relationships

First, resettlement plans should include provisions that help people maintain existing relationships and develop new ones (depending on relocation distance). We emphasize this factor, given its significant impact on the relationship pattern of affected households. Experience shows that short-distance relocation (for example, relocation within the same commune) or relocating together with acquaintances can reduce the impact on social networks. In our study, only households in Son La had to relocate a long way from their old villages to another district (from Muong La to Quynh Nhai). As noted earlier, this long distance prevented households from visiting members of their extended families.

Colson (1971) argues that families try to find ways to maintain old relationships after relocation, because they constitute significant sources of support – especially when the resettlement home is still new to them. Frequent in-person visits are the most preferred option because exchanging letters seems less effective in addressing problems. People often utilize these visits to perform spiritual rituals, collect fees, and seek help. Studies of social capital in Vietnam suggest that family bonds and links with friends and neighbors are the most important relationships that individuals can rely on during difficult times (Nguyễn Đức Chiện 2015; Nguyễn Tuấn Anh 2013; Nguyễn Thị Minh Phương 2011). Therefore, having to remain far away from parents, relatives, and friends would disrupt these relationships. This disruption may cause disproportionate impacts on women as, after marriage, men are more likely to maintain relationships with their own families than are their wives.

A study in India indicated a similar situation where resettled women were relocated to a new home far away from their parents and siblings. As a consequence, assistance from their parents was out of reach, and relocating made Indian women more dependent on their husbands and their husbands' families (Palit 2009). In short, relocation widens the distance between displaced persons and their family members, discouraging regular or frequent visits.

Colson (1971) found that, for the people in Gwembe Tonga in Zambia, an overwhelming reliance on the kinship and acquaintance system made the threat of losing it a primary concern when families learned about their required relocation. Not being recognized as "kinsmen" (due to lack of interaction) significantly affected both their kinship ties and their religious rituals (needed to maintain the relationship with the supernatural – *matundu*).

However, in the long run, people may question the usefulness of maintaining such relationships at all costs, given the demands of long-distance travel:

> Despite frequent reaffirmations of solidarity, people come to question the utility of going to great lengths to maintain contact with those who are torn out of the context of community interaction which makes the system viable.
> (Colson 1971:88)

In fact, in the new place of residence, resettled households must choose between maintaining a network of acquaintances at a distance or expanding their networks in their new area. Usually, the longer people have been in the relocation site, the higher the likelihood that they opt for the second scenario. On-site acquaintances have a great advantage of knowing and understanding local conditions. Of course, this is not an abrupt transformation: Colson found that it was gradually tested and applied by resettled households through a series of transactions (1971).

Social capital and social participation

Second, resettlement programs should provide a platform for displaced persons to enrich their social capital through increasing social participation. The earlier analysis indicated a decreasing participation level of relocated people in community activities and social organizations in the new living places. The community's stigma and discrimination toward newcomers would worsen this situation.

A concern over resource sharing is probably the leading cause of potential conflict between them. Scudder (2005) argued that the success of a resettlement program depends on the resilience of displaced households in competition with the host community or other migrant groups. In this competition, displaced communities are always in a weaker position, especially when elite migrants (politicians, senior government officials, businessmen) have access to privileged project-related information that helps them convert locations in the project area into economically profitable ones. Scudder (2005) observed such occurrences at the Kariba (Zimbabwe, Zambia) and Khao Laem (Thailand) dams in his survey of 50 major dams around the world. Previously, Chamber (1970), when synthesizing experience from the Volta River hydropower project, stressed the importance of relationships with host communities. These include existing tribal and ethnic conflicts that, in some cases, may result in an abrupt halt to progress in project implementation.

In terms of relocation, conflicts and land disputes are unquestionably predominant. Analyzing factors that affect rejection or acceptance by a host community, Geekiyanage et al. (2021) show that livelihoods and access to resources occupy the most important positions (13 percent of the total variance). This factor includes variables related to roads, public buildings, schools, and water sources. Other factors are the influence of displaced people in political power balances (9 percent of the total variance) and accessibility to public services and social security (7 percent of the total variance).

Increasing social participation is, in our opinion, a multi-targeted arrow. It both creates conditions for resolving conflicts (if any) and, at the same time, increases the social capital of displaced people, which they can eventually use to improve their integration. Data from the World Values Survey (WVS) showed that, on average, each individual is a member of two or three groups in Vietnam. Some reports (Nguyễn Văn Nghiêm 2005; Chu Tiến Quang 2005) have estimated that between 100,000 and 200,000 groups exist in Vietnam. Most of these are small, spontaneous groups, but some have been formed, maintained, and sustained through development projects. The survey also shows that the most engaged-in activities are mainly informal and related to recreational and physical activities, or sports, social, and cultural events. Other activities include sharing experience in trading, irrigation management, or environmental protection. In principle, these groups operate separately, but strong interorganizational networks exist, as a person may have multiple memberships in associations or groups.

Respondents could also be members of formal organizations at the community level, such as the Youth Union, Women's Union, Farmers' Union, or Fatherland Front. However, the role of these government-sponsored organizations in supporting relocated households post-resettlement is limited (Kim 2011; de Wit et al. 2012; Nguyen et al. 2015) or not relevant to land-related debate (To et al. 2019). The role of these organizations would mainly be to support local authorities in implementing land acquisition policies, persuading people to hand over the affected land to the project quickly. They may also contribute to mediation of disagreement or disputes between government agencies and affected households. In many cases, if they are members of a formal organization, resettlees may face pressure from that organization to cede the land, showing their compliance with government regulations.

Previous studies have confirmed the correlation between social participation and social capital (Pelling 1998; Coulthard et al. 2001) and their likely contribution to problem-solving (Brown & Ashman 1996). Wollebaek and Selle (2003) contend that participation in associations would undoubtedly enhance social capital in terms of both social trust and civic engagement. The authors also asserted that the depth of participation has a more significant impact on social capital (civil trust and commitment) than its frequency. Moreover, when the level of activities is constant, participation in multiple groups contributes more to social capital formation. In the process of participation, social capital can impact a group's activities and operations by promoting exchanges and transactions between individuals and groups (Grootaert & Bastelar 2002). As members of an activity or group, individuals engage in social interactions with others outside as well as inside the group. These interactions contribute to establishing weak ties (Granovetter 1973), an essential element of social capital. If individuals can genuinely participate in group activities, they can become contact points for networks between the different groups they belong to. Of course, these relationships are not for immediate usage; they constitute "intangible assets" that might be called upon in relevant contexts, such as relocation and adaptation in the post-relocation era.

Livelihood restoration planning

Third, resettlement planners should factor in the livelihood patterns of resettled households and the socioeconomic opportunities in the new residential area, to inform the livelihood restoration plan. Even though it may have been incorporated in the policy, restoring livelihoods for displaced households remains unsatisfactory. Most planners in Vietnam use a one-size-fits-all approach in developing livelihood restoration programs – programs that are not adapted to livelihood patterns found either in the original or in the post-relocation host communities.

Newcomers require a more extended adaptation period in which to properly understand livelihood opportunities in the host communities. Colson (1971) has pointed out that, in Gwembe Tonga, in the first few years resettled households needed to find a way to "understand" the new environment in order to identify resources (for example, for timber, edible green plants) or soils (quality, suitable crops). Children also need to learn about poisonous and edible plants in their surroundings.

The lack of proper understanding of the current livelihood activities also causes resettlement program failures. Chambers (1970) has pointed out that one of the reasons why displaced people are often absent from the resettlement site is the lack of nearby sources of livelihood, which people need to find elsewhere. People lack land and are not enthusiastic about participating in novel project-supported agricultural production programs (livestock, cropping). They can find better opportunities elsewhere to continue using the skills they are good at, such as fishing.

As Qian and Xue (2017) have shown in their study of three urbanized small cities in China, the integration and transformation levels depend on the households' pre-relocation livelihood pattern. Before the land acquisition, most people had jobs in the non-agricultural sector in a nearby town, so farmland was perceived as an asset, not as a source of livelihood. Therefore, their integration process was not disturbed by the land-taking because these households' livelihoods were virtually unchanged.

Conclusion

Smooth integration into the new community requires displaced people's efforts and preparedness, and facilitation from other stakeholders, during the entire resettlement process. Resettlement can turn terribly wrong if integration issues are not taken into account. It may cost the lives of resettlees, as observed in Beles Valley, Ethiopia, due to long-distance travel (1,000 km) and hot and inhospitable weather, coupled with lowland diseases (Abutte 2000); and it led to a high rate of depression among resettlees in the Three Gorges Project (Xi 2016).

Resettlement constitutes "a temporary reordering of space, time, relationships, norms, and psycho-socio-cultural constructs" (Downing & Garcia-Downing 2008).[6] A post-relocation life often begins in new homes that are far away from relatives and neighbors. New relationships must be established and reinforced to regain balance in their lives. In this context, individuals, families, and communities (in both old and new places) seem to be poorly prepared to deal with displacement and potential hazards. They may overlook (if not ignore) the need to create new social networks and to adapt to new norms and values – leading to an uncertain, confusing, and unpredictable post-resettlement life.

We want to emphasize that cultural, psychological, and social dimensions are equally important for a successful resettlement program. Downing and Garcia-Downing (2008) argue that the transition and adaptation process can be strengthened through a solid understanding of people's needs, expectations, fears, and doubts and through appropriate attention to vulnerable groups. A program that maximizes the participation of displaced persons in the decision-making process and mirrors the local social, economic, and cultural contexts can accelerate the land-taking process and project implementation. Addressing integration-related aspects early on can help ensure smooth transitions; minimize adverse impacts, including post-relocation poverty; and enhance the quality of life of resettled people.

Engagement and integration in a new community are essential parts of the recovery process. Resettlement programs need to achieve a better balance between the "visible" items (such as land, buildings/structures, and crops, and so forth) and the "invisible" elements (such as culture, lifestyle, customs, and social capital). Dealing with intangible impacts is often challenging but critical, and there is no general formula for such interventions. The project implementing agency and stakeholders must work closely to customize mitigation measures to the cultural, economic, and social conditions.

We call for a change of paradigm that places affected people at the center of resettlement processes. They are potential beneficiaries, and the resettlement program should provide them with opportunities for development and shared prosperity.

Notes

1 This hydropower project, the largest in Southeast Asia, affected more than 20,000 households. Relocated households could opt for either back-and-up resettlement or moving to a pre-determined site. The former means households can reorganize within their leftover land and move up to a level higher than the reservoir area.
2 See also Decree No 132/2003/ND-CP of the Government dated November 6, 2003, on the establishment of Hoang Mai district.
3 See also Resolution No. 132/NQ-CP of the Government dated December 27, 2013, on the geographical boundaries adjustment of Tu Liem district.
4 This location might not represent the whole project because the survey was conducted in Thuan Chau district, which hosts displaced persons relocated from Quynh Nhai district. The geographical distance between these two districts is 60 km.
5 Small standard deviations in transport and urban development projects indicated that the observed values (distance and travel time) were close to the mean. Therefore, it may imply that the new residences were not too far from the original location.
6 Downing T.E. and Garcia-Downing C. (2009), Routine and Dissonant Culture in Anthony Oliver-Smith (ed), *Development and Dispossession: The crisis of forced displacement and resettlement*. Santa Fe: School for Advanced Research Press.

References

Abutte, Wolde-Selassie. 2000. "Social re-articulation after resettlement: Observing the Beles Valley scheme in Ethiopia." In *Risks and Reconstruction: Experiences of Resettlees and Refugees, by Michael M Cernea and Christopher McDowell*, 412–431. Washington, DC: The International Bank for Reconstruction and Development/THE WORLD BANK.

Ager, Alastair, and Alison Strang. 2008. "Understanding Integration: A Conceptual Framework." *Journal of Refugee Studies* 166–191.

Brown, L. David, and Darcy Ashman. 1996. "Participation, social capital, and intersectoral problem solving: African and Asian cases." *World Development* 1467–1479.

Cernea, Michael. 1995. "Social integration and population displacement: The contribution of social science." *International Social Science Journal* 91–112.

Cernea, Michael. 2008. "Compensation and benefit sharing: Why resettlement policies and practices must be reformed." Journal of *Water Science and Engineering* 89–120.

Chambers, Robert. 1970. *The Volta Resettlement Experience*. London: Pall Mall Press.

Chu, Tiến Quang. 2005. *Khuôn khổ pháp lý và chính sách để phát triển các tổ chức kinh tế hợp tác trong lĩnh vực nông nghiệp của Việt Nam*. Hà Nội: Báo cáo trình bày tại hội thảo PPWG 'Các nhóm hợp tác nông thôn'.

Colson, Elizabeth. 1971. *The Social Consequences of Resettlement*. Manchester: The University Press.

Coulthard, Melissa, Alison Walker, and Morgan Antony. 2001. *Assessing People's Perceptions of Their Neighbourhood and Community Involvement (Part 1)*. London: London: Health Development Agency.

de Wet, C. (ed). 2006. *Development-Induced Displacement: Problems, Policies and People*. Oxford: Berghahn Books.

de Wit, Joop, Viet Sang Luong, Van Chien Le, Thu Hien Luong, Viet Hung Ha, Thi Anh Tuyet Dang, Ngoc Bau Dao, Hoa Quang, and Thi Thanh Tam Mai. 2012. *Assessing Decentralised Policy Implementation in Vietnam: The Case of Land Recovery and Resettlement in the Vung Ang Economic Zone*. Working Paper No. 546. The Hague: Institute of Social Studies.

Downing, T.E. and Garcia-Downing, C. 2008. "Routine and dissonant cultures." In *Development & Dispossession: The Crisis of Forced Displacement and Resettlement*, ed. by A. Oliver-Smith. Santa Fe: SRA Press.

Drèze, J., Samson, M., and Singh, S. (eds). 1997. *The Dam and the Nation: Displacement and Resettlement in the Narmada Valley*. New Delhi: Oxford University Press.

Fernandes, W. and Thukral, E.G. 1989. *Development, Displacement and Rehabilitation: Issues for a National Debate*. New Delhi: Indian Social Institute.

Geekiyanage, Devindi, Kaushal Keraminiyage, Terrence Fernando, and Thilini Jayawickrama. 2021. "Factors influencing acceptance or rejection regarding being the host community for post-disaster resettlements in developing countries." *International Journal of Disaster Risk Reduction* 1–12.

Granovetter, Mark S. 1973. "The strength of weak ties." *American Journal of Sociology* 1360–1380.

Grootaert, Christiaan, and Thierry Van Bastelar. 2002. *Understanding and Measuring Social Capital: A Multidisciplinary Tool for Practitioners*. Washington, DC: The International Bank for Reconstruction and Development/The World Bank.

Kim, M. Annette. 2011. "Talking back: The role of narrative in Vietnam's recent land compensation changes." *Urban Studies* 493–508.

Laurentsyeva, Nadzeya, and Alessandra Venturini. 2017. "The social integration of immigrants and the role of policy – A literature review." *Intereconomics* 285–292.

Mahaptra, L.K. and Mahapatra, Sheela. 2000. "Social re-articulation and community regeneration among resettled displacees." In *Risks and Reconstruction: Experiences of Resettlees and Refugees*, ed. by Michael M. Cernea and Christopher McDowell, 431–444. Washington, DC: The International Bank for Reconstruction and Development/The World Bank.

Nguyễn, Đức Chiện, 2015. "Mạng lưới xã hội trong phát triển kinh tế hộ gia đình nông thôn hiện nay: Phác thảo từ kết quả nghiên cứu định tính tại hai xã đồng bằng sông Hồng." *Tạp chí Xã hội học, số 4/2015* 25–36.

Nguyen, Quang Phuc, Annelies Zoomers, and vanWesten, A.C.M. 2015. "Compulsory land acquisition for urban expansion: A study of farmer's protest in peri-urban Hue, Central Vietnam." In *Land Grabbing, Conflict and Agrarian-Environmental Transformations: Perspectives from East and Southeast Asia*. Chiangmai: Chiang Mai University.

Nguyen, Quy Nghi, Nguyen, Thi Minh Phuong, and Do, Le Hang. 2018. *Social Readiness of Resettlement Programs in Vietnam: Gender Sensitivity, Participation and Community Cohesion*. Hanoi: World Bank Office in Vietnam.

Nguyễn, Thị Minh Phương. 2011. "Vốn xã hội của nông thôn Việt Nam đương đại (Nghiên cứu trường hợp tại xã Giao Tân, huyện Giao Thủy, tỉnh Nam Định)." *Tạp chí Xã hội học – Số 4/2011* 67–79.

Nguyễn, Tuấn Anh. 2013. "Thuê và cho thuê đất sản xuất nông nghiệp giữa các hộ gia đình ở Bắc Trung bộ." *Tạp chí Xã hội học, số 2/2013* 59–70.

Nguyễn, Văn Nghiêm. 2005. *Các nhóm Nông dân trong Nông nghiệp và ở các Khu vực Nông thôn. – các vấn đề còn tồn tại*. Hà Nội: Báo cáo trình bày tại hội thảo PPWG 'Các nhóm hợp tác nông thôn'.

Palit, C. 2009. "Displacement, gender justice and people's struggles." In *Displaced by Development: Confronting Marginalisation and Gender Injustice*, ed. by L. Mehta, 282–94. New Delhi: Sage Publications.

Pelling, Mark. 1998. "Participation, social capital and vulnerability to urban flooding in Guyana." *Journal of International Development* 469–486.

Picciotto, R., Van Wicklin, W., and Rice, E. 2001. Involuntary Resettlement: Comparative Perspectives. New Brunswick: Transaction Publishers.

Qian, Zhu, and Jianhong Xue. 2017. "Small town urbanization in Western China: Villager resettlement and integration in Xi'an." *Land Use Policy* 152–159.

Scudder, Thayer. 2005. *The Future of Large Dams: Dealing with Social, Environmental, Institutional and Political Costs*. London: Earthscan.

To, Phuc, Sango Mahanty, and Andrew Wells-Dang. 2019. "From 'land to the tiller' to the 'new landlords'? The debate over Vietnam's latest land reforms." *Land* doi:10.3390/land8080120.

UN High Commissioner for Refugees (UNHCR). 2002. *Refugee Resettlement. An International Handbook to Guide Reception and Integration*. UNHCR, September. Accessed September 10, 2021. www.refworld.org/docid/405189284.html.

Wang, Yang, Meiling Gao, Jian Zua, and Katharine Bartsch. 2020. "Social capital and social integration after project-induced displacement and resettlement: Exploring the impact on three life stages in the three gorges project." *The Social Science Journal*. https://doi.org/10.1080/03623319.2020.1728503.

Wollebaek, Dag, and Selle Per. 2003. "Participation and social capital formation: Norway in comparative perspective." *Scandinavian Political Studies* 67–91.

World Bank. 2011. *Compulsory Land Acquisition and Voluntary Land Conversion in Vietnam: The Conceptual Approach, Land Valuation and Grievance Redress Mechanisms*. Ha Noi: World Bank.

Xi, Juan. 2016. "Types of integration and depressive symptoms: A latent class analysis on the resettled population for the Three Gorges Dam project, China." *Social Science & Medicine* 78–86.

Part 4

Addressing emerging and dormant issues in resettlement programs

11 Breaking the vicious cycle

How the private sector can contribute to solving resettlement dilemmas

Dinh Thi Ngoc Bich

Introduction

This study was undertaken in response to two of the most critical development problems in transitional economies like Vietnam: involuntary resettlement (IR) and social conflict. Inspired by the increased role of the "private actor" in sustainable development, this chapter explores the collaboration between public and private actors in the field of compulsory land conversion in Vietnam, with an emphasis on "good practice" – in which the gains and not just the pains of development are shared (Cernea 1999). Over the past few decades, the Vietnamese government has drawn on international perspectives to improve its compulsory land conversion measures, by easing administrative procedures and adopting principles of consensus on benefit sharing between the involved parties (WB 2011). Thus, it is essential for policy makers to be able to access abundant empirical study results on how this principle can be adopted in practice and how it may resolve problems associated with social conflict in IR.

Land conversion in Vietnam: policy advocacy versus controversies

In Vietnam, land policies in general, and land conversion policies in particular, are characterized by the government ideology of "public ownership of land" as well as by continuous change under the influence of international donors.

To understand land policy and land management, including land conversion mechanisms in Vietnam, it is useful to begin with the key ideology stated in the Vietnamese Constitution, which has shaped the "public attitude about access to, control over, and use of land" (McPherson 2011:138). Indeed, the Vietnamese Constitution (2013) explains that "public ownership" over land gives the right to manage all land to the state, which represents the ownership of the entire people. As a result, the terms "land conversion," "compulsory land conversion," and "land takings" (Kim 2009), often used in policy frameworks in Vietnam, refer to the transformation of land from one purpose to another, and ownership is implicitly understood as governmental instead of private/personal land use.

DOI: 10.4324/9781003165774-16

Since the first decade of the twenty-first century, government policies on compensation, assistance, and relocation have been revised and improved significantly under pressure from international donors such as the World Bank and the Asian Development Bank (ADB). These donors set prerequisite conditions, in line with strict international policies for official development assistance (ODA)-funded infrastructure investment projects (Wells-Dang 2013). The basic legal framework for land conversion lies with Vietnam's *Land Law 2013*, which has been revised over time (in 1993, 2003, and 2013) with additional clauses relating to land acquisition (1998, 2001). Particularly, developments in resettlement, support and compensation policies have been guided by Decree 197/2004, Decree 84/2007, and Decree 69/2009, and more recently, the revised *Land Law 2013* was followed by Decrees 43, 45, 46 and 47/2014 for implementation.

Box 11.1 shows that policies of the Government of Vietnam have become more consistent with donor policies for IR (Nguyen & Nguyen n.d.)

Box 11.1 The development of compensation, support, and resettlement policies in Vietnam

Decree No. 17/2003/ND-CP: the exercise of democracy in communes, including requirements for consultation with and participation of people in communes.

Decree No. 197/2004/ND-CP: compensation, rehabilitation, and resettlement in the event of land recovery by the state.

Decree No. 84/2007/ND-CP: supplementary stipulations on issue of land use right certificates (LURC), land acquisition, land use right implementation, procedures for compensation, assistance in the event of land recovery by the state, and grievance redress.

Decree No. 69/2009/ND-CP: land use, cost of land, land recovery, compensation, and resettlement. This decree offers assistance to severely affected households, especially households that need to be relocated or that will lose agricultural land.

Circular 14/2009/TT-BTNMT: guidance on implementation details for compensation, resettlement and resettlement assistance, process of land acquisition, land allocation, and land leasing.

Land Law 2013 followed by Decrees 44, 46, 47/2014/ND-CP: more precise provisions regarding increased participation of the affected people, the state's accountability in land use planning, land acquisition, compensation, assistance, relocation arrangements, and vocational training as well as job creation and income generation.

(Updated by author from Dinh 2015)

Officially, regulations on compensation and resettlement have been properly defined since enactment of the third revised *Land Law 2003* and further refined in the revised *Land Law 2013*. These have been specifically set out in Provision 62 (land recovery by the state) and Provision 73 (land recovery by investors). The discrepancy between voluntary and compulsory land conversion mechanisms introduced in the policy framework has attracted considerable attention in public policy debates.

- The voluntary land conversion mechanism (which encourages the principle of negotiation between investors and affected stakeholders) is generally implemented in investment projects by domestic investors for commercial purposes.
- Compulsory land conversion is land recovery by the state for projects undertaken for national and public purposes. These include foreign direct investment (FDI) projects, ODA projects, and private business projects with national or public economic development impacts. Under the compulsory land conversion mechanism, the land prices are stipulated by the Provincial People's Committee (PPC) and must be based on the "market prices" of land (WB 2011). The relevant state authorities at the provincial or district levels (depending on the scope of projects) are responsible for the implementation of compensation, support, and resettlement.

Thus, the ongoing debate focuses both on projects with political and social purposes and on projects with a commercial purpose (making profit only for the investors), which are defined by the same land policy framework. Especially, the concept of "investment projects with socioeconomic development impacts" (Hung Vo 2009) appears ambiguous to implementation practitioners (Tran 2020). There has been a little improvement since the initial enactment of *Land Law 2013*, *Investment Law 2014*, and other related legislative documents (such as Decree 11/2013/NĐ-CP) that govern compulsory land conversion by the state for socioeconomic development and public purposes. They are subject to three decision-making levels: the National Assembly, the Prime Minister, and the Provincial People's Council.

The two processes in compulsory land conversion and implementation dilemmas

In IR literature, "involuntary resettlement" encompasses two distinct but related processes:

(i) Displacement, compensation, and relocation as an administrative procedural process, and
(ii) Economic restoration and implementation of social-safeguard policies, recognized as forms of socially responsible programs in IR (Wicklin III 1999).

In Vietnam, the revised policy framework defined in Decree 84 and re-emphasized in Decree 69 captures important features of IR by determining compulsory land conversion to be a more complex process that comprises "compensation, support and resettlement." Policy revisions in Decree 84/2007 and Decree 69/2009 allow for the process of implementation for land acquisition, assistance, and resettlement. A greater level of support is provided to people severely affected by land acquisition for economic development, especially for people losing productive land.

Experience suggests that the most striking problems found in the practice of implementation of compensation, support and resettlement in Vietnam relate to:

(i) increased complaints and grievances about compensation prices and administrative procedures; and
(ii) the failure of economic rehabilitation.

According to a World Bank report (2011), the majority of complaints and grievances in Vietnam were related to "improper execution of land compensation and resettlement" (accounting for 70 percent of all administrative complaints) and to land prices (accounting for 70 percent of all complaints on land compensation and resettlement). This suggests that the implementation of compulsory land conversion remains uneven. The evidence about social conflicts in land conversion is presented by a variety of media channels.

The problems of income generation and impoverishment risks for project-affected persons (PAPs) and project-affected communities (PACs) have been critically debated in the public media and by policy making bodies such as the National Assembly. As shown in a World Bank report (2011) and in academic literature (see Wells-Dang 2013; McPherson 2011; and Hung Vo 2009), the fundamental reasons for the problems noted earlier derived from policy ambiguity and from the limited awareness of the implementation practitioners. Indeed, it has been found that precise understanding of economic restoration and social safeguards provisions are virtually nonexistent during implementation, given that appropriate measures are often interpreted as "good practice" rather than "compulsory." The modes of assistance, which can either be "in kind" (non-monetary) or "in cash" (monetary) are not clearly stated in the related provisions. Additionally, there is a misconception about resettlement among state agencies and project developers. Many project developers view "resettlement" as referring only to relocation sites, housing and accompanying infrastructure – while the reconstruction of people's lives tends to be somewhat overlooked. Further, the value of entitlements and package benefits are often claimed to be too limited to meet the needs of effective economic restoration.

Furthermore, the two processes of displacement and economic rehabilitation tend to be closely integrated without distinctive measures for each process. Practice shows that the majority of land conversion projects combine economic restoration and other social-safeguard entitlements with cash compensation packages – whereas the implementation of economic restoration programs (including job creation and vocational training) is often in pro forma manner (Hung Vo 2009).

Seeking alternative solutions: can Public-Private Partnerships (PPPs) serve as good practice?

Based on the author's observations, PPP approaches in land conversion in Vietnam can involve:

(i) land conversion service provision (Hung Vo 2009);
(ii) partnership between private land developers and local governments for local infrastructure development (Kim 2009); and
(iii) the greater involvement of private actors in economic restoration and benefit sharing under the impacts of ODA-funded projects.

My focus is this third form of PPP in land conversion projects, which takes the form of a noticeable and increased involvement by the private sector as an actor and beneficiary in the implementation of compulsory land conversion (De Wit et al. 2012; WB 2011).

The implementation of livelihood rehabilitation programs and other social-safeguard policies take place with government or ODA-financed resettlement projects for big hydropower dams or industrial zones in Vietnam – such as the Son La hydropower dam, the Trung Son hydropower dam, and the Nghi Son and Vung Ang industrial zones. In addition, some forms of benefit sharing take place in private business projects such as the Vincom project, which offered a share of equity to the PAPs (Cernea 2008) and the Nui Phao resettlement project for mining operations, which endeavored to provide income generation and job creation for the PAPs. Especially, benefit sharing was strongly recommended for projects that have significant environmental and social impacts, such as such as mining, industrial cluster construction, large irrigation systems, and so forth (WB 2011:40).

Benefit sharing raises a critical question about the degree of involvement of the government and of private investors during the implementation process, so that both sides mutually benefit. To be more specific, can the problem of mining-induced displacement and resettlement, which are seen as engendering major risks to societal sustainability (Downing 2002; Nguyen 2016), be fixed through benefit sharing mechanisms? In Vietnam, although the international conference on economic management in mineral activities (EMMA) has been organized annually since 2015, there is still a lack of in-depth research about how resettlement dilemmas can be resolved in mining projects.

With this in mind, this research has aimed to identify this type of PPP in the practice of policy implementation of private business resettlement projects under the mechanism of compulsory land conversion. Arguably, since compulsory land conversion is still applicable for projects with a commercial purpose, the implementation process should attract increasing involvement by private investors in order to realize benefit sharing principles.

Method and analytical framework

This chapter is drawn from my PhD thesis, completed in 2015 at the Katholieke University of Leuven, entitled *PPP in practice: Contributing to conflict resolution in compulsory land conversion in Vietnam*. The method used for the research is qualitative, single case design based, encompassing qualitative fieldwork and participant observation in the Nui Phao resettlement project (the NP project) during the period 2008–2013.

This chapter offers an exploration of the PPP approach in the field of compulsory land conversion in Vietnam and its possible contributions to resolving resettlement dilemmas from a "network" perspective (as discussed later). First, in order to justify defining the NP project as a type of PPP, I apply the simplest definition of PPP as "a partnership which involves public and private actors who work or act together" (McQuaid 2000:11). Second, PPP is regarded as a type of policy network (Klijn 1997), a concept used to "indicate patterns of relations between interdependent actors involved in the process of public policy making" (Kickert et al. 1997:6). At the analytical level, the involvement of the actors encompasses resources and resource interdependence, powers, and perceptions. The collaborative structure encompasses rules, interaction patterns, and goals (Dinh 2015). In addition, PPP features both institutional and process factors.

In this chapter, I adopt the key elements of the analytical framework developed in my PhD thesis to assess the PPP process in IR under the network theory (see Figure 11.1). As a result, this simplified framework envisages three major components: input (actors and structures); throughput (processes and content); and output (results). Part of the findings, which assess the outcomes of the NP project collaboration model, are discussed here, as they (the outcomes) were particularly influenced by institutional and process factors.

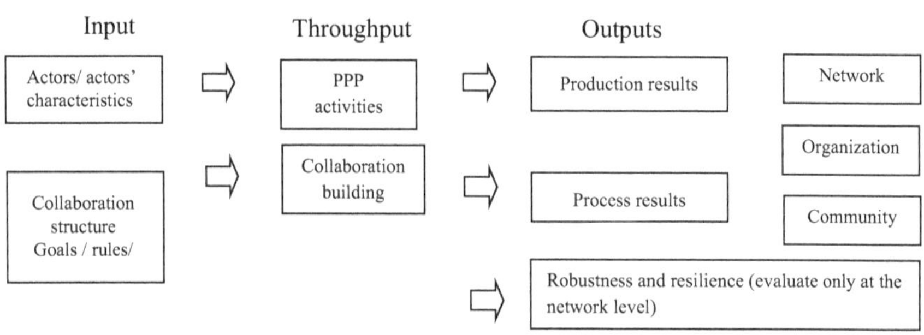

Figure 11.1 Analytical framework to assess PPP in NP project developed by Dinh (2015)

The Nui Phao resettlement project (the NP project): An introduction

The Nui Phao[1] mine is a conventional open pit mine. The primary commodities produced at Nui Phao are tungsten and fluorspar, and its secondary metals include bismuth, copper, gold, and silver. Nui Phao has one of the world's largest identified tungsten deposits outside China, with 55.4 million tons of ore.

Nui Phao mine is located within the Dai Tu District of Thai Nguyen Province, which is approximately 80 km northwest of the capital of Ha Noi and about 150 km south of Vietnam's northern border with China. Dai Tu District is a semi-mountainous district, with a population of about 168,000 people, 94 percent of whom practice agriculture. The district has the largest area devoted to rice and tea cultivation in the province. Despite the potential of the area, 24.63 percent of total households are poor, which is considerably higher than the national average rate of 14 percent and the provincial rate of 18 percent (Thai Nguyen PPC 2011). The district is home to eight ethnic minority groups beside the majority Kinh. The area of the Nui Phao mining project is characterized by a narrow economic base, and it is heavily dependent on subsistence agriculture as the predominant livelihood activity. The natural environment in the project area has been polluted by poorly managed mining operations in the past, and therefore, some of the significant local development needs are related to health issues and safe water supplies.

Historical uncertainty regarding a world-class mining project

The Nui Phao Joint Venture was established in 2004 between Tiberon, a Canadian company, and two local companies (one private and the other one state-owned) with total investment capital of 150 million USD. The project was subject to FDI laws. In 2007, the project was acquired by Dragon Capital, a domestic private investment company. The project has since become a 100 percent domestic investment. Due to the economic crisis in 2010, the project was transferred to another private company, Nui Phao Mining (later changed to "Masan Resources"), which belongs to the Masan Group, a leading private company in Vietnam specializing in consumer products, banks, and mineral resources. In 2011, earthworks commenced, followed by construction of a processing plant and other mining facilities. The mine was ready for operation in 2013. Masan Resources is currently listed on the Hanoi stock exchange as the largest producer of tungsten and among the largest producers of acid-grade fluorspar and bismuth in the world (Mining Global Online 2020).

A segmented and long-lasting land conversion process for mine operation

The complicated ownership history of the project has affected the compensation and resettlement activities, which began in 2006 and have been suspended upon every change of ownership.

Due to its size and significant influence on national and provincial socioeconomic development, the NP project was subject to the *Land Law* (2003) on compulsory land conversion and to subsequent decrees such as Decree 197/(2004), Decree 84/(2007), and Decree 69/(2009) during the seven years of the resettlement and compensation stage, from 2006 to 2013.

The Resettlement Action Plan (RAP) was developed as a collaborative effort with local and regional authorities and PAPs. During the compensation and resettlement process, the RAP was monitored and revised by internal and external (including international) audits. In the meantime, the Public Consultation and Disclosure Plan (PCDP) and the Community Development Plan (CDP), as well as more specific economic restoration programs, have been developed by the Company in order to comply with international norms (as outlined in Box 11.2).

Box 11.2 International policies applied in the NP project

A number of international norms, often regarded as social safeguards, have been set up as key instruments to guide practices in resettlement projects.

Examples of such policies include:

- World Bank Group Operational Policies (OPs) and Operational Directives (ODs) 4.30, including OP 4.01 on Environmental Assessment and OP 4.12 on Involuntary Resettlement
- IFC's Good Practice Manual (1998), Doing Better Business through Effective Public Consultation
- IFC's Investing in People: Sustaining Communities Through Improved Business Practice – A Community Development Resource Guide for Companies
- The International Council on Mining & Metals (ICMM) and World Bank Group, "Community Development Toolkit," prepared specifically to address community development in oil and gas and mining projects.

(The Nui Phao RAP 2005)

Comprehensive resettlement activities in the NP project began in 2006, due to the large scale of land acquisition involved. According to the RAP, updated in 2007 for the NP project, the project comprises approximately 478 ha, of which 40.9 ha is residential land and 367.2 ha is agricultural and other land. The total area required for the resettlement sites was 156.7 ha. There were 3,313 project-affected households (PAHs), of which 1,231 households needed to move their

Figure 11.2 The landscape at the NP project site before land acquisition

houses. Of these households, 985 preferred the resettlement sites while 246 preferred self-resettlement. The estimated and approved cost for compensation, assistance and resettlement was VND (Vietnamese đồng) 885,434,422,000 (equivalent to US$40 million) in 2007 – a large increase over the initial budget of US$26 million agreed in the first RAP in 2005. As of 2013, this amount has further increased, with the total updated cost of VND 1,400 billion (equivalent to approximately US$60 million).

The project area extends mainly over four communes in the Dai Tu District, Ha Thuong, Hung Son, Tan Linh, and Cat Ne, with 23 villages fully or partly affected by land acquisition (see Figure 11.2). Ha Thuong is the most severely affected commune, with more than 776 houses having to relocate; the loss of about one-third of its population; and removal of 100 percent of the population of two villages in the commune. In 2012, with a need for expansion of the project footprint and some additional areas required for engineering works or for mitigation of environmentally adverse impacts, the total area of land needed increased to 678 ha.

Social conflict in the NP project

The concept of *conflict* employed in this research, and as broadly used in IR literature, implies *resistance, tensions*, and *complaints* (Hung Vo 2009; Kim 2009; Oliver-Smith 1996). Participatory observation used in this research illuminated the status of conflicts in various forms – including latent, emerging, and manifest conflict – and revealed the root causes of these conflicts. The figures used later were mainly summarized from company reports and from the reports of the task force group for complaint resolution[2] between 2008 and 2013.

In general, the conflict observed in the NP project can be divided into two stages: before and after construction work began in 2011. As shown in Figure 11.3, letters expressing grievances were viewed as an "emerging" form of conflict, which could potentially turn into "manifest" conflict should the original inquiries not be appropriately addressed by the project. Figure 11.3 also demonstrates that, in the earlier stages, less evidence of conflict was found, while the number of grievances and request letters significantly increased in later stages.

The "latent" form of conflict in NP project is understood to refer to the tensions between the project and the PAPs/PACs during project implementation. These

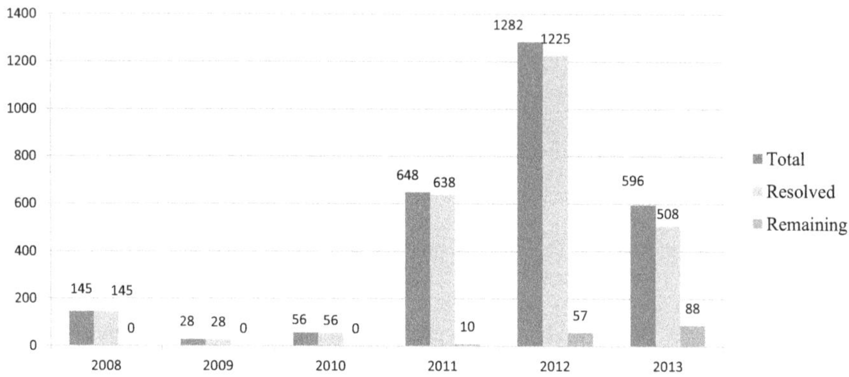

Figure 11.3 Summary of grievance letters, by year, in the NP project

tensions could be found during the community meetings, where expectations or demands over land conversion prices, procedures and additional entitlements were raised by the PAPs and PACs. It was also found that some degree of dissatisfaction over the compensation packages or the performance of the public and private actors also induced the latent form of conflict in the NP project. "Manifest" conflicts in the NP project refer to cases of resistance, demonstrations, and violence. Such expressions of conflict were relatively rare, however. Examples of manifest conflicts included a group of resistant households residing along National Road 37 who refused the detailed measurement surveys (DMSs) and compensation payments, asking for market prices for their residential land; a collective demonstration by various PAPs, who asked for increased compensation payments in October 2011; and resistant households who behaved uncooperatively in the task force group without reaching any agreement (Dinh 2015).

The root causes of conflict in the NP project appeared to be relatively diverse, deriving from policy problems, the implementation process, and the awareness and capability of the stakeholders. First, policy problems were a source of conflict in the NP project in the following respects: inadequate policy content, comprising imposed, non-market-based prices; complicated administrative procedures; and changes of policies during project implementation.

Although Figure 11.3 shows that complaints about compensation prices made up less than 10 percent of all complaint issues, they were associated with critical, active, and ongoing disputes, causing project activities to be interrupted. Procedures for authorization of compensation, support, and resettlement for a household comprised 17 discrete steps that appeared to be difficult for the relevant actors to follow properly, causing the highest number of letters of request. Within the seven-year period (2006–2013) of NP project preparation and implementation, the *Land Law* was revised three times with additional provisions, including Decree 197/2004, Decree 84/2007, and Decree 69/2009 (see Box 11.1). In general, these new policies were revised to realize higher prices and better assistance entitlements than the former policies. However, the PAPs who had already received compensation under the earlier prices realized that they had been paid too little and began to return to their land asking for greater compensation payments.

Second, conflict over implementation resulted from the capacity of the implementation agencies, the project types, and the complexity of local circumstances. To be more specific, the high number of complaints as shown in Figure 11.3 implies disagreement by the PAPs and PACs with the compensation calculation results. Also, the project took many years, resulting in disrupted procedural steps, changes in land status, and the disappearance of documents. Moreover, the DMSs took place several years before payments were fully made, and there were changes in housing structures, crop diversification, and methods of measurement.

Finally, an important point that helps explain PAPs' concerns about the NP project is the negative implications of using the compulsory land conversion mechanism. According to the PAPs, private projects with commercial purposes – like the NP project – should have employed the voluntary land conversion mechanism. Therefore, despite being aware of the policy requirements, many PAP grievances tended to demand a more adequate compensation mechanism, with one affected person noting:

> This project belongs to the company . . . the benefit from the project comes to their pockets . . . it is not a state-owned project. The district and the province only assist the company to acquire the land.

In particular, the PAPs requested more entitlements from the company in terms of income stabilization allowances, bonuses, and employment. These can be viewed as "latent" conflicts, in the sense that if the company is unable to properly handle the expectations and the requests of PAPs, it may lead to uncooperative behavior and resistance by the PAPs. As stated by one PAP in a community meeting:

> The company takes our land being used for cultivation from generation to generation . . . their responsibility is to provide us with new income generation opportunities, not just compensation payments.

Thus, the PAPs and PACs strongly requested additional compensation from the company, asking for better living conditions and more opportunities for income restoration. These requests have been implicitly and explicitly supported by the local authorities, especially at the commune level.

Understanding PPP in the NP project: A network perspective

In this research, the emergence of the PPP approach in the NP project can be viewed as a development in the implementation of compulsory land conversion in the context of Vietnam. The PPP approach signals the increased participation of private actors in response to the weakness of governmental institutional arrangements, which were found to be inadequate for major mining projects.

The voluntary nature of the private actors' participation with their additional resources stems from their dependence upon existing public services for timely acquisition of land for mining activities.

PPP inputs: mapping the actors and inter-playing their roles in the NP project

In the NP project, the "public actors" are the multilayered authorities at the provincial, district, or communal levels where the project is located.

Thai Nguyen Provincial People's Committee (Thai Nguyen PPC) and functional departments

Representing decision-making power at the provincial level, the Thai Nguyen PPC is allowed to issue (or revise) relevant policy guidelines on the basis of standing national laws and relevant public policies. The Thai Nguyen PPC is allowed to issue new policies and regulations based on proposals by its functional bodies (such as the Department of Natural Resources and Environment (DONRE), the Department of Finance (DoF), the Department of Construction (DoC), and others). The Thai Nguyen PPC is responsible for issuing decisions and granting approvals for compensation, support, and resettlement.

Dai Tu District People's Committee (DPC)

The Dai Tu DPC is authorized to manage administrative procedural supervision, appraisal, and implementation and to delegate decision-making power to provincial levels. In particular, the Dai Tu DPC has been authorized to make decisions on land recovery relating to compensation, support, and resettlement only for the affected households; to identify and approve procedures for relocation sites; and to provide official responses to complaints and grievances from PAPs (Nui Phao RAP 2005). Decision-making on matters such as land recovery for collectives – and approvals of compensation, support, and resettlement for households and collectives – is therefore delegated to the Thai Nguyen PPC and to the provincial administrative level – causing complications and fragmentation in policy implementation for this project. The executive of the district government was the Dai Tu Board for Compensation, Support and Resettlement (BCSR).

Communal People's Committees (CPCs) and mass organizations

The Communal People's Committees of the affected communes are the lowest level of the state administrative system in the NP project. The communal actors, the CPCs, and mass organizations (such as the Fatherland Front) are responsible for acknowledging and confirming eligibility for each PAH and details of each compensation package and are in charge of information disclosure and relevant implementation activities in every affected village and commune.

These communal actors also represent PAPs and PACs, and they may also be project-affected people themselves. Due to their dual roles of public authority and PAPs, there is no doubt that the communal actors play crucial roles in enabling the implementation of land conversion in the NP project.

Project-Affected Persons (PAPs) and Project-Affected Communities (PACs)

In land conversion, it seems that public and private actors are highly dependent on important resources that belong to a third party – the PAPs and PACs as the land users. Thus, the PAPs and PACs should also be treated as "actors" in my analysis, despite the fact that PPP theory refers only to "public" and "private" actors. As required by law, the PAPs and PACs are eligible for fair compensation, economic restoration measures, and benefit sharing from investors. The guiding principle is that PAPs should not be left worse off as a result of compulsory land conversion.

The company

As a private business investor, Nui Phao Mining Company (NPM or "the Company") was tasked with supporting the government in moving ahead with the necessary procedures for compensation, support, and resettlement. However, the Company has sought partnerships with public actors and is willing to provide more resources in order to facilitate the process of land acquisition for mining operations. The Company's position was explained by a NPM manager, who said:

> In order to execute the land conversion process for mining activities in the NP project, we definitely cannot rely on the local government to carry out this task on our behalf. This large-scale project exceeds the capabilities of the province and the district. We and our stakeholders mostly benefit from the project outcomes; thus, we should be most responsible.

Other related actors participated and acted on an as-requested basis, including mass organizations, consultation partners, and external auditors (both social and financial). NPM has been also subject to the Multilateral Investment Guarantee Agency's policies in regard to the international social-safeguard policies.

Throughput: collaboration content in the NP project

The structural complexity of the PPP in the NP project suggests two different interaction patterns shaping the two distinct styles of collaboration. These patterns are determined by the nature of the IR and are associated with two distinct but related processes:

(i) Displacement/resettlement, named as the first sub-network (SN1); and
(ii) Livelihood rehabilitation, named as the second sub-network (SN2).

From a network perspective, the two processes of collaboration can also be viewed as sub-networks of a single PPP model involving the same public and private actors, encompassing multilayered relationships and multi-task dimensions in a specific policy implementation domain (see O'Toole in Kickert et al. 1997). In this research, SN1 and SN2, as explained later, are regarded as the sub-units of my analysis of the PPP aspect of the NP project.

Sub-Network 1 (SN1): displacement and compensation procedures

In this sub-network, the members were defined by the application of strict administrative collaborative mandates. The main function of the sub-network is to carry out displacement-related activities, including both on-site works (such as DMS, calculation of compensation, compensation-making, support, and resettlement plans for PAHs) and administrative procedural work. (Administrative procedural work includes information dissemination; acknowledgment and approval for compensation and support; and the RAP, which legitimizes displacement procedures). Relocation site selection, design, and supervision of construction also involve the members of SN1.

However, by additional policy and entitlements, the company is involved as a key player (rather than a "supporter") – making relations between NPM and the multi-layer public actors more collaborative in nature (see Mandell & Keast 2007). An example of this collaboration was provided by a well-known national newspaper, which analyzed NPM policies and claimed that:

> the compensation for the forestland at 260 million VND per hectare, and for agricultural land (paddy land) at 65 million VND per sào, has been multiplied 2.5 times in comparison to the baseline rates set by government policies.
> (Nguyen 2013)

At the implementation level, the Company is linked to all public actors at all levels. The BCSR is a responsible executive agency under the immediate supervision of the DPC. In fact, the district BCSR was assigned to carry out technical work (such as DMS) in only two sectors of project areas (Sector 1 and Sector 3); the NPM hired other professional consulting companies to carry out technical work on land conversion in other sectors of project areas (Sectors 2, 4, 5, and 6). NPM has a big team (as outlined in Box 11.3) providing day-to-day support for various consulting firms as well as for the BCSR and accelerating progress in resettlement and compensation in line with the company schedule. However, all inputs from the land conversion service contracts with the consulting companies must receive appraisal and administrative approval by the district BCSR, which further reports to district authorities and provincial functional departments to carry out land acquisition procedures. In other words, the district authority, provincial functional departments, and its executive BCSR are legally responsible for inputs for land conversion in the NP project, including inputs from the consulting companies hired by NPM.

Box 11.3 Resources of NPM for land conversion activities

NPM has established a compensation and resettlement section with more than 60 qualified staff and associates (increasing to 80 at the most critical stage) – accompanied by well-staffed site offices specializing in land compensation, resettlement, and economic rehabilitation. Notably, modern office equipment such as computers, printers, photocopy machines, and cameras were provided to the office of the state partner. The organizational chart shows that the Deputy General Director of NPM, who was a former senior World Bank officer, is also the leader of the Department of External Affairs. The department is divided into different functional teams such as Community Liaison and Economic Restoration, the DMS, Mapping, Calculations, Land Recovery and Relocation, and the Monitoring and Evaluation sections, to name a few.

Annual reports 2010–2013 of NPM Department of External Affairs

Regarding relocation arrangements for the PAHs, the administrative departments of the Dai Tu District and Thai Nguyen Province, together with NPM, investigated suitable areas for relocation sites. NPM designed the selected relocation sites in accordance with Vietnamese standards for physical infrastructure and social services. The administrative department and district authorities appraised and approved the construction of the relocation sites. As the result, three feasible relocation sites were identified, in Nam Song Cong, Hung Son, and Dong Bong. Affected households had a choice of which site they preferred and were also given the opportunity to self-relocate to a site of their choice. Some wished to make arrangements with elderly or other family members living in the vicinity; others wished to construct a new house on land they purchased elsewhere. Self-relocating households were given a special allowance, as their actions reduced the cost of developing the relocation sites.

In SN1, consultation and disclosure activities played an important role in resettlement, in line with the PCDP developed in 2006 by an international consulting group. The plan was viewed as an integral part of the RAP and would maintain its functions throughout the project life – suggesting that the PCDP was not limited to RAP implementation. Implementation of the PCDP had a double purpose. It was aimed at maintaining two-way communication between the company and various stakeholders, especially the PAPs and PACs. It was also meant to provide evidence, to financiers, investors, and other stakeholders, that NPM is implementing its project based on consultation and with the participation of stakeholders in a transparent way.

Information disclosure took place at the grassroots level, through various channels and tools, including television, newspapers, community information spots, and community loudspeakers, in all 23 affected villages and in the four communal headquarters. In particular, the NPM Information Centre, established in 2006, was visited daily by PAPs and other interested people. In addition, community meetings took place in every affected village and commune. The main topics for community meetings were policy dissemination and explanations and questions about resettlement policies and project information. In addition, community capacity building and awareness-raising activities were provided through workshops and seminars with the participation of external partners.

In line with the PCDP, a complaint mechanism for PAPs in the project was established, disseminated, and implemented. In October 2011, the task force group comprised suitable personnel from the province, the district, and the company, and it operated as an administrative group for solving complaints and grievances.

The collaborative style of the first process (SN1) characterizes the so-called "symbolic PPP" (Mandell & Keast 2007), in which hierarchical governance dominates and public administration is involved in order to carry out compensation and resettlement procedures. This is viewed as short-term collaboration, especially with the highly institutionalized structure of the task force group. Indeed, the task force group demonstrates the unique role of government actors in SN1 while including all the public members of the task force group, as encouraged by NPM. NPM, in turn, strongly pushed to speed up the complaint resolution process. The interaction patterns in SN1 are characterized by tight and close links between public and private actors.

In SN1, there was also a relatively high level of transparency in regard to access to information at the community level, thanks to the effective information disclosure channels instituted in the NP project. In particular, PAPs were encouraged to raise their concerns and uncertainties through the complaint mechanism and PCDP activities to some extent. This engendered high expectations by the PAPs and the larger public audience regarding the performance of the public and private actors, which partly explains the high number of complaints and grievances recorded by the NP project.

Sub-Network 2 (SN2): economic rehabilitation and social-safeguard activities

This sub-network – referred to as a development partnership – was formulated through the company's corporate programs: the Economic Restoration Programs (ERPs) and the Community Development Plan (CDP). In SN2, apart from the predominant role of the NPM, other actors joining this network were the PAPs and local authorities, mass organizations and administrative departments, and consulting and training organizations.

In line with government policies, the involvement of public actors such as the district BCSR and the Provincial and District Department of Labour, Invalids and Social Affairs (DoLISA) was quite ambiguous in regard to the dimensions of economic restoration and social safeguards, which allowed them to simply include these entitlements in cash in the compensation package. This practice can be explained by the "public policy vacuum," which (as pointed out in IR literature) stems from the absence of explicit policy guidelines for implementation in this regard (Cernea 1996:1521). This also explains why the public actors appear to be rather inactive in SN2.

As stated in the Nui Phao RAP (2007), the economic restoration activities derived from the fact that the majority of the people experienced full dispossession – not only losing their residential land but also their agricultural land. Furthermore, if agricultural land for replacing agricultural land loss was not available, affected households would lack productive land to allow them to continue with farming activities or would need to settle for smaller areas of productive land for farming activities. For the PAPs, compensation for lost property was not sufficient to help them to generate income after land acquisition. Income generation through different activities (farm- and non-farm-based activities) needed to be implemented to make sure that project-affected people would, at least, not be worse off.

The ERPs have been diversified to include vocational training and job creation; agricultural service extension (husbandry, tea planting, porcupine raising, mushroom farming); non-farming activities including business and outsourcing service development (shops, laundry, car washing, and construction service); and funding for self-employment – depending on people's preferences. One of the main types of ERPs involved recruitment of PAPs for NPM and contractors. In addition, economic restoration activities have included assistance to vulnerable groups (female-headed households, ethnic minorities, and poor households).

Such collective models encourage efforts to generate income through outsourcing, procurement, and supplying services for project development. Local supply of bags, pallets for tungsten products, and NPM employees' uniforms has accelerated as NPM instituted company procurement priority rankings. Meanwhile, partnership models (such as the Phu Gia mushroom company, a Taiwanese investor) have proven to be a promising avenue for the continuation of economic restoration activities over the long term.

A CDP is also needed to support the ERPs in long-term sustainable development. The CDP was composed in 2006 by international consulting groups. The plan is regarded as the realization of the company's corporate social responsibility through community development and social-safeguard programs in the local area, particularly within its host communities. In particular, the scope of CDP activities in the NP project encompassed gender-based micro-finance programs; an economic restoration fund (CDP 2013)[3] for PAPs; the construction or improvement of infrastructure (roads, schools, and health care centers); programs for ethnic minorities; capacity building activities that bolster the ERPs; and other corporate social responsibility (CSR) contributions.

Thus, differing from the strictly mandated collaborative process of SN1, SN2 is characterized by cooperative relationships between the involved actors. This means that in the cooperative patterns of relations, as clarified by Mandell and

Keast (2007:576), the involved actors are less interdependent and the actors might react with each other only when necessary, such as for exchanges of information and expertise.

PPP output: the public value gained in the PPP model in the NP project

Study of the results of the PPP reveals the importance of the public value generated by collaboration instead of being created by single actors alone, as argued by Bryson et al. (2006:51). The public values identified in the PPP results were drawn from the complete sets of compensation procedures; the decrease in conflicts and complaints; and the positive effects of economic restoration and income generation. These achievements should be interpreted as the collective benefit of the actors as well as evidence of the effectiveness of the PPP in the NP project.

The SN1 resulted in increased benefit for the PAPs, especially for complainants

Recognizing task accomplishment to be crucial for both public and private actors in SN1, the investor was successful in having the land acquired for mining operations while the public actors overcame workload and resource deficiencies in order to hand over the land to the investor.

The positive land compensation results were publicly documented in 2012 by a well-known national newspaper (Thu 2012), including two compelling statistics: 99.6 percent of the total land area had been acquired and a total of 2,700 households had been resettled. Such results addressed local people's concerns regarding the feasibility of resettlement projects with commercial purposes. In one interview, conducted at the time (2010) that the third investor (the Masan Group) began re-activation of the project, a PAP stated that:

> They (the investors) are only interested in the sale of the project, instead of focusing on compensation activities. We are not sure whether they will acquire the land as planned or just keep waiting for a better sale. Particularly, the new investor is a Vietnamese company. We don't think they can carry out this big project while other foreign investors had to withdraw their capital.

In general, in terms of physical infrastructure, the status of the Nam Song Cong relocation site is relatively clear evidence of the achievements of the NP resettlement project (see Box 11.4): the project met the international requirement (Operational Policy 04-WB) that "the PAPs should have better living conditions than the ones before the project." The majority of those interviewed in a 2013 survey commented that the Nam Song Cong and Hung Son 3 relocation sites were the best relocation sites in Thai Nguyen province in terms of physical and social infrastructure – and are often showcased as resettlement models to visitors, including governmental leaders.

Box 11.4 Resettlement in Nam Song Cong relocation site

The Nam Song Cong relocation site comprises 425 plots. Currently, 50 percent of these are occupied by resettled people. The Nam Song Cong relocation site was designed with all necessary physical, social, and cultural infrastructure, namely, a market, community house, health clinic, cemetery, and school, along with amenities such as electricity and clean water. There was also a Catholic church built that was bigger than the original church. Social Audit Report (2012) (Nui Phao Mining) also found that the sales price for household plots at the relocation sites varied from VND 250 million to 550 million, which is 2–3 times higher than the original price (the price per plot sold by NPM was VND 125 million). Notably, 100 percent of the resettled households have been provided with an LUC (Land Use Certificate) for their plots.

The survey results show that the resettlers seem to be satisfied with their more solidly constructed and accommodating houses in the relocation site. However, some of them are frustrated with the smaller residential plot in comparison with their former land. They are also concerned about job opportunities in the new areas since they have no land for cultivation and may lack the ability to learn other non-farm skills. Notably, the elderly purported greater dissatisfaction with their mundane lives at the relocation site since they have nothing to do there. In addition, many elderly people reported that they missed their old villages and neighbors.

(NPM Audit Report: first half 2012, 2013)

Results for complaint resolution were clearly observable in the NP project as the task force group was monitored by issuing monthly reports (see Figure 11.3). It was found that 90 percent of the complainants had their compensation packages revised and gained increases in total cash awards. The majority of the complaints were found to have not conformed to legal procedures and entitlements. Discussion with the NPM and the district staff revealed certain degrees of flexibility in the interpretation of legal procedures and entitlements, which were purposely adapted to benefit the complainants. In addition, more than 20 percent of complaints initially remained unresolved, due to a lack of policy guidelines, which risked creating a major blockage in resolution or agreement between the project and the complainants. To resolve this problem, the NPM issued new policies to provide additional compensation for disputed cases, which had not been clearly addressed by provincial policies. Apart from additional policy measures, there is some evidence that complaints and tensions were resolved in the NP project by other measures as well, such as by negotiation for more entitlements and job procurement. In the words of one NPM human resources manager:

> We offer priorities in hiring to the PAPs who have been severely affected and also to the resisting people, since their requests cannot be resolved by policy.

> We often used this strategy to assist the disadvantaged PAPs and reduce tensions due to resistance. In addition, owing to the priority recruitment policies for PAPs, NP can have more support from the PAPs and their relatives, as they are now our employees.

Local leaders, who had expressed concern about the tendency of PAPs to demonstrate resistance during the last quarter of 2011, showed their satisfaction with the complaint resolutions, in which "no forcible measures were used although we were, at times, about to do so," according to a commune leader.

Finally, it was observed that some resistance and constraints could not be completely resolved in the NP project. Cases of resistance by a minority of the households located along National Road 37 were still ongoing in 2014 and 2015. According to the local authorities and NPM, these households found that they could personally negotiate with the project for more compensation benefits, due to their exceptional location. My investigation revealed that these households requested compensation rates that were approximately ten times higher than the proposed government prices and much higher than the market prices for other plots in the same condition.

The SN2 resulted from an ongoing struggle for long-term stability

The study found different degrees of success between the agricultural and the non-agricultural activities in the NP project, suggesting that the results of the economic restoration activities should be accurately evaluated.

In general, positive results were achieved through non-agricultural activities encompassing vocational training, job creation, and recruitment – viewed as an effective measure to secure income for the PAPs in a timely manner (see Box 11.5). According to the company's sustainability report in 2014, more than 950 PAPs (equivalent to 38 percent of the total workforce including contractors) were employed at the company, thanks to company training and recruitment priority programs. However, my observation showed some tensions caused by increased demand for job creation for the PAPs, which the Company could not afford. The imbalance between the large number of PAPs and the limited number of needed employees for the NPM and its contractors – in combination with the low level of education of the PAPs – was seen as problematic for these training and recruitment initiatives.

Box 11.5 Vocational training and recruitment in the NP project

In mid-2012, Nui Phao completed a training program for 230 project-affected people. As part of the negotiation for land access, and in preparation for commencement of operations, the group of trainees embarked on a 15-month program to learn the technical requirements of operating a polymetallic processing plant. Most of the participants had no previous experience in the mining industry. The training program required participants' attendance at college, visits to other mines in the province, and on-the-job-training. Salaries, accommodation, and other costs were paid for by Nui Phao. At the conclusion of the program, participants received a vocational qualification or trade certificate and were guaranteed a job at Nui Phao. All of the participants who completed the training remained working at Nui Phao throughout 2013. Approximately 22 percent of the group were women.

(NPM Sustainability Report 2013)

In comparison to the success demonstrated by the non-agricultural activities, the agricultural service extension activities did not present equivalent positive results. Although traditional agricultural activities such as tea plantations and the partnership model with the Social Policy Bank for the Economic Restoration Fund (project financed by the Company) showed promising results, other livelihood programs – such as organic vegetable plantation, mushroom plantation, and cattle raising – were introduced but later discontinued due to lack of participation.

The discontinuation of those programs explains, to some extent, the failure of livelihood diversification. Initial results of the economic restoration activities reveal that limited awareness by the PAP participants and a low level of participation by local authorities influenced the activity results in SN2. Indeed, despite the fact that the new agricultural programs were often successful in the pilot stages, many PAPs still wanted to work as casual workers or to be recruited by the NPM. More critically, some PAPs were not interested in the economic restoration activities after receiving large compensation payments. Reports from the NPM economic restoration team and interviews with local officers showed that the majority of PAPs wanted to have cash from economic restoration entitlements instead of joining the programs.

Regarding assessment of the company's performance of CSR (encompassing the CDP and ERPs) in the NP project, I found high levels of satisfaction and acknowledgment by external observers of the tangible results. This was expressed in media articles, audit reports, and presentations by leaders at all levels (from national to provincial and local) (see Box 11.6 and Figure 11.4). Yet interviews with PAPs and communal authorities reveal more complexity. While some interviewees acknowledged the extra support provided to their community by the project, others found that these efforts fell short when compared to the negative impacts of displacement caused by the project. In particular, in the view of the communal authorities, the CDP initiatives should be seen as additional compensation to the affected community rather than as benefit sharing or CSR by the Company.

As a communal leader said:

> we cannot deny that there is much additional support from the project such as the construction of schools, community houses, clinics. . . . However, we

expect more than these since the company will benefit greatly from mining operations and our share is not adequate.

This attitude/standpoint partly explains the limited participation of the local authorities in the SN2, while demanding more responsibility of the company in this regard. The implementation processes, including supervision, promotion, and evaluation, were mainly carried out by the NPM staff.

Box 11.6 The establishment of the Cao Lan ethnic minority display corner

The Cao Lan ethnic group originated from a mountainous part of Thai Nguyen province in northern Vietnam and moved to Hamlet 5 and Hamlet 6 of Ha Thuong commune. During the land acquisition phase of the NPM project, the majority of the PAHs (nearly one hundred households) from Hamlet 5 decided to resettle in Hamlet 6, whose population was also mainly Cao Lan.

In 2013, NPM helped the Cao Lan ethnic minority group in Hamlet 6 celebrate their heritage by establishing a display of artifacts and cultural material. Over the years, the Cao Lan people's lives have changed considerably, and the establishment of this display helped to reinvigorate discussions about the group's background and cultural heritage. Moreover, the resettled and the host population can share their cultural heritage in this sense, facilitating social integration.

Figure 11.4 The Cao Lan ethnic minority display

In general, although it is voluntary and philanthropic in nature, the SN2 is viewed as an instrument for achieving the primary goal of acquiring land for mine operations. Since SN2 invested in socially responsible activities in land conversion, the positive results attained in SN1 helped to minimize conflicts of interest between the Company and the PAPs/PACs. The evidence regarding complaint resolution in SN1 also shows that many complaints were addressed owing to the recruitment and the income generation initiatives described earlier.

Discussion: can everybody win in IR?

> All involuntary resettlement projects should be conceived and executed as development programs, with resettlers provided sufficient investment resources and opportunities to share in project benefits.
>
> (World Bank Operational Directive 4.30)

The experience of the NP project underscores the challenges that arise in realizing an IR project as a development project – since displacement and resettlement further short-term objectives, while development is perceived as a long-term journey. However, the parallel implementation of SN1 and SN2 in the NP project suggests a promising PPP approach to obtain dual goals in IR. This section discusses the feasibility of PPP in IR, based on assessment of the outcomes of the NP project, encompassing both successes and failures in implementation.

Success in compulsory land conversion comes at a price

The experience of the NP project demonstrates the fact that resettlement expenses are often underestimated and thus increase due to the long-term nature of this type of project, as argued by Cernea (1999, 2008).

The whole process of compensation, support and resettlement in the NP project did not come cheaply. Indeed, the project started in 2004 and it was expected that the compensation and resettlement phase would have been completed by 2007. Further investigation of the history of the project showed that the prolonged preparation phases and the impacts of the national and regional financial crisis caused severe tensions that forced two previous project owners (Tiberon and the Dragon Capital) to withdraw their capital from the project. Consequently, disruption of the NP project meant a great loss to the former investors and to the affected people. It is important to note that Masan was not the original investor and that they benefited from the failure of the previous investors by re-acquiring a project which had been in preparation for a long time. However, strong and resilient financial capability proved to be crucial to the success of the company.

Risk taking in the company's strategy

As stated earlier, the failure of previous investors in the NP project underscores the high risk characterizing investment in land conversion projects, which require appropriate land conversion strategies. The company regarded PPP in the NP project as a means to achieve their business goals. The private actor is most concerned with the progress of the project, which is significantly determined by the relevant public service providers and the authorities, as well as by resistance by the PAPs, which may increase transaction costs. Therefore, the company's strategies included increased financial investments for capacity building and for lobbying the authorities and corporate social responsibility initiatives for the PACs. Thus, it can be inferred that the strategies of the private actor were characterized by risk taking and innovations, particularly considering that there were few lessons to draw from other similar resettlement projects in the district and provinces.

Rethinking public actors' accountability

The positive PPP results seem to have enhanced the reputation and credibility of the public actors, of the government authorities related to the public service provider, and of the social safeguards body in compulsory land conversion. The results of the economic restoration programs and other sustainable development initiatives support the view that the public goals were largely achieved in the NP project and are in line with the national goals – being socioeconomic development and social security as a whole. Notably, the positive results of the task force group make them a convincing example of successful PPP in conflict resolution, characterized by a decline in complaint letters; a high degree of acceptance by complainants of proposed grievance adjudication; and making the complaint mechanism more effective and reliable for the PAPs and PACs. However, observation revealed limited leadership by the public actors in regard to project execution, or in resolving difficult cases of displacement, given that the public actors were endowed with full formal authority for land conversion. Similarly, public actors became involved to a limited extent in implementing economic restoration and social safeguards, due to an absence of the institutional capacity needed (for a similar argument, see Hung Vo 2009). Indeed, some public members (as they were not dedicated actors) had a tendency to become "free riders" in the network, since they perceived that the private actor should be the key player in the NP project with "private business" goals. I therefore argue that the robustness and resilience of the PPP project in IR should be improved through greater accountability for public actors.

Access and mechanism of public participation

At the implementation level of the compulsory land conversion policies in the NP project, the study indicates that a high degree of participation was generated through PCDP, which has created a real impact. It is interesting to observe that new or additional formal rights and benefits for PAPs and PACs were developed gradually, evolving from participation and consultation in the preparation phase (under RAP preparation); in the implementation phase; and in the conflict resolution phase. Through the PCDP, which encompassed the complaint mechanisms, the PAPs and PACs were encouraged and guided to voice uncertainties, concerns, grievances, and disagreements. As a result, the NP project experienced an unusually high number of complaints and grievances, compared with other IR projects in Vietnam. However, all complaints and grievances were recorded, monitored, and fully addressed by different proposed solutions, which went beyond government policies and entitlements. Finally, the complainants gained additional benefits and, notably, there were no forced measures applied in cases of resistance in the NP project.

Conclusion

The study of the PPP in the NP project is meaningful in the IR literature, particularly with regard to the contribution of the PPP in developing alternative approaches to mitigate the adverse impacts of involuntary resettlement. Assessment of the public values in the NP project shows that PPPs can produce results, solutions, and processes that otherwise would not have been possible with single, hierarchical organizations (Agranoff & McGuire 2001).

However, the emergence of the PPP in the NP project may raise a question about the definition of PPP, since hierarchy with "commands and controls" still dominate the relationship between the actors. In response to this question, I have discussed the special features of PPP in sustainable development, which involve not only the provision of additional services but also separate value-added activities voluntarily developed by the private actor. Thus, empirical analysis of the outcomes of the NP project shows that this type of PPP shares features with the CSR type of PPP, which are not emphasized in the accepted policy framework for PPP. In other words, the value-added activities increase the contribution of the PPP in IR. Finally, it is important to note that the NP project suggests that the PPP-CSR approach is not always a panacea, since the core nature of forced displacement still exists and must be addressed at a policy level.

Notes

1 In English the term "Nui Phao" means "artillery mountain."
2 The task force group comprising suitable personnel from the province, district, and the company operated as a selective and a functional group for solving complaints and grievances (Dinh 2015).
3 CDP report 2013: From 2013 NPM committed to fundraising from 100,000 to 150,000 USD annually.

References

Agranoff, R., & McGuire, M. (2001). Big questions in public network management research. *Journal of Public Administration Research and Theory*, *11*(3), 295–326.

Bryson, J. M., Crosby, B. C., & Stone, M. M. (2006). The design and implementation of Cross-Sector collaborations: Propositions from the literature. *Public Administration Review*, *66*(S1), 44–55. Special Issue.

Cernea, M. (1996). Public policy responses to development-induced population displacements. *Economic and Political Weekly*, 1515–1523.

Cernea, M. (Ed.). (1999). *The economics of involuntary resettlement: Questions and challenges*. World Bank Publications. doi:10.1016/S1674-2370(15)30021-1.

Cernea, M. (2008). Compensation and benefit sharing: Why resettlement policies and practices must be reformed. *Water Science and Engineering*, *1*(1), 89–120. doi:10.1016/s1674-2370(15)30021-1.

De Wit, J., Sang, V., Van Chien, L., Hien, T., Hung, V., Ha, H., & Mai, M. (2012). Assessing decentralised policy implementation in Vietnam: The case of land recovery and resettlement in the Vung Ang economic zone. *ISS Working Paper Series/General Series*, *546*(546), 1–55. Retrieved from https://ideas.repec.org/p/ems/euriss/32910.html.

Dinh, T. N. B. (2015). *Public private partnership (PPP) in practice: Contribution to conflict resolution in involuntary resettlement in Vietnam* (PhD Dissertation). KU Leuven. Institute of Public Governance.

Downing, T. E. (2002). *Avoiding new poverty: Mining-induced displacement and resettlement* (Vol. 52). International Institute for Environment and Development.

IFC's Good Practice Manual. (1998). Doing better business through effective public consultation. https://www.ifc.org/wps/wcm/connect/topics_ext_content/ifc_external_corporate_site/sustainability-at-ifc/publications/publications_handbook_doingbetterbusiness__wci__1319576642349

Kickert, W. J., Klijn, E. H., & Koppenjan, J. F. M. (Eds.). (1997). *Managing complex networks: strategies for the public sector*. Sage. http://dx.doi.org/10.4135/9781446217658.

Kim, A. M. (2009). Land takings in the private interest: Comparisons of urban land development controversies in the United States, China, and Vietnam. *Cityscape*, *11*(1), 19–31. www.jstor.org/stable/20868688

Klijn, E. H. (1997). Policy networks: An overview. *Managing Complex Networks. Strategies for the Public Sector*, 14–34.

Mandell, M., & Keast, R. (2007). Evaluating network arrangements: Toward revised performance measures. *Public Performance & Management Review*, *30*(4), 574–597. https://doi.org/10.2753/pmr1530-9576300406

McPherson, M. F. (2011). Land policy in Vietnam. *Journal of Macromarketing*, *32*(1), 137–146. https://doi.org/10.1177/0276146711427447

McQuaid, R. W. (2000). The theory of partnership: Why have partnership? In S. Osborne (Ed.), *Public-private partnerships: Theory and practice in international perspective*. Advances in Management and Business Studies 19 (pp. 9–35). Routledge.

Mining Global Online. (2020). Masan resources Nui Phao Mine: The world's largest tungsten mine. *Mining*. https://miningglobal.com/smart-mining/masan-resources-nui-phao-mine-worlds-largest-tungsten-mine.

Nguyen, H. (2013). Hình mẫu Núi Pháo Mining. *Nong Nghiep Vietnam*. https://nongnghiep.vn/hinh-mau-nui-phao-mining-d117496.html

Nguyen, T., & Nguyen, T. (n.d.). Review of resettlment policies and research. *ISEE*. www.isee.org.vn/Content/Home/Library/ethnic-minorities/review-of-resettlment-policies-and-research.pdf.

Nguyen, T. K. N. (2016). *The conflict between residents and business in mining operations-Situations and solutions*. EMMA Proceedings. Hanoi, Vietnam.

Oliver-Smith, A. (1996). Fighting for a place: The policy implications of resistance to development-induced resettlement. *Understanding Impoverishment: The Consequences of Development-Induced Displacement*, 77–97.

Thu, H. (2012). Dự án Núi Pháo: Những con số "biết nói". *Saigon Giải Phóng*. www.saigondautu.com.vn/doanh-nghiep-doanh-nhan/du-an-nui-phao-nhung-con-so-quotbiet-noiquot-27208.html.

Tran, L. (2020). Thu hồi đất để phát triển kinh tế- xã hội vì lợi ích quốc gia, công cộng. Thực trạng và kiến nghị sửa đổi. *Viện Kiểm Sát Nhân Dân Tỉnh Khánh Hoà*. http://vkskh.gov.vn/thu-hoi-dat-de-phat-trien-kinh-te-xa-hoi-vi-loi-ich-quoc-gia-cong-cong-thuc-trang-va-kien-nghi-sua_1783_381_2_a.html.

Van Wicklin, W. A. III (1999). Sharing project benefits for improving resettlers's livelihoods. In M. M. Cernea (Ed.), *The economics of involuntary resettlement: Questions and challenges*. World Bank Publications. doi: 10.1016/S1674-2370(15)30021-1.

Vietnam National Assembly. (2003). The law on land. Vietnam. https://data.vietnam.opendevelopmentmekong.net/laws_record/lu-t-d-t-dai-2003

Vietnam National Assembly. (2013). The constitution of socialist Republic of Vietnam. Vietnam. https://constitutionnet.org/sites/default/files/tranlation_of_vietnams_new_constitution_enuk_2.pdf

Vietnamese Government. (2004). Decree No. 197/2004/ND-CP of the Government on compensation, support and resettlement when land is recovered by the state. https://leap.unep.org/countries/vn/national-legislation/decree-no-1972004nd-cp-compensation-support-and-resettlement-when

Vietnamese Government. (2007). Decree No. 84/2007/ND-CP additionally stipulating the grant of land use right certificates, recovery of land, exercise of land use rights, order and procedures for compensation, support and resettlement upon land recovery by the State, and settlement of land related complaints. https://leap.unep.org/countries/vn/national-legislation/decree-no-842007nd-cp-additionally-stipulating-grant-land-use

Vietnamese Government. (2009). Decree No. 69/2009/ND-CP additionally providing for land use planning, land prices, land recovery, compensation, support and resettlement. https://leap.unep.org/countries/vn/national-legislation/decree-no-692009nd-cp-additionally-providing-land-use-planning

Vo, D. H. (2009). *Improving land acquisition and voluntary land conversion in Vietnam. Policy note*. The World Bank. https://openknowledge.worldbank.org/handle/10986/18611.

WB. (2011). *Compulsory land acquisition and voluntary land conversion in Viet Nam*. WB Ha Noi.

Wells-Dang, A. (2013). *Promoting land rights in Vietnam: A multi-sector advocacy coalition approach*. Paper prepared for presentation at the "Annual World Bank Conference on Land and Poverty" The World Bank – Washington, DC, April 8–11. https://data.opendevelopmentmekong.net/dataset/043f479e-9fc6-40e0-ad1c-b579c984b6ff/resource/aaf8f1c3-a03d-4912-9d4d-261dcaac2b62/download/wells-dang2355.pdf.

Documents for review

Masan Resources Sustainability Reports 2013, 2014.

NPM Audit Report 2012 & 2013.

NPM Community Development Plan (CDP).

NPM Community Development Report (CDP) (2013).

NPM Economic Restoration Programs (ERPs).

NPM Public Consultation and Disclosure Plan (PCDP).

Nui Phao Mining (NPM) Resettlement Action Plan (2005, 2006, 2007).

Thai Nguyen PPC. (2011). Thai Nguyen province and Dai Tu district: Statistics and socio-economic report 2011.

12 Excitement or anxiety

Psychological aspects of development-induced resettlement

Do Thi Le Hang, Nguyen Quy Nghi and Nguyen Thi Minh Phuong

Introduction

Development-induced resettlement affects the daily lives of families in many ways, ranging from lifestyles, structure, working conditions, social networks, customs, and traditions to losses of assets, income, and livelihoods (Ben-Sira 1997; Chakrabarti & Dhar 2009; Hwang et al. 2007; Verma 2004; Mehta 2009). In such a turbulent context, families face multiple impoverishment risks, as Cernea (1997, 2000) has described in his foundational analytical work. While there is abundant literature on losses of assets, livelihood disruption, and compensation measures, little research has focused on the mental health impact of development-induced resettlement (Xi 2016). Scholars, however, widely acknowledge that this stressful process would have significant psychological impact on affected people (Scudder 2005; Good 1996; Xi 2016). Negative feelings during relocation could eventually affect individual and group behaviors (Cernea 1997). In Vietnam, domicile (accommodation) plays a vital role in the social norms system, as people consider stable accommodation a prerequisite for career development and life stability. Building a house constitutes one of three critical milestones in a farmer's life in a traditional society. Therefore, relocation or resettlement is always a major upheaval for families, especially when it results from involuntary land acquisition for development projects.

Using a portion of a cross-sectional study in Vietnam, this chapter presents the psychological experiences of resettlees who cede their lands (and associated houses) to infrastructure projects. We argue that the current land acquisition practices primarily focus on the "hard" component of compensation (resettlement site and physical infrastructure on the site; compensation packages for affected people (in cash or in-kind); and livelihood restoration and income generation activities). The "soft" aspects of the relocation process (psychological and social support programs) are currently thin or absent in mitigation programs. Successful integration into new living environments depends heavily on mental preparedness and psychological adaptability. Lack of information and preparation may create psychological damage for affected people, leading to other more severe mental health concerns. Action from resettlement planners is needed to consider these soft aspects, making resettlement more comprehensive and building resilience for affected people in the course of settling into the new site.

DOI: 10.4324/9781003165774-17

Research samples, methodology, and locations

In this chapter, we used data related to the psychological experiences reported in a survey described in the methodology section of Chapter 10: Post-resettlement integration into host communities: Evidence from a cross-sectional survey of large infrastructure projects in Vietnam. In this cross-sectional research, respondents (one person per household) were asked to recall their emotional and mental conditions at specific critical times during the resettlement process, especially when learning of the land taking impacts and relocation. The study was carried out in four provinces and cities in Vietnam with households affected by a hydropower project (Son La), a road project (Quang Ngai), and urban development projects (Binh Duong, Hanoi). Each project was unique in its approach to implementing land acquisition and resettlement. A total of 787 households responded to the survey, of which 61.4 percent were displaced (235 out of 237 households resettled in Son La; 132 out of 133 resettled in Hanoi; 87 out of 228 resettled in Quang Ngai; and 29 out of 189 resettled in Binh Duong).

Findings

This section will describe the psychological impacts that affected households reported during the resettlement process. The first two subsections will focus on the sources of the psychological states (emotions/feeling upon hearing news of resettlement activities and subsequent concerns). The final two sections will explore the level of participation of those who reported negative emotions and their levels of satisfaction with resettlement outcomes.

Reported feelings upon learning of project activities and resettlement impacts

Emotions are people's psychological states or mental experiences, based on the recognition and evaluation of situations that occur to them (Lewis 1993; Cabanac 2002). They are often associated with thoughts, feelings, and degrees of pleasure or displeasure. Negative emotions manifest when emotional stress exceeds the tolerance level associated with an event/situation. If these emotions continue for an extended period, they can cause psychological damage. In our survey, we asked people to report their first feeling when learning about the impact of resettlement for their families.

Nearly 70 percent of survey respondents said they were apprehensive when they heard about the family's upcoming resettlement (see Figure 12.1). Among the respondents, 73.4 percent (578 households) said they had at least one negative feeling when they heard about it, while 26.6 percent of respondents – or 209 households – said that they had a positive feeling.

A chi-square test indicates that the relationship between the research locations and respondents' feelings was statistically significant ($\chi 2= 0.000$, Cramér's $V = 0.221$ percent). People living in Hanoi and Son La had a higher likelihood of having negative feelings (Table 12.1). Meanwhile, affected people in Quang Ngai

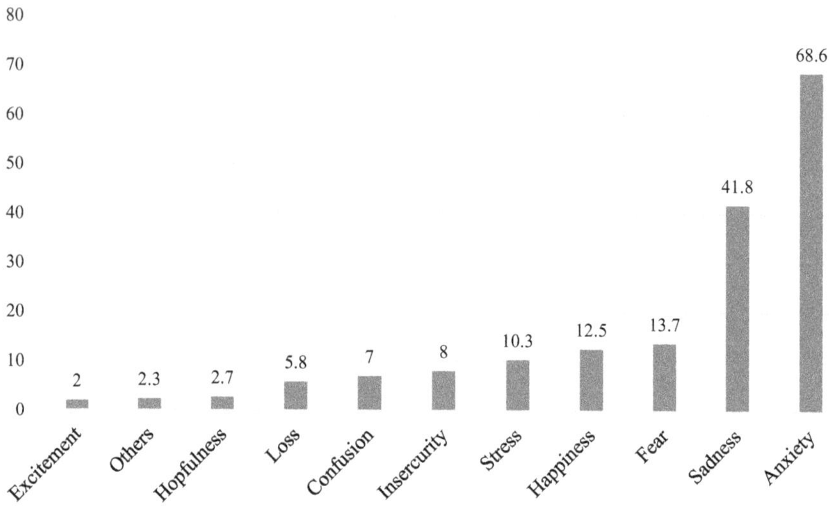

Figure 12.1 Respondents' mood when learning of a project's impact on their land (with or without physical relocation)

Table 12.1 Respondents' feelings upon the announcement of land acquisition

	Number		*Positive*		*Total*	
	Number	*%*	*Number*	*%*	*Number*	*%*
Province**						
Son La	195	82.3	42	17.7	237	100.0
Quang Ngai	163	71.5	65	28.5	228	100.0
Binh Duong	110	58.2	79	41.8	189	100.0
Ha Noi	110	82.7	23	17.3	133	100.0
Gender						
Male	309	72.9	115	27.1	424	100.0
Female	269	74.1	94	25.9	363	100.0
Displaced**						
Yes	391	81.0	92	19.0	483	100.0
No	187	61.5	117	38.5	304	100.0
Total	578	73.4	209	26.6	787	100.0

Note: ** = statistical significance level with $p<0.05$.

and Binh Duong had fewer negative and more positive feelings. The relation with Cramér's V = 0.221 percent was moderately strong.

These data confirm that a person living in Hanoi or Son La would have experienced more negative than positive feelings when learning that their land would be acquired; a person in Binh Duong and Quang Ngai would have experienced more positive than negative feelings. Only 19 percent of the displaced households reported a positive mood compared with 38.5 percent of non-displaced households. The chi-square test result indicates a higher likelihood of relocated households having a negative feeling ($\chi 2 = 0.000$, Cramér's V = 0.214 percent). However, the test coefficient shows that this relationship is moderately strong.

Conversations with resettlees from different land acquisition projects allowed us to sense the high levels of anxiety and fear of the resettled people. In the context of considerable uncertainty relating to compensation and resettlement policy at the beginning of project implementation, the concerns and unease of the households are completely understandable. In addition, a lengthy transition period (from ceding their land to receiving a house) also caused resettled households to suffer discomfort with temporary housing conditions that did not meet their requirements.

> At that time, I rented two rooms of a cement concrete-roof house. Our family of eight people lived in a 20 square meter rented house. We had no choice but to live in a tiny area. Clothes were hung everywhere. Sometimes, the roof leaked when it rained, and we had to cover ourselves and our things to avoid getting wet. It was miserable! We only wished to be allocated a piece of land quickly so we could set up a tent for a new living place. The adults in our family even slept on the floor to let the children sleep on two beds. This situation worried all of us adults, although the kids were still too young to know what was going on. We could not foresee how our livelihoods and houses would be affected when the government acquired the land. I was only 60 years old then, I worried and lost weight, experiencing headaches and illness. Home moving was very tiring. We had to pull our house down, too. Pulling our home down and moving to another place was really hard.
>
> (In-depth interview with a resettlee, Nam To Liem district, Hanoi)

Even after the households received land plots as compensation from the authorities and the project, they continued to meet obstacles when building their new houses. The construction of the house could be stopped if an inspection of the allocation of land use in the resettlement site was required.

> I built my house earlier, and nothing happened. Some houses built later were destroyed. They would demolish a house immediately if the house owner did not have a land use certificate. Though the government allocated the land, they still forced the demolition. It was enforced as part of the land allocation inspection process, and it was so hard for us to build a house – what a miserable time! There were so many investigations while the government acquired our land. Even parcels with land use certificates signed and stamped by competent agencies were under investigation.
>
> (In-depth interview, female, Nam Tu Liem district)

Many of the households whose land was acquired in Binh Duong were waiting for the certificate of land allocation for the land plot that they would receive as compensation. They might not need the land, but they could sell the certificate. The value of the certificate might be higher or lower depending on when they sold it. Some people became wealthier if they speculated on this certificate and sold it at the right time, because the resettlement land plots were often sold more cheaply than the market price to affected households.

Anxiety and sadness were the prevailing moods, regardless of relocation status. The proportion of people who recorded anxiety was higher for those in the displaced group than for those in the non-displaced group (75.2 percent versus 58.2 percent). Likewise, the proportion of non-displaced people who reported a positive mood was more than twice as high as the proportion of displaced people with the same mood (18.4 percent versus 8.7 percent). As it was with the resettlees from Binh Duong (most of whom did not have to relocate), it was a positive indicator if families were able to keep their housing intact, along with the possibility that they might receive residential land as compensation for the lost agricultural land. Under the current legal system of Vietnam, residential land (especially urban land) is generally much more valuable than agricultural land.

The data (see Table 12.2) also shows a gender difference regarding psychological experiences when hearing information about land acquisition and relocation. The proportion of women with feelings of anxiety was higher than that of men, but this difference was not statistically significant. This may mean that both men and women, when faced with such a change, feel anxious and depressed. The data for "single women" or "female-headed" households also show similar nuances. However, the existing evidence is insufficient to conclude that female-headed households had a greater sense of vulnerability than those headed by males. Differences in the gender of household heads are more evident for positive emotions: male heads of households tended to report higher positive feelings than female heads of households. Specifically, the proportions of male-headed households that recorded feelings of joy, excitement and hope were 12.2 percent, 2.3 percent, and

Table 12.2 Comparison of moods among groups during resettlement process

	Displacement		*Head of household*		*Head of household*	
	Displaced	*Non-displaced*	*Male*	*Female*	*Single mother*	*Female head of household*
Happiness	8.7	18.4	13.5	9.6	4.1	13.3
Excitement	1.9	2.3	2.4	1.0	0.0	2.4
Hopefulness	2.9	2.3	3.1	1.4	0.0	1.3
Sadness	42.0	41.4	41.9	41.6	51.4	26.7
Anxiety	75.2	58.2	67.5	71.8	67.6	66.7
Fear	18.0	6.9	14.0	12.9	14.9	5.3
Stress	13.3	5.6	10.4	10.0	6.8	9.3
Loss	9.3	0.3	5.9	5.7	6.8	4.0
Insecurity	11.2	3.0	9.3	4.3	2.7	4.0
Confusion	10.1	2.0	8.0	4.3	5.4	2.7
Others	2.9	1.3	2.6	1.4	4.1	13.3
Total	61.4	38.6	73.4	26.6	41.7	40.0

4.8 percent, respectively. The respective percentages for female-headed households were 9.8 percent, 1.3 percent, and 0.7 percent.

According to marital status, further analysis of the level of psychological trauma in the female-headed household group shows that single women were more severely traumatized than other female-headed households. There are almost no positive emotions in this group, and only three respondents confirmed that they were happy to know about the land taking decision. Among female-headed households, those headed by single women also had a higher rate of reporting other negative emotions. In fact, women are often assessed as "less agile" than men in land-price determination and compensation in the resettlement process. Single women are even more disadvantaged (for example, ethnic minority, female and single), resulting in double or triple vulnerabilities (see Box 12.1).

Box 12.1 Psychological portraits of resettlement groups

Common emotions experienced	Key psychological features
Anxiety Sadness Fear Stress Loss Insecurity Confusion	➔ The household head, either male or female, faces psychological trauma. ➔ Female household heads do not have as many positive feelings as male household heads. ➔ Single mothers suffer more severe psychological trauma compared to other household heads. ➔ Single mothers report few if any positive emotions.

Affected people's concerns about land acquisition[1]

Regardless of the psychological feelings of individuals, displacement is, in many cases, inevitable. Therefore, sooner or later, families must consider relocation options for themselves. This section will present our research findings on people's concerns about relocation. Their three biggest concerns were (i) decrease in family income (60.5 percent); (ii) adequacy of the compensation package (45.5 percent); and (iii) a loss of productive land (44.4 percent). Other concerns included (i) work disruption (20.6 percent); (ii) lack of clean water (12.4 percent); and (iii) separation from relatives or friends (11.3 percent).

Household concerns may vary, depending on the socioeconomic group (see Table 12.3). For farming households, their biggest concern was a decline in income (72.5 percent), followed by a loss of productive land (40.0 percent) and the adequacy of the compensation package (33.3 percent). It is clear that, for these households, land is vital as it is the foundation for income-generating activities for the whole family. A loss of land reduces the family's income source and disrupts the employment of family members. It is even a concern for households

Table 12.3 Concerns of affected households upon land acquisition/resettlement (by household types)

	Farming	*Mixed*	*Non-farming*	*Number*	*Total*
Compensation rate	33.3	49.6	47.7	260	42.1
Income reduction	72.5	64.7	48.6	345	58.0
Impacts on children's study	12.5	9.7	8.4	56	9.3
Disruption of work	23.3	24.4	14.5	117	19.9
Separation from relatives/ friends	18.3	9.2	9.8	65	11.2
Access to medical services	3.3	1.3	0.0	7	1.2
Lack of clean water	19.2	15.1	5.6	71	13.8
Reduced productive land	40.0	52.1	37.9	257	44.9
Adverse impacts on health	3.3	0.4	0.9	7	1.2
Security and safety in new place	2.5	5.0	7.5	31	5.4
Others	13.3	10.1	24.8	93	16.6

with mixed sources of income that is partially land-based. Households with mixed and off-farm sources of income are more concerned with the appropriateness of compensation than farming households, as their livelihood and income does not heavily depend on the land. In addition to these major concerns, households with off-farm sources of income pay more attention to security factors in the new places of residence than do other groups of households.

Analyzing the differences by survey area (see Table 12.4), we found that, although affected households in the provinces under study tended to share the same main concerns, the level of interest in specific issues was different for each province.

For example, the adequacy of the compensation package was of more concern for households in Quang Ngai, Hanoi, and Binh Duong. Determining compensation prices is always the most controversial issue, especially in urban areas (Hanoi) or peri-urban areas (Binh Duong). Residents in these localities often assume that the proffered compensation package will be lower than the market transaction price, and this is a primary cause of prolonged litigation.

Meanwhile, most households in Son La (67 percent) were concerned about a decline in income after land acquisition. In Binh Duong and Hanoi, the percentage of households concerned about this issue was 50.9 percent and 50.5 percent, respectively. The issue of "reduced land for business" concerned only about 15.7 percent of affected households in Hanoi. The corresponding percentages in Quang Ngai and Binh Duong were 60.1 percent and 62.4 percent, respectively.

Finally, it was surprising to learn that Son La and Hanoi, which are at two opposite poles of development level – the least- and most-developed among studied locations – have a higher proportion of affected households worrying about clean water and family/kindship separation. This may be partly due to the characteristics of settlement arrangements in each of the participating provinces in this study.

Table 12.4 Concerns of the affected households upon land acquisition/resettlement (by research location and relocation status)

	Province				*Situation*	
	Son La	*Quang Ngai*	*Binh Duong*	*Ha Noi*	*Displaced*	*Non-displaced*
Compensation rate	38.7	52.1	41.3	51.9	46.1	44.1
Income reduction	67.0	65.6	50.5	50.9	59.8	61.8
Impacts on children's study	17.5	2.5	3.7	13.0	13.4	2.2
Disruption to work	27.8	19.0	11.9	18.5	22.7	16.1
Separation from relatives/friends	20.1	4.3	0.9	16.7	16.2	1.1
Access to medical services	3.6	0.0	0.0	0.0	1.8	0.0
Lack of clean water	26.8	4.9	0.0	10.2	17.8	1.1
Reduced productive land	9.3	0.3	5.9	5.7	6.8	4.0
Adverse impacts on health	11.2	3.0	9.3	4.3	2.7	4.0
Security and safety in new place	10.1	2.0	8.0	4.3	5.4	2.7
Others	2.9	1.3	2.6	1.4	4.1	13.3
Compensation rate	61.4	38.6	73.4	26.6	41.7	40.0

Analysis by relocation status shows a clear difference in the concerns of displaced and non-displaced households. The former cared more about income decline while the latter paid attention to compensation adequacy and land for business. In addition, those in relocated households tended to worry more about a lack of clean water and the possibility of family/kindship disruption. Fear of disruption to family and kinship is not surprising, as this is unique to the displaced group.

Participation and consultation

People's participation, which has become increasingly required in resettlement-related national and international guidelines, can contribute to the success of resettlement programs. It gives affected people the opportunity to access accurate and complete information, which helps to alleviate their anxieties. Participation in resettlement consultations has four dimensions: meeting attendance, discussion, implementation, and decision-making. In this study, these four dimensions accounted for 14 Yes/No sub-questions, with each "Yes" response equaling 1 point. Each dimension reflects a participation level that ranges from meeting attendance (the lowest level) to decision-making. Therefore, to reflect the hierarchy of the participation ladder, we assigned a multiplier to each dimension (1 for meeting attendance, 2 for discussion, 3 for implementation, and 4 for decision-making). The participation score is the sum of all sub-questions after being multiplied, ranging from 0 to 36. The Cronbach's Alpha coefficient of the participation scale is 0.846.

When looking at whether emotional experience affects participation, the results showed that people with negative feelings had an average participation score of 18.8 points compared with 16 points among those having positive emotions ($p = 0.002$). This result shows that anxiety motivates families to seek and receive project-related information to a certain extent.

Restoring income sources, social networks, and other meaningful life circumstances could alleviate anxiety for displaced people. In other words, once they have been integrated into the economy and society, resettlees will be less likely to experience symptoms of depression and anxiety caused by moving. On the other hand, scholars believe that the relocation experience itself plays a significant role in causing psychological distress because it often includes a subjective or emotional aspect, such as "grief for one's lost home" and "worry about an uncertain future" (Colson 1971; Scudder 2005). Relocation disrupts traditional culture and puts people in a position to redefine "who they are" and "where they belong" (Downing & Garcia-Downing 2009). Mentally healthy individuals tend to maintain control over their lives and their social environment and maintain a high level of interactions with people in their communities (Ryff 2014). Displacement might cause great disorder in people's mental health. It can only be restored when new cultures and practices are established. In other words, without full integration, resettled people may still experience depressive symptoms due to relocation.

Satisfaction

Satisfaction with the new place of residence certainly affects the psychology and adaptability of displaced people. Juan Xi (2016) has argued that displaced people who cannot integrate into the new community and places of residence might develop depression. In this study, the satisfaction level of displaced people is measured on a scale from 0 (completely dissatisfied) to 10 points (completely satisfied). The obtained results (see Table 12.5) show that the average level of satisfaction with new accommodations is 6.21 points ($SD = 2.16$). Among the respondents, 28.1 percent rated their satisfaction level at 8 points or more, and 13.9 percent rated their scores at a relatively low level of 0 to 4 points. These scores suggest that the satisfaction level with new places of residence would be between 5 and 7 points. Among relocated people, men rated their satisfaction levels higher than women did, with average scores of 6.4 ($SD = 2.07$) and 5.5 ($SD = 2.24$), respectively ($p= 0.02$). People with a low level of education tended to be more satisfied than those with secondary school or higher education.

The results of one-way ANOVA (analysis of variance) on educational attainment and satisfaction level show no correlation between these two factors [$F (4, 448) = 1.25$, $p=2.089$]. However, post hoc comparisons using the Tukey HSD (Honestly Significant Difference) test indicated a statistically significant difference between the group with high school education ($M=5.55$, $SD=2.09$) and those with middle school education ($M = 6.12$, $SD = 2.43$). There is no statistically

Table 12.5 Comparison of satisfaction with new living places among various population groups

		Number	*Mean*	*SD*
Gender of respondents**	Male	263	6.4	2.07
	Female	199	5.5	2.24
Level of education of respondents	Illiteracy	48	6.04	2.04
	Primary education	103	6.23	1.89
	Lower secondary education	162	6.41	2.19
	Secondary education	107	6.12	2.43
	Post-secondary education*	33	5.55	2.09
Respondents' age group	<= 35 years old*	79	6.44	1.72
	36–45 years old**	122	6.08	2.10
	46–55 years old***	122	5.99	2.20
	56–65 years old***	87	5.85	2.52
	Above 66 years old	52	7.29	2.48
Total		462	6.21	2.15

Notes:
* = statistical significance level with p < 0.1
** = statistical significance level with p < 0.05
*** = statistical significance level with p < 0.001

significant difference between groups with other educational attainments and those with a high school education. This result suggests that those with a high school education are less satisfied with their new accommodation than those having lower qualifications. Among all age groups, those over 66 years old have the highest average satisfaction score (7.29 points). The difference with other age groups is statistically significant.

Comparing satisfaction by mood shows that people with positive emotions have a higher level of satisfaction in their new sites than those with negative emotions. The mean score for comparison between the two groups was 6.82 and 6.0, respectively ($p = 0.03$). The correlation between participating in preparation activities during relocation and satisfaction levels shows that people who are more actively involved have higher levels of satisfaction. These data demonstrate the intricate link between individual emotions, levels of participation, and adaptation to the new community of displaced people. Active participation in activities before, during, and after the resettlement of the affected people increases the likelihood that they will be satisfied with the new residence, contributing to their rapid adaptation to the surrounding living space and community.

Integration

The resettlement process is considered successful only when the displaced person is fully integrated into the host community. However, integration is not easy, as resettlees may face risks of impoverishment, discrimination, and segregation (Kessler et al. 1999; Borjas 2015), disruptions in their social networks, and adverse changes in their lifestyles (Tan et al. 2009). Host communities are not always welcoming to new members due to conflict over resources (Lu & Wang 2013). Compensation and support usually only deal with tangible impacts, yet most resettlees struggle to reconstruct their lives in their new community (Xi & Hwang 2011).

Researchers suggest that acquaintance with the social and cultural environment of local communities (for example, language and food) is often the first step in the integration process (Alba & Nee 1997). Next, they strive to achieve economic and social status, in the job market and the educational system, equivalent to that of local people (Alba & Nee 1997). After relocation, the quality of resettlement housing often increases, ranging from informal housing to apartments with reinforced concrete structures, tap water, garbage-treatment stations, and other facilities (Li et al. 2001). Satisfaction with housing conditions, commercial conditions, and infrastructure all positively affect the elimination of discrimination. Reduced social stratification, greater emotional attachment, and a sense of belonging to a new home are indicators of achieving the final stage in integration (Alba & Foner 2014). However, even when relocated people feel comfortable with the local culture and have reached equal socioeconomic status, they may not develop an emotional attachment to the host society (Amit 2011). In this case the resettlement arrangement remains incomplete and partially unsuccessful.

An improvement in the conditions found at resettlement sites has greatly helped displaced people in their daily lives. That has helped them integrate into the local community and has reduced discrimination. The host community has become a small, fully functional society, providing enough space and opportunity for members to interact and perform activities that restore their lifestyles (Aaen et al. 2016; Cernea 1997; Oshio & Urakawa 2012).

Conclusion

The "soft factors" that contribute to community cohesion are often not fully recognized as the top priorities of stakeholders who focus on compensation package, infrastructure development, and benefit-sharing. Meanwhile, integration requires economic success and re-establishing interlinkages between people, environment, and society (Downing & Garcia-Downing 2009). This is also the time when affected people redefine where they belong. Unfortunately, these subjective aspects of resettlement have never been central to the discussion of project-induced resettlement.

There are few studies of the psychological impacts and integration of resettled people in Vietnam. Most resettlement studies address issues around lessons learned on compensation and site clearance. However, our research findings are not complete outliers in the literature. We initially assessed people's emotional experience with land expropriation and their ability to adapt to new circumstances. The results show that psychological stabilization is much slower than economic recovery. Emotional trauma is experienced by newcomers as well as host communities during the early stages of reconfiguring life. Social support is an important mediator of stress and psychological responses. It also contributes to effective mental health protection and reduces feelings of loneliness for the resettled group (Furman & Buhrmester 1992). Finally, this study calls for the inclusion of a customized psychological support component in resettlement programs to enhance people's preparedness during such an unsettled time in their lives.

Note

1 The research team identified 11 different sources related to people's interests when hearing about land acquisition. Respondents were asked to select three sources of anxiety for the household.

References

Aaen, S., Kerndrup, S., & Lyhne, I. (2016). Beyond public acceptance of energy infrastructure: How citizens make sense and form reactions by enacting networks of entities in infrastructure development. *Energy Policy*, *96*, 576–586. https://doi.org/10.1016/j.enpol.2016.06.031.

Alba, R., & Foner, N. (2014). Comparing immigrant integration in North America and Western Europe: How much do the grand narratives tell us? *International Migration Review*, *48*(1_suppl), 263–291. doi:10.1111/imre.12134

Alba, R., & Nee, V. (1997). Rethinking assimilation theory for a new era of immigration. *The International Migration Review*, *31*(4), 826–874. https://doi.org/10.2307/2547416.

Amit K. (2012). Social integration and identity of immigrants from western countries, the FSU and Ethiopia in Israel. *Ethnic and Racial Studies*, *35*(7), 1283–1310. doi:10.1080/01419870.2011.602091.

Ben-Sira, Z. (1997). *Immigration, stress, and readjustment*. West Port, CT: Praeger.

Borjas, G. (2015). Immigration and globalization: A review essay. *Journal of Economic Literature*, *53*(4), 961–974. https://doi.org/10.1257/jel.53.4.961

Cabanac, M. (2002). What is emotion? *Behavioural Processes*, *60*(2), 69–83. doi:10.1016/s0376-6357(02)00078-5. PMID: 12426062

Cernea, M. (1997). The risks and reconstruction model for resettling displaced populations. *WorldDevelopment*, *25*(10), 1569–1587. https://doi.org/10.1016/s0305-750x(97)00054-5

Cernea, M. (2000). Risk, safeguards and reconstruction: A model for population displacement and resettlement. In M. Cernea & C. McDowell (Eds.), *Risk and reconstruction: Experiences of resettlers and refugees*. Washington, DC: The World Bank.

Chakrabarti, A., & Dhar, A. (2009). *Dislocation and resettlement in development: From third world to the world of the third*. New York and London: Routledge.

Colson, E. (1971). *The social consequences of resettlement*. Manchester: The University Press.

Downing, T. E., & Garcia-Downing, C. (2009). Routine and dissonant culture: A theory about the psycho-socio-cultural disruptions of involuntary displacement and ways to mitigate them without inflicting even more damage. In A. Oliver-Smith (Ed.), *Development & dispossession*. Santa Fe: School for Advanced Research Press, pp. 223–320.

Furman, W., & Buhrmester, D. (1992). Age and sex differences in perceptions of networks of personal relationships. *Child Development*, *63*(1), 103–115. https://doi.org/10.1111/j.1467–8624.1992.tb03599.x.

Good, Byron J. (1996). Mental health consequences of displacement and resettlement. *Economic and Political Weekly*, *31*(24), 1504–1508. www.jstor.org/stable/4404273.

Hwang, S.S., Xi, J., Cao, Y., Feng, X., & Qiaa, X. (2007). Anticipation of migration and psychological stress and the three gorges dam project, China. *Social Science & Medicine*, *65*(5), 1012–1024.

Kessler, R., Mickelson, K., & Williams, D. (1999). The prevalence, distribution, and mental health correlates of perceived discrimination in the United States. *Journal of Health and Social Behavior*, *40*(3), 208–230. https://doi.org/10.2307/2676349.

Lewis, M. (1993). The emergence of human emotions. In M. Lewis, J. M. Haviland-Jones, & L. F. Barrett (Eds.), *Handbook of emotions*. Third edition. New York: Guilford Press, pp. 304–319.

Li, H., Waley, P., & Rees, P. (2001). Reservoir resettlement in China: Past experience and the Three Gorges Dam. *The Geographical Journal*, *167*, 195–212.

Lu, Y., & Wang, F. (2013). From general discrimination to segmented inequality: Migration and inequality in urban China. *Social Science Research*, *42*(6), 1443–1456. https://doi.org/10.1016/j.ssresearch.2013.06.006

Mehta, L. (2009). *Displaced by development: Confronting marginalisation and gender injustice*. New Delhi: Sage Publications India Pvt Ltd.

Oshio, T., & Urakawa, K. (2012). Neighbourhood satisfaction, self-rated health, and psychological attributes: A multilevel analysis in Japan. *Journal of Environmental Psychology*, *32*(4), 410–417. https://doi.org/10.1016/j.jenvp.2012.07.003

Ryff, C. D. (2014). Psychological well-being revisited: Advances in the science and practice of eudaimonia. *Psychotherapy and Psychosomatics*, *83*(1), 10–28. https://doi.org/10.1159/000353263.

Scudder, T. T. (2005). *The future of large dams: Dealing with social, environmental, institutional and political costs*. London: Earthscan.

Tan, Y., Chen, Y., & Hugo, G. (2009). Displacement and economic consequences of the three gorges project: A case study of resettlers in Sichuan province. *Asian and Pacific Migration Journal*, *18*(4), 473–496. https://doi.org/10.1177/011719680901800402

Verma, M. (2004). *Development, displacement and resettlement*. Jaipur, India: Rawat Publications.

Xi, J. (2016). Types of integration and depressive symptoms: A latent class analysis on the resettled population for the Three Gorges dam project, China. *Social Science & Medicine*, *157*, 73–86. ISSN 0277–9536. https://doi.org/10.1016/j.socscimed.2016.03.045

Xi, J., & Hwang, S. (2011). Relocation stress, coping, and sense of control among resettlers resulting from China's three gorges dam project. *Social Indicators Research*, *104*(3), 507–522. https://doi.org/10.1007/s11205-010-9758-5

13 Gender-impact assessment

Toward a universal application in large development projects in Vietnam

Pham Thi Dieu My

Introduction

Although hydropower can bring potential benefits in terms of economic development, it can also bring difficulties (WCD 2000). Large-scale projects trigger unexpected changes in the lives of downstream communities and often force their physical relocation. As the World Commission on Dams (WCD) noted in 2000 in its influential report *Dams and development: A new framework for decision-making*, there is a strong link between equitable and sustainable water and energy development. In the last two decades, hundreds of hydropower projects have been developed in many regions of Vietnam, with the highest density of projects of any size found in the Central and Central Highlands regions. These hydropower schemes have contributed significantly to satisfying the country's electricity demands, primarily for industrial and domestic consumption. However, they also bring negative environmental and social impacts, including deforestation; biodiversity loss; river-flow regime fluctuation; reduced downstream availability; and involuntary agricultural and residential land acquisition. For people affected by loss of land, displacement and resettlement, livelihood support and compensation are often inadequate. As well, affected communities are often unable to share equitably in the financial benefits of hydropower development.

While the importance of social and environmental impact assessments in hydropower development is rarely questioned (Sneddon & Fox 2008), using impact assessments to address social and gender-related impacts is not straightforward. Vietnam has improved its policies on land acquisition, compensation, and resettlement, but people's livelihood benefits and rights are not always safeguarded by hydropower investors and local governments.

Moreover, investors in large-scale projects often survey and report on the most commonly found overall impacts on communities, without also analyzing gender aspects or impacts on other specific groups. The perspectives of local communities and related stakeholders (including the poor, women, and ethnic minorities) have not been fully addressed, and most stakeholders have given little attention to gender-related effects and to gender roles, relations, and rights (GIZ 2013).

For water governance to equally benefit women and men living in poverty, their voices need to be taken into account (Hill et al. 2017): this is necessary for us to

DOI: 10.4324/9781003165774-18

be able to recognize rights, assess potential risks, and plan for risk mitigation for all groups of affected people. The widespread inequality and higher vulnerability experienced by women in affected communities is fully reflected in hydropower development in Vietnam and in case studies examined by the NGO Centre for Social Research and Development (CSRD) in the Central and Central Highlands regions.

Some international NGOs have conducted gender-impact assessments (GIAs) in developed countries to respond to the *Beijing Declaration and Platform for Action* (BDPA), a resolution adopted by the UN at the end of the Fourth World Conference on Women on September 15, 1995. This resolution, which promulgated a set of principles concerning the equality of men and women, has been regarded as a key policy tool for consideration of gender in decision-making (Verloo & Roggeband 1996; Roggeband & Verloo 2006). Based on its previous reports, Oxfam introduced and piloted a GIA implementation manual, *Balancing the scales: Using gender impact assessment in hydropower development* (Oxfam Australia & CPWF 2013). A GIA manual for mining and extractive industries was developed in 2009 and updated in 2017 (Hill & Newell 2009; Hill et al. 2017). The GIA manual for hydropower development has adapted many proven gender-impact tools that can be used in evaluating hydropower development in the Mekong region. It provides developers with assessment checklists at different stages of project cycles, aiming for equally positive outcomes for women and for men (Hill et al. 2017).

Vietnam's *Law on Gender Equality 2006* did not explicitly include a requirement to conduct GIAs for large-scale projects (including hydropower projects). However, the CSRD has been working on this issue since 2011, using different approaches in assessing several projects. This chapter presents the CSRD's experience in applying gender-impact assessment to hydropower development projects in the Central and Central Highland regions of Vietnam, analyzes the gaps, and introduces recommendations for introducing GIAs into developers' social impact assessments and corporate social responsibility (CSR) programs.

Gender-impact analysis methodologies

In 2013, Oxfam introduced GIA practice to Vietnam through its Water Governance Project, providing hydropower investors and government officials with some basic GIA tools for consideration in project cycles, and setting out six basic steps to be followed to inform analysis and planning in the early stages of project development (Oxfam Australia & CPWF 2013). These six steps are summarized below, followed by a description of some of the most commonly used tools.

Step 1: Gathering the data: Establishing a project-specific baseline that analyzes gender

This step is to inform the scope and terms of environmental and social assessment incorporating gender analysis, in order to:

> check that any baseline data that were established early in the feasibility assessments are robust enough to enable understanding of the gender context.

> If there are gaps [in] data for project development, a data-gathering process may need to be undertaken, revised or updated.

To better understand the gender context:

> many other demographic factors within the river basin and project-impact zone should be considered, including ethnicity and language groups; socio-economic status; education; literacy; cultural norms and decision-making processes; marginalization; social norms and domestic violence; disability; and how any of the multiple forms of vulnerability intersect with gender.

Step 2: "Understanding the context"

> A thorough context analysis for the hydropower project will help the company – and its backers in finance and government – [to] understand the communities that will be affected by the dam; how they are structured; how they function; how they interact with other communities and with the natural environment that will be affected by the dam. . . . This context analysis should consider the practical needs and interests of both women and men: good practice means that there should be a clear understanding of the roles, responsibilities and relationships between men and women in the affected communities and river user groups.

Step 3: "Identify issues introduced by the dam"

As an outcome of Step 2, project developers will have a better understanding of the capacity of women and men to respond to the changes imposed by the dam.

> [Drawing] initially from community consultation and engagement, this will take the form of a set of assumptions about men's, women's and community assets, resources, strengths and vulnerabilities. As such, an iterative process of community engagement should be facilitated so these assumptions are tested with the community and with men's and women's groups.

Step 4: "Understand women's (and men's) needs and aspirations"

> Having undertaken the baseline assessment, gathered the sex-disaggregated data and identified the issues that the project will introduce from a gendered perspective." . . . [It is necessary to] understand women's needs and interests. And from this, consider how the project can respond to these needs.

Step 5: "Gender strategy and action plan"

> It is recommended that a stand-alone gender action plan and strategy should be developed. . . . By developing a project specific gender action plan informed by the gender-impact assessment, the project should have a clear roadmap with specific, measurable and targeted interventions.

Step 6: "Review, audit and respond"

> This [step] . . . looks at the importance of monitoring and reporting; emphasising the importance of a participatory process to ensure that the planned and predicted outcomes achieve what they intended.
>
> (Oxfam Australia & CPWF 2013)

GIAs for hydropower projects can be carried out at several stages: during the river basin planning process; at the beginning of the project; and after the dam begins operation. To satisfy the research objectives and requirements of gender-impact assessment, the CSRD uses different methods for data collection, validation and reporting.

Oxfam's six gender-impact assessment tools

The main component of the GIA research proposed by Oxfam is a field survey using six gender-impact assessment tools:

(1) Community profiles of hydropower-affected communities in production, and community activities, by gender.
(2) Profiles of resource access, use and control, by gender, to identify who has control over the resources and their use.
(3) Institutional analysis to identify the impact, by gender, of policies and project implementation in the project areas.
(4) Gender-impact analysis: How would the hydropower dam affect men and women (in terms of its environmental, social, and economic impact) during its construction and operation phases?
(5) Gender needs assessment: What do women need to help them in their roles and responsibilities? What structural or institutional change is required to achieve greater equality in the community?
(6) Use of the Oxfam Women's Empowerment Framework (WEF) tool in order to evaluate the impacts of hydropower projects on women's status in terms of "welfare, access, conscientization, participation or mobilization, and control."

The purpose of the WEF tool is to record what project activities and programs have been established and why. It encourages project staff to be explicit in their assessment of why these initiatives are important, and to think through how they could be strengthened or enhanced to positively contribute to women's empowerment.

The key questions used are as follows:

- Have women been consulted in the establishment of the project response or activity?
- Have they been involved in decisions based on full information and with options?

- Have women been engaged in planning the activity?
- Have project staff considered how the initial activity from other projects could be supported over time to be more empowering for project-affected women?

The research team led by CSRD core staff used Tool 2 and Tool 6 to identify women's participation in the planning and decision-making processes to bring about equitable benefits for women in society. These aspects were included in the report writing as well as in policy recommendations.

Piloting locations

In 2015, the CSRD (as the main partner of Oxfam Vietnam) undertook a GIA for hydropower dam impacts in the Central and Central Highland regions of Vietnam. The overall goal was to support hydropower companies and relevant government agencies in considering the impact, by gender, of hydropower development along the Srepók, Sesan, and Sekong (3S) river basins.

This project focused on:

(1) applying GIA tools in practice and writing GIA reports;
(2) sharing the results of GIA implementation with local and national stakeholders and communities, by organizing a series of workshops and dialogues; and
(3) working with selected hydropower producers in using the GIA results and then supporting them in developing gender action plans for their organizations.

For this chapter, two representative areas from the CSRD project – the A Luoi dam in Thua Thien Hue province and dams on the Srepók river system in Dak Lak province – have been used to illustrate the GIA contribution to impact assessment.

The A Luoi hydropower project

Located about 70 km from Hue City, the A Luoi hydropower plant was built on the A Sap River, one of the Mekong River's two major third-level tributaries (along with the Ta Rinh) (CSRD & CORENARM 2014). The length of the main river from the western side of the South Annamite Mountain Range to the hydropower dam is 43 km, and the catchment area is 331 km^2. Major components of the A Luoi hydropower project include the main dam, a spillway, and a powerhouse (with two installed generating units of 170 MW). The maximum flow (Qmax) through the plant is 43.3 m^3/s.

The CSRD project aimed to investigate gender impacts for local people. In the A Luoi hydropower project, this research was conducted in two villages in the Hong Thuong commune (A Sap and A Den) affected by the construction of the resettlement area and in Quang Ngan village in Son Thuy commune, which was partially affected by impoundment of the reservoir.

The Srepók River and communities affected by hydropower construction

The Srepók River stretches for 126 km within Vietnam. There are ten hydropower plants built on this river (Dray H'linh 0, 1, 2 and 3; Srepók 3, 4 and 4A; Buon Kuop; Buon Tua Srah; and Drang Phok), with a combined installed capacity of 870 MW. This cascade of dams blocks water flow on a 20 km stretch of the Srepók River running through the Buon Don District (Trung Duong 2016).

The GIA was conducted in communities affected by three hydropower plants: Srepók 3, 4 and 4A in the Buon Don District, Dak Lak Province. This area is home to many ethnic minority groups, such as the Ede and M'Nong, who have lived there for a long time. Each ethnic group has a unique cultural identity, creating the rich cultural diversity that is characteristic of the Central Highlands.

The Srepók 3 Hydropower Project

Srepók 3 Hydropower, a 220 MW plant, was approved by the Prime Minister in Decision No. 1225/TTg-CN dated 25 August 2005. There are two resettlement sites developed in Dak Nong and Dak Lak provinces to serve this project.

RESETTLEMENT IN EA PO COMMUNE

The resettlement village in Ea Po commune, Cu Jut District, hosts 70 relocated households from the Srepók 3 Hydropower Project. Land acquisition started in 2007 and relocation activities were implemented from 2009 to 2010. However, only 7 households built their houses by themselves and about 20 households have received land-use rights certificates.

RESETTLEMENT IN EA NOUL AND TAN HOA COMMUNES

The resettlement area in Ea Noul and Tan Hoa communes hosts 44 relocated households, including 18 households who rebuilt their homes on their remaining land, 26 who moved to the resettlement site, and 60 who lost agricultural land but not houses.

The Srepók 4 and Srepók 4A Hydropower Projects

For the Srepók 4 Hydropower Project, following a decision on 13 April 2007 by the MOIT (Vietnamese Ministry of Industry and Trade), the Dalak Provincial People's Committee granted an investment license to the Dai Hai Electricity Investment and Development Joint Stock Company to implement the Srepók 4 Hydropower Project. It acquired 556.72 hectares of land in two districts: 447.87 hectares in the Buon Don District and 108.85 hectares in the Cu Jut district.

Srepók 4A Hydropower Plant was financed by Buon Don Hydropower Joint Stock Company with 2 units with a capacity of 64MW/year. It was started in

October 2010. The total investment budget was 1,876.739 billion, of which 335 billion is the company's own capital; the rest consists of loans from credit institutions. The investor directly manages the project's implementation.

Without damming the river, the Srepók 4A Hydropower Project dug a 10 km waterway from the back of the Srepók 4 hydropower plant and a 4 km discharge channel to bring water back to the Srepók River (Le 2016). The area of usable land is 400.3 hectares, located across Ea Wer, Ea Huar, and Krong Na communes of the Buon Don District, Dak Lak province. The plant has been in operation since January 2014.

By September 2015, 294 households were eligible for compensation and support. Payments have been made to 292 households (209.48 ha) and are pending for the remaining two households (4.48 ha).

Main gaps identified through these GIA projects

The research results were synthesized and published (in both Vietnamese and English) by the Thuan Hoa Publishing House in the 2018 report *Hydropower impacts from environmental, social and gender perspectives – Evidence from the Central and Central Highlands, Vietnam* (Pham & Nguyen 2018). This section also presents CSRD's review of GIA tools for better practice in the future. The following are some major findings.

Lack of community participation and of gender perspectives

Xu et al. (2015) have argued that a techno-economic paradigm strongly drives hydropower development. Because of this, limited attention has been paid to social and institutional issues, community involvement, or gender impacts. However, gender, hydropower, and sustainable development – as well as constructivist ecofeminism (Cabo 2010; Holy et al. 2021) – are now emerging as areas of discourse. Gender-based analysis can take into account the different gender roles, in production and in life, that are associated with differing impacts of hydropower development. Constructivist ecofeminism considers the relationship of women in a social construct linked to the sexual division of labor that sustains capitalist patriarchal societies – often labeled as "men's work" and "women's work."

Patriarchal norms have had a strong influence on gender inequality in our project communities. In our research, we investigated whether hydropower development is sustainable when its impacts – on the community in general and on women in particular – are taken into account during the project cycle and whether there any plans to minimize negative impacts.

The pilot projects conducted by the CSRD found that gender gaps exist in the application of the impact assessment process and that gender-related issues require attention. In the case of both the A Luoi and Srepók projects, the assessment conducted by investors was incomplete, while the evidence we gained from surveys more fully reflects the issues that arise when women's roles and voices are neglected.

Consultation processes for the A Luoi Dam project

There was no clear evidence of local participation (especially women's involvement) in important steps of the project process, including planning, implementation, and monitoring.

Some key issues emerged:

- Only the household head (usually a man) was invited to the pre-compensation meeting. Women did not have the opportunity to voice their needs and concerns. Additionally, no opportunity was provided for dialogue in which both men and women could participate and openly discuss their issues.
- Some of the ethnic minority women (Cotu) explained that they were not aware of compensation from the company because their husbands participated in the meeting and received the money. Some men used that money for family needs, while others used it to fund drinking habits.
- Although the investor in the A Luoi dam project made strong efforts to improve the compensation process in the area, not enough attention was given to gender issues and gender sensitivity during the planning and implementation process. The compensation and housing construction practices merely followed the suggestions of the local government without proper gender consideration.

  As a result, most of the buildings did not accommodate the practical needs of women residents. For example, constructing bathrooms too far away from the house resulted in decreasing their use by women, due to safety concerns. The majority of the women surveyed expected to have a bathroom inside the house. Additionally, the long distance between residential areas and the market discouraged small-scale commercial trading by older women and young girls.

Consultation processes for the Srepók Dam project

Similarly, in the communities affected by the A Luoi dam, women rarely had access to information, meetings, or training due to their heavy work burdens and to social norms. This was fundamentally inequitable for women.

This assessment again confirms the distinctive differences in division of labor, roles, and needs of men and women throughout the development history of the researched communities. Under the impact of hydropower development on the Srepók River, local women – even in matrilineal communities – have faced increased and emerging difficulties in economic development, health and social engagement.

These communities shared common issues in terms of women's advancement:

- Regarding labor division, women are expected to take on housework and family care as the "heavenly responsibilities" of a mother and a wife (rarely recognized by family, community, and society) – while maintaining full participation in production activities for domestic economic development.

- In addition, although women could have participated in more meetings, their husbands often decided to represent the household in important meetings. As a result of many unanticipated adverse impacts from hydropower projects, women in all researched communities were found to have become more vulnerable.

Gender gaps in impact assessment

The surveys found that the hydropower projects had both negative and positive impacts on affected communities in general, and on women in particular:

- On the one hand, the respondents acknowledged that improved living conditions had resulted from the dam construction projects. In Tan Phu village (resettlement area), people reported strengthened social interaction and better access to schools, electricity, information, and healthcare. One hundred percent of children are going to primary school, compared with rates of 60 to 70 percent before the project.
- On the other hand, there is concrete evidence of personal setbacks caused by the dam projects in both A Luoi and Srepók. Several of these were gender-related impacts that had not been mentioned in the project-impact assessment reports, including depression due to unstable livelihoods; health and health-care problems; food security issues; and impacts on community activities and social life.

Depression among men and women due to unstable livelihoods

According to Le et al. (2018) and Nguyen et al. (2018), surveyed communities confirmed that reduced and unstable income; limited access to land for livelihood activities; and debt led to depression for both men and women and to increased burdens on women's household duties.

In the three surveyed areas in A Luoi, the main livelihoods of local people were formerly agricultural production and non-timber forest product exploitation. After resettlement, they were provided with less land, and with land suffering from poor irrigation infrastructure and poor-quality soil, causing difficulties for agricultural production.

According to the experience of affected communities, during the rainy season, nearly all of the local land became inundated and could not be used for cultivation. In addition, people could not invest in livestock due to unusual flooding and a lack of grazing land and food. Most affected people lost income and become unemployed. The consequence was an increased number of people working as hired laborers.

As was the case in the Srepók River basin, people at the other three sites in the study suffered impacts that included income decline, river pollution, difficulties in cultivation, and declines in animal husbandry. This was exacerbated by the need for increased expenditure on water for food and domestic use (instead of a self-supply as before).

In addition, the landscapes changed, causing a drop in the number of tourists. This eventually affected the incomes of companies and local households involved in tourism services.

In essence, workers in all the resettled communities studied had transitioned from having stable livelihoods to being hired laborers. The transient nature of this employment caused anxiety and depression for both men and women.

Srepók research sites

In the Srepók research sites, the construction of hydropower projects has led to adverse changes in the environment and landscape. Future floods will most likely be more devastating, and erosion may be more serious. Forest loss has led to dramatic changes in the way people farm and live compared with their traditional practices, which featured a "forest culture" and "life of shifting cultivation" (Le et al. 2015). Loss of productive land due to dam construction and hydroelectric projects, land submerged in the reservoir, and landslides have made it impossible for local people to cultivate crops in Tan Phu village. In downstream communities, dry rivers prevent people in Tri A village from using them for transportation and irrigation.

Tan Phu village

In Tan Phu village, families previously had no debt; however, a survey revealed that 100 percent of the households had taken out bank loans due to the increasing need for capital for livelihood-related investments. A greater work burden is thus put on women's shoulders, as they often play a key role in taking care of all family members.

When life becomes more difficult, women and men with different roles and responsibilities are subject to different impacts. Some men were found to have illegally exploited forests or collected scrap metal for income. When men work far away, the family burdens that fall on women's shoulders become heavier. (Among the matrilineal families in Tri A village, Krong Na commune, the study found that women do 95 to 100 percent of family care and housework.) Women take care of their families and ensure food security for all members, leading to them feeling more stressed and vulnerable when a food shortage occurs.

A Luoi research sites

In the studied sites in A Luoi, agricultural land and forests were the most important assets for farmers. Loss of agricultural land and reduced agricultural productivity have resulted in a lack of jobs, food insecurity, and reduced income generation in the locality. Difficult living conditions affected all members of every family. They have to buy more rice or eat cassava at certain times of the year.

Health and health-care problems

Water and health

During the survey, the research team also found some health impacts caused by hydropower projects. All the studied communities reported health problems due to water shortages, water pollution, poor living conditions, and limited health-care services in the resettlement areas. Most expressed the desire to leave the resettlement sites to live and work in their old locations.

Negative changes in water resources included water quality and availability of surface water and groundwater for irrigation and domestic use. In addition, the hydroelectric dam caused water stagnation that encouraged algal blooms. In the resettlement areas, the water from wells contains limestone, which is not safe for drinking and cooking. The water supply system is insufficient for basic personal hygiene needs. The water quality of the A Sap River was found to be very poor: polluted by production activities and waste from upstream communes (A Roang, Huong Lam, Dong Son, and A Dot). In the resettlement villages of A Sap and A Den of A Luoi, the water was reported to have a strong odor, to be discolored and to be polluted by naturally occurring aluminum – but for three consecutive years, many residents used it for household consumption.

The heavily odorous water affects the whole community's health, especially for children and women, who are more susceptible than adult men to respiratory infections. Women and children suffered health risks more than men and young people. Water shortages caused an increasing incidence of gynecological diseases for women and negative psychological impacts on men and women. (For Quang Ngan village, Hong Thai commune, gynecological diseases have also become common among women.) Pollution of open well water also dramatically increased skin diseases among children.

Disease prevalence and access to health services

The number of people suffering from diseases has been increasing. Many children and the elderly suffer from malaria, diarrhea, and skin diseases, while women suffer from gynecological diseases. For the sites affected by the Srepók Dam projects, communities face similar issues. In Tan Phu village, dengue fever and viral fever often occur, and the local hospital is thus always overburdened. The incidence of gynecological disease has increased as, according to local people, they still use water from rivers and streams with poor quality.

Regarding health-care services, the A Luoi hydropower company has already built a community health clinic, but local residents explained that it has not been put into use effectively, because children and the elderly could not access the community health clinic due to costs and its inconvenient location. Local people must still travel long distances for medical treatment.

Precarity among women due to food insecurity

The lack of land and other livelihood resources triggered food insecurity and precarity for women at the studied sites.

A Luoi research sites

In A Luoi, at the time of the survey, food shortages were widespread, affecting most of the households. Eighty percent of the surveyed households lacked rice because production for domestic consumption only sufficed for one or two months. Land for cassava and cash crops was limited, and non-timber forest products (NTFPs) could only be secured far from their settlements, requiring time for travel and threatening food shortages all year round. The lack of food has forced people to secure loans to support their lives.

In Quang Ngan village, the volume of land used for rice cultivation has decreased due to reservoir construction. Seven out of nine hectares of the original rice fields were inundated when reservoir impoundment occurred, so food shortages usually occur. About 50 to 60 percent of households with food shortages have had to purchase food, adding to the debt burden for women, who are primarily responsible for providing the household meals.

Many residents, especially young people, have lost their jobs when being relocated to a new area. The unsuccessful outcomes of some livelihood promotion programs and vocational training activities have caused new gender-related issues. In the new resettled areas, due to a lack of job opportunities and access to productive land, the available labor (such as manual labor, hunting, and illegal logging) can only be carried out by men. In addition, because of their low level of education, many women struggle due to limited agricultural potential and a lack of jobs, and many women have come to depend heavily on their husbands financially.

With lack of employment has come an increase in alcoholism and gambling, with many men losing confidence or hope since they are unable to support their families financially. Household conflicts about finances now occur more frequently. If there is no solution for these issues, more social problems and domestic violence may occur. Domestic violence has increased, and women have become more vulnerable.

Social life changes

According to the affected communities, the many changes in access to resources, livelihoods, and health mentioned above have contributed to emerging social problems in families, communities and ethnic groups. In A Luoi, the affected people stated that a growing number of men are working far away due to difficult local living conditions, and it is mainly women, the elderly, and children who remain in the community.

This absence of men has had an effect on conducting community activities. In the case of Srepók, affected people confirmed that it has been difficult to conserve and promote traditions and culture. For example, changes in water sources have led to difficulties in organizing traditional festivals and in promoting local cultural and spiritual activities.

According to animistic belief, waterfalls and forests are associated with legends about gods who dominate the productive and spiritual activities of the communities. Apart from supplying water for domestic use and production, a village's freshwater spring is also a place for cultural and spiritual activities of the community. Each ethnic minority village has a spiritually significant water spring. Ethnic minority villages hold spring worship ceremonies every year, when they pray for good weather, good health, and good luck in their labor. Freshwater springs are associated with the cultural and spiritual life of E De and Gia Rai people in the Central Highlands.

Because of the hydropower dam development, it is difficult to organize such ceremonies, as the river does not provide enough water during the festival. Springs used for local religious activities have been adversely affected and abandoned in many places.[1]

Conclusion and recommendations

Conclusion

The inclusion of GIA in consultations and impact assessment projects allows us to have a much better understanding of how hydropower development affects women and men differently. Gaps in understanding could be bridged if the GIA process was applied correctly. It would also be helpful if various stakeholders, especially hydropower developers, included gender-sensitive measures to mitigate adverse impacts.

Although the hydropower projects undertook strong efforts to implement appropriate compensation measures in the affected area, an assessment of gender-based needs and aspirations was lacking and there was not enough concern about gender issues and gender sensitivity during the planning and implementation process.

This research project revealed that one of the most significant barriers was limited local participation by affected people – especially women – in the project planning, implementation, and monitoring process. Women did not have the opportunity to raise their voices and to discuss their interests and needs. Additionally, there was no open dialogue that allowed both men and women from affected communities to discuss issues of concern.

Women's limited role in household financial management also led to disadvantages for women post-resettlement. The unsuccessful outcomes of some livelihood promotion programs and vocational training activities have also been implicated in emerging gender-related issues, as many men were severely alienated and lost confidence when they could not support their families financially. If there is no solution for these issues, more social problems and domestic violence may occur, because women will increasingly depend heavily on their husbands for financial reasons.

Our research has suggested that participation in a GIA process may empower women to speak up about the issues of concern to them. GIA can validate the lived experiences of women and men and provide the evidence needed to persuade government – and hydropower developers – that they ought to act more responsively.

Recommendations for GIA implementation

Based on experience with GIA gained through these CSRD pilot projects, the following recommendations have been proposed:

Recommendation 1

Awareness of gender and development needs to be raised. Gender perspectives should be deployed in evaluating large development projects, including hydropower development. Better resettlement outcomes are impossible if gender inequality is not minimized or if women become more vulnerable. The advancement of women should be an important criterion for assessing impacts and evaluating results of hydropower projects and other development projects.

Recommendation 2

The practice of gender-impact assessment for large-scale projects should be promoted. GIA should be carried out systematically, together with environmental impact assessments and social impact assessments, for projects that potentially impact people and the environment, such as hydropower projects. This would allow men and women to raise their concerns and help Vietnam to achieve the sustainable development of affected communities and of the energy sector.

Recommendation 3

Based on gender-impact assessment reports, local economic, social, and cultural development initiatives should be carried out to mitigate the impacts of hydropower projects while satisfying the short-term and strategic development needs of the affected communities. It is essential to identify and mobilize the participation of communities from the first stages of hydropower projects.

All stakeholders – including investors, project owners, government agencies at all levels, social organizations, businesses, and men and women from local communities – should be invited for consultations. Stakeholder trust-building, responsibilities, and functions and communication mechanisms should be established, fostering impact assessment action plans that are formulated and monitored by the local authorities and communities.

Recommendation 4

GIA should be considered as both a process and practice. After a GIA report is completed, action plans should be developed and monitored, and gender equality and women's empowerment should be integrated in project activities, approaches, business ethics and codes of conduct.

Recommendation 5

Gender-impact assessment is a new approach in Vietnam's development context. It should be piloted; improved through practice and lessons learned; and promoted as good practice for businesses in terms of corporate social responsibility (CSR), social safeguards, inclusive growth, and sustainability. GIA should be regulated and enforced within a more comprehensive environmental impact assessment (EIA) of natural-resource extraction industries or pioneering provinces before being incorporated into practice at a higher level.

Recommendations for GIA integration into CSR of the energy sector

According to Carroll (2015), "corporate social responsibility" refers to the need for companies to respond to societal concerns and values regarding the social, economic, and environmental development of the system in which we live (see Figure 13.1). CSR is generally understood to be policies and practices that a business takes to ensure that society and external stakeholders are considered and protected when companies carry out their business strategies and activities. Companies have many reasons for developing CSR strategies. These include establishing a positive reputation, ensuring benefits for employees, taking care of the local environment,

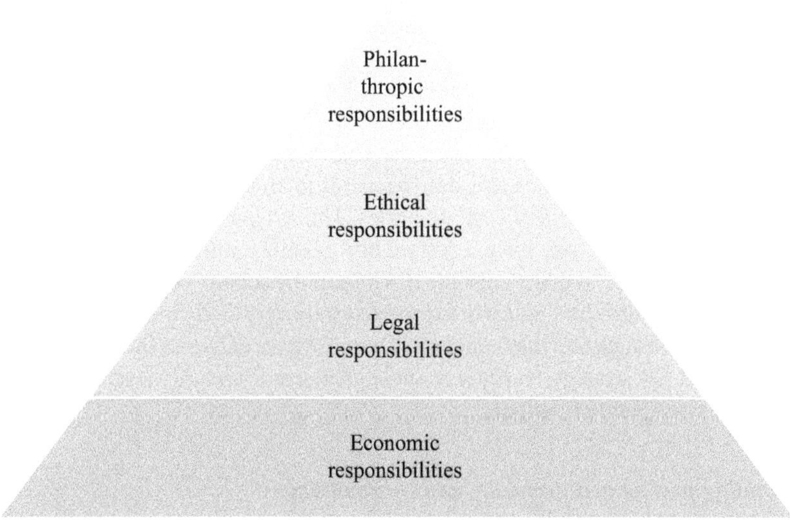

Figure 13.1 The corporate social responsibility (CSR) pyramid

Source: Carroll (1991) adapted by Hediger (2018)

complying with regulations, reducing costs and improving labor efficiency, showing concerns for their customers, and supporting stakeholders' interests.

Businesses should invest in their local communities. Therefore, CSRD aims to promote CSR in hydropower development to gain more sustainable support for affected communities, including gender needs. Communities in an area where a hydropower project operates are often resettled, and companies must question how they take responsibility for people displaced or affected by their activities. However, more importantly, they need to interact and work with communities to develop common social goals, so-called shared values. This helps build common benefits and impacts that resonate with both the company and the community. Stakeholders are no longer just passive recipients of goods, services, and experiences.

Businesses need to find ways to engage their customers as co-creators at every stage in the process. Moreover, CSR calls for shared responsibility between the government and private businesses. This directly applies to the management of water resources, which is generally regarded as a shared responsibility of public and private actors and thus to activities in the hydropower industry. The CSR of hydropower companies must be evaluated and implemented in the concrete context of their economic, institutional, geographical, and political spheres.

Recommendations for building partnership and advocating for women rights by local NGOs

Research by CSRD associates Pham and Nguyen (2018) and Pham et al. (2016) showed that companies introduced many supportive activities for local communities, yet they did not lead to the expected positive results. For example, the A Luoi Hydropower Company built new houses for local people, but these houses failed to meet the necessary quality requirements. In particular, the kitchen design did not suit local customs and needs, leading to people building new kitchens. A health center built in the resettlement area has not been used, as it did not meet village-level health center operation regulations.

These examples highlight the need for collaboration between the companies and the affected communities and state agencies to create shared social goals that maximize the effectiveness of CSR activities. The A Vuong hydropower company is a positive example: they have a community relations office to support affected communities on special occasions like the start of the school year and New Year's, and they have established an early warning system for flood risk mitigation. This type of evidence suggests that companies would be receptive to the integration of GIA in their CSR strategy, in order to meet local needs and the needs of the most vulnerable community members.

Evaluating project achievements and shortcomings

In the Central Highlands area, CSRD is the first NGO actively working on hydropower development topics. This was an advantage as well as a challenge for us and our partners. Over approximately a decade, we collaborated with our partners to effect positive impacts on several communities affected by hydropower dam development. We helped relevant stakeholders to have a better overall understanding of hydropower dam development, sought justice for affected people and improved policy-making processes.

There have been both achievements and shortcomings for the main hydropower-related projects implemented by CSRD in accordance with the strategies of our main donors. CSRD has evaluated the contribution of our projects to changes in hydropower-related communities and stakeholders, including outcomes for local communities, the private sector, and public sector decision-makers at all levels. The outcomes we have achieved vary from project to project and place to place in accordance with project scope, the goals of the program and the objectives of projects.

Identifying achievements

For affected communities, raising awareness, building capacity, raising local voices, and networking are important steps. We have obtained considerable achievements in this respect in Central and Central Highland Vietnam. For example, CSRD has organized a range of communication activities to provide communities with relevant knowledge on issues such as environmental impacts, social impact, gender equity, policy, and human rights. This improved their ability to articulate their needs and views. The affected communities were encouraged to consider different perspectives in understanding the problems and impacts they were facing and to find ways to identify their own solutions and raise concerns with the company – with support as needed from civil society organizations, media, and government agencies. The projects have made a connection between the communities and the state agencies and hydropower investors, helping people to raise their voices at forums and seminars. Support is provided to local people to self-implement monitoring and evaluation of hydropower impacts.

A network of dozens of communities affected by hydropower development in the Central and Central Highland regions of Vietnam has been established to exchange information and advocate for action to address adverse environmental impacts of hydropower development, as well as for participation in the hydropower development process and in monitoring of environmental protection implementation. Via meetings, workshops, and training organized within the project framework, network members have chances to build their capabilities, exchange information and experiences, and learn more from each other. As a result, the network has been firmly strengthened.

More importantly, we have significantly enhanced women's leadership. Our project partners have gained notable successes in changing the status, positions, and capabilities of women in the targeted project sites. A total of 972 women have been engaged in the project activities, which consist of technical trainings; studies; regional and national policy dialogues; local planning workshops; and research. With the activities implemented by the project, approximately 50 percent of the network members have participated in our project activities. Many residents and local government staff can now make clear presentations about the impacts of hydropower on their livelihoods, environment, and social life. This shows that women in our project sites are more aware of their roles and their rights in monitoring environmental protection implementation.

Meanwhile, improved awareness by the private sector and policy makers needs to be achieved as well. During the time of project implementation, CSRD engaged investors from large hydropower development companies to improve their understanding of the social impacts of hydropower development. More importantly, we have communicated concerns about dam-related problems to local authorities and policy makers by raising local voices in various forums. We have also sent reports, policy briefs and other publications to relevant agencies so that our information will be taken into account by policy makers.

Acknowledging shortcomings

The shortcomings of projects should be fully acknowledged. Regarding the sustainability of projects, due to the limited duration of projects, our efforts are sometimes blocked. Normally, we have to bring projects to a conclusion quickly, then prepare a new phase or new project to continue supporting our communities. This discourages people and wastes resources. After evaluation, we concluded that the main challenges or limitations have been in achieving sustainability and policy advocacy for social change. Policy advocacy associated with our projects has failed to meet our expectations in solving problems facing affected communities and preventing similar problems for future dam construction.

In addition, the space to influence policy change is still limited. The roles of an NGO are not fully recognized by the public or by authorities at all levels. Therefore, our inputs for policy making and implementation are not effectively used, and our influence is sometime inadequate for reaching all stakeholders in hydropower development or for mobilizing the participation of other stakeholders, apart from the affected local community. Most leaders and officials are in favor of economic development, but skeptical about the cost of hydropower, and they hesitate to make dramatic changes.

Overall, however, the authorities support poor people and vulnerable groups and are open to improvement of mechanisms to limit the negative effects of hydropower projects. So far, the topic of hydropower dams is still a sensitive issue for the national policy agenda. We encourage all parties to comply with government requirements and expectations, collaborate, and create real sustainable development.

Note

1 This refers to freshwater springs where the ethnic minorities in the Central Highlands of Vietnam used to take good quality water for their daily life. They have unique value in the life and culture of the minority groups. Each village has its own spring, which represents the soul of the village. Every year they used to have a water spring worship ceremony.

References

Cabo, MA., 2010. Environmental Governance from a Gender Perspective: Theoretical Reflections and Case Studies. Doctoral thesis. Universitat de Girona.

Carroll, AB., 1991. The Pyramid of Corporate Social Responsibility: Toward the Moral Management of Organisational Stakeholders. *Business Horizons* 34 (4): 39–48.

Carroll, AB., 2015. Corporate Social Responsibility: The Centrepiece of Competing and Complementary Frameworks. *Organizational Dynamics* 44: 87–96.

CSRD and CORENARM (Centre for Social Research and Development and Consultative and Research Center on Natural Resources Management), 2014. Social Impact Assessment of A Luoi Hydropower. Technical Report.

GIZ (Deutsche Gesellschaft für Internationale Zusammenarbeit), 2013. Regional Scoping Workshop on Gender and Sustainable Hydropower. Workshop Report, 20–21 June, Bangkok.

Hediger, W., 2018. The Corporate Social Responsibility of Hydropower Companies in Alpine Regions-Theory and Policy Recommendations. *Sustainability* 10: 3594. DOI: 10.3390/su10103594.

Hill, C, Phan, TNT, Storey, J and Vongphosy, S., 2017. Lessons Learnt from Gender Impact Assessments of Hydropower Projects in Laos and Vietnam. *Gender and Development* 25 (3): 455–470.

Hill, C and Newell, K., 2009. Women, Communities and Mining: The Gender Impacts of Mining and the Role of Gender Impact Assessment. *Guidelines and Toolkits*. https://oxfamilibrary.openrepository.com/handle/10546/293093.

Holy, M, Zeman, MG and Zeman, Z., 2021. From Ecofeminist Theories to Ecofeminist Practice: Women, Sustainability and Ethical Consumerism. In *The Sustainability Debate (Critical Studies on Corporate Responsibility, Governance and Sustainability, Vol. 14)*, eds. M. Topić and G. Lodorfos. Bingley: Emerald Publishing Limited, pp. 123–140. https://doi.org/10.1108/S2043-www.emerald.com/insight/content/doi/10.1108/S2043-9059 20210000015007/full/html.

Le, TH., 2016. *Tác động của hồ chứa thủy điện Srepók 4 và kênh Srepok 4A đến chế độ dòng chảy vùng hạ lưu sông Srepok. Trong 55 năm Viện quy hoạch thủy lợi1961-2016.* Hà Nội: Nhà xuất bản Khoa học và Kỹ thuật. http://iwrp.gov.vn/img-svc/files/bai30(1).pdf

Le, VK, Ngo, DT and Nguyen, QL., 2015. *Phong tục tập quán cổ truyền: Một số dân tộc thiểu số Nam Tây Nguyên.* Hà Nội: Viện Nghiên cứu Văn hóa, Viện Khoa học Xã hội Việt Nam.

Le, TNN, Nguyen, TMV and Lam, TTS., 2018. Gender impact assessment of A Luoi hydropower in Thua Thien Hue Province. In *Hydropower Impacts: From Environmental, Social and Gender Perspectives – Evidence from the Central and Central Highlands, Vietnam*, eds. Pham Thi Dieu My and Nguyen Quy Hanh. Hue: Thuan Hoa Publishing House.

National Assembly of Vietnam., 2006. Law on gender equality No. 76/2006/QH11 dated 29 November 2006.

Nguyen, QH, Pham, TDM, Storey, J, Nguyen, TT and Nguyen, TNT., 2018. Understanding and Responding to the Hydropower Impacts: From Conceptualization to Practice. In *Hydropower Impacts: From Environmental, Social and Gender Perspectives – Evidence from the Central and Central Highlands, Vietnam*, eds. Pham Thi Dieu My and Nguyen Quy Hanh. Hue: Thuan Hoa Publishing House.

Pham, TDM and Nguyen, QH (eds.), 2018. *Hydropower Impacts: From Environmental, Social and Gender Perspectives – Evidence from the Central and Central Highlands, Vietnam*. Hue: Thuan Hoa Publishing House.

Oxfam Australia and CPWF. 2013. *Balancing the Scales: Using Gender Impact Assessment in Hydropower Development*. Retrieved from https://asia.oxfam.org/policy-paper/gender-impact-assessment-gia-manual

Pham, TDM, Lam, TTS and Tran, BQ (eds.), 2016. *Thủy điện miền Trung và Tây Nguyên: Mối quan tâm của người dân và trách nhiệm của các bên liên quan*. Huế: NXB Thuận Hóa.

Roggeband, C and Verloo, M., 2006, October. Evaluating Gender Impact Assessment in the Netherlands (1994–2004): A Political Process Approach. *Policy & Politics* 34 (4): 615–632(18). Publisher: Policy Press. https://doi.org/10.1332/030557306778553097. Sneddon, C and Fox, C., 2008. Struggles Over Dams as Struggles for Justice: The World Commission on Dams (WCD) and Anti-Dam Campaigns in Thailand and Mozambique. *Society and Natural Resources* 21 (7): 625–640.

Trung Duong, 2016. Cơn khát dưới chân hồ đập thủy điện. Vietnamnet ngày 17/4/2016. http://vietnamnet.vn/vn/thoi-su/con-khat-duoi-chan-ho-dap-thuy-dien-299066.html

Verloo, M and Roggeband, C., 1996. Gender Impact Assessment: The Development of a New Instrument in the Netherlands. *Impact Assessment* 14 (1): 3–20.

Xu, J, Ni, T and Zheng, B., 2015. Hydropower Development Trends from a Technological Paradigm Perspective. *Energy Conversion and Management* 90: 195–206. DOI: 10.1016/j.enconman.2014.11.016. www.researchgate.net/publication/278323019_Hydropower_development_trends_from_a_technological_paradigm_perspective.

WCD (World Commission on Dams), 2000, November. *Dams and Development: A New Framework for Decision-Making. The Report of the World Commission on Dams*. London and Sterling, VA: Earthscan.

Index

absolute right, private land ownership as 13
access to health services and disease prevalence 265
active noncompliance 43
advocacy groups 168–69
advocacy *versus* controversies in Vietnam land conversion 215–17
African Development Bank (AfDB) 177
Ager, Alastair 186
agricultural land appropriation 82–96; *see also* Phú Điền village agricultural land appropriation case study; Đổi Mới policies 83–7; introduction to 82–3; loss of agricultural livelihoods from 90–1; market adaptations for new livelihood strategies 92–3; Phú Điền village case study 87–96; socialist-oriented market economy and 86–7; state and 85–6
Ali, S. 128
A Luoi hydropower project 259, 262, 264, 266
Anderson, C. 46
Appendini, K. 139
Arhem, K. 124–25
Aronsson, Inga-Lill 178
Asian Development Bank (ADB) 67, 177, 178, 216
assistance, "in cash" (monetary) and "in kind" (non-monetary) 218
authoritative tools 50–2

Bắc Từ Liêm 95
balance between private/public interests ideology 14–15
Balancing the scales: Using gender impact assessment in hydropower development (Oxfam) 256
Batterbury, S. 139
Baulch, B. 122
Bebbington, A. 138–39
Beijing Declaration and Platform for Action (BDPA) 256
Bemelmans-Videc, M. 46
benefit-sharing principle 68
Bentham, Jeremy 13–14
Binh Duong host community survey 186–87; *see also* host communities, post-resettlement integration into
Blackstone, William 12, 14
Board for Compensation and Ground Clearance (BCGC) 49
Bo Hon village resettled community: cultural capital differences 132–34; described 125; living conditions and livelihoods 126–27; non-farm employment 128; reported monthly income 128; social capital changes 129–31
Bramwell, Baron 14–15
Brinkerhoff, W. 45
Brundtland Commission 160
Bryson, J. M. 232

Capano, G. 57
Carroll, A. B. 269
Centre for Social Research and Development (CSRD) 256, 259
Cernea, M. 123, 129, 242
Cernea, M. M. 2, 161, 171
Chambers, R. 139
Citizen Reception Office 43
civil society organizations (CSOs) 76
cohesion: community 129, 187, 194, 199, 252; social 134
collaboration, public and private 215
collaboration processes, NP project 227–32; displacement/compensation 228–30; economic rehabilitation/social-safeguard activities 230–32; overview of 227–28

collective interests-based ideology 13–14
collective resistance, role of 76
Colson, E. 179, 205
common property resources 123
Communal People's Committees (CPCs) 226–27
communication 34
communities of origin, uprooted from 187–90; distance between old/new residence and 187–88; distance from parents/parents-in-law and 188; family visit frequency and 188–90
community capitals framework 123
community cohesion 129, 187, 194, 199, 252
community disarticulation 129
community engagement 167, 196–99, 200–201, 209
community rebuilding, integration and 196–99
community relations, integration and 199–201
compensation, hard component of 242
compensation rates 24; determination of 67–8; setting 34–5
complaints: filing 18–19; land acquisition 11
compulsory land acquisition: fair compensation for landholders and 19–20; identifying procedures for 18–19; limiting purposes of 16–18; purposes of, limiting 22; tangible *vs.* intangible interests and 20; in Vietnam Constitution 16
compulsory land conversion 215; processes in, and implementation dilemmas 217–20
conflict, integration process success and 190–92
conflict concept, described 223
constructivist ecofeminism 261
consultation 169–71
consultation processes 262–63
controlling rights 83
Conway, G. 139
Cook, C. Cynthia 169
corporate social responsibility (CSR) programs 68, 256, 269–70; pyramid 269
Cotu communities 124–25; *see also* peri-urban resettlement
Council of Land Price Evaluation 18
Crosby, B. 45
cultural events participation, integration and 201–3
culturally appropriate 177, 178
culture: of migration 128; resettlement programs and 177–79
Cutchrun resettled community 127; Cao Lan as ethnic minority groups 236–37; cultural capital differences 132–34; described 125; living conditions and livelihoods 127; main sources of income 128; reported monthly income 128; social capital changes 129–31

Dams and development: A new framework for decision making (WCD) 255
Dang Ngoc Quang 171
de-collectivization of land tenure system 42
Denhardt, R. 45
Department of Environmental and Natural Resources 29, 34
depression: among resettlees 208; unstable livelihoods and 263–64
De Soto, Hernando 14, 22
development-induced peri-urban resettlement 121–34; benefits and challenges for 123–24; Bo Hon village living conditions and livelihoods 126–27; cultural capital differences 132–34; cultural identity differences 132–34; Cutchrun village living conditions and livelihoods 127; dress/weaving differences 132; Gian Bi village living conditions and livelihoods 126; human/financial capital comparison 128–29; introduction to 121–22; language differences 132–34; methodology/data 124, 125; outcomes and location 122–23; religion practice differences 132; research sites 124–25; social capital changes following 129–31
development-induced resettlement, psychological aspects of *see* psychological aspects of development-induced resettlement
development partnership 230
direct noncompliance 43
disbursement, self-construction and 174
discrimination, integration process success and 190
disease prevalence, access to health services and 265
displacement: economic 1; reasons for, in Vietnam 1; and resettlement, introduction to 1–6
District People's Committee (DPC) 226
diversification 138–40; *see also* Son La Dam-induced resettlement; for

accumulation 140; determinants of 140; introduction to 137–38; livelihood, defined 139; study site and methods 140–45; Tan Lap resettlement site 143–44
Đổi Mới: agricultural land appropriation policies 83–87; economic reforms 1, 100, 106
Doi village 146–47
Dong Tam (Hanoi City) land-taking case study 47–8; *see also* policy tool-based approaches
Downing, T. E. 208
dual ownership 21

Ea Noul resettlement commune 260
Ea Po commune resettlement village 260
economic displacement 1
economic reforms 1, 100, 106
Ellis, F. 139, 150
eminent domain 29
empowerment process 171, 176, 258–59
environmental impact assessments (EIAs) 28–9, 178, 255, 268, 269
Equator Principles 177
ERDB 177
ethnic minorities, resettlement programs and 177–79
ethnic minority group, Cao Lan 236–37
ethnic minority languages, information disclosure and 34
everyday politics approach 85

fair compensation 24; for landowners 19–20
fair urbanization 78
Fazal, S. 66
fighting, integration process success and 190–92
Food and Agriculture Organization (FAO) 67
food insecurity and precarity among women 266
free, prior and informed consent (FPIC) 67

Garcia-Downing, C. 208
gender gaps 263
gender-impact assessments (GIA) 178, 255–72; access to health services and disease prevalence 265; achievements, identifying 271–72; at A Luoi hydropower project 259, 262, 264, 266; community participation, lack of 261–62; depression, unstable livelihoods and 263–64; at Ea Noul and Tan Hoa communes 260; at Ea Po commune resettlement village 260; gender gaps in 263; gender perspectives, lack of 261–62; health/health-care issues 265; introduction to 255–56; methodologies 256–58; Oxfam's six tools for 258–59; piloting locations for 259–61; precarity among women, food insecurity and 266; recommendations for implementation of 268–69; shortcomings, identifying 272; social life changes and 266–67; at Srepók 3 Hydropower project 260; at Srepók 4 and 4A Hydropower projects 260–61; Srepók River and communities 260–61, 262–63; in Tan Phu village 264; water, health and 265
gender-impact assessment tools, Oxfam 258–59
gender strategy 257
General Statistics Office 65
GIA *see* gender-impact assessments (GIA)
Gian Bi village resettled community: children accessing secondary/tertiary education 128–29; cultural capital differences 132–34; described 125; living conditions and livelihoods 126; non-farm employment 128; reported monthly income 128; social capital changes 129–31
Gill, R. 160
Gofen, A. 43
"good" *versus* "bad" urbanization case studies 100–116; appropriation/compensation, La Ca village 104–5; appropriation/compensation, La Tinh village 105–6; division, La Tinh village 111–12; infrastructure improvement 106–8; La Ca village research site described 102; La Tinh village research site described 102–3; livelihood transformation 108–10; local residents' perceptions of urbanization and land appropriation 112–14; low-wage manufacturing/service-sector work, La Ca village 110; overview of 100–101; protest/division, La Ca village 110–11; rental accommodation, agriculture and trade, La Ca village 108–9; research method described 101–2; retail, manufacturing and service-sector work, La Tinh village 110; selling service land, La Ca village 108; urbanization/agriculture, La Tinh village 110;

urbanization patterns/land appropriation 103–4; vocational training, La Ca village 109–10
governance: issues of 68–9; UNDP definition of 68
government information portal 54
grievance redress mechanism (GRM) 39–40
guol 125, 127, 133

Hanoi: collective resistance in 76; host community survey in 187 (*see also* host communities, post-resettlement integration into); land appropriation in 84, 87, 90; Nam Từ Liêm urban district of 95, 96, 187; real estate in 92
hard component of compensation 242
Hartmann, D. 128
Hay, M. 174–75
Hazell, P. 150
Herschon, R. 124
Ho Chi Minh City: collective resistance in 76; land appropriation in 84; Thu Thiem project and 49, 51, 54
home construction, resettlees flexibility in 173–74
host communities 149
host communities, post-resettlement integration into 185–209; barriers to 190–92; communities of origin and 187–90; community rebuilding 196–99; distance between old/new residence and 187–88; distance from parents/parents-in-law and 188; family visit frequency and 188–90; introduction to 185–86; livelihood patterns, changes in 194–96; livelihood restoration planning 207–8; from Nga Tu So to Dong Tau example 195; relationships, maintaining/developing 204–6; research survey locations 186–87; resettlement apartments, maintenance services for 192–94; social capital 206–7; social organizations/cultural events participation 201–3; social participation and 206–7; three-tiered resettlement program 203–4; travel time between old/new residence and 187–88; trust and support 199–201
household economies, models of 149
Howlett, M. 46–47
Hue's peri-urban areas case study 69–75; benefits/costs allocation imbalances 71–2; compensation for livelihood reconstruction and 73–5; data collection/analysis 70; desktop research 70; findings 70–5; household surveys 70; in-depth interviews 70; land acquisition, unequal participation and 72–3; research site background 69; unfair pricing framework 73, 74
human rights 6, 185, 272
Hung Yen, collective resistance in 76
hydroelectricity 160
hydropower development in Vietnam 160–79; *see also* resettlement program in hydropower development, elements of; introduction to 160–61; *Land Law 2013* handling of 164–66; resettlement impacts of 161–64; social impacts of 161; successful resettlement program, elements of 166–79; trends for, to 2045 162

Impoverishment Risk and Reconstruction model 123
indigenous communities 178
indigenous community house 133
indigenous culture 173, 178
indigenous language skills 123
indigenous people 5, 123, 177
indirect noncompliance 43
information-based tools 53–5
information disclosure 32–4, 33; communicating to stakeholders 34; ethnic minority languages 34; information leaflets 33–4; timely disclosure 33
information leaflets 33–4
infrastructure development 28–9; *see also* resettlement outcomes, local governments as catalysts for
Institute of Energy 161
institution strengthening 75–6
intangible losses 20
integration; *see also* host communities, post-resettlement integration into: barriers to 190–92; communities of origin uprooting factors 187–90; elements of 186; into host community 251–52; measuring 186
Inter-American Development Bank (IADB) 177
International Energy Agency (IEA) 160
international financial institutions 2, 6, 166, 167, 169
International Hydropower Association (IHA) 161
involuntary resettlement (IR) 215; PPPs in, feasibility of 237–39; processes 217;

public actors' accountability, rethinking 238; public participation, access/ mechanism of 238–39; risk taking and 237–38
Ivarsdotter, Kristine 169

Keast, R. 231–32
Kerkvliet, B. J. T. 85, 86
Korten, D. C. 67

La Ca village urbanization case study: appropriation/compensation 104–5; infrastructure improvement 106–8; low-wage manufacturing/service-sector work 110; protest/division 110–11; rental accommodation, agriculture and trade 108–9; research site described 102; resident perceptions of urbanization/land appropriation 112–14; selling service land 108; vocational training 109–10
land acquisition 215; *see also* noncompliance with land acquisition; challenges, institutional approach to 44–5; complaints 11; described 11; farmer resistance to 67; involuntary 1; legal framework in Vietnam 11–24; positive/negative effects of 66–7; unequal participation and 72–3; for urban development debate 66–9 (*see also* urbanization)
land acquisition legal framework 11–24; balance between private and public interests 14–15; compulsory, identifying procedures for 18–19; compulsory, limiting purposes of 16–18; fair compensation for landholders 19–20; future improvements to 24; introduction to 11–12; land ownership issues 21–2; private ownership-based ideology 12–13; public (or collective) interests-based ideology 13–14; reform, in Vietnam 20–24; in Vietnam, themes in analysis of 15–20
land acquisition/resettlement concerns, affected people's concerns about 247–49
land allocation 174
land appropriation 103–4
land conversion, Vietnam 215; *Land Law 2013* 216; policy advocacy *versus* controversies 215–17; policy changes, donor policies and 216–17; PPPs and 219–20
land for infrastructure policy 143
Land Fund Development Center (LFDC) 29, 30, 49; building capacity for 38–9; calculating land value and compensation 35–6; compensation rates, setting 34–5; consultation process 32, 39; information disclosure and 32–4; legal requirements of 31; resettlement implementation capacity 31, 37–8; socioeconomic surveys and 32
landholders, fair compensation for 19–20
Land Law 3, 15, 83; amendments to 11; compulsory land acquisition and 22; land appropriation 103–4; land groups in 83; land-use rights 42; livelihood restoration and 36; public dialogue and 55; resettlement circulars of 29–30
Land Law 2013 handling of hydropower development in Vietnam 164–66
land-lost farmers 91
land ownership 12, 15, 42, 83; issues 21–2
land recovery term use 16
land-taking *see* land acquisition
land titling 21
land use rights 83
land-use rights certificates 84
land users 42
land value and compensation, calculating 35–6
Lang, Lo Van success story 152–53
Lao Dong (Trade Union) 76–7
Lascoumes, P. 47
La Tinh village urbanization case study: appropriation/compensation 105–6; division 111–12; infrastructure improvement 106–8; research site described 102–3; resident perceptions of urbanization/land appropriation 112–14; retail, manufacturing and service-sector work 110; urbanization/agriculture 110
Law on Complaints 30
Law on Gender Equality 2006 256
Law on Housing 2014 172
Le, T. N. N. 263
Le Gales, P. 47
legal framework, resettlement programs and 166–68
LFDCs *see* Land Fund Development Centers (LFDCs)
life satisfaction 130, 131
Lippi, A. 57
livelihood; *see also* Son La Dam-induced resettlement: definitions of 138–39; diversification, defined 139; introduction to 137–38; research 139–40; strategies

138–40; study site and methods 140–45; sustainable 139; Tan Lap resettlement site 143–44
livelihood patterns, displacement and changes in 194–96
livelihood restoration: outcomes 36; planning 207–8; planning in post-resettlement period 174–76
livelihood strategies 138–40
Locke, John 12
Lodhi, A. H. A. 42
Long Coc village 147–48
Lund, Michael S. 46
Luu, H. 133
Luu, T. D. C. 178

Magna Carta 15
Mandell, M. 231–32
marginal farmers 150
market value 67; compensation model 78
Marx, Karl 13–14
Mehta, L. 179
Meppem, T. 160
migration 122, 128, 140; labor 126, 128–29; rural-urban 66
Ministry of Industry and Trade 162
Ministry of Natural Resources and the Environment (MONRE) 11
Mintrom, M. 46–7
Mintz, Alex 45

Nam Song Cong relocation site resettlement 233
Nam Từ Liêm 95, 96, 187
Nattapoolwat, S. 91
natural law 12
natural right, private land ownership as 12–13
NGOs *see* non-governmental organizations (NGOs)
Nguyen, H. T. 122
Nguyen, Q. H. 263
Nguyen Tan Dung 142
noncompliance with land acquisition 42–57; *see also* policy tool-based approaches; authoritative tools 50–2; cross-case analysis research method described 48–9; defined 43; economic explanation of 45; explanations of 44–6; financial tools 52–3; governance approach to 45–6; information-based tools 53–5; institutional approach to challenges of 44–5; introduction to 42–3; land-taking cases of 47–8; organizational tools 49–50; policy 43–4; policy tool-based approaches to 46–7
non-farm employment 4, 66, 123, 128, 134
non-governmental organizations (NGOs) 5, 49, 50, 76, 133, 185, 256, 270, 272
NP project *see* Nui Phao (NP) resettlement project
Nui Phao Joint Venture 221
Nui Phao Mining Company 227
Nui Phao (NP) resettlement project 220; collaboration content in 227–32; Communal People's Committees role in 226–27; Dai Tu DPC role in 226; international policies applied at 222; introduction to 221; Nui Phao Mining Company role in 227; PAPs/PACs role in 227; PPP approach in, understanding 225–26; PPP inputs 226–27; public actors and roles in 226–27; public value gained 232–37; as segmented and long-lasting process 221–23; social conflict in 223–25; TN PPC role in 226; uncertainty regarding 221; vocational training/recruitment in 234–35

O'Brien, K. J. 85
official development assistance (ODA) 216; agencies 127
organizational tools 49–50
Our common future (UN) 160
ownership rights 83
Oxfam GIA: *Balancing the scales: Using gender impact assessment in hydropower development* 256; *Bao Cong An Nhan Dan* (newspaper) 77; *Bao Giao Thong Van Tai* (newspaper) 77; GIA manual for hydropower development 256; identify issues introduced by dam step 257; review, audit and respond step of 258; understanding context step of 257; understand women's (and men's) needs and aspirations step of 257
Oxfam Vietnam 256; six tools for gender-impact assessments 258–59; Water Governance Project 256–58

PACs *see* project-affected communities (PACs)
Paine, Thomas 14
PAPs *see* project-affected persons (PAPs)
participation 169–71; in resettlement consultations 249–50
passive noncompliance 43

Payments for Forest Environmental Services (PFES) 127
people-centered development approach 67
peri-urban resettlement 121–34; benefits and challenges for 123–24; Bo Hon village living conditions and livelihoods 126–27; cultural capital differences 132–34; cultural identity differences 132–34; Cutchrun village living conditions and livelihoods 127; dress/weaving differences 132; Gian Bi village living conditions and livelihoods 126; human/financial capital comparison 128–29; introduction to 121–22; language differences 132–34; methodology/data 124, 125; outcomes and location 122–23; religion practice differences 132; research sites 124–25; social capital changes following 129–31
peri-urban zones, defined 122
Phú Điền village agricultural land appropriation case study 87–96; government program failures and 91–2; implications of political action/contestation and engagement with market choice 95–6; implications of villagers' move into real estate/rental 94–5; income comparisons 94; land compensation rates 88–90; livelihood strategies 92–3; loss of agricultural livelihoods 90–1; online information/social media use 95; overview of 87–90; post land acquisition challenges 90–1; real estate livelihood strategies 92–3; retail/service provision livelihood strategies 93; scale of change 94
plural activity 139
PMUs *see* Project Management Units (PMUs)
policy advocacy *versus* controversies in Vietnam land conversion 215–17
policy implementation 43
policy legitimacy 46
policy mechanisms 47
policy noncompliance: described 43–44; types of 43
policy noncompliance with land acquisition 43–4; described 43; policy tools in cases of, analyzed 47–8; tool-based approaches to 46–7
policy tool-based approaches: analysis of, in land-taking cases 47–8; authoritative tools 50–2; financial tools 52–3; information-based tools 53–5; to noncompliance with land acquisition 46–7; organizational tools 49–50
poverty alleviation 123, 125, 133, 139
PPPs *see* Public-Private Partnerships (PPPs)
precarity among women, food insecurity and 266
pricing frameworks 73, 74
primary ownership 21
private land ownership: as absolute right 13; as natural right 12–13
private ownership-based ideology 12–13
private sector, compulsory land conversion and 215–20; *see also* Nui Phao (NP) resettlement project; Public-Private Partnerships (PPPs); dilemma types 215
proclamation 54
project-affected communities (PACs) 218, 227
project-affected persons (PAPs) 218, 227; SN1 and increased benefit for 232–34
Project Management Units (PMUs) 33, 168, 171; building capacity for 38–9; consultation with affected people 39; resettlement implementation roles of 37
Provincial People's Committee (PPC) 18, 49; executive order 54; LFDCs and 29
psychological aspects of development-induced resettlement 242–53; concerns of resettlement activities 245–46; emotions experienced 247; emotions/feeling upon hearing of resettlement activities 243–46; gender difference regarding 246–47; integration into host community and 251–52; introduction to 242; land acquisition/resettlement concerns 247–49; participation levels of those reporting negative emotions 249–50; research methods and locations described 243; satisfaction levels with resettlement outcomes 250–51
public actors' accountability, rethinking 238
public dialogue 55
public interest investment, land acquisition for 17–18
public interests-based ideology 13–14
public ownership 42
public participation, access/mechanism of 238–39
public policy vacuum 231
public poster 54
Public-Private Partnerships (PPPs) 219–20; *see also* Nui Phao (NP) resettlement

project; definition of 220; involuntary resettlement and feasibility of 237–39; in Nui Phao resettlement project 225–27; as policy network 220; public value gained, in NP project 232–37; research method/analytical framework for 220; structural complexity of, in NP project 227–32
public resistance concept 86

Quang Ngai province host community survey 186; *see also* host communities, post-resettlement integration into

real estate livelihood strategies 92–93
"Red Book" (sổ đỏ) 84
reforming Vietnamese land acquisition legal system 20–4; compensation rates and 24; compulsory land acquisition purposes and 22; land ownership and 21–2; transparency and 23–4
relationships, maintaining existing/developing new 204–6
relocation process, soft aspects of 242
replacement cost 67; compensation model 78–79
replacement land 121, 122, 123, 145, 167
resettlement apartments/buildings 192–94; common spaces and 193; elevators and 193; funding for maintenance issues with 193–94; garbage and 193; maintenance/management issues with 192–93; noise and 193; parking and 193; pets and 193
resettlement areas 18
resettlement impacts, handling of 164–66
resettlement impacts of hydropower development in Vietnam 161–64; described 162–64; handling of 164–66; sectoral context 161–62
resettlement outcomes, local governments as catalysts for 28–40; *see also* Land Fund Development Centers (LFDCs); background of 29–30; building capacity for PMUs/LFDCs 38–9; compensation rates, setting 34–5; consultation process 32; consultation with affected people 39; grievance redress mechanisms 39–40; information disclosure 32–4; introduction to 28–9; key stakeholder roles in 36–40; Land Fund Development Centers and 29, 30; land value and compensation, calculating 35–6; legal requirement issues 31; LFDC resettlement implementation capacity 31, 37–8; livelihood restoration process 36; peri-urban 122–23; project management units and 37, 38; resettlement implementation issues 31; SIAs and 28–9; socioeconomic surveys 32; technical factors 32–6
Resettlement Policy Framework (RPF) 30, 31
resettlement program, management of 171–74
resettlement program in hydropower development, elements of 166–79; adaptative management of 171–74; consultation, participation, and stakeholder engagement 169–71; disbursement, compliance/satisfactory progress and 174; legal framework 166–68; livelihood restoration planning in post-resettlement period 174–76; PMU/local authority commitment 168–69; resettlees flexibility in home construction and 173–74; site selection and 173; sufficient allocation of land and 174; vulnerable groups/local culture, attention to 177–79
resettlement program structure *see* three-tiered resettlement program structure
retail/service provision livelihood strategies 93
Rigg, J. 91
rightful resistance 85–6
The rights of man (Paine) 14
risk taking 237–38
Royal Institution of Chartered Surveyors (RICS) 23

Salamon, L. 46
satisfaction levels with resettlement outcomes 250–51
Scott, J. 85
Scudder, T. 169
secondary ownership 21
selective compensation 79
service land 88, 105
shortcomings, identifying 272
SIAs *see* social impact assessments (SIAs)
Simon, H. 45
Singer, J. 169
site selection 173
social capital/social participation 206–7
social cohesion 134
social conflict 215; in Nui Phao (NP) project 223–25

social connection 186
social costs of urban expansion 71–2
social impact assessments (SIAs) 28–9
social integration, described 185; *see also* host communities, post-resettlement integration into
socialist-oriented market economy, adapting to 86–7
socialist principles 70
social life changes 266–67
socially sustainable development model 160; *see also* hydropower development in Vietnam; resettlement program in hydropower development, elements of
social organization participation, integration and 201–3
socioeconomic development, land acquisition for 17
socioeconomic surveys 32, 79
soft aspects of relocation process 242, 252
Son La Dam 141
Son La Dam-induced resettlement 137–57; challenges 145–49; displacement stages 142; Doi village story 146–47; farming and livelihood prior to 144–45; farming land shortages 145–46; introduction to 137–38; Lang success story 152–53; learning new ways of living in 149–55; Long Coc village story 147–48; organizing, and policy 142–43; research study site/methods overview 140–45; in Tan Lap 143–44
Son La province host community survey 186; *see also* host communities, post-resettlement integration into
Srepók 3 Hydropower project 260
Srepók 4 and 4A Hydropower projects 260–61
Srepók River and communities affected by hydropower construction 260–61, 262–63
stakeholder engagement 169–71
stakeholder roles in resettlement implementation 36–40; communication 34; consultation with affected people 39; grievance redress mechanism 39–40; LFCDs and 37–8; PMUs 37
state ownership 42
Statistical Package for the Social Sciences (SPSS) 187
stigma, integration process success and 190
Stone, D. 45
Strang, Alison 186
sustainable development 160; in hydropower sector 161
sustainable development, form of urban development and 79
sustainable livelihoods 139

tangible losses 20
Tan Hoa resettlement commune 260
Tan Lap resettlement project 143–44; land for infrastructure policy 143; land use and agricultural structure in 140
Tan Lap resettlement site 143–44
Tan Lap Tea Cooperative 151
Tan Phu village 264
Taylor, P. 86
temporary residence 93
Thai Nguyen PPC *see* Thai Nguyen Provincial People's Committee (Thai Nguyen PPC)
Thai Nguyen Provincial People's Committee (Thai Nguyen PPC) 226
Thanh Nien (Youth Union) 76–77
threat of state-enforced sanctions 50–1
three-tiered resettlement program structure 203–4; livelihood restoration planning 207–8; relationships, maintaining/developing 204–6; social capital/social participation 206–7
Thu Thiem (Ho Chi Minh City) land-taking case study 47–8; *see also* policy tool-based approaches
title security 22
tool-based approach *see* policy tool-based approaches
tools, defined 46
transparency 23–4
Từ Liêm 95
Tuoi Tre (Youth News) 76–7
Tu Son (Bac Ninh Province) land-taking case study 47–8; *see also* policy tool-based approaches

United Nations Declaration on the Rights of Indigenous Peoples 177
United Nations Development Program (UNDP) 67, 68
urban development, sustainable development and form of 79
urban embellishment 16
urbanization 65–79; *see also* agricultural land appropriation; "good" *versus* "bad" urbanization case studies; Hue's peri-urban areas case study; civil society role 76; collective resistance role 76; determination of compensation and

67–8; governance issues with 68–9; Hue's peri-urban areas case study 69–75; introduction to 65; land acquisition debate 66–9; media role 76–7; policy recommendations for 77–9; positive/negative effects of land acquisition 66–7; strengthening institutions and 75–6

Vietnam: Government Inspectorate of 43; land conversion in 215–17; public ownership of land ideology 215
Vietnam Electricity (EVN) 127, 161
Vietnam Renewable Development Project 163
Von Meding, J. 178
vulnerable groups 33, 39, 169, 177–79, 231, 264, 266, 270

Wallman, S. 138
water, health and 265
Williamson, O. 45
Wilmsen, B. 123
women, resettlement programs and 177–79
Women's Empowerment Tool (WEF) 258–59
World Bank 2, 67–8, 75, 122, 127, 172, 177, 216, 218; Environmental and Social Standard (ESS) 166–68
World Commission on Dams (WCD) 255

Xi, Juan 250
Xu, J. 261

Zhou, M. 66–7

For Product Safety Concerns and Information please contact our EU
representative GPSR@taylorandfrancis.com
Taylor & Francis Verlag GmbH, Kaufingerstraße 24, 80331 München, Germany

www.ingramcontent.com/pod-product-compliance
Ingram Content Group UK Ltd.
Pitfield, Milton Keynes, MK11 3LW, UK
UKHW020152200926
475702UK00016B/2672
9780367761660